IN DEFENSE OF PLURAL MARRIAGE

With more than half of Americans now in favor of marriage equality, it is clear that societal norms of marriage are being quickly redefined. The growing belief that the state may not discriminate against gays and lesbians calls into question whether the state may limit marriage to couples and exclude other kinds of marital unions. While much has been written about same-sex marriage, as of yet, there has been no book-length legal treatment of unions among three or more individuals.

The first major study on plural marriage and the law, *In Defense of Plural Marriage* begins to fill this lacuna in the scholarly literature. Ronald C. Den Otter shows how the constitutional arguments that support the option of plural marriage are stronger than those against. Ultimately, he proposes a new semicontractual marital model that would provide legal recognition for a much wider range of intimate relationships.

Ronald C. Den Otter is an associate professor of political science at California Polytechnic State University, San Luis Obispo. Professor Den Otter has previously taught courses in public law, political theory, and American politics at Cal State (Los Angeles), UCLA, Pepperdine University, and UC Santa Cruz. His first book, *Judicial Review in an Age of Moral Pluralism* (2009), was published by Cambridge University Press.

In Defense of Plural Marriage

RONALD C. DEN OTTER
California Polytechnic State University, San Luis Obispo

CAMBRIDGE
UNIVERSITY PRESS

CAMBRIDGE
UNIVERSITY PRESS

32 Avenue of the Americas, New York, NY 10013–2473, USA

Cambridge University Press is part of the University of Cambridge.

It furthers the University's mission by disseminating knowledge in the pursuit of education, learning, and research at the highest international levels of excellence.

www.cambridge.org
Information on this title: www.cambridge.org/9781107087712

First published 2015

A catalog record for this publication is available from the British Library.

Library of Congress Cataloging in Publication Data
Den Otter, Ronald C., author.
In defense of plural marriage / Ronald C. Den Otter, California Polytechnic State University, San Luis Obispo.
pages cm
Includes bibliographical references and index.
ISBN 978-1-107-08771-2 (Hardback)
1. Polygamy–Law and legislation–United States. 2. Polygamy–Social aspects. I. Title.
KF519.D46 2015
346.7301′6723–dc23 2014050300

ISBN 978-1-107-08771-2 Hardback

To my (only) wife, Grace, who has helped me through
the most difficult part of my life and continues to do so.

I love you very much and I am grateful for everything
you have done for me in the past.

Without you, this book, and many other important things, would
not have been possible.

"If you liked it, then you shoulda put a ring on it."

– Beyoncé Knowles, "Put a Ring on It"

Contents

Acknowledgments

I owe so many people so much for so many things that it is hard to know where to begin. But here goes . . . I would like to thank the following scholars, all of whom assisted me in one way or another with my thinking, research, and writing about marriage: Carlos Ball, Mark Kleiman, Paul Fymer, Eileen Scallen, Andrew Lister, Scott Bowman, Jude Egan, Adam Winkler, Bill Niemi, William Sokoloff, Steve Shapiro, Mark Sawyer, Chris Den Hartog, Craig Arceneaux, Martha Ertman, Mark Goldfeder, Andrew Sabl, Diane Klein, Dave Lowenthal, Janet Bennion, Andrew Koppelman, Brian Walker, and Victor Wolfenstein. Sonu Bedi and Matt Moore went above and beyond the call of duty by helping me through some of the most difficult stages of this project. A special thanks to Elizabeth Brake, who generously shared her work, philosophical insights, and time with me to make this book much better than it otherwise would have been. Andrew Sabl was a wonderful mentor when I was a graduate student at UCLA; I would not be where I am today professionally but for his concern about my development as a scholar and his ongoing generosity. I have been blessed with some wonderful friends who were there when I really needed them: Chris Bickel, David Lowenthal, Matt Moore, Chris Den Hartog, Beth Lowham, Anika Leithner, Erin Clemons, and Mike Latner. The staff in the political science department – Suzy Black, Charlotte Lopez-Schermer, Andrea Nash, and Kristin Ventresca – has been fantastic. During the production stage, I owe debts of gratitude to copy editor Christopher Stolle; project managers Britto Fleming Joe and Ezhil Sugu Maran; production editor Mark Fox; the typesetters at SPi Global; Robert Swanson; and Stephen Acerra. My editor, John Berger, could not be better at his job. Several years ago, he took a chance on me and my first book when I was completely unknown. I will always be in his debt for his doing so.

I would also like to acknowledge the constructive criticism of the two anonymous external reviewers and the encouragement I received at the

UCLA political theory workshop where I first presented some of the ideas developed in this book, particularly those found in the last chapter. Cal Poly provided me with a one-quarter paid sabbatical that helped me put the final touches on the manuscript. I would also like to note here how much I learned from Tamara Metz's *Untying the Knot* and Elizabeth Brake's *Minimizing Marriage*, which are two of the best books ever written on what "marriage" could be. My family members – Grace, Doug, Debra, and Jason – deserve considerable credit for whatever I have been able to accomplish professionally. It always has been and always will be a team effort. Last but not least, my maternal grandmother, Eleanor Allen, who financed my legal education, should not be forgotten.

Introduction

In this book, I take seriously the idea of plural marriage.[1] While many legal scholars have written about same-sex marriage, none of them have produced a sustained treatment of marriages among three or more individuals. The state's continuing and extensive involvement in the institution of marriage, coupled with the growing belief that the state may not discriminate against gays and lesbians, puts into some doubt whether the state may limit marriage to couples. As progressive, important, and successful as the marriage equality movement has been, it is parochial by focusing on same-sex marriage at the expense of other kinds of intimate relationships that may also deserve legal recognition. This book begins to fill the lacuna in the scholarly literature by elaborating on why the constitutional arguments that support the option of plural marriage are better than the constitutional arguments against it.[2] A fair evaluation of such marriage is imperative when even the most open-minded of us are socialized in a society that venerates monogamy and too often self-righteously condemns unconventional beliefs and practices without adequate information or understanding.

It is not too much to ask from those who oppose plural marriage to formulate their respective positions without relying on prejudice, disgust, negative stereotypes, dubious empirical claims, speculation about adverse consequences, fear of difference, or controversial religious views.[3] Even the

[1] In the rest of this book, when I refer to "marriage," I mean civil marriage – that is, marriage the state treats as a legal status. By "plural marriage," I mean being legally married to more than one person at the same time.

[2] Because they do not resonate in modern liberal democracies, I do not address some of the traditional arguments used to defend plural marriage, such as guaranteeing a husband for every woman, reducing adultery and prostitution, and increasing the number of children.

[3] For a detailed history of the religious origins of marriage in the West, see John Witte Jr., *From Sacrament to Contract: Marriage, Religion, and the Law in the Western Tradition* (2nd ed.) (Louisville, KY: Westminster John Knox Press, 2012).

most deferential standard of review – rational basis – demands that the state have a legitimate interest in limiting marriage to couples.[4] Unfortunately, public opinion about plural marriage has not changed much since the nineteenth century. Many Americans still cling to a sentimental notion of monogamous marriage, overlook its flaws, and refuse to consider the possibility that a plural marriage might work better for some persons under some circumstances or that those involved in a multiperson relationship might love one another and be happy together. As I shall show, opponents of such marriage ought to have the burden of persuasion to demonstrate that the state's failure to recognize plural marriage is constitutionally permissible, which is a way of saying that discrimination against polygamists who would marry if they were allowed to do so should trigger a heightened standard of review or a stronger form of rational basis. As it turns out, none of the state's interests in not permitting plural marriages are either compelling or important. In fact, they may not be legitimate. According to one scholar: "The legal arguments against polygamy . . . are extremely weak."[5] Under existing constitutional doctrine, a strong presumption in favor of marital choice has existed for a while.[6] In a constitutional democracy like our own, competent adults should be able to marry more than one person at the same time unless the state can prove that it has adequate reasons for denying such choice.

In this book, I have three main aims. First, I invite readers to think about plural marriage in the first place if they have not done so already. The ongoing debate about same-sex marriage is not only about gay and lesbian couples and their constitutional right not to be legally discriminated against, but it is also about the even more complicated question of the most appropriate definition of marriage under the conditions of moral pluralism that characterize America. At stake is nothing less than how the law should treat those who

[4] Constitutionally, animus – understood as visceral dislike, disgust, or hatred – cannot count as such an interest. See *U.S. Department of Agriculture v. Moreno*, 413 U.S. 528 (1973), *Cleburne v. Cleburne*, 473 U.S. 432 (1985), *Romer v. Evans*, 517 U.S. 620 (1996), and *United States v. Windsor*, 570 U.S. _ (2013). Dale Carpenter refers to these four cases as the "animus quadrilogy." Dale Carpenter, "'*Windsor* Products': Equal Protection From Animus": http://papers.ssrn.com/sol3/papers.cfm?abstract_id=2424743.

[5] Martha C. Nussbaum, "A Right to Marry?" *California Law Review*, 98 (2010), 688.

[6] In this book, I do not have much to say about the decriminalization of polygamy. Rather, my concern is about the lack of official recognition by the state of consensual multiperson intimate relationships through a licensing scheme. The removal of criminal prohibitions would be the first stage in the process of legalization. Polygamy has never been effectively regulated. Such regulation might mitigate its worst aspects and therefore might be better public policy. See Mark Goldfeder, "It's Time to Reconsider Polygamy": www.cnn.com/2013/12/16/opinion/goldfeder-polygamy-laws/index.html?htp=op_+1.

have unconventional ideas about intimate relationships, want the freedom to live accordingly, and desire equal legal treatment. At first, plural marriage may seem to be unequivocally morally disturbing due to its historical association with patriarchal practices, its recent connection to Warren Jeffs, and its continuing role in the practice of Fundamentalist Latter-Day Saints (FLDS) polygyny.[7] A closer examination of its various forms, though, reveals that it deserves a second look. American history contains numerous examples of behaviors that were once widely thought to be immoral and are now considered to be morally permissible or even morally praiseworthy. Because we have often been wrong in the past, we should not be so confident that our contemporary moral judgment is infallible. With the benefit of hindsight, Americans may look back at a norm, which at the time seemed unproblematic, and conclude it made no sense. Not that long ago, many of them could not stomach same-sex marriages. In those days, most Democrats took positions on the issue that an increasing number of Republicans would not embrace in 2015. For years, Barack Obama's "public posture" with respect to same-sex marriage had been "all over the map."[8] Such relationships are now more visible and less foreign.[9] In the minds of many Americans and especially younger ones, same-sex marriages signify what is best in human life when two persons commit to sharing their lives with each other. The fact that the couple consists of two men or two women is increasingly irrelevant.

Second, I would like readers to evaluate the possible forms of plural marriage more objectively, as hard as that may be to do.[10] For too long, antipolygamists have framed the issue to make it seem as if to be open to the idea of plural marriage is to endorse Hugh Hefner's lifestyle or to condone Jeffs's crimes. If monogamous marriage is to remain the only kind of marriage that bears the imprimatur of the state, those who care about treating others fairly should examine the case against plural marriage more closely before rendering a judgment. Although a lot of what I have to say gestures toward the disestablishment of civil marriage and its replacement with a more inclusive alternative, I devote most of my attention to plural marriage, with an

[7] On Jeffs, see Stephen Singular, *When Men Become Gods: Mormon Polygamist Warren Jeffs, His Cult of Fear, and the Women Who Fought Back* (New York: St. Martin's Press, 2009).

[8] Mark Halperin and John Heilemann, *Double Down: Game Change 2012* (New York: Penguin Press, 2013), 57.

[9] For the story of how this state of affairs came to be, see Michael J. Klarman, *From the Closet to the Altar: Courts, Backlash, and the Struggle for Same-Sex Marriage* (New York: Oxford University Press, 2013).

[10] Scholarship concerning marriage more generally tends to be politicized. Hendrick Hartog, *Man and Wife in America: A History* (Cambridge, MA: Harvard University Press, 2000), 3–4.

emphasis on its legal aspects.[11] In the final chapter, I explain why I do not advocate abolition, which is understood as the complete privatization of marriage and reliance on private marital contracts the state is supposed to enforce, and introduce a semicontractual alternative I believe would enable people to customize their marriages as much as possible.[12]

My proposal may remind readers of Sir Henry Maine's famous remark: "The movement of the progressive societies has hitherto been a movement from Status to Contract."[13] However, as Mary Anne Case notes: "The state has been a relative latecomer in the regulation of marriage. ... [T]he history of marriage in Anglo-American law seems thus far to have been one of movement from contract to status and only part way back again."[14] I do not mean that status would be entirely dispensed with. Instead, my suggestion is that more nuanced contractual alternatives should not be ruled out without assessing their advantages in the midst of growing familial diversity and economic uncertainty. At present, marriage is a hybrid of status and contract, with default rules that can be contracted around. For example, in California, a married couple can avoid the consequences of community property law through a valid prenuptial agreement to protect the inheritance of their children from a previous relationship. Postnuptial agreements are becoming more common than they used to be.[15] In states that still refuse to recognize same-sex marriage or even civil unions, gay and lesbian couples who seek to protect their intimate relationship have no choice but to use legal instruments like private contracts. The very idea of marital contracts is not nearly as otherworldly as it initially may appear to be. While such contracts can hinder freedom and equality, they can promote each of these values and serve other ends depending on their terms. They also provide the kind of

[11] In the literature, "disestablish" is a term of art. Normally, it does not entail the elimination of the legal status of a marriage-like relationship (abolition or complete privatization) but the creation of a new, more inclusive status the state would continue to recognize, subsidize, and compel such third parties as government agencies, employers, and hospitals to acknowledge.

[12] At the outset, I want to acknowledge how much my contractual account of marriage owes to its first serious treatment – more than thirty years ago – found in Lenore J. Weitzman, *The Marriage Contract: A Guide to Living With Lovers and Spouses* (New York: The Free Press, 1981). For a more recent and equally insightful discussion of contracts and the role they play (and can play) in family law more generally, see Martha M. Ertman, *Love's Promises: How Formal and Informal Contracts Shape All Kinds of Families* (forthcoming from Beacon Press).

[13] Henry Sumner Maine, *Ancient Law*, (3rd American edn.) (Sioux Falls, SD: NuVision Publications [2009] 1888), 165.

[14] Mary Anne Case, "Marriage Licenses," *Minnesota Law Review*, 89 (2005), 1766.

[15] Jacoba Urist, "Postnups Becoming More Popular, but They're Not for Everyone," www.thedailybeast.com/articles/2012/05/20/postnups-becoming-more-popular-but-they-re-not-for-everyone.html.

flexibility that can accommodate individual differences. As such, they deserve serious attention. They also cannot be dealt with by the mere assertion that they would be bad for women and children.

The recent arguments in support of disestablishment, which Tamara Metz, Elizabeth Brake, and Sonu Bedi have advanced, are consistent with the legal recognition of various kinds of plural marriage.[16] By "disestablish," most scholars mean eliminating civil marriage as a legal status and putting in its place state-recognized caretaking relationships or private contracts that would empower the parties to devise most of the terms of their legal relationship. In the marital regime I favor, people would be able to form marriages that could contain more than two persons, could be same sex, and would not require love, physical intimacy, caregiving, or any other substantive value. A marriage could be premised on the emotional closeness that comes with an old friendship.[17] They could form just about whatever kind of intimate relationship they desire and tailor it to meet their particular needs, provided they do not violate other valid laws. The state would subsequently treat the contractual relationship as a marriage-like status – whatever its form – and require other entities, such as hospitals and employers, to recognize them.

Third, I argue that as long as states continue to license monogamous marriages – different sex or same sex – they must provide the option of different kinds of plural marriages to fulfill the constitutional mandate of nondiscriminatory treatment.[18] In doing so, they would give the same legal recognition that is already accorded to different-sex monogamous marriage in all states and same-sex marriage in some states, putting all marriage-like relationships on the same footing. I refer to this state of affairs – equal legal treatment of all marital arrangements (notwithstanding their structure or dynamics) – as "external equality," whereas the kind of equal treatment within the intimate relationship that may occur is "internal equality." The latter is

[16] Tamara Metz, "The Liberal Case for Disestablishing Marriage," *Contemporary Political Theory*, 6 (2007), 196–217; Metz, *Untying the Knot: Marriage, the State, and the Case for Their Divorce* (Princeton, NJ: Princeton University Press, 2010); Elizabeth Brake, "Minimal Marriage: What Political Liberalism Implies for Marriage Law," *Ethics*, 120 (2010), 317; Brake, *Minimizing Marriage: Marriage, Morality, and the Law* (New York: Oxford University Press, 2012); Sonu Bedi, *Beyond Race, Sex, and Sexual Orientation: Legal Equality Without Identity* (New York: Cambridge University Press, 2013), especially 208–51.

[17] The idea of marriage as friendship is underappreciated but hardly new. See, for example, Ruth Abbey and Douglas J. Den Uyl, "The Chief Inducement? The Idea of Marriage as Friendship," *Journal of Applied Philosophy*, 18 (2001), 37–52.

[18] I borrow the term "mandate of nondiscriminatory treatment" from Pamela S. Karlan, "Let's Call the Whole Thing Off: Can States Abolish the Institution of Marriage?" *California Law Review*, 98 (2010), 701.

what people are usually referring to when they object to plural marriage because it is supposed to be too inegalitarian.

I do not limit myself to the tools of legal analysis – narrowly construed – but I also draw upon arguments of political morality found in contemporary normative political theory scholarship. I take this approach due to my belief that American constitutional practice incorporates something like a neutrality or public justification requirement that demands that states offer sufficiently public reasons on behalf of laws that infringe on fundamental rights or permit unequal treatment. Before it may do so, the state must be able to articulate a rationale that all reasonable persons could share so the law in question is legitimate. That public justification requirement precludes appeals to the alleged superiority of a particular way of life or to empirically questionable claims or speculation about adverse consequences.[19] In the context of the debate over how to define marriage as fairly as possible, one cannot simply argue that monogamous marriage is intrinsically better than all the alternatives. First, it may not be so, given the well-known pathologies of monogamous marriage and intimate relationships. Second, even if it were better, generally speaking, that fact would still not necessarily justify not having the option of marital multiplicity. People are allowed to form and stay in all kinds of unhealthy personal relationships, including violent ones. That some or perhaps many marital choices are less than wise does not entail that either person should be denied the right to marry or stay in the marriage. One does not have to be a Libertarian to appreciate why some and probably most of the most personal of personal choices are best left to the people who are most directly affected by them. Usually, they are in a better position to make such choices due to the likelihood they know themselves and their personal needs better than anyone else does.

At times, it can be difficult to discern where an argument of political morality ends and where a constitutional argument begins because the implications of abstract constitutional language may not be evident. As I see it, in hard cases, what the Constitution means is really about what it should mean more often than not. The constitutional text itself and external sources, such as case law, history, structure, and moral theory, cannot answer the most challenging questions in a manner that is beyond reasonable dispute. Arguments of political morality have always been and always will be relevant to judging and understanding the nuances of constitutional practice. In such cases, judges have considerable discretion and thus can construct new

[19] For an overview of the philosophical concept of public justification, see Kevin Vallier and Fred D'Agostino, "Public Justification," http://plato.stanford.edu/entries/justification-public.

constitutional meanings.[20] Like it or not, that is judicial lawmaking – however judges describe their actions. As long as judges retain the power of judicial review and do not let all the laws they could invalidate stand, they will be legislating. The only remaining issues are how often they do it, when they should do it, and whether it is justified in particular instances.

Although the task of providing answers to hard constitutional questions seems to fall only on judges, it is also the responsibility of lawyers, public officials, political elites, and the rest of us to decide which new constitutional meanings will be conceived. This country might benefit from a frank discussion about the nature of judging in hard constitutional cases and the inevitability of judicial lawmaking so that ordinary Americans at the very least, ordinary Americans can be better informed about the constitutional choices that are made in their name. It is troubling, if not pernicious, to mislead the public by pretending that judging is always like umpiring or that the law always produces deductively valid answers. The implication is that someone who disagrees with the outcome of a particular case must be acting in bad faith in the sense of not caring what the law is.

Initially, for purely practical reasons, many people would reject the view, which I shall develop and defend in this book, that the Constitution requires states – as long as they remain in the marriage business – to provide alternatives to dyadic marriage.[21] But one cannot simply respond to any normative claim by insisting it is unrealistic, as if doing so were enough to end the conversation. At one moment in American history, the abolition of slavery and the enfranchisement of women looked unrealistic. At least one legal scholar believes that family law could accommodate marital multiplicity quite easily.[22] Another scholar introduces some interesting proposals about how the tax system could be reformed if states were to recognize polygamous relationships.[23] It should not be too easy to summarily dismiss any proposed

[20] See, for example, Richard A. Posner, *Reflections on Judging* (Cambridge, MA: Harvard University Press, 2013).

[21] Nonetheless, concerns about the possible unconstitutionality of laws that criminalize polygamy or fail to recognize multiperson relationships as marriages have arisen in other countries. See, for example, Martha Bailey et al., "Expanding Recognition of Foreign Polygamous Marriages: Policy Implications for Canada." *Queens University Legal Studies Research Paper* No. 7-12. Prepared for Status of Women Canada. Available at http://papers.ssrn.com/sol3/papers.cfm?abstract_id=1023896. The report recommends that "Canada prepare for a constitutional challenge to the limitation of marriage to two persons." Recently, the British Columbia Supreme Court issued an advisory opinion regarding Section 293 of the Criminal Code of Canada, which keeps polygamy illegal, and concluded it was constitutional.

[22] Goldfeder, *Legalizing Plural Marriage: The Next Frontier in Family Law*, 149 (forthcoming, University of New England Press), esp. 162–187.

[23] Samuel D. Brunson, "Taxing Polygamy," *Washington University Law Review*, 91 (2013), 113–68.

reform – marital or otherwise – on the grounds it is utopian. After all, in constitutional controversies, public opinion can shift rapidly.[24] Anyone with specialized legal knowledge and imagination – when the law is unsettled and the timing is right – can put together a legal argument that arguably justifies the outcome he or she prefers. This phenomenon appears over and over again. American history demonstrates that forecasting our constitutional future must be done with humility. Certain constitutional understandings, which the legal community used to consider farfetched, are now widely accepted.[25] Not long ago, the claim that same-sex couples have a constitutional right to marry would have been met with derision by most legal experts.[26] From the standpoint of world history, the very idea of (monogamous) same-sex marriage is far more unprecedented than certain forms of polygamy. We should try to avoid having too selective of a memory.

Before I proceed any further, I want to clarify some of the terminology that appears in this book. According to anthropologists, "polygyny" is a man with multiple wives, "polyandry" is a woman with multiple husbands, and "polygynandry" (or group marriage) is any combination of three or more persons.[27] "Polyamory" also covers such arrangements and is not pejorative.[28] "Polyfidelity" emphasizes the possibility of individual choice and equality when three or more persons form such a relationship.[29] I will use "polygamy" to refer to any situation in which three or more adults consider themselves to be a unit, they are not legally married, and each of them is physically intimate with at least one of the other persons, even when they do not live together.[30] For the most part, I use "polygamy" and "polyamory" interchangeably,

24 According to a recent Pew Center poll, 14 percent of Americans surveyed proclaimed they had changed their minds in favor of permitting same-sex marriage. www.people-press.org/2013/06/06/homosexuality-opinion.

25 See Jack M. Balkin, *Living Originalism* (Cambridge, MA: The Belknap Press of Harvard University Press, 2011).

26 Klarman, *From the Closet to the Altar*, 19.

27 Miriam Koktvedgaard Zeitzan, *Polygamy: A Cross-Cultural Analysis* (New York: Berg, 2008), 3.

28 See Deborah Anapol, *Polyamory in the Twenty-First Century: Love and Intimacy With Multiple Partners* (Lanham, MD: Rowman & Littlefield, 2010). However, some commentators caution against using "polyamory" and "polygamy" interchangeably. See, for example, D. Marisa Black, "Beyond Child Brides: Polygamy, Polyamory, Unique Familial Constructions, and the Law," *Journal of Law and Family Studies*, 8 (2006), 498.

29 Maura I. Strassberg, "The Challenge of Post-Modern Polygamy: Considering Polyamory," *Capital Law Review*, 31 (2003), 452.

30 Historically, the meaning of "polygamy" has varied. In some places, "polygamy" referred to a man (or, less frequently, a woman) who had abandoned his first spouse without divorcing her and then had "married" another woman. What made polygamy wrong, then, is what made adultery wrong. See, for example, John Witte Jr., *The Western Case for Monogamy Over Polygamy* (forthcoming from Cambridge University Press).

even though many scholars would not conflate them. I do so due to my belief that even inegalitarian marriages, including traditional polygynous ones, are entitled to legal protection as long as they involve consenting adults do not violate other valid laws. A "triad" or a "thruple" involves three partners who are sexually connected. A "hinge" or "pivot" exists when only one of the partners has a sexual relationship with the other two persons. "Quads" contain four persons and "moresomes" include five or more adults.[31] Group marriages can be configured in multiple ways.[32] While my definition of polygamy is probably underinclusive, it captures the basic distinction between monogamy and polygamy in the minds of most Americans: open sexual nonexclusivity.[33]

While "polyamory" implies a more egalitarian relationship, I deliberately use "polygamy" to cover all multiperson intimate relationships among adults the state refuses to recognize as a legal status. I do so because I doubt (a) the state should recognize only marriages that are sufficiently internally egalitarian; (b) even if the state wanted to do so, it could determine with much precision whether the prospective marital partners are likely to meet the minimum equality criteria when they apply for a marriage license; (c) and the state could effectively oversee people's behaviors during their marital relationship without intolerable invasions of privacy. As a practical matter, according legal status to polyamorous relationships also entails according such status to polygynous ones.[34]

In referring to being married to more than one person simultaneously, then, my preference is to use "plural marriage" – not only to avoid connoting polygyny rooted in patriarchal religious or cultural traditions but to eschew a premature evaluation of the rights and wrongs of such relationships. Americans too frequently make snap judgments about beliefs and practices that seem exotic to them. I suspect this term is about as neutral as possible to

[31] Arin Greenwood, "Who Are 'The Polyamorists Next Door'? Q&A With Author Elisabeth Sheff," *Huffington Post*, March 5, 2014.

[32] See Diane J. Klein, "Plural Marriage and Community Property Law," *Golden Gate University Law Review*, 41 (2010), especially 48–53.

[33] It may not be as easy to define monogamy as it initially may seem because different couples may understand infidelity or appropriate boundaries differently. See Meg Barker and Darren Langdridge, "Introduction," in *Understanding Non-Monogamies*, ed. Meg Barker and Darren Langdridge (New York: Routledge, 2010), 3–20.

[34] Legal scholars cannot afford the luxury of assuming ideal conditions given the intractable imperfections of human beings and their institutions. That a real liberal democracy could never ensure internal equality in marriages in the absence of draconian measures is an independent and probably decisive reason for not incorporating equality into its licensing criteria.

American eyes and ears and I will employ it to cover any legal status where at least three persons constitute a single marital unit – notwithstanding its configuration and gender composition. Furthermore, this book addresses whether consenting adults should be able to have such a marital relationship and only touches upon whether any kind of plural marriage is better than its monogamous counterpart, which is not the real issue, constitutionally speaking. For my purposes, polygamy is an intimate relationship among three or more adults that the state does not recognize as a marriage or its legal equivalent. By this definition, right now, there could be as many as 500,000 polygamous households in the United States.[35] As of this writing, no state has decriminalized polygamy or come close to doing so. What is left of the Defense of Marriage Act (DOMA) discriminates not only against same-sex couples but also against all polygamous unions.[36] For my purposes, the only difference between polygamy and a plural marriage is that the state recognizes the latter as a legal status.

The definition of marriage, which I defend in subsequent chapters and believe to be constitutionally required, would dramatically change the current legal meaning of marriage by covering a much wider variety of intimate relationships. Only by making marriage considerably more inclusive can states respect the marital choices of all adults and treat them equally without making controversial moral judgments about their respective ways of life. With this new definition of marriage in place, irrespective of their gender, two or more adult siblings or close friends could marry each (or one) another. Such marriage would not have to be premised on any sort of sexual intimacy, and it also would include incestuous relationships between or among consenting adults.[37]

I. CONTEMPORARY POLYGAMY

Whatever names they go by, the ideas of polygamy and plural marriage are not new. The Hebrew Bible refers to multipartner relationships, such as those of Moses, Abraham, David, and Solomon.[38] In the past, certain Christian sects

[35] Sherif Girgis, Ryan T. Anderson, and Robert P. George, *What Is Marriage? Man and Woman: A Defense* (New York: Encounter Books, 2012), 51.

[36] Martha M. Ertman, "Race Treason: The Untold Story of America's Ban on Polygamy," *Columbia Journal of Gender and Law*, 19 (2010), 357–62.

[37] For a qualified defense of (adult) incestuous marriage, see Andrew F. March, "What Lies Beyond Same-Sex Marriage: Marriage, Reproductive Freedom and Future Persons in Liberal Public Justification," *Journal of Applied Philosophy*, 27 (2010), 39–58.

[38] 1 Samuel 25: 43–44; and 1 Kings 7: 8. The *Talmud* also allows polygamy. In Western Europe, the practice was banned around 1000 CE. Norman Solomon, *Judaism: A Very Short*

engaged in polygamy.[39] Some Native Americans have also done so and still do.[40] Polygamous practices continue to exist in Africa.[41] In one interpretation of the Islamic tradition, men are allowed to marry up to four wives – subject to certain conditions.[42] In the United States, it is estimated that 75,000 Muslims have polygynous relationships.[43] Polygamy has not disappeared from the Hmong culture.[44] Those who identify themselves as FLDS continue to believe that polygyny is a religious duty.[45] In some parts of the world, polygamy is more prevalent than monogamy.[46] According to one study, in societies that legally permit polygyny, 5 to 10 percent of men actually practice it.[47] Several years ago, Canadians debated whether polygamy must be decriminalized under the Canadian Charter of Rights and Freedoms.[48] Almost fifty countries perform plural marriages.[49] Several democracies, such as Great Britain, Australia, France, and New Zealand, give some degree of legal protection to those involved in plural marriages entered into in countries that allow them.[50] In the past decade, South Africa created the option of plural marriage for men from certain tribes.[51] While the Netherlands does not perform its own plural marriages or accord them civil union status, it allows

Introduction (New York: Oxford University Press, 1996), 91. Judaism was unenthusiastic about polygamy but was willing to permit the practice under some circumstances.

39 John Cairncross, *After Polygamy Was Made a Sin: The Social History of Christian Polygamy* (London: Routledge and Kegan Paul, 1974). There are few references to polygamy in the *New Testament*. The Catholic Church unequivocally banned the practice in 1563. See Goldfeder, *Revisiting Polygamy*, 13.

40 Jonathan Turley, "Expert Report Prepared for the *Amicus Curiae*," October 20, 2010, p. 5. Hereinafter, "Turley Report."

41 See Zeitzan, *Polygamy*, 157–64.

42 Those conditions include the consent of the wives and their being treated equitably. Needless to say, the issue is controversial in Islamic thought about the family. www.islamology.com/Overview/Women/Polygamy in Islam.htm. The prophet Muhammad may have married as many as thirteen women. Malise Ruthven, *Islam: A Very Short Introduction* (New York: Oxford University Press, 2012), 110.

43 Barbara Bradley Hagerty, "Some Muslims in U.S. Quietly Engage in Polygamy," May 27, 2008. www.npr.org/templates/story/story.php?storyId=90857818.

44 http://hmongamerican.blogspot.com/2011/08/polygamist-marriages-in-hmong-culture.html

45 Richard Lyman Bushman, *Mormonism: A Very Short Introduction* (New York: Oxford University Press, 2008), 14, 86–91.

46 See Stephanie Coontz, *Marriage, A History: How Love Conquered Marriage* (New York: Penguin Books, 2005), 10.

47 See Philip L. Kilbride, *Plural Marriage for Our Times: A Reinvented Option?* (Westport, CT: Bergin & Garvey, 1994), 31.

48 Janet Bennion, *Polygamy in Primetime: Media, Gender, and Politics in Mormon Fundamentalism* (Waltham, MA: Brandeis University Press, 2012), 5.

49 Ibid., 247.

50 Ibid.

51 See Judith Stacey, *Unhitched: Love, Marriage, and Family Values From West Hollywood to Western China* (New York: New York University Press, 2011), 10.

polygamists to protect their relationship to some extent through private cohabitation contracts.[52]

American attitudes toward sexuality and marriage have been changing slowly but surely to the point where it is now much harder to ascertain what kinds of intimate relationships, marriages, or families are normal. In this country, "normal" tends to mean morally correct or socially acceptable. Multiperson intimate relationships are more visible than they used to be and that visibility – in conjunction with the ongoing debate about the meaning of marriage – may eventually prompt Americans to question the legitimacy of numerical restrictions. For one scholar, "postmodern polygamy" or polyamory differs from traditional polygyny in important respects and deserves its own analysis.[53] As I grow older, I am less convinced I know normal when I see it and more convinced that most of us only know what our own personal lives are like; those of others' remain opaque. Public figures used to have to keep all their unconventional beliefs or behaviors a secret for fear of exposure. Eleanor and Franklin Roosevelt had an atypical marriage and did everything they could to conceal it from the public. For all we know, prior to the Monica Lewinsky scandal, Bill and Hillary Clinton may have had an understanding, so to speak. During the 2012 Republican presidential primary, Newt Gingrich had to defend himself against accusations he had asked his wife for an open marriage.[54] In the 2012 general presidential election, Mitt Romney suffered some political embarrassment when the media reported that some of his ancestors had been polygamists.[55]

Moreover, a serious conversation about the very possibility of plural marriage may seem premature when the American public remains divided over same-sex marriage.[56] In 2013, the U.S. Supreme Court stopped short of declaring that the Constitution mandates such marriage or even civil union status when a state already gives marriage licenses to opposite-sex couples.[57]

[52] In the Netherlands, the first thruple did so in 2005. www.brusselsjournal.com/node/301. See also John Corvino, *What's Wrong With Homosexuality?* (New York: Oxford University Press, 2013), 133.

[53] Strassberg, "The Challenge of Post-Modern Polygamy," 440–41; see also Mark Goldfeder and Elisabeth Sheff, "Children of Polyamorous Families: A First Empirical Look," *Journal of Law and Social Deviance*, 5 (2011), 155.

[54] Halperin and Heilemann, *Double Down*, 252.

[55] www.csmonitor.com/USA/Elections/President/2012/0421/Mitt-Romney-addresses-a-touchy-subject-about-his-religion

[56] The most recent national polls reveal that a majority of Americans support same-sex marriage. Klarman, *From the Closet to the Altar*, 204.

[57] *United States v. Windsor*, 570 U.S. __ (2013) (reviewing the Second Circuit's decision to invalidate part of DOMA) and *Hollingsworth v. Perry*, 570 U.S. __ (2013) (reviewing the Ninth

No state has ever recognized any kind of plural marriage.[58] Nor will any legislature or court do so in the near future. In 2007, the Supreme Court denied a petition for a *writ of certiorari* in such a case.[59] At most, the decriminalization of polygamy in some states may be off in the distance. As one writer observes: "We live in a society that presumes that marriage is between one man and one woman, and even though many polygamous cultures exist, we take it for granted that a marriage involves two people and only two people."[60] No influential social movement or legal organization currently advocating such a dramatic revision in the legal definition of marriage exists. At this moment, the extension of the right of marriage to thruples and larger marital groups would generate enormous controversy. For the most part, Americans do not discuss plural marriage openly or fairly, as if the topic were undeserving of serious thought.

My hope is that this situation will change sooner rather than later. That may be wishful thinking, but one of the goals of this book is to induce readers to imagine that marriage in the future could be a much more inclusive institution that acknowledges the reality of the diversification of the family and the need for greater flexibility in family arrangements. People are similar in some respects but very different in others when it comes to what they want from their intimate relationships. For this reason, one size never has and never will fit all. Americans are becoming more accustomed to the possibility that it may not be wrong for people to have an unconventional intimate relationship, provided that everything is consensual and between or among those who are legally capable of giving consent. Under existing constitutional doctrine, most deeply personal choices are presumptively entitled to protection.

Marriage is one of those choices that almost all people want to make for themselves. The institution remains very important to the vast majority of Americans.[61] On average, it is likely to be in one way or another an essential component of their conception of the good. For some of them, it may be more

Circuit's decision to invalidate California's Proposition 8 and deciding that on appeal, the petitioners lacked standing to challenge the district court's order to enjoin the enforcement of Proposition 8).

58 Andrew Koppelman, *Same Sex, Different States: When Same-Sex Marriages Cross State Lines* (New Haven, CT: Yale University Press, 2006), 131.

59 *Holm v. Utah*, 127 S. Ct. 1371 (2007).

60 Barbara J. Risman, "Families: A Great American Institution," in *Families As They Really Are*, ed. Barbara J. Risman (New York: W. W. Norton, 2010), 456.

61 Martha C. Nussbaum, *From Disgust to Humanity: Sexual Orientation and Constitutional Law* (New York: Oxford University Press, 2010), 127.

important than anything else. Marriage could be an achievement for some individuals, the foundation of the family life they desire, or a symbol of genuine commitment. *Loving v. Virginia* does not have to be read narrowly to only be about interracial marriages; it can stand for the principle that the state may not infringe on marital choice unless it has a compelling justification for doing so.[62] Under conditions of moral pluralism, some Americans may want to marry differently and not have the state refuse to provide them with a menu of marital options to select from. Difference is not always bad or to be feared; it deserves a presumption in its favor under most circumstances. Unfortunately, many Americans do not make the effort to familiarize themselves with the lives of different kinds of minorities. For too long, gays and lesbians had to put up with vicious stereotypes that served as the legal basis of their unequal treatment and social marginalization. In David Chambers's words: "One of the lessons to be derived from exploring the history of reactions to Mormon polygamy is that all of us, including those of us who favor same-sex marriage, find difference threatening, and that all of us, including those who favor same-sex marriage, need to work harder to understand those who are different from us."[63]

Given the human tendency to be suspicious of difference and to find certain kinds to be frightening, one should not be surprised that acceptance – if it comes about at all – occurs gradually. What is less excusable is the unwillingness of so many otherwise bright and conscientious people to make an effort to do so when such judgments adversely impact the quality of the lives of those who belong to the minority in question. The day may come when almost all American voters might accept candidates for public office who are openly gay, lesbian, bisexual, or transgender or have unconventional personal lives. Millennials seem to be less concerned with following traditional sexual mores, more willing to experiment, and less interested in what occurs in the privacy of their neighbors' homes. Today, very few Americans favor making consensual same-sex sex a crime.[64] Open marriages exist, adultery is not uncommon, alternative lifestyles are not as hidden as they used to be, the meaning of sexual identity is being contested, and premarital sexual activity is less likely to be frowned upon as long as neither person is too young nor in a committed or exclusive relationship. In an era of no-fault divorce, almost all Americans tolerate "serial polygamy," in which many people have more than one marital

[62] *Loving v. Virginia*, 388 U.S. 1 (1967).

[63] David L. Chambers, "Polygamy and Same-Sex Marriage," *Hofstra Law Review*, 26 (1997), 54.

[64] Nussbaum, *From Disgust to Humanity*, 67. That said, post-*Lawrence*, some states have still not repealed their antisodomy laws.

partner during their lifetimes. The actor Mickey Rooney and the actress Elizabeth Taylor were each married eight times, yet no one thinks of either of them as polygamists. A growing number of Americans have blended families – which one might describe as *de facto* polygamy – than ever before. In the African-American community, some women favor the option of non-monogamy due to a shortage of marriageable African-American men.[65] For African-Americans, there is a disparity between the rates of interracial marriage, with such marriage taking place much more often for men.[66] Johnny Cochran and Jesse Jackson were involved in concurrent relationships, where they were not simply having affairs but had two families.[67] Former U.S. congressman Vito Fossella also had more than one family at the same time.[68]

Increasingly, the very idea of plural marriage is no longer taboo. In 2009, *Newsweek* presented polyamory in a more favorable light.[69] Such television programs as HBO's *Big Love*, TLC's *Sister Wives*, TLC's *My Five Wives*, and NGC's *Polygamy USA* have illuminated the unique challenges of multipartner intimate relationships; they have also revealed that in some respects, such families may not be so different and, in doing so, have humanized them. Showtime's *Polyamory: Married and Dating* is even more welcome because it is not about a cliché – that is, about a religiously motivated, inordinately large polygynous family – thereby helping more Americans to appreciate that a plural marriage need not be polygynous. In 2013, a U.S. district court partially invalidated Utah's antibigamy law.[70] In the wake of this judicial decision, the *New York Times* broached the plural marriage question.[71] The more charitable media portrayal of polygamy – in the midst of the ongoing battle over same-sex marriage – has finally created space for academics to discuss the quality of the rationale for not extending the right of marriage beyond couples. After all, it could be true that limiting the size of a marriage is just as constitutionally objectionable as restricting marriage to same-race or opposite-sex couples. Several law professors have begun to address how multiperson intimate

65 See, for example, Patricia Dixon-Spear, *We Want for Our Sisters What We Want for Ourselves: African American Women Who Practice Polygyny by Consent* (Baltimore, MD: Inprint Editions, 2009).

66 Ralph Richard Banks, *Is Marriage for White People?: How the African American Marriage Decline Affects Everyone* (New York: Dutton, 2011), 33.

67 See Adrien Katherine Wing, "Polygamy in Black America," in *Critical Race Feminism: A Reader* (2nd ed.), ed. Adrien Katherine Wing (New York: New York University Press, 2003), 190.

68 See Stacey, *Unhitched*, 123–24.

69 Jessica Bennett, "Polyamory: The Next Sexual Revolution?" *Newsweek*, July 29, 2009. www.newsweek.com/polyamory-next-sexual-revolution-82053.

70 *Brown v. Buhman* (2013) (Case No. 2:11-cv-0652)

71 www.nytimes.com/roomfordebate/2013/12/17/should-plural-marriage-be-legal

relationships or plural marriages might be regulated to serve the ends of family law.[72] Because the expansion of marriage to include same-sex couples is bound to cover a broader range of marital relationships, lawmakers, judges, and the rest of us will eventually have to decide which kinds of intimate relationships will be legally recognized as marriages and which kinds will be left out.

According to Section 1.3 of the 2012 Libertarian Party Platform: "Government does not have the authority to define, license, or restrict personal relationships."[73] The ACLU advocates the decriminalization of polygamy.[74] A couple well-known and highly regarded legal academics – Laurence Tribe and Sanford Levinson – have come out in favor of an even more radical view – namely, a constitutional right to plural marriage.[75] And they have company. Cass Sunstein has some sympathy for eliminating the numerosity requirement but believes that such changes ought to be left to the democratic process.[76] Richard Posner insists that a polygynous marriage with the consent of all the women involved could benefit them by widening their range of choices.[77] Sarah Song believes that "qualified recognition" of polygamy can serve the interests of women by facilitating their exit from polygamous communities.[78] Martha Nussbaum maintains that such marriage may be acceptable when women may also marry more than one person at the same time.[79] Elsewhere, she notes that gender equality in personal relationships is not normally considered to be a compelling state interest, which is what a heightened standard of

[72] See, for example, Klein, "Plural Marriage and Community Property Law," 33–89; Adrienne D. Davis, "Regulating Polygamy: Intimacy, Default Rules, and Bargaining for Equality," *Columbia Law Review*, 110 (2010), 1955–2046; Martha M. Ertman, "The Business of Intimacy: Bridging the Private-Private Distinction," in *Feminism Confronts Homo Economicus: Gender, Law, and Society*, ed. Martha Fineman and Terrance Dougherty (Ithaca, NY: Cornell University Press, 2005), 467–500; and Mark Goldfeder, *Legalizing Plural Marriage*.

[73] www.lp.org/platform

[74] The official ACLU policy is that "criminal and civil laws prohibiting or penalizing the practice of plural marriage violate constitutional protections of freedom of expression and association, freedom of religion, and privacy for personal relationships among consenting adults." Policy #91, National ACLU Policy on Polygamy, April 1991: www.worldpolyamoryassociation.net/worldpolyamoryassociation.com/wiki/mywikidb/page/A/ACLU_Strategy.db.

[75] Laurence H. Tribe, *American Constitutional Law* (2nd ed.) (New York: Foundation Press: 1988), 521–28; Sanford Levinson, "The Meaning of Marriage: Thinking About Polygamy," *San Diego Law Review*, 42 (2005), 1049–58.

[76] Cass Sunstein refers to this understanding of marriage as "maximalist." See Cass R. Sunstein, "The Right to Marry," *Cardozo Law Review*, 26 (2005), 2110.

[77] Richard A. Posner, *Sex and Reason* (Cambridge, MA: Harvard University Press, 1992), 257.

[78] Sarah Song, *Justice, Gender, and the Politics of Multiculturalism* (New York: Cambridge University Press, 2007), 162.

[79] Martha C. Nussbaum, *Women and Human Development: The Capabilities Approach* (New York: Cambridge University Press, 2000), 230.

review would call for.[80] Some political theorists who are sympathetic to multicultural critiques of liberalism disparage polygyny yet are less hostile to polyandry.[81] Andrew March defends plural marriage in the language of Rawlsian public reason.[82] Elizabeth Emens reminds us that some people may only be happy in a polygamous relationship.[83] Several economists who study marriage markets find that polygamy enhances women's bargaining power prior to marriage.[84] Judith Butler favors the abolition of marriage.[85]

As the debate over the meaning of marriage unfolds, those who oppose plural marriage can be expected to draw upon the same kinds of arguments that conservatives have deployed against same-sex marriage. When all is said and done, there may be adequate reasons for not changing the status quo, but conservative opponents of plural marriage will have to articulate their normativity. They will have to do more than consult a dictionary, refer to religious understandings, conduct survey research, embrace "tradition," or determine how most people happen to use the "m" word. Equally importantly, it is incumbent upon liberals who seek to treat the two kinds of marriage differently to defend the constitutionality of unequal legal treatment, which is easier said than done. There has to be a legally relevant difference between them or else the state must cease to privilege one at the expense of the other. In the past, liberals who favored same-sex marriage hesitated to join forces with those who advocated decriminalizing polygamy or legally recognizing plural marriages. In fact, some of them went out of their way to distinguish sharply between discrimination against gays and lesbians and discrimination against polygamists.[86] At present, my impression is that the rhetorical imperative of drawing such a distinction and thereby avoiding guilt by association is not nearly as powerful as it used to be. A plural marriage need not be a different-sex situation or even sexual.[87] In explaining why marriage ought to be defined in one

[80] Martha C. Nussbaum, *Liberty of Conscience: In Defense of America's Tradition of Religious Equality* (New York: Basic Books, 2008), 197–98.

[81] See, for example, Bhikhu Parekh, *Rethinking Multiculturalism: Cultural Diversity and Political Theory* (2nd ed.) (New York: Palgrave Macmillan, 2006), 282–92.

[82] Andrew F. March, "Is There a Right to Polygamy? Marriage, Equality and Subsidizing Families in Liberal Public Justification," *Journal of Moral Philosophy*, 8 (2011), 244–70.

[83] Elizabeth F. Emens, "Monogamy's Law: Compulsory Monogamy and Polyamorous Existence," *New York University Review of Law and Social Change*, 29 (2004), 363.

[84] See, for example, Gary S. Becker, *A Treatise on the Family* (Cambridge, MA: Harvard University Press, 1993), 80–107.

[85] Judith Butler, "Competing Universalities," in *Contingency, Hegemony, and Universality: Contemporary Dialogues on the Left* (New York: Verso, 2000), 176–77.

[86] See, for example, William N. Eskridge Jr., *Gaylaw: Challenging the Apartheid of the Closet* (Cambridge, MA: Harvard University Press, 1999), 280–81.

[87] Gregg Strauss, "Is Polygamy Inherently Unequal?" *Ethics*, 122 (2012), 518.

particular way, both sides will have to address the normative question of whether marriage ought to be restricted to couples and defend their respective positions. In doing so, if they care about trying to convince those who disagree with them, they should avoid relying on unduly controversial reasons.

II. DOUBLE STANDARDS

By definition, a double standard involves applying different principles to similar situations. The term implies that the application at issue is unfair because if the principle applies in one way in one situation, then it also ought to apply the same way in another similar situation. Most Americans are aware that the double standard, which emerges when the state limits marriage to different-sex couples, needs a defense. These days, many of them are concluding that the legal status quo in most states can no longer be adequately defended. The strong dignity language of the recent *Windsor* decision (and how some lower federal court judges have been interpreting it subsequently to invalidate bans on same-sex marriage in certain states) indicates that future courts will be more skeptical of the rationale for defining marriage as only being between one man and one woman when the definition is designed to demean sexual minorities.[88] The Supreme Court will probably hear another same-sex marriage case within the next few years in the midst of so much disagreement among the lower federal courts about the constitutional implications of *Windsor*.

Another double standard, which this book underscores, concerns why the state allows almost all different-sex and increasingly more same-sex couples to marry but refuses to acknowledge any plural union.[89] Those who care about gays and lesbians being discriminated against cannot ignore whether those who would marry multiple partners – if they were allowed to do so – are also being treated unfairly.[90] The former kind of discrimination may be more widespread and worse than the latter, but that does not mean the latter is morally or legally acceptable.[91] It never ceases to amaze me just how upset smart people can get about discrimination that directly affects them or others

[88] *United States v. Windsor*, 570 U.S. __ (2013) (Scalia, J., dissenting).

[89] This argument is also called the "argument from inconsistency." Andrew Lister, *Public Reason and Political Community* (London: Bloomsbury Publishing, 2013), 171.

[90] Elizabeth Brake refers to this kind of discrimination – where the state recognizes only two-person amorous relationships – as "amatonormativity." Brake, *Minimizing Marriage*, 5.

[91] Polygamists still face numerous legal disadvantages. For example, under current U.S. immigration law, a polygamist cannot become a naturalized citizen. In addition, such a person could be deported for having such a relationship. www.nolo.com/legal-encyclopedia/will-you-be-denied-us-citizenship-based-polygamy-bigamy-multiple-marriages.html.

who are close to them while being so unsympathetic to other kinds that lie outside their personal experience. We should have to go through the pain of discrimination ourselves before we can begin to appreciate how much it diminishes the lives of its victims.

Ultimately, the constitutionality of any restriction on marriage turns on its public justification – that is, on the quality of the reasons the state advances on its behalf.[92] In the case of plural marriage, those who want such marriage to receive a fair hearing must be wary of how easy it is to believe we have been fair when we have not been so. According to Nussbaum: "Disgust . . . often prevents us from looking for . . . good reasons . . . creating the misleading impression that the policy already has been well defended."[93] From any liberal standpoint, all the reasons conservatives use to defend their opposition to same-sex marriage miss the mark. What too many liberals fail to see is that the compelling reasons that support same-sex marriage, such as the value of personal choice in selecting a marital partner and the importance of equal legal treatment, also support a right to plural marriage. The slope from same-sex to plural marriage may be slipperier than many liberals notice or are willing to admit.[94] Anyone who rejects their constitutional equivalence will not only have to prove that the two kinds of marriage differ in relevant respects but additionally that the state may treat them differently without acting unconstitutionally. Despite their professed tolerance of difference, most liberals have made little effort to do so. Although many of them act as if they wished that the possibility of plural marriage did not exist, they should not let themselves be manipulated into choosing between only caring about one kind of discrimination, particularly when a plural marriage could be same sex, bisexual, or asexual.

III. THE CONSTITUTIONAL RIGHT TO MARRIAGE

While all legal scholars acknowledge a constitutional right to marriage, they do not agree on its scope, which is to say that only some restrictions are permissible.[95] In *Loving*, the Supreme Court ruled that the state's asserted

[92] See Ronald C. Den Otter, *Judicial Review in an Age of Moral Pluralism* (New York: Cambridge University Press, 2009); Bedi, *Beyond Race, Sex, and Sexual Orientation*.

[93] Nussbaum, *From Disgust to Humanity*, 20.

[94] See Kent Greenfield, "The Slippery Slope to Polygamy and Incest," *The American Prospect*, July 15, 2013. http://prospect.org/article/slippery-slope-polygamy-and-incest.

[95] See, for example, *Loving v. Virginia*, 388 U.S. 1 (1967) (the unconstitutionality of laws that ban interracial marriages); *Boddie v. Connecticut*, 401 U.S. 371 (1971) (the unconstitutionality of laws that require unreasonably high filing fees and court costs to divorce); *Zablocki v. Redhail*, 434 U.S. 374 (1978) (the unconstitutionality of laws that prohibit those who are delinquent on

interest in preserving white supremacy could not limit the right of marriage to same-race couples.[96] Other restrictions, such as those involving sexual orientation, remain controversial but are increasingly difficult to defend. Prior to the *Windsor* decision, several lower federal courts found Section 3 of DOMA to be unconstitutional.[97] *Perry v. Schwarzenegger* and *Perry v. Brown* indicate that such courts are more receptive to a broader definition of marriage than they used to be.[98] Several state supreme courts have also moved in this direction.[99] *Romer v. Evans* establishes that animus against gays and lesbians cannot warrant unequal treatment.[100] *Lawrence* makes it much more difficult for a state to enact morals legislation.[101] The Supreme Court did not reach the merits of the law being challenged in *Hollingsworth*, but it let stand the lower federal courts' decisions to invalidate Proposition 8.[102] In his majority opinion in *Windsor*, Justice Anthony Kennedy extends the rationale, which he first announced in *Romer*, to the denial of federal benefits to married same-sex couples: A bare desire to harm a politically unpopular group cannot constitute a legitimate state interest.[103]

While what follows from the holding is not automatically that states can no longer limit marriage to only two persons, it is becoming increasingly more constitutionally challenging for the state to treat what Bedi calls "plural marriage enthusiasts" differently if that differential treatment reflects an intention to stigmatize them.[104] Indeed, these days, those who seek to practice polygamy may need more judicial protection than other sexual minorities.[105] Just like discrimination against gays and lesbians, discrimination against polygamists may call for a heightened standard of review. And that includes the marital discrimination that all plural marriage enthusiasts continue to

their child support payments from remarrying); and *Turner v. Safley*, 428 U.S. 78 (1987) (the unconstitutionality of laws that prevent prisoners from marrying).

96 *Loving v. Virginia*, 388 U.S. 1 (1967).

97 See, for example, *Gill et al. v. Office of Personnel Management*, 682 F. 3d 1 (1st Cir.) (2012); *Golinsky v. Office of Personnel Management*, 824 F. Supp. 2d 968 (N.D. Cal.) (2012).

98 See *Perry v. Schwarzenegger*, 704 F. Supp. 2d. 921 (N.D. Cal. 2010); and *Perry v. Brown*, 671 F. 3d 1052 (2012).

99 See, for example, *Baehr v. Lewin*, 852 P. 2d 44 (Haw. 1993); *Baker v. Vermont*, 744 A. 2d 864 (Vt. 1999); *Goodridge v. Department of Health*, 798 N.E. 2d 941 (Mass. 2003); *In re Marriage Cases*, 43 Cal. 4d 757, 183 P. 3d 384, 76 Cal. Rptr. 3d 683 (2008); *Kerrigan v. Commissioner of Public Health*, 289 Cnn. 135, 957 A. 2d 407 (2008).

100 *Romer v. Evans*, 517 U.S. 620 (1996).

101 *Lawrence v. Texas*, 539 U.S. 558 (2003).

102 *Hollingsworth v. Perry*, 570 U.S. __ (2013).

103 *United States v. Windsor*, 570 U.S. __ (2013).

104 Bedi, *Beyond Race, Sex, and Sexual Orientation*, 220–24.

105 That is not to say, of course, that gays and lesbians are no longer subject to different kinds of unjustified discrimination in many places in this country.

experience. Historically, antipolygamy discourse and activism has a disturbing racial dimension.[106] A numerical limitation may lack support unless the state can enunciate a more persuasive rationale for not having plural marriages. One argument against polygamy is that it is more likely than monogamy to harm women and children.[107] Another argument is that polygamy undermines gender equality.[108] More than a century ago, Justice Stephen Field wrote: "They [bigamy and polygamy] tend to destroy the purity of the marriage relation, to disturb the peace of families, to degrade woman, and to debase man. Few crimes are more pernicious to the best interests of society and receive more general or more deserved punishment."[109]

Those days are not over. Many Americans continue to associate plural marriages with the subordination of women – and this association is not baseless, given the particular pedigree of polygyny in this country and elsewhere and the dynamics of some and perhaps a fair number of polygynous relationships.[110] As I shall show, though, none of the arguments that are designed to undermine a constitutional right to plural marriage are strong enough to justify a numerical restriction, especially when regulation remains a viable option. Such arguments do not override the strong presumption in favor of the state's having to respect the autonomy of competent adults by allowing them to make their own marital choices. First, the state cannot merely assert harm or base its policy on a small sample of illegal polygynous relationships. The alleged harm in question must not only be serious but must also be proven before the state's interest in preventing it is strong enough to justify a criminal prohibition or unequal treatment of all plural relationships. The harms associated with certain kinds of polygyny often reflect the conditions under which such arrangements exist, including the state's failure to regulate them effectively, and the beliefs that the participants have internalized and act on. Second, women and children can be protected from possible harm in more direct ways that are independent of marital status.[111] Constitutionally, the issue ought to be whether competent adults should be

[106] See Martha M. Ertman, "Race Treason: The Untold Story of America's Ban on Polygamy," *Columbia Journal of Gender and Law*, 19 (2010), 287–366.

[107] Thom Brooks, "The Problem With Polygamy," *Philosophical Topics*, 37 (2009), 111.

[108] Susan Moller Okin, "Is Multiculturalism Bad for Women?" in *Is Multiculturalism Bad for Women?* ed. Joshua Cohen, Matthew Howard, and Martha C. Nussbaum (Princeton, NJ: Princeton University Press, 1999), 587–97.

[109] *Davis v. Beason*, 133 U.S. 333, 341 (1890) (Field, J., majority).

[110] However, the historical antipolygamist discourse in this country is complicated because of its being about so many other things: race, gender, citizenship, and political power. See Martha M. Ertman, "Race Treason," 287–366.

[111] Cass R. Sunstein and Richard H. Thaler, "Privatizing Marriage," *Monist*, 91 (2008), 384.

free to choose such a marital relationship and not whether it would be wise for most people to do so, whether the legal recognition of different types of plural marriages would irreparably damage the traditional institution of marriage, or whether the licensing of only two-person marriages would produce better overall consequences. Constitutionally, their personal reasons are their own and should be presumed to be valid.

Those reasons do not have to be religious.[112] As one commentator remarks: "It seems perfectly possible for someone to have the most serious religious or personal reasons for wanting [plural marriage]."[113] True, at present, the vast majority of those who advocate for plural marriage are religiously motivated. Some FLDS believe that polygyny remains a religious duty.[114] In this book, I hope to convince the reader that such marriage need not involve such notorious figures as Warren Jeffs, Tom Green, or Brian David Mitchell, the man who kidnapped Elizabeth Smart. To equate polygyny more generally with plural marriage is to mistake the part for the whole and to transform polygamy into its worst possible manifestations, thereby ruling out the likelihood that unconventional marital arrangements may work well in some instances and preempting a serious discussion about their possible merits. As Diane Klein notes, those who object to plural marriage are almost always objecting to what she names "asymmetrical polygyny," where the male is married to the other female spouses but they are not married to each or one another.[115] In Bedi's words, "one man and many women may be the more popular instance of plural marriage but certainly not the only kind."[116] Moreover, some people may be more satisfied in nonmonogamous marital relationships than they would be in more traditional monogamous ones.[117] Their personal lives can then be more honest inasmuch as they have polygamous desires yet no longer have to conceal them from their partners.[118] An adult may prefer a multiperson marital arrangement – however it may be constituted – to any of the alternatives. That possibility should not be too hard to imagine in light of how different people are and how different their circumstances may be.

In the past, states have imposed few restrictions on marriage, and right now, they impose even fewer. To be legally recognized, a two-person marriage

[112] Jon Mahoney, "Liberalism and the Polygamy Question," *Social Philosophy Today*, 23 (2008), 162.

[113] Ralph Wedgwood, "The Fundamental Argument for Same-Sex Marriage," *Journal of Political Philosophy*, 7 (1999), 242.

[114] Bennion, *Polygamy in Primetime*, 7.

[115] Klein, "Plural Marriage and Community Property Law," 46, n. 53.

[116] Bedi, *Beyond Race, Sex, and Sexual Orientation*, 222.

[117] Emens, "Monogamy's Law," 284.

[118] Ibid., 277–376.

does not have to be companionate; it can begin in that way but later cease to be so without automatically dissolving. As one commentator observes: "The law determines who is eligible for marriage ... but it says almost nothing about what marriage itself consists in; it is a contract without content."[119] A prenuptial agreement empowers a couple to contract around many of the rules that would otherwise govern their future divorce proceedings. Postnuptial agreements can perform a similar function if they are enforced.[120] In three states, couples can opt for a covenant marriage, which requires premarital counseling and additional counseling if problems arise during the marriage and limits the grounds of divorce.[121] Without much trouble, they can personalize many aspects of their marital relationship to suit their particular preferences.

Nevertheless, every state claims to have an interest in how a marriage is configured; it must be between two and only two persons. Under the status quo, people have fewer options than they would have if they could marry multiple persons or just one person who is already married. In all fifty states, as long as an individual meets the age, consanguinity, and mental competence requirements, that person may marry another person of the opposite gender.[122] As of this writing, depending on the metric used, in thirty-five states (and counting) of those states and in Washington, DC, he or she may marry a person of the same gender.[123] With the exception of a fraudulent marriage –

[119] Brook J. Sadler, "Re-Thinking Civil Unions and Same-Sex Marriage," *Monist*, 91 (2008), 580–81.

[120] In California, for example, such agreements are used very frequently but are enforceable if they achieve mutual advantage. They also require the higher standard of care required in a prenuptial agreement – that is, more than just contract principles but also that they not be voided for "encouraging dissolution" (for example a payout if the marriage does not work, such as a *mahr*, a Muslim agreement that requires the husband to give the wife a set amount of money upon divorce, which is *void ab initio* because it encourages divorce). Postnuptial agreements can cover a wide variety of areas – from separating community and separate property, allocating limits on spousal support, and providing for ownership of community businesses and the like. I thank Jude Egan for his insights here and some of the wording in this footnote.

[121] So far, only Louisiana, Arizona, and Arkansas have adopted such legislation, which makes it harder to enter a marriage and harder to exit it. See, for example, Louisiana Revised Statute Section 9:272 (2009). See also Brake, *Minimizing Marriage*, 13.

[122] William Burnham, *Introduction to the Law and Legal System of the United States* (5th ed.) (St. Paul, MN: Thomson West, 2011), 518–19.

[123] Alaska, Arizona, California, Colorado, Connecticut, Delaware, Hawaii, Idaho, Illinois, Indiana, Iowa, Kansas, Maine, Maryland, Massachusetts, Minnesota, Montana Nevada, New Hampshire, New Jersey, New Mexico, New York, North Carolina, Oklahoma, Oregon, Pennsylvania, Rhode Island, South Carolina, Utah, Vermont, Virginia, Washington, West Virginia, Wisconsin, and Wyoming.

where a U.S. citizen "marries" a noncitizen so that the noncitizen can become a permanent resident – the law not only overlooks the reasons that individuals have for marrying, but it also pays little attention to how the couple plans to interact with each other. Their personal reasons are their own and thus are not subject to further examination.

They need not love or even like each other to be eligible to marry. A gay man could marry a woman to be covered by her health insurance plan or to hide his sexuality to advance his career. The married couple does not have to live together or see each other on a regular basis. They are free to have an open marriage or be celibate if they so desire. They can structure their finances however they please. A monogamous marriage could be nothing more than a mutually beneficial business arrangement or a very close friendship for mutual emotional support during inevitable hardships. Today, almost any opposite-sex couple can marry for the most idiosyncratic of reasons. They can remain married even when their relationship lacks any intimacy, and receive all the material and expressive benefits that come with marriage. As Case puts it, "we do not only license those marriages entered into only for certain enumerated or even only for worthy purposes."[124] Baltimore Ravens running back Ray Rice knocked out his then-girlfriend (and now wife) in an altercation and dragged her unconscious body out of an elevator. By contrast, regarding plural marriage, the state may treat one's most serious personal reasons for wanting to marry more than one person at the same time very differently than another's frivolous reasons for wanting to marry only one person. And when the marriage begins, couples are pretty much free to interact with each other however they please. At most, their mutual ethical duties are imperfect, as Kantians like to say; they can be fulfilled in multiple ways at the discretion of the person who is supposed to perform them because marital arrangements tend to be contextual. A couple can cease being a couple, so to speak, and still receive all the benefits that come with marriage – as long as they do not legally separate or divorce.

Upon reflection, it is not evident why this egregious unequal legal treatment is allowed. This double standard – where the personal reasons for a monogamous marriage are almost always good enough and the personal reasons for a plural marriage are always bad as far as the state is concerned – is too often presupposed to be morally and legally correct. Either this judgment needs a rigorous defense or those who oppose plural marriage will have to concede that the state may scrutinize the personal reasons of couples when

[124] Mary Anne Case, "Marriage Licenses," *Minnesota Law Review*, 89 (2005), 1782.

they apply for marriage licenses to determine which prospective marriages are likely to be at least minimally meritorious. I say that half in jest. In a liberal society that values personal choice, the meaning of marriage is best left to competent adults who can decide for themselves what they want their marital relationship to be. That proposal aligns with the constitutional principle that we let people form, revise, and pursue their different conceptions of the good with as little interference as possible by the state. They could choose a traditional two-person opposite-sex marriage; a nontraditional more egalitarian two-person opposite-sex marriage; a two-person same-sex marriage; or a two-person nonsexual marriage – regardless of its gender composition. By contrast, they cannot choose any sort of plural union – notwithstanding its possible merits. We let people have different religious beliefs and practices. We let them select different educational institutions and professions. We let entrepreneurs form different business associations. But we do not let them marry differently, so to speak, and that state of affairs must change.

Marriage can be about many things; it is not just about sexual gratification or procreation but may also include other kinds of intimacy and human goods. Marriage does not have to contain a romantic element. In fact, it might be preferable – all things considered – for more people to put one or more close friendships at the center of their personal lives and cease overvaluing amorous relations that are fraught with peril. At any rate, the choice should be theirs – and theirs alone. That is not to say people will always make thoughtful choices. The point is surely not that a particular individual's personal reasons for wanting an unconventional marital arrangement are always admirable or even intelligible. Instead, the state must consider the likelihood that such an arrangement may be the best way of respecting their autonomy and meeting their particular needs, thereby fostering their well-being. The participants of a plural marriage may find such a relationship to be more emotionally satisfying, intellectually stimulating, and sexually fulfilling. In an economic crisis, it may not be a bad idea for more people to pool their resources, such as some extended families do. Children may be more likely to flourish in a family environment that has multiple caregivers, a more efficient division of domestic labor, better parental supervision, and greater financial stability.[125]

[125] The effects of bankruptcy on children can be devastating. See Elizabeth Warren and Amelia Warren Tyagi, *The Two-Income Trap: Why Middle-Class Parents Are Going Broke* (New York: Basic Books, 2003), 178. Unfortunately, there is little data on polygamous families and their effects on children. One recent study emphasizes that (a) polygynous and polyamorous families must be disaggregated and (b) even the harms that allegedly take place in polygynous

The elderly may benefit from the kind of caregiving network a plural marriage could provide.[126] In the event of the death or exit of one of the participants, the presence of more than two people in a marriage-like relationship may make the emotional and financial transition to the new situation easier for everyone than it otherwise would be.

Unfortunately, until recently, media coverage of plural marriage has been superficial – rarely going beyond occasional law enforcement raids on polygynous communities, such as the infamous one in Eldorado, Texas, in 2008, and salacious accounts of older men sexually assaulting underage girls and fathering their children.[127] The public is led to believe that plural marriage can be reduced to other illegal or immoral behaviors. While this *reductio* is not fair, it reflects the mixed feelings that some Americans have about living arrangements they believe to be wrong, although perhaps not so wrong they deserve to be criminalized. In the nineteenth century, John Stuart Mill expressed such ambivalence toward Mormon polygyny when he reluctantly defended the practice.[128] It is important to keep in mind that if a state were to permit plural marriage, it could continue to impose consent and age requirements and prosecute people for such crimes as forcible or statutory rape, underage marriage, incest (between an adult and a minor), intimate partner violence, or fraud. Serious crimes are serious crimes – regardless of the context in which they take place. Even if polygamy itself were decriminalized, crimes that are sometimes associated with it would remain crimes.[129] To be open to the idea of plural marriage is not to believe that all its forms are morally or legally acceptable. Any plausible defense of the option of plural marriage must be qualified. With effective regulation, almost all plural marriages in a liberal democracy like ours would not resemble the polygynous marriages in undeveloped countries that raise well-known concerns about how women and children are being treated.

In this book, I develop and defend what I describe as a pro-choice position based on fundamental rights and equal protection considerations.[130] When it

families are uncertain. See Mark Goldfeder and Elisabeth Sheff, "Children of Polyamorous Families: A First Empirical Look," *Journal of Law and Social Deviance*, 5 (2011), 150–243.

126 Levinson, "The Meaning of Marriage," 1057.

127 See Bennion, *Polygamy in Primetime*, especially 163–94.

128 John Stuart Mill, "On Liberty," in *On Liberty and Other Writings*, ed. Stefan Collini (Cambridge, UK: Cambridge University Press, 1989), 91–92.

129 Bigamy is against the law in all fifty states. For a concise compilation of each state's particular antipolygamy statute, see Klein, "Plural Marriage and Community Property Law," 81–89 (appendix).

130 In my analysis, I abstain from freedom of association analysis, even though this claim has arisen in such state polygamy cases as *Green* and *Holm*, because rightly or wrongly, the Supreme

comes to something as important as marriage, simply put, the more options, the better. The state exceeds its authority when it tries to save competent adults from their ill-conceived personal choices, assuming probably incorrectly that the decision to marry more than one person is always or likely to be misguided. Such a choice may not be any worse than the decision to marry only one person, to remarry, or to remain single. The state may also not justify its discrimination against any minority group by asserting the mere possibility that equal treatment would produce an intolerable future state of affairs when the empirical situation is so uncertain. If there is one thing we should have learned from the recent litigation involving the constitutionality of Proposition 8, it is that the state's alleged interests need not be taken at face value, even under rational basis standard of review. Judges can investigate their sincerity.

Plural marriage is nothing more than a monster under our bed. Ultimately, my belief is that states, which issue marriage licenses to couples, must issue marriage licenses to polygamists so that they can form a multiperson marriage if they so desire.[131] As we shall see, the state's interests are not strong enough to privilege monogamous marriage – opposite sex or same sex. Indeed, the state's purported interests in restricting marriage to couples turn out to be surprisingly weak. The meaning of marriage, then, can be left to individuals, who frequently have very different ideas about what a marriage should be and will only flourish when the law becomes considerably more pluralistic about marriage.

Court has limited freedom of association to speech and assembly protected by the First Amendment. On this point, see Erwin Chemerinsky, *Constitutional Law: Principles and Policies* (4th ed.) (New York: Wolters Kluwer, 2011), 1198. As such, freedom of association is not as directly related to plural marriage compared with these lines of analysis. Additionally, I abstain from free exercise of religion analysis. First, a free exercise claim will probably be more promising when the defendant has been prosecuted for religiously motivated conduct – namely, cohabitating with multiple persons and treating them as wives or "marrying" them in a religious ceremony – when not being able to marry more than one person substantially burdens the free exercise of religion, and the state has purposefully discriminated against a religious minority group. If polygamists are denied the right to marriage, an equal protection claim arises and the state may not invidiously discriminate against religious minorities. Second, there may be no such thing as a free exercise argument because constitutionally, there is no principled way of distinguishing between personal religious and nonreligious reasons for wanting to do or not do certain things. In other words, religion may not be constitutionally special. On this point, see Brian Leiter, *Why Tolerate Religion?* (Princeton, NJ: Princeton University Press, 2013).

[131] At one time, polyamorists were not very interested in marrying. See Hadar Aviram, "Make Lover, Not Law: Perceptions of the Marriage Equality Struggle Among Polyamorist Activists," *Journal of Bisexuality*, 7 (2008), 264. However, new research reveals that a majority of them would marry more than one person simultaneously if doing so were a legal possibility.

I approach the question of plural marriage from an undeniably liberal angle that underscores personal choice, embed the question in the ongoing debate over same-sex marriage, and call attention to the unfairness of the double standard that underlies the disparate legal treatment of monogamous and plural marriage. My assumptions are that (1) at least in the foreseeable future, the state will not leave the marriage business; (2) marriage does not have an essence, natural function, or inherent purpose[132]; (3) it is not necessarily a heterosexual institution nor necessarily tied to procreation or raising children; (4) it does not require sexual exclusivity; (5) it does not have to be predicated on romantic or sexual intimacy ; (6) American constitutional law incorporates something like a neutrality requirement in which laws that infringe on people's personal lives or treat politically vulnerable minorities unequally must be publicly justified; and (7) Americans value autonomy or freedom of choice with respect to their most important personal decisions. While one could take issue with any of these assumptions, those who favor same-sex marriage are keen to endorse them and the arguments I make in this book are addressed to an audience that is already convinced that our Constitution requires states to give marriage licenses to same-sex couples.

Here, I should add that I fully recognize that the constitutional conclusion that competent adults have the right to marry more than one person simultaneously will strike many readers as so radical that it might as well be nothing more than a thought experiment when no state has yet decriminalized bigamy. My response is that (a) just because a proposal is radical does not mean it is wrong constitutionally or morally; (b) what is radical at a particular moment can change over time, as the evolution of the debate over same-sex marriage nicely illustrates; (c) to call something "radical" frequently serves as an excuse for not taking its potential merits seriously; (d) thought experiments are the heart and soul of constitutional theory; and (e) history or political reality may seem to limit what is possible, but it also suggests that one should not be overly pessimistic. Above all, even if one believes that my proposal is unrealistic, I hope the reader can conceive of a possible world in which marriage law is truly nondiscriminatory. Some radical ideas may be bad, but others may turn out to be good. For some readers, then, this book can be read as an attempt to examine the implications of the same-sex marriage debate – whatever the future holds.[133]

[132] Contractual views assume "there is no decisive moral reason for a particular marital structure." See Elizabeth Brake, "Marriage," 5. http://plato.stanford.edu/entries/marriage.

[133] I thank Martha Ertman for urging me to be more concrete about exactly what I am trying to do in this book.

IV. PLAN OF THIS BOOK

In the first chapter, before dealing with the case against plural marriage and identifying its weaknesses, I explore an aspect of constitutional theory to explain why my view that the Constitution requires such marriage is not as farfetched as it may seem. The resources for making such an argument already exist and the public discourse about same-sex marriage raises the deeper question of why marriage has to be between two – and only two – persons. My objective is to show how the indeterminacy of the constitutional text and the inevitability of constitutional constructions in hard cases mean that someday, if public opinion changes, there may be a constitutional right to plural marriage (or its equivalent on equal protection grounds).

In the second chapter, I begin to sketch the case that opponents of plural marriage have formulated and elaborate on why it is not persuasive. I begin in this manner because most Americans probably assume that the state's not providing such an option needs no defense. I then evaluate what I take to be the strongest arguments against plural marriage, such as those that reference gender inequality, other harms, and the appropriateness of paternalism on the part of the state to save women from making what may be poor marital choices.

In the third chapter, I address the remaining arguments that are supposed to cut against a constitutional right to plural marriage: the welfare of children, administrative considerations, tradition, nature, and the new natural law. In terms of constitutional standards of review, the state's interests in not permitting plural marriage may not be important or compelling, which is what a heightened standard of review would require. These interests may not even be legitimate if they reflect moral disapproval or animus. My aim is to demonstrate that none of the reasons offered against plural marriage have crossed the threshold of any standard of review.

In the fourth chapter, I stop playing defense and begin to articulate why the freedom to choose one's marital partner(s) should not be compromised. My strategy is to show that this kind of marital choice is just as important as other types of personal choices the Supreme Court already protects from legislative encroachment, such as whether to use birth control, to have a child, to have consensual sex with another adult, or to end one's life. The more personal the decision is, the more likely the state cannot presumptively interfere with it. That constitutional right of decisional autonomy includes the right to marry multiple persons simultaneously – notwithstanding the quality of one's personal reasons for wanting to do so.

In the fifth chapter, I explain why the apparent unconstitutionality of laws that limit marriage to opposite-sex couples puts into considerable doubt whether the state may treat groups of three or more persons unequally when they seek a marriage license. If the reasons a state relies on to support a numerical restriction are unsatisfactory, then under the Equal Protection Clause, states must extend the right of marriage to polygamists or cease legally recognizing any marriage-like relationships – whatever they are called. Ultimately, not permitting same-sex marriages is sufficiently similar to not permitting plural marriage. In both instances, the state's rationale for using an unduly narrow definition of marriage fails to be convincing. As a result, restricting marriage to couples – same and opposite sex – is unconstitutional.

In the sixth chapter and final chapter, I argue that marriage should be disestablished and describe what form such disestablishment should take – namely, the institutionalization of a regime of semiprivate contracts that would allow competent adults to personalize their intimate relationship as much as possible. Such contracts would let them form just about whatever marriage-like relationship they want to form on the basis of the personal reasons they happen to have and would bind third parties. Marriage law already conveys the message that it is better to be married than unmarried. In doing so, it normalizes some intimate relationships while it marginalizes others that may be equally or more worthwhile. For liberals committed to neutrality, the state is not supposed to privilege traditional different-sex intimate relationships without adequate justification. Laws that do not treat same-sex couples equally imply their inferiority. To avoid such discrimination, most liberals favor the extension of the right of marriage to same-sex couples in the name of marital equality. At the same time, few of them recognize how their position may lead to something much more groundbreaking – namely, disestablishment, where the state must accord legal status to just about any marriage-like relationship that consenting adults want to form.

In the Conclusion, I reiterate why polygamy is not inherently evil or harmful and why the state must provide a much longer menu of marital options to choose from. The debate over same-sex marriage in this country is important and far from finished, but someday, that debate may also induce Americans to decide whether marriage must be limited to couples. Constitutionally, if the reasons the state offers to defend a numerical restriction turn out to be bad reasons, then the state must extend the right of marriage to groups of three or more persons. I may not convince anyone who is not already sympathetic to my view that the Constitution – properly understood – calls for the option of plural marriage. At the very least, though, I hope I will be able to show that such a view merits serious consideration.

1

The Constitutional Possibility of Plural Marriage

In this chapter, before identifying the weaknesses in the case against plural marriage, I delve into constitutional theory to explain why the view that the Constitution requires such marriage is not as implausible as it may initially seem. Not only do the resources for making such an argument already exist, but additionally, several well-known U.S. Supreme Court decisions – particularly *Windsor*, the most recent one concerning same-sex marriage – indicate that states are not free to define marriage however they please. Some of the reasons they typically offer on behalf of their definition are no longer constitutionally admissible. At the very least, that fact calls into question the failure of all states to recognize multiperson unions. My aim is to rebut the objection that no court would ever recognize such a right (or its equivalent on equal protection or other constitutional grounds), and thus any legal analysis of plural marriage would be futile. Presumably, any state could expand its definition of marriage to include multiple persons without acting unconstitutionally.[1] These days, as the ongoing debate over same-sex marriage reveals, the constitutional problems involving marriage stem from overly restrictive definitions and their controversial rationales.

Because the causes of constitutional change are complicated, are above my pay grade, and lie well beyond the scope of this chapter, my plan is not to make predictions. Rather, I illustrate how the flexibility of certain constitutional language enables various actors to develop novel constitutional positions that may gain adherents over time. As Sanford Levinson

[1] While most scholars believe a state could abolish marriage without violating the Constitution, there are some exceptions. See, for example, Pamela S. Karlan, "Let's Call the Whole Thing Off: Can States Abolish the Institution of Marriage?" *California Law Review*, 98 (2010), 697–707. I take up this question in the final chapter.

writes: "It is always the case that courts are perpetually open to new arguments about rights . . . that reflect the dominant public opinion of the day."[2] What counts as a defensible constitutional view is not fixed and can change over time in response to popular beliefs about its merits. The recent success of the reinterpretation of the Second Amendment and near success of the once implausible constitutional arguments deployed against the Affordable Care Act (ACA) nicely illustrate this point. Arguments that support a constitutional right to plural marriage or its equivalent, then, are not necessarily bad; their time may come. As I shall argue later in this book, constitutional arguments that justify giving people the option of different kinds of plural marriage turn out to be no worse than those that proponents of same-sex marriage advance to bolster what used to be – but no longer is – an unthinkable constitutional position.

This chapter will be divided into the following sections. First, I will discuss the possibility of a constitutional right to plural marriage (or something like it on equal protection grounds) and defend the view that it is not farfetched. I do so by underscoring how indeterminacy in the constitutional text, constitutional doctrine, and case law, coupled with shifts in public opinion, makes possible the development of new constitutional understandings. Second, in discussing contemporary constitutional theory, I use the new originalism and the concept of constitutional construction to spell out why judicial lawmaking cannot be avoided in hard constitutional cases.[3] The possibility of such lawmaking increases the likelihood that a court may someday require a state to allow adults to marry more than one person at the same time. Third, I close with some thoughts on the future of the meaning of marriage in this country by calling attention to how much it has already changed in a relatively short period.

2 Sanford Levinson, *Our Undemocratic Constitution: Where the Constitution Goes Wrong (And How We the People Can Correct It)* (New York: Oxford University Press, 2006), 5.

3 For a concise description of the new originalism, including how it differs from the older versions, see Lawrence Solum, "Legal Theory Lexicon 071: The New Originalism," http://lsolum.typepad.com/legal_theory_lexicon/2013/02/legal-theory-lexicon-071-the-new-originalism.html. The idea of construction has its origins in contract law. Its use by such new originalists as Keith Whittington and Randy Barnett is more recent, but Ronald Dworkin writes: "Roughly, constructive interpretation is a matter of imposing purpose on an object or practice in order to make of it the best possible example of the form or genre to which it is taken to belong." Dworkin, *Law's Empire* (Cambridge, MA: Belknap Press of Harvard University Press, 1986), 52. As such, it is not hard to see how legal theorists might use the idea in constitutional cases. For a concise explanation of Dworkin's view, see also Scott J. Shapiro, "The Hart-Dworkin Debate: A Short Guide for the Perplexed," in *Ronald Dworkin*, ed. Arthur Ripstein (New York: Cambridge University Press, 2007), 38–39.

I. CONSTITUTIONAL CHANGE

A. *The Possibility of a Constitutional Right to Plural Marriage*

In America, part of what makes legally defining marriage so complicated is that the public discussion surrounding it is about so many different things: single motherhood, the moral acceptability of divorce, cohabitation, homosexuality, the purported breakdown of the family, the welfare of children, the role of religion in public life, the value of tradition, appropriate gender roles, marriage as an antipoverty program, and the limits of the authority of the state. At times, then, disagreement about the meaning of marriage can be traced to other deeper disagreements rooted in political morality. Those differences are bound to shape constitutional discourse and affect how judges decide real same-sex marriage cases. It is not a coincidence that as public opinion changes in favor of legal recognition of same-sex marriage, lower federal court judges are finding that states that fail to permit them are acting unconstitutionally. Even though it is easy to become sidetracked, I believe that marriage is entitled to its own analysis, which entails addressing related issues while not letting them dominate the discussion to the point where marriage itself ceases to be the focal point.

In the Introduction, I tried to articulate why it is imperative for Americans to begin discussing plural marriage sooner rather than later with the kind of care the topic deserves. In American history, antipolygamy sentiments were tied to such political controversies as slavery, federalism, women's rights, citizenship, democracy, and the separation of church and state.[4] As a consequence of the federal government's crusade against polygamy, Mormon women lost their right to vote.[5] Inevitably, the debate over the meaning of marriage in this country will move forward as the public accepts same-sex marriage and views the lack of such a right as invidious discrimination. Eventually, even conservative judges will probably reject legal arguments against same-sex marriage because they are predicated on constitutionally impermissible unequal treatment. The writing is on the wall. Someday, lawmakers, judges, and ordinary people will have to rethink their basic assumptions about how to define marriage, including whether it only can be between two people and whether it presupposes sexual intimacy. When that happens, those who defend a numerical restriction will have to do more than consult their own dictionary.

4 Shayna M. Sigman, "Everything Lawyers Know About Polygamy Is Wrong," *Cornell Journal of Law and Public Policy*, 16 (2006), 101–85.

5 Jessie L. Embry, "Effects of Polygamy on Mormon Women," *Frontiers: A Journal of Women's Studies*, 7 (1984), 56.

Even if the judiciary were to avoid this constitutional question and leave it to the states in the name of federalism, any state that allowed a person to marry more than one person simultaneously within its own borders would have raised the question of whether other states that do not perform such marriages must treat them as legally valid when a multiperson intimate union visits or becomes residents.[6] A similar issue has already arisen with respect to same-sex marriage under the Full Faith and Credit Clause, which, when properly construed, may require states to recognize such marriages performed in other states.[7]

Of course, one might doubt the very possibility of a constitutional right to plural marriage in the midst of the ongoing political and legal battle over same-sex marriage.[8] Despite growing tolerance of sexual minorities, their intimate relationships and the increasingly common view that marriage does not have to be between a man and a woman, a substantial majority of Americans would not let competent, fully informed adults marry more than one person at the same time.[9] In their minds, a numerical limitation differs significantly from one based on sexual orientation and is consequently much easier to defend. Likewise, many scholars try to differentiate same-sex marriage from traditional polygyny.[10] For some of them, it is obvious that the constitutional right of marriage cannot be extended beyond couples.[11] Others maintain that a marriage must be between one man and one woman due to

[6] See Andrew Koppelman, *Same Sex, Different States: When Same-Sex Marriages Cross State Lines* (New Haven, CT: Yale University Press, 2006), 162, nn. 16–17. All states recognize valid two-person opposite-sex marriage from other states. D. Kelly Weisberg and Susan Frelich Appleton, *Modern Family Law: Cases and Materials* (3rd ed.) (New York: Aspen Publishers, 2006), 234–44.

[7] In an unlikely but theoretically possible scenario, a person could be legally married to two different people at the same time. Imagine a man marries another man in California, which once again allows same-sex couples to marry, and then the couple moves to Arizona, which does not recognize their same-sex marriage (and does not have to do so under DOMA), and establishes legal residency. Because both of them are single as far as Arizona is concerned, they are eligible to marry someone of the opposite gender. One of them then marries a woman. As a result, he would be legally married to a man in California but to a woman in Arizona. However, Section 4 of DOMA, which was not challenged in the *Windsor* case, may turn out to be unconstitutional.

[8] However, legal recognition of same-sex marriage in all states seems to be inevitable. Michael J. Klarman, *From the Closet to the Altar: Courts, Backlash, and the Struggle for Same-Sex Marriage* (New York: Oxford University Press, 2013), 202.

[9] According to a Gallup poll, 90 percent of them believe the practice of polygamy is immoral. Gallup poll, May 8–11, 2008; N = 1,017 adults nationwide; margin of error: +/– 3 percent. www.gallup.com/poll/108115/americans-evenly-divided-morality-homosexuality.aspx.

[10] See, for example, Maura I. Strassberg, "Distinctions of Form or Substance? Monogamy, Polygamy, and Same-Sex Marriage," *North Carolina Law Review*, 75 (1997), 1615–18.

[11] See, for example, Marci A. Hamilton, *God vs. the Gavel: Religion and the Rule of Law* (New York: Cambridge University Press, 2005), 68.

their natural sexual complementarity.[12] Others allege that compared with a couple, a thruple or a larger marital group would pose unique challenges to family law.[13]

Nonetheless, there are three basic reasons why a constitutional right to plural marriage (or its equivalent) cannot be ruled out. First, in the past, one could have been equally skeptical of the claim that the Constitution forces states to let same-sex couples marry. For most of American history, almost all legal experts would have summarily rejected what they would have seen as a bizarre constitutional position.[14] In 1972, the Supreme Court dismissed an appeal of the Minnesota Supreme Court's decision denying a right to same-sex marriage "for want of a substantial federal question."[15] Not that long ago, in *Bowers v. Hardwick*, the Supreme Court ruled that states could criminalize same-sex sex between consenting adults.[16] As Michael Klarman writes, "the notion that gay couples would one day be permitted to legally marry must have seemed a pipe dream."[17] In 1986, most experts would not have predicted that in less than thirty years, a U.S. district court judge would decide that the Constitution requires states, which grant marriage licenses to different-sex couples, to also give marriage licenses to same-sex ones and that a U.S. Court of Appeals would affirm the decision.[18] *Hollingsworth* may not be close to the decisive victory that proponents of same-sex marriage had hoped for, but *Windsor* directly connects the rationale of *Romer* with marriage, establishing that the federal government's denial of numerous benefits to married same-sex couples cannot reflect animus against an unpopular group.[19]

Second, several developed countries are moving in the direction of decriminalizing polygamy and legally protecting multiperson intimate relationships. While their doing so is not the same as creating a right of plural marriage or something like it, these legal changes open the door to more sweeping reforms in the future. After all, if such change occurs at all, it will be incremental. What is happening abroad is bound to influence how Americans think about their own definition of marriage and increase the probability that more of

[12] See, for example, Sherif Girgis, Ryan T. Anderson, and Robert P. George, *What Is Marriage? Man and Woman: A Defense* (New York: Encounter Books, 2012).

[13] See Diane J. Klein, "Plural Marriage and Community Property Law," *Golden Gate Law Review*, 41 (2010), 33–89; Adrienne D. Davis, "Regulating Polygamy: Intimacy, Default Rules, and Bargaining for Equality," *Columbia Law Review*, 110 (2010), 1955–2046; and Goldfeder, *Legalizing Plural Marriage*, esp. 162–87.

[14] Klarman, *From the Closet to the Altar*, 19.

[15] *Baker v. Nelson*, 409 U.S. 810 (1972).

[16] *Bowers v. Hardwick*, 478 U.S. 186 (1986).

[17] Klarman, *From the Closet to the Altar*, 39.

[18] See *Perry v. Schwarzenegger*, 704 F. Supp. 2d. 921(N.D. Cal. 2010); and *Perry v. Brown*, 671 F. 3d 1052 (2012).

[19] *Hollingsworth v. Perry*, 570 U.S. __ (2013); *United States v. Windsor*, 570 U.S. __ (2013).

them will believe that change is possible and desirable. It is much harder to argue that the sky is going to fall in our own country if we were to enact a particular reform when that reform has already been successful elsewhere under similar conditions.

Third – and most importantly – if there is one truth about American constitutional development, it is that it is nearly impossible to forecast what is likely to happen in our distant constitutional future. True, the Supreme Court usually does not bring about novel constitutional understandings on its own.[20] In *Hollingsworth*, the Supreme Court eschewed the more radical "fifty state" solution, where all states would have to allow same-sex couples to marry, by deciding the case on procedural grounds and limiting its ruling to California.[21] Instead, the Supreme Court is far more likely to not contravene public opinion and to come on the scene belatedly to confirm a new constitutional understanding that has already come into being. Anyone who expects the Supreme Court to ride to the rescue is probably engaging in wishful thinking, given its historical failure to do so more often than not. As Judith Stacey observes: "In the end, the fate of legal gay or plural marriage or of any other state-sponsored brand of marriage will not hinge on abstract logic or on legal precedents but on complex social forces and political alliances that are either painstakingly forged or foolishly foresworn."[22] Constitutional change does not simply result from the behaviors of lawyers and judges but can be traced to social developments where various legal and nonlegal actors play their respective roles in our constitutional drama.

B. *The Current Political and Legal Climate*

Although many Americans no longer think twice about interracial couples and slowly but surely are becoming used to same-sex ones, they normally do not extend that tolerant attitude toward any kind of polygamist. For the most part, our culture remains hostile to multipartner unions, which I suspect has less to do with polygamy itself and more to do with their faith in the superiority of monogamy and the inappropriateness of sexual nonexclusivity. Monogamy remains the standard by which most of them judge the quality of intimate relationships.[23] But for internalizing the belief that one can only be truly

[20] Klarman, *From the Closet to the Altar*, x. [21] *Hollingsworth v. Perry*, 570 U.S. __ (2013).

[22] Judith Stacey, *Unhitched: Love, Marriage, and Family Values From Hollywood to Western China* (New York: New York University Press, 2011), 120.

[23] Elizabeth Brake, *Minimizing Marriage: Marriage, Morality, and the Law* (New York: Oxford University Press, 2012), 5.

intimate with one other person at the same time, they might be more receptive to the possibility of marital multiplicity and why it might work better for some people in some situations. In the near future, polygamists will continue to encounter numerous legal difficulties due to their way of life, such as risking criminal liability, being fired or not hired in the first place, being disadvantaged in custody disputes (where a family law judge may rule that exposure to such a lifestyle is not in the best interests of the child), and in immigration matters. Also, second and third "spouses" are usually not legally entitled to marital assets and spousal support when the "marriage" ends, leaving them dangerously unprotected unless they have an explicit and enforceable cohabitation agreement or a court finds the existence of a common-law marriage.[24]

This disturbing state of affairs should not go unnoticed. First, no person should have to remain in any unhealthy, abusive, or otherwise miserable intimate relationship because she does not have a real option to leave and start a new life. To favor the legalization of plural marriage is not to believe that the state should remove itself completely from the institution and endorse an "anything goes" marital regime in which the state has no interest in any aspect of intimate relationships. Second, from a liberal standpoint, absent compelling reasons to the contrary, people should be able to think and act unconventionally in their pursuit of their most important ends. Not only do they have different needs, desires, and preferences, but they also have different visions of what makes a human life worthwhile. Usually, they are not indifferent to their marital status. As Martha Nussbaum writes: "For many if not most people, ... marriage is not a trivial matter. It is a key to the pursuit of happiness, something people aspire to. . . ."[25] In a society like ours that venerates the institution yet disputes its meaning, some Americans may want the flexibility that comes with plural forms of marriage to achieve their life plans – whatever they happen to be. For the most part, American constitutional law maximizes choice when it comes to profoundly personal decisions. It is not evident why marriage remains an exception to that general rule that people prefer options when they know circumstances differ, including their own, and feelings can change over time. Those who care about treating others fairly must take more seriously the possibility that the constitutional right of marriage should not be limited to couples.

[24] See Martha M. Ertman, *Love's Promises*, chapter 6, "The Basics of Cohabitation Agreements" (April 11, 2014: draft). Only nine states retain common-law marriages.

[25] Martha C. Nussbaum, "The Right to Marry?" *California Law Review*, 98 (2010), 668.

If Americans are going to evaluate plural marriage more objectively, they cannot simply see what they want to see based on their preconceptions, which may have little basis in reality, or wrongly assume that to be in favor of the legal option of plural marriage is to ignore other crimes, endorse irresponsible promiscuity, or celebrate child brides. They also need to (a) disaggregate polygyny from polyamory and other multiperson unions or networks to appreciate their diversity; (b) cease demonizing polygamists as if their identities could not be acceptable or their lives could not be worthwhile; (c) concede that the members of a polygynous family could care for and love one another even if its structure and dynamics are unequal; (d) acknowledge the empirical uncertainty that characterizes the alleged harms of certain polygynous relationships; and (e) stop assuming that the structure of the relationship alone explains the alleged harms and begin investigating the other possible causes with more enthusiasm.[26] Patriotism may be the last refuge of a scoundrel, but when it comes to polygamy, prejudice has a similar function. Equal treatment under the law would allow polygamists to live the kind of life they want to have without being legally discriminated against. A liberal society that is committed to enhancing the quality of the lives of everyone has to be aware that idiosyncratic beliefs and behaviors may have considerable value and that tolerance is always harder to accomplish in practice than in theory. As I shall show, the state may commit a serious wrong by unduly restricting the freedom of people to marry unconventionally.

How such a double standard – in which all states treat monogamous and plural marriages so differently – came into existence is not part of my agenda. But I suspect that part of the unease that many Americans feel toward plural marriage has to do with its connection to Mormonism. As noted in the Introduction, the difficulty with this narrow view of plural marriage is that Fundamentalist Latter-Day Saints (FLDS) polygyny is only one of the many forms a plural marriage could take. After all, other (but less prominent) religious minorities also believe that polygamy is either a religious duty or permissible.[27] FLDS polygyny itself exhibits considerable variance.[28] A plural marriage is not synonymous with FLDS polygyny or even polygyny more generally. Such marriage can have a secular basis, may be configured in

[26] In the British Columbia polygamy case, Chief Justice Robert Bauman accepts the state's interest in preventing harm to women, children, society, and the institution of marriage. Section 293 of the Criminal Code of Canada, BCSC 1588, 1.

[27] That list includes some evangelical Christians, African Hebrew Israelites of Jerusalem, and Muslims affiliated with the Nation of Islam and Sunni sects. Davis, "Regulating Polygamy," 1970.

[28] Bennion, *Polygamy in Primetime*, xvii.

multiple ways, and does not have to be polygynous, different sex, or even sexual. Also, not all polygamy is abusive or harmful.[29] Even though a particular plural marriage could be dysfunctional, the same could easily be said about many monogamous marriages and other intimate relationships. Couples may be dishonest, insensitive, and cruel to each other, whereas the participants in a plural marriage may love one another and be truthful, thoughtful, selfless, and caring in their daily interactions. Being in a more traditional two-person intimate relationship hardly magically transforms ordinary human beings into saints. Indeed, polyamorous relationships may be characterized by better communication, less jealousy, and more honesty than most monogamous ones. They may have unique virtues, such as fostering female bonding.[30] It is inexcusable to compare the worst types of polygynous relationships with ideal monogamous ones that in reality often leave so much to be desired. By way of analogy, just because some religions are dangerous cults does not mean that all religions should be banned.

C. *Past Political Theorizing on Plural Marriage*

According to Elizabeth Brake, "there is a long tradition of philosophical thought on marriage."[31] By contrast, with respect to plural marriage, most political theorists have not had much to say about multiperson intimate relationships and few of them – even those who approach the issue from a more secular angle – have been charitable in the sense of acknowledging its possible merits. At best, their treatment of plural marriage is limited to polygyny, is superficial, and often reflects the contempt of their day for anything other than opposite-sex monogamy. In the *Persian Letters*, Montesquieu facetiously claims that the problem with polygamy is that a normal man cannot sexually satisfy all his wives, leading to depopulation.[32] Mary Wollstonecraft writes that "polygamy is another physical degradation" women must suffer.[33] David Hume recognizes that marriage can take different forms at different times in different places but rejects the practice of polygamy.[34] Immanuel Kant mentions polygyny but concludes that the arrangement, like concubinage (his term), is not the equivalent of monogamous marriage

[29] Ibid., 241. [30] See Davis, "Regulating Polygamy," 1972.
[31] Elizabeth Brake, "Marriage," http://plato.stanford.edu/entries/marriage.
[32] Montesquieu, *Persian Letters*, trans. C. J. Betts (London: Penguin Books, 1973), 206–08.
[33] Mary Wollstonecraft, "A Vindication of the Rights of Woman," in *Political Writings*, ed. Janet Todd (Toronto: University of Toronto Press, 1993), 148–49.
[34] David Hume, "Of Polygamy and Divorces," in *David Hume Essays: Moral, Political, and Literary*, ed. Eugene F. Miller (Indianapolis: Liberty Fund, 1985), 181–87.

because "each wife ... ought ... to be entitled to the whole man."[35] One scholar reads Hegel as regarding polygyny as the foundation of a tyrannical state.[36] In *The Souls of Black Folk*, in discussing African-American social history, W. E. B. Du Bois reminds his readers that during slavery, "a new polygamy and polyandry appeared."[37]

On the other hand, a handful of political thinkers have been more willing to countenance alternative marital arrangements or the elimination of marriage. In *The Republic*, Plato proposes that the family be abolished and reproduction be managed for the good of the state.[38] In defending the permissibility of divorce, John Locke apparently holds the that under some circumstances, a man who is already married may marry another woman.[39] Karl Marx and Friedrich Engels predict the end of the bourgeois family with the advent of communism.[40] John Stuart Mill entertains the possibility that plural marriage may have some value when he halfheartedly defends what he refers to as the "Mormonite Doctrine."[41] One scholar writes that "Mill's defense of the Mormons, despite his feminist opposition to Mormon polygynous marriages, is a striking attempt to reconcile tensions between liberalism's commitments both to individual autonomy and to religious and cultural pluralism."[42] Bertrand Russell does not explicitly advocate plural marriage but writes that "people are generally polygamous in their instincts" and favors what today would be called an open marriage to keep families together.[43] None of these thinkers endorse plural marriage as I conceptualize it, but at least they suspect that conventional understandings of marriage are relative to time and place and therefore may be incomplete.

35 Immanuel Kant, "Duties Towards the Body in Respect of Sexual Impulse," in *Lectures on Ethics*, trans. Louis Infield (Indianapolis: Hackett Publishing, 1963), 167–68.

36 See Strassberg, "The Challenge of Post-Modern Polygamy," especially 474–86.

37 W. E. B. Du Bois, *The Souls of Black Folk* (ReadaClassic.com, 2010), 118.

38 *The Republic of Plato*, trans. Francis MacDonald Cornford (New York: Oxford University Press, 1945), 155–68.

39 John Locke, *The Second Treatise of Government*, ed. Peter Laslett (Cambridge, UK: Cambridge University Press, 1993), 321, section 81, especially Laslett's footnote. I thank Andy Sabl for bringing this point to my attention.

40 Karl Marx and Friedrich Engels, *The Communist Manifesto* (New York: Penguin Books, 1967), 100–01. Additionally, at the end of the passage on the bourgeois family, they refer to bourgeois marriage "as a system of wives in common" (101).

41 John Stuart Mill, "On Liberty," in *On Liberty and Other Writings*, ed. Stefan Collini (Cambridge, UK: Cambridge University Press, 1989), 91–92.

42 Bruce Baum, "Feminism, Liberalism and Cultural Pluralism," *Journal of Political Philosophy*, 5 (1997), 230.

43 Bertrand Russell, *Marriage and Morals* (New York: Liveright, 1970), 139–42.

The trouble with relying too heavily on religious sources in evaluating the rights and wrongs of plural marriage is not only that they may be outdated or hard to verify, but they are also likely to be problematically sectarian in the midst of so much disagreement over what kind of human life is most worthwhile. Many academics do not believe that religious arguments should have a place in public debates about, say, how civil marriage should be defined. Those who describe themselves as political liberals believe that religious reasons should not be incorporated into law. Such reasons are too controversial under conditions of moral pluralism to serve as the basis of the legal definition of marriage that everyone is subject to because they are too closely linked to a conception of the good. In this book, I work from the assumption that past theorists did not understand polygamy (and its multiple configurations) nearly as well as we do today. One cannot possibly translate the historical case against polygamy, then, into a contemporary one without considerable effort. The issue of polygamy is just too morally and empirically complex in such a pluralistic society as ours for commentators to appeal to an old religious text that sees polygamy as sinful or inherently harmful or treats it more like serial polygamy or fornication and less like multiperson intimate unions that may not even be sexual in any manner. Polygamy cries out for a sustained treatment that takes seriously all its possible forms and not just traditional polygyny, which is almost always, regrettably, the target of antipolygamy advocates. Today, "there are diverse stakeholders in the plural marriage debate."[44]

D. *The Contemporary Debate*

By comparison, what those who support the option of plural marriage have to say can no longer so easily be dismissed. That said, those who want such marriage to be discussed fairly do not only have to worry about conservatives' tiresome invocation of "tradition." Many individuals and organizations on the left also continue to reject plural marriage.[45] For liberals, though, appeals to dictionary definitions, public opinion, or past practices cannot justify limiting marriage to opposite-sex couples. Thus, they cannot employ similar reasoning in the coming debate over plural marriage if they oppose such a marital option but want to remain consistent. Liberals who refuse to accept plural marriage, then, will either have to change their minds

[44] Davis, "Regulating Polygamy," 1975–79.

[45] See Evan Gerstmann, *Same-Sex Marriage and the Constitution* (New York: Cambridge University Press, 2004), 100. See also Emens, "Monogamy's Law," 282.

about same-sex marriage or will have to look elsewhere for normative assistance, which is why some of them fall back on purported state interests in promoting gender equality, stopping the coercion of women and the abuse of children, and preventing welfare and tax fraud.

While the constitutional right to marriage is well established in case law, experts disagree about its exact meaning. Some restrictions would be undeniably acceptable, such as those involving age, competence, and species, due to the undeniably important legal inability to consent, whereas others would be unacceptable, such as those based on race.[46] Others still spark controversy, such as those based on sexual orientation.[47] At least one scholar believes that incestuous marriages between consenting adults should be allowed in some circumstances.[48] One writer has gone considerably farther, explaining how marriage between humans and robots could occur in the future.[49]

At one time, some sexual minorities eschewed marriage as a patriarchal or heterosexual institution.[50] For the most part, though, those days seem to be over and plenty of members of the lesbian, gay, bisexual, and transgender (LGBT) community do not want to marry only so that they can reap the benefits of a legal relationship that a married opposite-sex couple already enjoys. They could be entitled to many of those benefits through civil union status (in some states) or a series of private contracts (to some extent). Understandably, they also want to be treated as legal equals because they do not want the state to act as an ethical authority that marginalizes their intimate relationships and in doing so diminishes their lives. In 2008, before the passage of Proposition 8 in California (which was overturned in 2013 by the U.S. Supreme Court), the California Supreme Court declared that civil unions for same-sex couples could not substitute for marriages.[51] In 2012, in his decision to affirm the lower federal court's decision, Judge Stephen Reinhardt

[46] *Loving v. Virginia*, 388 U.S. 1 (1967) (bans on interracial marriage are unconstitutional).

[47] According to a March 12–16, 2009, CBS News poll, 35 percent favor legal marriage for same-sex couples, 27 percent favor civil unions, and 35 percent favor no legal recognition. N = 1,142 adults nationwide. www.cbsnews.com/htdocs/pdf/poll_040309.pdf.

[48] See, for example, Andrew F. March, "What Lies Beyond Same-Sex Marriage? Marriage, Reproductive Freedom and Future Persons in Liberal Public Justification," *Journal of Applied Philosophy*, 27 (2010), 39–58.

[49] See David Levy, *Love + Sex With Robots: The Evolution of Human-Robot Relationships* (New York: HarperCollins Publishers, 2007), 151–59.

[50] See, for example, Claudia Card, "Against Marriage and Motherhood," *Hypatia*, 11 (1996), 1–23; Paula Ettlebrick, "Since When Is Marriage a Path to Liberation?" in *Same-Sex Marriage: The Moral and Legal Debate* (2nd ed.), ed. Robert M. Baird and Stuart E. Rosenbaum (Amherst, NY: Prometheus Books, 2004), 257–61.

[51] *In re Marriage Cases*, 43 Cal. 4d 757 (2008) (George, J., majority).

underscored the symbolic importance of the difference between taking away a right to marriage from same-sex couples, which Proposition 8 did, and the state's not extending it to such couples in the first place.[52]

It is not beyond dispute that the state's failure to grant marriage licenses to interracial or same-sex couples constitutes the moral or legal equivalent of not doing likewise for plural marriage enthusiasts. One could object that a person who seeks to marry more than one person has technically not been denied the right to marry but has only been denied the right to marry additional persons when that person is already married. This kind of argument rings hollow; it resembles the old assertion that gays and lesbians have not been denied the right to marry because a gay man may marry a woman and a lesbian may marry a man. Such an argument is not only disingenuous but also misses the point. When someone is asking for the right to marry more than one person simultaneously, he or she is not only asking the state to treat the marital relationship he or she wants to form equally. He or she is also requesting that the state respect his or her freedom of choice in a deeply personal matter and to let him or her be the judge of who his or her intimate partner is going to be – perhaps for the rest of his or her life. The failure to permit plural marriage would deny that choice to someone who is already married to only one person, and it would also deny that choice to those who are not already married as to their first choice of a marital partner.

E. *The Current Legal Situation*

By contrast, under the status quo, different-sex couples can marry in all states for just about any personal reasons they happen to have. Those reasons could be trivial, but for purposes of being eligible to marry, they would suffice.[53] A man could want to marry because he wants a trophy wife, to do the "right thing" in the case of an unplanned pregnancy, to please his parents or relatives, to conceal his sexual orientation, to help him to run for public office, to obtain a higher standard of living, or to never have to shop for his own clothes ever again. Legally, none of these reasons are good or bad or better or worse; their quality is irrelevant. All that seems to matter is that each person has his or her own reasons for wanting to form such a legal relationship and believes them to be good enough for the time being.

While the option of plural marriage would probably increase the number of people who practice nonmonogamy, it is difficult to predict the magnitude of

[52] *Perry v. Brown*, 671 F. 3d 1052 (2012).

[53] Nussbaum, "The Right to Marry?" 670.

such an increase or which forms plural marriage would take even in the near future. Different people would have different personal reasons for wanting different types of marital arrangements. Such legal recognition would open the door to a woman being married to multiple men, multiple women, or multiple men and multiple women – and the participants in such an arrangement would not have to be sexually exclusive or even romantically involved with one another. I would expect marital diversity to grow as multipartner relationships become less exotic and consequently more socially acceptable, but that is hard to know in advance. The existing polyamory community in this country is somewhat demographically diverse, and the forms and dynamics of their nonmonogamous intimate relationships vary.[54] Polygyny would most likely be increasingly uncommon over time when women living in America would have a much longer list of marital options to choose from and might prefer nonsexual marriages with other women, with close friends, or with adult family members. It is possible, of course, that a plural marriage could exceed five persons or be composed of a number of interconnected networks. At some point, though, such a marriage – due to its overly complex dynamics – would be unattractive. Also, economic development may eventually eradicate traditional polygyny in less developed countries.[55] The likely consequence of that trend is that fewer immigrants who come to the United States would be interested in forming or maintaining such a marital arrangement for religious or cultural reasons.

F. *The Basic Case Against Plural Marriage*

Some people worry that the state's permitting plural marriages may cause or contribute to gender inequality. The basic problem with this view, which I shall elaborate on in Chapter 2, is that it is not evident that the problem lies with polygamy per se, as in the form or structure of the intimate relationship. First, a more effective regulatory scheme may improve the lives of the women who are a part of such relationships. In other words, oversight or regulation, not prohibition, may be the best solution in an imperfect world by protecting those who are most likely to be exploited.

Second, the patriarchal beliefs, which the participants in traditional polygynous relationships often hold, and the behaviors that follow from them, are just as likely to cause the unequal treatment of women, particularly under certain conditions. If that is the case, then the argument from gender inequality

[54] See Anthony D. Ravenscroft, *Polyamory: Roadmaps for the Clueless and Hopeful* (Santa Fe, NM: Fenris Brothers, 2004), 1.

[55] Miriam Koktvedgaard Zeitzen, *Polygamy: A Cross-Cultural Analysis* (New York: Berg, 2008), 9.

proves too much: Far more numerous monogamous couples hold such regressive beliefs and also act on them. To avoid arbitrariness, then, the state should deny marriage licenses to couples who aspire to an inegalitarian marriage. After all, it is not as if many of those who adhere to traditional religious or cultural beliefs have particularly progressive views with respect to women and their place in the family and in society.[56]

Third, no state requires a couple – married or not – to have an egalitarian personal relationship, even if such internal equality would be morally preferable. Under current family law, the enforcement of equality only becomes a concern when a marriage ends and a family law judge has to decide how to divide the marital property, whether to award spousal support, and so on. A plural marriage would not always be opposite sex, polygynous, or rooted in traditional religious and cultural ways of life and thus would not necessarily reinforce traditional gender roles. It might turn out to be as subversive to such roles as some same-sex marriages have proved to be depending on the forms it takes and its visibility. Also, if it were polygynous, a plural marriage could deemphasize male–female amorous interactions and foster female cooperation, friendship, and compassion. A woman in such a family may find herself being emotionally closer to her sister wives than to her husband. It is a mistake to assume, then, that all polygynous marriages are the same, even if they share some characteristics. Each monogamous marriage – same or different sex – has the same form, but that surely does not mean their respective dynamics are identical. Patterns of behaviors between two married persons – for better or for worse – tend to be idiosyncratic. Couples cooperate in different ways, deal with conflict in different ways, and have different expectations and aspirations. Even a traditional religious dyadic marriage, which is premised on different gender roles, cannot be reduced to a stereotype. Some of them will be functional and some of them will not be so. Some of them will exhibit high marital satisfaction and others will not. Some persons in a polygamous relationship will be happy and others will be miserable. In this sense, a plural marriage resembles its monogamous counterpart: Considerable variance is unavoidable. And we should not forget that the best polygynous marriages are better than the worst monogamous ones.

Even if the legal recognition of plural marriage would exacerbate gender inequality or harm children, which makes the issue of such marriage more vexed than it otherwise would be, the state will most likely not be able to demonstrate that the kind of inequality or harm that exists in some plural

[56] See Susan Moller Okin, "Is Multiculturalism Bad for Women?" in *Is Multiculturalism Bad for Women?* ed. Joshua Cohen, Matthew Howard, and Martha C. Nussbaum (Princeton, NJ: Princeton University Press, 1999), 9–24.

marriages is unique or worse than that of far more numerous monogamous marriages, especially more patriarchal or high-conflict ones. In terms of the degree and kind of inequality, a plural marriage among, say, three lesbians or three close friends is much less troubling than a traditional difference-sex monogamous marriage rooted in so-called natural differences between men and women. Today, different-sex couples are having trouble implementing their egalitarian ideals.[57] Despite ample evidence that traditional marriage is bad for gender equality, most feminists do not want the state to remove itself completely from the institution or its analogues.[58] Rather, they prefer regulation to protect women and children, favor more effective enforcement, and do not see abolition as a plausible solution because such intimate relationships will continue to exist – with or without legal recognition. When they speak about disestablishing marriage, they usually do not mean complete privatization in the sense of leaving the institution to individuals and private religious organizations. Even though monogamous, opposite-sex marriage has patriarchal origins, it does not have to continue to be a patriarchal institution if it can be reformed along more egalitarian lines.

On the other hand, marriage does not have to be premised on a commitment to eradicating all kinds of gender inequality at all costs, and it does not have to posit that all women are committed feminists who only want a certain sort of marriage. A strong presumption in favor of respect for personal choice cannot suddenly disappear in a liberal society when an adult woman chooses a more traditional kind of marriage. The state does not step in and prevent her from marrying only one person who is likely to be a poor match for her or abuse her. What the state can do is to ensure her consent is as voluntary as possible and make her less economically vulnerable so she can exit if necessary before a bad situation becomes even worse. Gender equality is undeniably important, but it is not the only consideration a lawmaker or judge should take into account when deciding what is to be done. Contemporary family law reflects the belief that a trade-off between personal choice and gender equality is appropriate. Despite how radical advocacy of plural marriage appears to be, the even more radical position would involve the state's imposing a gender equality requirement on all couples as a condition of their being able to marry each other.

When it comes to marriage, formal legal equality has been an achievement, but real equality in intimate relationships has proved more elusive. As in the

57 Stephanie Coontz, *Marriage, A History: How Love Conquered Marriage* (New York: Penguin Books, 2005), 300.

58 Tamara Metz, "Why We Should Disestablish Marriage," in *Just Marriage*, ed. Mary Shanley (New York: Oxford University Press, 2004), 103.

past, there is an unfortunate tendency on the part of contemporary opponents of plural marriage to emphasize how inegalitarian polygamous relationships are without being nearly as harsh on their monogamous counterparts, as if only the form of a marriage should concern us. Some of the alleged problems of plural marriage may turn out to be real, but at this juncture, too much factual uncertainty exists. Researchers should not extrapolate from such a small sample size of illegal polygynous and polyamorous units to what could be the case in the future if all states were to decriminalize polygamy, put a regulatory structure in place, cease demonizing polygamists, let them choose from a variety of marital options, and treat their marital relationships equally. Nor should antipolygamy advocates simply rely on so-called expert testimony from a handful of polygamy trials when prosecutors cherry-pick to find someone who has certain credentials and will testify in a way that supports the state's legal position. Some studies indicate that polyamorous relationships better serve the welfare of children.[59] Most of the reasons critics of plural marriage advance in defense of their position are speculative or apply equally to monogamous marriages. It would be unimaginable to use the same reasoning regarding traditional two-person marriages and conclude that the state may not permit them. No one has yet satisfactorily defended this double standard, but it remains in place on the dubious assumption that it requires no defense.

G. *Scalia's Slippery Slope*

While no state has ever created a right to plural marriage and no American court has ever recognized such a right, judges are aware that rationales used to deny or support a constitutional right to same-sex marriage may be relevant in the coming debate over plural marriage. As early as 1996, in his testimony supporting DOMA before the House Judiciary Committee, Hadley Arkes compared same-sex marriage and polygamy to discredit the former.[60] That same year, in his dissent in *Romer v. Evans*, Justice Antonin Scalia favorably equated laws that discriminate against gays and lesbians to those that prohibit polygamy.[61] In his dissent in *Lawrence v. Texas*, he criticized the majority's decision to protect same-sex sex acts between consenting adults

[59] See, for example, Elisabeth Sheff, *The Polyamorists Next Door: Inside Multi-Partner Relationships and Families* (Lanham, MD: Rowman & Littlefield, 2014).

[60] Testimony on the Defense of Marriage Act: Hearing on H.R. 3396 Before the House Committee on the Judiciary, 104th Congress (1996) (statement by Hadley Arkes, professor, Amherst College), 1996 WL 256693 at 11.

[61] *Romer v. Evans*, 517 U.S. 620, 648–52 (1996) (Scalia, J., dissenting).

for implying that state laws that ban bigamy are invalid.[62] In *Brown v. Buhman*, U.S. district court judge Clark Waddoups used the privacy rationale of *Lawrence* to invalidate part of Utah's antibigamy law.[63] Scalia is not alone among conservatives in calling attention to how slippery the slope from allowing same-sex marriage to allowing plural marriage may be. Robert Bork writes: "If homosexuality may not be discouraged by state constitutions, it is difficult to see how the provisions of various state constitutions banning polygamy can stand."[64] More recently, during the trial in U.S. district court, Charles Cooper, the lead attorney for the groups defending Proposition 8, raised the polygamy question.[65] In the moot courts prior to oral arguments in front of the justices concerning the constitutionality of Proposition 8, Ted Olson, the lead attorney for the plaintiffs, prepared for the same kind of question.[66] These slippery slope arguments are premised on a *reductio ad absurdum*: If the recognition of same-sex marriage invariably leads to plural marriage, which is supposed to be ridiculous, then the premise that there is a right to same-sex marriage must be false.[67] This approach appears to be a scare tactic and that is probably why those on the left who advocate same-sex marriage have not been nearly as enthusiastic about any form of plural marriage.[68]

Even when those who advance slippery slope arguments are sincere, such arguments may be flawed for three main reasons. First, the term *slippery slope* is ambiguous; it can mean that one thing logically follows from another or it can mean that one event is likely to cause another sooner or later. In formal logic, no connection between same-sex and plural marriage is present.[69] One cannot deduce the right to plural marriage from the right to same-sex marriage when some relevant differences between them may exist. The reasons for having the option of the latter but not the former may be adequate. Also, as any social scientist knows, in the midst of so many independent

[62] *Lawrence v. Texas*, 539 U.S. 558, 590 (2003) (Scalia, J., dissenting).

[63] *Brown v. Buhman* (2013) (Case No. 2:11-cv-0652).

[64] Robert H. Bork, *Slouching Towards Gomorrah: Modern Liberalism and American Decline* (New York: Regan Books, 2003), 113.

[65] See Jo Becker, *Forcing the Spring: Inside the Fight for Marriage Equality* (New York: Penguin Press, 2014), 91.

[66] Ibid., 369.

[67] See, for example, Jeff Jordan, "Contra Same-Sex Marriage," in *Same-Sex Marriage: The Moral and Legal Debate* (2nd ed.), ed. Robert M. Baird and Stuart E. Rosenbaum (Amherst, NY: Prometheus Books, 2004), 170–72.

[68] See Judith Stacey and Tey Meadow, "New Slants on the Slippery Slope: The Politics of Polygamy and Gay Family Rights in South Africa and the United States," *Politics and Society*, 37 (2009), 168–69.

[69] John Corvino, "The Case for Same-Sex Marriage," in *Debating Same-Sex Marriage*, ed. John Corvino and Maggie Gallagher (New York: Oxford University Press, 2012), 70.

variables, making causal inferences should be done with caution. In the politically charged debate over the most appropriate definition of marriage, no one should eagerly embrace the "facts" that either side offers in defense of its position.[70] That is a lesson that should have already been drawn from the continuing debate over same-sex marriage and the questionable social science that was offered to support the conclusion that children do better when they have two different-sex parents. The view that straight couples provide an optimal environment for the raising of children was not only called into question during the trial in *Perry v. Schwarzenegger*, but it also came close to being completely discredited.[71] Some recent research suggests that same-sex parents parent better.[72] Second, even when it is evident that the person using the term is making an empirical prediction, the slope may not be slippery or even wet. Indeed, there may be no slope at all. Third, when the slope is slippery, people still have to consider whether the aggregate costs outweigh the benefits of sliding to the bottom.[73] In other words, even when a slope between same-sex and plural marriage exists, it does not necessarily follow that the former should not be permitted just because it would lead to the latter.

As I shall explain in a subsequent chapter, one version of the slippery slope argument is more cogent than many people on the left realize and its conclusion – that people have a constitutional right to marry more than one person simultaneously – is not as ridiculous as those on the right believe. I take Scalia's slippery slope seriously because the recognition of a constitutional right to same-sex marriage implicates the kinds of reasons that would justify redefining marriage to include different kinds of plural marriages. Americans could then do something that is long overdue: Evaluate the quality of the arguments for and against plural marriage on their merits. The lack of a sustained explanation of why persons who want to have such marital relationships may be excluded should not be overlooked in a society that usually demands much stronger justification for legal discrimination. Ultimately, the main liberal reasons that work in favor of recognizing same-sex marriages also apply to plural marriages.[74]

70 See Andrew J. Cherlin, "One Thousand and Forty-Nine Reasons Why It's Hard to Know When a Fact Is a Fact," in *Families as They Really Are*, ed. Barbara J. Risman (New York: W. W. Norton, 2010), 10–14.

71 Becker, *Forcing the Spring*, especially 132–42.

72 See, for example, Carlos A. Ball, *Same-Sex Marriage and Children: A Tale of History, Social Science, and Law* (New York: Oxford University Press, 2014).

73 See Andrew Lister, *Public Reason and Community* (London: Bloomsbury Publishing, 2013), 139.

74 Some natural law opponents of same-sex marriage also recognize this point. See, for example, Girgis et al., *What Is Marriage?* 18–19.

H. *The Double Standard*

Nonetheless, the correctness of this double standard – where the law privileges monogamous marriages at the expense of its other potentially valuable forms – lies at the heart of opposition to plural marriage and too often escapes scrutiny. Under alternative social circumstances, this state of affairs might be more controversial. Although monogamous marriage has a checkered past, few contemporary scholars maintain that the state should leave the marriage business altogether or abolish traditional two-person marriage because it is positively correlated with the subordination of women, intimate partner violence, child abuse and neglect, or other sociopathic behaviors. When the legal system does not make room for plural marriage, this omission restricts the freedom of those who are denied the option of marrying the person(s) of their choice. Therefore, they may not be able to have as good a life as they could have had or achieve their most important ends.

When it comes to the legal recognition of plural marriage, then, the fundamental question is whether a restriction on the right to choose a particular partner is sufficiently justified to override the normally strong presumption in favor of letting adults make their own decisions about how they want to live. That distinctly liberal approach, which is also found in our constitutional tradition, would begin to make some sense of our well-entrenched beliefs as to why some restrictions – but not others – are unobjectionable. As a rationale for the denial of the right to same-sex marriage, heteronormativity – no longer suffices. Those who want to retain a numerical restriction would have to prove that plural marriage – unlike other forms of marriage that already receive legal recognition – is intrinsically bad, directly harms the participants, indirectly injures third parties or puts them at risk, or has other awful consequences. Since the nineteenth century, the U.S. Supreme Court has not addressed the possibility of a constitutional right to polygamy or plural marriage. The Utah Constitution prohibits such a practice.[75] In the past decade, the Utah Supreme Court has dealt with the issue twice but has not found such a right under the U.S. Constitution or in its own constitution.[76]

[75] Utah Constitution, Article III, Section 1 (removing polygamy from the scope of constitutional protection for free exercise of religion)

[76] See *Arthur v. Utah*, 2004 UT 76, 99 P. 3d 820 (2004); *Utah v. Holm*, 2006 UT 31; 137 P.3d 726 (2006).

II. CONSTITUTIONAL CONSTRUCTION

A. *The New Originalism*

In this section, I explain how a constitutional right to plural marriage or its equivalent could come into being someday. I do so by showing how even originalism, which is supposed to fix constitutional meaning, still leaves considerable room for judges to make law in the kinds of cases the Supreme Court often takes. The appeal of any originalist theory of interpretation in a constitutional democracy like our own that constitutionalizes contested issues of political morality – such as affirmative action, same-sex marriage, abortion, privacy, health care, campaign finance reform, speech more generally, gun control, religion, capital punishment – lies in its promise to curb judicial discretion. Unelected federal judges with life tenure are supposed to interpret the law and not make it, as we have often been told. When they engage in the latter, they usurp the authority of lawmakers, put the legitimacy of their decisions into doubt, and may make serious mistakes that are not easily corrected.

This portrayal of judging in America in which judges either follow the law or make it up as they go along is not only oversimplified, but it also distorts constitutional practice by making it seem as if the Constitution always dictates the legal conclusion, where the judge rendering the decision is an umpire who could not sincerely and reasonably have reached the opposite result. One of the most pernicious ideas still in circulation is that in hard constitutional cases, there is a legally correct answer – independent of deeper judgments of political morality – that a judge could uncover, provided he or she actually looks for it and resists the temptation to decide what the law should be.[77] This way of thinking about what judges do invites the public to assume they are not making law when they are and encourages ordinary Americans to conclude that when judges reach decisions they disagree with, those judges must have been acting in bad faith. My point is not that all constitutional cases are hard. Nor is it that judges always make egregiously partisan decisions with complete indifference to whether they have any legal support for their positions. Rather, how they discern constitutional meaning is bound to be shaped by their deepest political convictions.

That is not a mere empirical observation or an indictment of judges for being insidiously political despite their protestations to the contrary. American constitutional law is moralized; it contains abstract principles like freedom and

[77] See Ronald Dworkin, *Freedom's Law: The Moral Reading of the American Constitution* (Cambridge, MA: Harvard University Press, 1996), 37.

equality that require moral judgments when judges apply them to new fact patterns. The kinds of cases the Supreme Court takes and people care most about frequently do not yield obviously legally correct answers in the sense that everyone in the legal community would concur with the result or with the reasoning. That state of affairs helps explain the existence of 5–4 decisions and why the political beliefs of the judges are good – but far from perfect – predictors of how they will vote in particular cases. In hard constitutional cases, they can invalidate the law whose constitutionality is being challenged and in doing so make law. Their other option is to leave the law alone. The obvious problem with judicial restraint is that it seems to defeat the very purpose of judicial review – namely, to limit what legislative majorities are allowed to do. When the justices let the law stand, in a sense, they are still making law because they could have invalidated it. To decline to veto a law can be seen as a kind of lawmaking because the justices are indirectly responsible for its continuing existence. In 1944, in *Korematsu*, the Supreme Court constitutionalized one of the worst instances of racial profiling in America history. The majority could fall back on the fact it did not enact the internment order. As such, the other branches of government and the military were to blame. However, that would be cold comfort to the Japanese-Americans whose lives were ruined or, in a few instances, ended. Thus, notwithstanding how they would describe what they are doing, the justices are deciding what the law should be and not what it is in hard constitutional cases because there is no "is" there. There is only normative space that somehow has to be filled.

According to Larry Solum, in such situations, one must grasp the critical constitutional difference between interpretation and construction and appreciate that judging involves each of them.[78] First, the judge tries to discern the semantic meaning of the constitutional language at issue. At this stage, he or she can try to resolve any linguistic ambiguity. Next, he or she determines the legal effect of the text by applying it to the particular fact pattern.[79] To discern the linguistic meaning of the constitutional text, then, is not to answer the constitutional question at hand, as the old originalists, such as Justice Scalia, believed. At most, it is the beginning of the analysis.

These days, originalism takes many forms and any judge or law professor who describes him or herself as an originalist must specify exactly what he or she means by the term or risk being misunderstood. As Solum writes:

[78] Lawrence B. Solum, "The Interpretation-Construction Distinction," *Constitutional Commentary*, 27 (2010), 95–118.

[79] Lawrence B. Solum, "We Are All Originalists Now," in *Constitutional Originalism: A Debate* (Ithaca, NY: Cornell University Press, 2011), 3, 22–24.

"Originalism is . . . an evolving family of constitutional theories."[80] For the old originalists, the purpose of relying heavily on original expectations – how most people of that time would have expected the constitutional language in question to be applied – was to preserve the relevance of the original public meaning so that history could answer contemporary constitutional questions. A judge need not know anything about, say, the morality of the state's putting to death those who had been convicted of capital crimes. He or she only needed to discover how the practice would have been understood by most people in 1791 and whether they would have seen it as "cruel and unusual." In that way, interpretation and construction are more closely related than they otherwise would be. The other option would be to eschew such expectations, which has the advantage of according the interpreter more latitude in determining the implications of the constitutional language in question. For example, Keith Whittington believes that "[s]pecific expectations about the consequences of a legal rule are distinct from the meaning of the rule itself."[81]

However, it is doubtful that such expected applications could so easily be divorced from their meaning when how the rule is used may more or less constitute its meaning. The judge's understanding of the application of the rule to new circumstances has to make at least some use of past applications, even when he or she is not particularly concerned with trying to follow precedent. After all, two persons probably do not agree about the meaning of a rule if they did not converge on how it ought to be applied more often than not. Whittington concedes that widespread agreement on applications "may be reflective of the content of the rule in question."[82] The more discretion the judge has in the application process, the less history can guide him or her toward an answer. Also, the rejection of past applications would push her much closer to the nonoriginalist camp that the old originalists ad endeavored to distance themselves from.

This much is increasingly evident: The enterprise of so-called originalist judges involves something more than merely discerning the meaning of certain words at a particular moment in American history. They are not simply interpreting constitutional language but are also grappling with its vagueness and in doing so – whether they realize it or not – are also constructing new constitutional meaning that may gain adherents over time. The new

80 Lawrence B. Solum, "Originalism and the Natural Born Citizen Clause," p. 3 (April 18, 2010: draft), http://ssrn.com/abstract=1263885.

81 Keith E. Whittington, "Originalism: A Critical Introduction," *Fordham Law Review*, 82 (2013), 383.

82 Ibid., 385.

originalism is considerably more sophisticated than its predecessor. To their credit, the new originalists acknowledge the nuances of judicial decision making.[83] At times, the old originalists cast certain constitutional principles at a higher level of generality to avoid unpalatable results, such as the conclusion that *Brown* was wrongly decided, and defended this move as being consistent with how most people would have understood the constitutional language in question. Their doing so is more than convenient; it allows them to be fainthearted when they do not want to decide a case on strictly historical grounds because the outcome would be at odds with well-accepted constitutional understandings. In a hard case, then, it is not evident what kind of work originalism does in just about any semioriginalist constitutional argument other than establishing loose semantic parameters for their imminent constructions.

In one form or another, nonoriginalists already accept the need for such construction – whatever they may call it – because they do not believe they have any other choice when the text and case law run out. Additionally, they seem to be more willing to ignore original meaning – even when it is crystal clear – if following it would produce objectionable political outcomes. What I want to highlight here is just how much ground the new originalists have conceded to their nonoriginalist critics. One of the defining characteristics of the new originalism is frank recognition of the fact that judges must fill the gaps in underdetermined constitutional language through constructing new constitutional meaning.[84] As Whittington states: "Interpretation has an important role to play in the elaboration of constitutional meaning, but it is a limited one."[85] The need for construction arises because the original meaning, even if it can be discerned, cannot dictate how certain constitutional language ought to be applied. According to Jack Balkin: "Constitutional construction builds out the Constitution-in-practice, fleshing out and implementing vague and abstract language through doctrine. . . ."[86]

The old originalism – which assumes that original, widely accepted practices, such as capital punishment, cannot be unconstitutional – fails to take into account that constitutional meaning can be fixed but that applications may extend beyond how most people would have applied them at the time of their enactment.[87] Other new originalists, such as Solum and Randy Barnett,

[83] Ibid., 375–409. [84] Whittington, "The New Originalism," 612.
[85] Whittington, *Constitutional Interpretation*, 5.
[86] Jack M. Balkin, "The New Originalism and the Use of History," 1–91, August 1, 2013.
[87] See Mark D. Greenberg and Harry Litman, "The Meaning of Original Meaning," *Georgetown Law Journal*, 86 (1998), 569–619.

concede that constitutional construction involves fleshing out constitutional provisions beyond simply determining their original linguistic meaning in applying them to new circumstances.[88] They accept that a judge cannot merely fall back on original expected applications, as if judging were an exercise in channeling the beliefs of eighteenth-century Americans. In Whittington's words, "... the textual principle should not be reduced to the founders' scope of beliefs about that principle."[89] And if they did so, they would still be engaged in construction.

Today, some of the new originalists are more inclined to use the theory offensively and are no longer so obsessed with judicial restraint.[90] Barnett has deployed a particular kind of originalism in advancing Libertarian causes.[91] Frequently, it feels like debates over constitutional interpretation are a sideshow in the following respect: In hard constitutional cases, the primary focus should be on constitutional construction (the legal effect of the constitutional language) and not on constitutional interpretation (its linguistic meaning). For Solum, originalism is only a theory of the latter.[92] As part of his indictment of Justice Scalia for not being a consistent originalist, Barnett points out that Scalia leaves himself with several escape routes to avoid having to adhere to original meaning when he does not want to do so.[93] Scalia seems to be too willing too often to indulge in what amounts to nonoriginalist methods of legal reasoning, defeating the very purpose of being an originalist – that is, being committed to curbing judicial discretion to avoid controversial moral judgments that are better left to elected officials in a democracy.

The point is not that Scalia or other like-minded originalists are engaged in an elaborate ruse but rather that how they construct constitutional meaning is not simply a matter of retrieving linguistic meaning. The distinction between interpretation and construction calls into question the very coherence of the old originalism; to interpret the constitutional text is one thing, but to apply it in

88 Not all new originalists acknowledge the need for constitutional constructions. See, for example, John O. McGinnis and Michael B. Rappaport, "A New Theory of Interpretation and the Case Against Construction," *Northwestern University Law Review*, 103 (2009), 751–801; John O. McGinnis and Michael B. Rappaport, *Originalism and the Good Constitution* (Cambridge, MA: Harvard University Press, 2013).

89 Keith E. Whittington, "The New Originalism," *Georgetown Journal of Law and Public Policy*, 2 (2004), 610.

90 Ibid., 607–08.

91 Randy E. Barnett, *Restoring the Lost Constitution: The Presumption of Liberty* (Princeton, NJ: Princeton University Press, 2004).

92 Solum, "We Are All Originalists Now," 71.

93 Randy E. Barnett, "Scalia's Infidelity: A Critique of 'Faint-Hearted' Originalism," *University of Cincinnati Law Review*, 75 (2006), 13.

contemporary circumstances to give it legal effect is another. At most, this distinction was latent in the old originalism. According to Barnett: "The more general or vague the term (determined historically), the more likely it is that uncertain applications will arise outside its core meaning . . . whether an object falls outside the ambit of a vague term is a matter of 'construction' rather than of interpretation."[94] This way of viewing judging dramatically alters the nature of the debate over how to discern constitutional meaning and decide hard constitutional cases. After all, for years, the main defense of originalism was predicated on how in theory – if not always in practice – original public meaning constrained judges so they would not substitute their own views for those of lawmakers and disrespect separation of powers and majority rule. Originalists purportedly accomplished this objectivity by denying that a judge has to exercise his or her own judgment in hard constitutional cases and insisting that the Constitution (its original meaning) made originalist judges do it.

Fortunately, some of the new originalists, such as Barnett and Whittington, developed a more plausible version of originalism that took into account the extent to which judges construct constitutional meaning but in a manner somehow constrained by original meaning.[95] While the focal point of Whittington's theory of construction is how new constitutional meanings come into being through the interaction of politics and the Constitution, Barnett's theory is unapologetically normative in the sense of guiding judges and other legal actors in deciding what the law should be. Unlike Barnett, Whittington believes that the judiciary is not the appropriate branch to make such constructions. While Barnett maintains that original meanings limit the range of acceptable constitutional constructions, he also admits that in some cases, it may be hard to distinguish between them.[96] Whittington shares this view.[97] For Solum, originalism does not "entail a particular theory of constitutional construction."[98]

That critical point must not be missed. Because it is difficult to see how the original meaning could more than minimally constrain the process of

94 Randy E. Barnett, "An Originalism for Nonoriginalists," *Loyola Law Review*, 45 (1999), 611–54; Barnett, *Restoring the Lost Constitution*, 120.

95 See, for example, Keith E. Whittington, *Constitutional Interpretation: Textual Meaning, Original Intent, and Judicial Review* (Lawrence: University of Kansas Press, 1991); Keith E. Whittington, *Constitution Construction: Divided Powers and Constitutional Meaning* (Cambridge, MA: Harvard University Press, 1999); Randy E. Barnett, *Restoring the Lost Constitution: The Presumption of Liberty* (Princeton, NJ: Princeton University Press, 2004).

96 Barnett, *Restoring the Lost Constitution*, 121–28.

97 Whittington, *Constitutional Interpretation*, 1–11.

98 Solum, "We Are All Originalists Now," 151.

constructing constitutional meaning in what Solum calls the "construction zone," it is hard to know what counts as a legitimate constitutional construction or why one would be better than the others without falling back on one's deepest beliefs about political morality. Judges and others can use history and other sources to defend various outcomes without obviously acting illegitimately. Different normative constructions, then, would be expected, and the new originalism would be a theory that many liberals could embrace if they care about maintaining some sort of loose fidelity to the constitutional text and reject even more open-ended living constitutionalist methodologies. Whittington also believes that "construction is essentially creative."[99] The relationship between original meaning and construction can vary markedly.[100] As James Fleming points out, Solum's inclusive new originalism has little in common with the old originalism of Edwin Meese, Robert Bork, and Scalia.[101] Indeed, it is so inclusive that it not only invites moral readings – broadly construed – but also probably requires them. The more abstract, vague, and underdetermined the constitutional language in question is, the less its original public meaning can contribute in more than a trivial way to any normative constitutional argument. There are too many places where the judge must exercise discretion to fill in the gaps.

As a result, we should doubt that constitutional interpretation – strictly speaking – matters as much in constitutional adjudication as we have been led to believe.[102] At least in hard cases, which are the ones that generate the most controversy, what happens in the construction zone ought to concern us more than anything else. Judges and others can construct constitutional meaning in multiple ways when they have so much material outside of the four corners of the text to draw upon, including adoption history, and they need not follow traditional originalist methods. At some point, in a given case, they even may have crossed the line between construction and creation.[103] Most of the time, though, it will be nearly impossible to ascertain whether judges have done so unless the connection between the original meaning and the construction is so attenuated that the result cannot be justified as a mere construction.

99 Whittington, *Constitutional Interpretation*, 5.

100 Solum, "We Are All Originalists Now," 69.

101 James E. Fleming, "The New Originalist Manifesto: Constitutional Originalism: A Debate," *Constitutional Commentary*, 28 (2013), 541.

102 Ibid., 547.

103 According to Whittington: "Constitutional creation invents wholly new meaning." Whittington, *Constitutional Interpretation*, 11.

While the old originalists did everything within their power to disassociate themselves from the activism they purported to despise, the record demonstrates they were increasingly eager to use originalist arguments to induce courts to overturn laws they oppose on political grounds. In real cases, it can be hard to pinpoint where an interpretation ends and a construction begins or, for that matter, where a construction ends and a creation begins. Whittington insists that the "crucial point of disagreement" among various kinds of originalists and various kinds of nonoriginalists is that the latter are willing to construct new constitutional meaning, even when it conflicts with the original meaning.[104] At best, this rejoinder only works in easy or moderately difficult cases. In hard constitutional cases, which invariably involve highly abstract constitutional language, conflicting precedent, and complex fact patterns, the original meaning will not be sufficiently clear to shape the process of constitutional construction. Today, many progressive legal scholars, such as Balkin, identify with originalism and do not see such an interpretive approach as incompatible with the pursuit of progressive political ends. Their doing so, I suppose, is a way of seizing the high ground but has made it even more difficult to know an originalist argument when one sees it. Recently, Bruce Ackerman has claimed that he – and not such justices like Scalia and Clarence Thomas – is the real originalist.[105] Increasingly, self-identified originalists do not see eye to eye about the correct outcome in real cases, which suggests that either they cannot converge on the original public meaning or, more likely, even when they have done so, they still have to apply it and thus will construct new constitutional meaning differently. Under such circumstances, particularly if judges fail to exercise restraint by leaving the law in question alone, then they may be engaged in something more like lawmaking than they care to admit or perhaps are aware of. As Barnett writes: "If originalism is [only] a theory of interpretation, then it may be of limited utility in formulating a theory of construction, other than in requiring that original meaning not be disregarded or undermined."[106]

This is not the same overstated claim that runaway judges can do whatever they please; it reflects a genuine concern about what judges are actually doing when they find themselves in Solum's "construction zone," H. L. A. Hart's "penumbra of uncertainty," or Richard Posner's "open area." In constructing

104 Keith E. Whittington, "Originalism: A Critical Introduction," *Fordham Law Review*, 82 (2013), 408.

105 Bruce Ackerman, *We the People: The Civil Rights Revolution* (Cambridge, MA: Belknap Press of Harvard University Press, 2014), 329.

106 Randy E. Barnett, "Interpretation and Construction," *Harvard Journal of Law and Public Policy*, 34 (2011), 65.

constitutional meaning, judges appear to make law in more than the minimal sense of producing a decision that may serve as a precedent in the future. Thus, the debate over judicial activism and restraint cannot be reduced to interpreting the Constitution or ignoring it to reach a preferred outcome, as many ordinary Americans continue to believe. The debate should really be about what normative considerations should be allowed. Under such circumstances, deeper political differences are bound to influence what people mean when they say a case has been rightly decided. As long as the power of judicial review continues to exist, I do not see how it could be any other way.

III. THE FUTURE OF MARRIAGE

A. *Beyond Same-Sex Marriage*

In the previous section, my primary aim was to underscore the extent to which even new originalist approaches create considerable space for judges to move constitutional law in new directions. If there has been one casualty in the war between different kinds of originalists and different kinds of nonoriginalists, it involves the notion that original public meaning can meaningfully constrain judicial discretion in hard cases and thus produce legally correct answers when the law is unsettled. As two legal scholars put it, "in deciding how to vote and what to say, the justices are moved by a dizzying array of considerations."[107] Historically, the Supreme Court's decisions have been inside of and outside of our existing constitutional practices.[108] Judges who claim that the Constitution forced them to answer the question the way they did are either disingenuous or lack self-awareness. At the very least, they should take responsibility for the choices they make.

Moreover, in hard cases, even if the original public meaning were clear enough to be beyond any reasonable dispute, judges still may not care when that meaning is so out of sync with precedent or with widely shared conventional moral understandings. Nobody thinks that in 1868, the drafters and ratifiers of the Fourteenth Amendment believed that the Equal Protection Clause had anything to do with marriage or the protection of gays and lesbians or other sexual minorities from legal discrimination. I doubt many scholars think that clause was meant to protect white people from so-called reverse

107 Laurence Tribe and Joshua Matz, *Uncertain Justice: The Robert Courts and the Constitution* (New York: Henry Holt, 2014), 4.

108 Stephen A. Simon, *Universal Rights and the Constitution* (Albany: State University of New York Press), 1.

discrimination. The framers would not have anticipated that the clause would have been applied by the Supreme Court the way it was in *Romer* and more recently in *Windsor*. An increasing number of legal scholars simply do not care about such a narrow original meaning, as if it were beside the point. The abstract principle of equality found in that clause covers situations that its authors and ratifiers did not envision, and constitutional change continues to take place outside of the formal amendment process.

The social meaning of marriage is currently evolving more rapidly in some places than in others. The analysis in the last section indicates that the constitutional text does not stand in the way of such change and even may facilitate it inasmuch as some of its most important language is highly abstract, thereby inviting various normative constructions. Even when some states are reluctant to expand their respective definitions of marriage, no one can rule out the possibility that courts may someday find a numerical limitation unconstitutional, especially if public opinion becomes less hostile to plural marriage, as it already has with respect to interracial marriage and same-sex marriage to some degree. *Windsor* provides considerable support for the view that when it comes to marriage, laws that demean sexual minorities (and other unpopular groups) are unconstitutional.[109]

As I shall show in a subsequent chapter, states demean plural marriage enthusiasts by refusing them to allow them to marry more than one person at the same time. There is nothing necessarily silly in wanting to be married to more than one person simultaneously. Today, for the most part, states could not care less about the personal reasons couples have to marry. Their respective personal reasons are their own and are not subject to being second-guessed. By contrast, regarding plural marriage, the state may treat one's most serious personal reasons for wanting to marry more than one person at the same time differently from another's most frivolous reasons for wanting to marry only one person.[110]

Sooner rather than later, this double standard, which so often evades scrutiny, needs to be defended more forcefully if it is to remain in place. Constitutionally, whether there is a right to plural marriage (or whether not permitting such an option constitutes a denial of equal protection of the law) comes down to the quality of the reasons that would justify a numerical

[109] *United States v. Windsor*, 570 U.S. __ (2013) (invalidating Section 3 of DOMA)

[110] Proponents of same-sex marriage have pointed out how odd it is that an opposite-sex couple could marry almost immediately after a one-night stand, whereas a same-sex couple, which had been together for twenty years and may have even raised a family together, would still not be eligible for a marriage license in most states. In the latter case, it is evident that that couple probably has much more serious personal reasons for wanting to marry.

limitation. This way of understanding the constitutional limits of the state is known in the legal literature as a public justification requirement.[111] As we shall see, these reasons turn out to be surprisingly weak. As a matter of fact, some of the most compelling reasons proponents of same-sex marriage have put forth in defense of their position, referencing the importance of personal choice and equal legal treatment, support the conclusion that states must provide the option of plural marriage.

In the rest of this book, my basic strategy is to illuminate how one cannot be consistent and still believe in a constitutional right to same-sex marriage (or its equivalent on equal protection grounds) without also believing in such a right to plural marriage. Upon closer inspection, the constitutionally relevant differences between them are superficial. The constitutional right to same-sex marriage (or its equivalent), then, implies the constitutional right to plural marriage. In Elizabeth Brake's words: "Liberal defenses of same-sex marriage have not followed the implications of their own reasoning far enough. Attempts within liberalism to produce a rationale for restricting legal marriage to different-sex partners have failed, but so have attempts to produce a rationale for restricting it to monogamous or amatonormative relationships."[112]

B. *Strategic Concerns*

This book is not about looking into a crystal ball and making predictions about the future of marriage or offering advice about the most efficacious way to advance the cause of plural marriage through a combination of social activism, media exposure, fundraising, political maneuvering, and litigation. However, one explanation for the lack of support for plural marriage on the part of advocates of same-sex marriage is pragmatic. A lot of them have not embraced plural marriage because their opponents will use the possibility of such marriage as evidence that no logical stopping point exists when Americans begin to tinker with the so-called traditional definition of marriage.[113] The attempt to make the public overlook the possible connection between same-sex and plural marriage is intelligible when many Americans still refuse to endorse a right to same-sex marriage even when they do not reject such alternatives as

[111] See, for example, Den Otter, *Judicial Review in an Age of Moral Pluralism*; Bedi, *Beyond Race, Sex, and Sexual Orientation*; and Wilfrid Waluchow, "On the Neutrality of Charter Reasoning," in *Neutrality and Theory of Law*, ed. Jordi Ferrer Beltran, Jose Juan Moreso, and Diego M. Papayannis (Dordrecht, Netherlands: Springer, 2013), 203–24.

[112] Brake, *Minimizing Marriage*, 6.

[113] Cheshire Calhoun, "Who's Afraid of Polygamy? Lessons for Same-Sex Marriage from the History of Polygamy," *San Diego Law Review*, 42 (2005), 1026.

civil unions or domestic partnerships. One of the lessons from the passage of Proposition 8 in California in 2008, which amended the California Constitution to take away the right of same-sex marriage, is that even in a blue state, it may be more difficult to frame such marriage as a civil rights issue than many proponents of that right had anticipated.[114]

I am not unsympathetic to the strategic concerns of the advocates of same-sex marriage and certainly would not want courts to foist plural marriage on states if doing so would produce a constitutional amendment restricting marriage to couples. One way to read what happened in *Hollingsworth* is to see even the liberal justices as being reluctant to move too quickly on a divisive issue when public opinion continues to evolve. Nothing I say in this book should be construed as advocating indifference to or contempt for political reality. As more and more states legally recognize same-sex marriages, though, the more likely it is that such advocates will no longer have to fear the slippery slope that some conservatives have made so much of. Only several years ago, several prominent liberal legal scholars were convinced that courts were moving too quickly on the issue and that judicial decisions mandating same-sex marriage would cause a backlash. Today, the probability that an anti-same-sex marriage constitutional amendment could be enacted through the procedures specified in Article V is just about zero.

In any event, this book concerns whether there is principled constitutional distinction between the two kinds of marriages – whatever happens in the future.[115] The debate about plural marriage is unavoidable, and Americans must eventually decide whether to expand the scope of marriage in the name of marriage equality so each person has a much longer menu of marital options to choose from. It would be surprising if the judiciary did not play some role in this prolonged decision-making process, even if it were only to ratify, in a manner of speaking, what had already happened socially and politically. Some of the old fears about plural marriage live on and the question of whether to expand the legal definition of marriage is not as uncomplicated as that of same-sex marriage because in the eyes of many people, a society that is committed to ensuring that women have all the opportunities that men have does not have a place for an institution that seems to be premised on exactly the kind of gender inequality that

[114] On November 4, 2008, the voters of California passed Proposition 8, which overturned the California Supreme Court's decision recognizing a constitutional right to same-sex marriage under the California Constitution. In *Strauss v. Horton*, the California Supreme Court declined to invalidate Proposition 8 on the grounds it was a constitutional revision.

[115] Recently, Cass Sunstein has given his theory of Burkean minimalism a distinctly utilitarian or consequentialist foundation by emphasizing outcomes. Cass R. Sunstein, *A Constitution of Many Minds: Why the Founding Document Doesn't Mean What It Meant Before* (Princeton, NJ: Princeton University Press, 2009), especially 72.

ought to be eradicated. The task ahead of us is to address this constitutional question in a manner that captures its complexity and considers the importance of protecting women from mistreatment and of the individual freedom to be able to marry more than one person at the same time.

In defending a constitutional right to plural marriage, I do not sharply distinguish between legal and policy arguments when no bright line between them exists in hard cases. One person's moral or policy argument can frequently be turned into another's legal argument without too much exertion. Now and then, judges have considerable latitude in deciding whether a particular legal argument is sound or better than its rivals. In hard cases, then, the constitutional text always requires supplementation, as I argued earlier, and one does not have to be a full-fledged realist to appreciate the extent to which judges in these situations not only can but must go beyond mere interpretation. Invariably, they will have to assess what the state's interest is, whether it is sufficiently compelling, and whether the legislative means fit the legislative end well enough. Such equal protection cases as *Romer v. Evans* and *Grutter v. Bollinger* indicate that even the official standard of review that the legislative classification in question triggers may not predetermine the outcome.[116]

CONCLUSION

Although the constitutional text is not an inkblot test, it contains unforeseen meanings because it can be legitimately applied in a manner that its authors and ratifiers did not anticipate. I do not feel I am saying anything that has not been said more eloquently by other legal scholars about constitutional possibilities. The implication is that the right to plural marriage (or its equivalent on other constitutional grounds) is not as farfetched as it may seem. While such marriage will not be recognized by any state anytime soon, those who would like to be a part of a plural marriage have been waiting too long for a fair hearing. Recent scholarship about possible changes to the legal status of marriage mainly concerns same-sex marriage or the elimination of civil marriage and its replacement with something like civil union status for everyone.[117]

[116] *Romer v. Evans*, 517 U.S. 620 (1996); *Grutter v. Bollinger*, 539 U.S. 306 (2003).

[117] On the former, see, for example, Gerstmann, *Same-Sex Marriage and the Constitution*; Andrew Koppelman, *The Gay Rights Question in Contemporary American Law* (Chicago: University of Chicago Press, 2002); Jonathan Rauch, *Gay Marriage: Why It Is Good for Gays, Good for Straights, and Good for America* (New York: Henry Holt, 2004); Evan Wolfson, *Why Marriage Matters: America, Equality, and Gay People's Right to Marry* (New York: Simon and Schuster, 2004); and William N. Eskridge Jr., *The Case for Same-Sex Marriage: From Sexual Liberty to Civilized Commitment* (New York: The Free Press, 1996).

Those who take the first route are reticent about plural marriage insofar as they fear the aforementioned slippery slope. Those who take the other route often do not pay close attention to the particulars of plural marriage.[118] The result is that scholars rarely treat the topic more than superficially, and when they do, they often utilize caricatures or make sweeping empirical generalizations based on a tiny sample of contemporary polygynous relationships and overlook the compelling personal reasons an individual might have for wanting a nonmonogamous marital relationship. It is about time that scholars, judges, and the rest of us stop reducing such marriage to other social problems, approach it on its own terms, and evaluate it on its own merits more objectively. That is not too much to ask in a society that prides itself on tolerating difference and respecting personal choice.

[118] A number of law professors have discussed the merits of disestablishing or abolishing civil marriage and replacing it with a more inclusive alternative, such as universal civil unions, but none of them have made plural marriage their focal points. See, for example, Martha Albertson Fineman, *The Autonomy Myth: A Theory of Dependency* (New York: The New Press, 2004); and Linda C. McClain, *The Place of Families: Fostering Capacity, Equality, and Responsibility* (Cambridge, MA: Harvard University Press, 2006).

2

Judging the Case Against Plural Marriage (Part I)

One of the serious problems with typical critiques of plural marriage is that critics take aim at traditional patriarchal polygyny – as if it were the only possible form – when plural marriage can be quite diverse. In an era of "postmodern polygamy," multiperson intimate relationships not only exist but also already exhibit considerable variance.[1] A plural marriage could be same sex or opposite sex and involves three or more siblings or three or more close friends. The participants would not have to be physically intimate, and such a marital arrangement could consist of partners who are romantically attached to some – but not all – of the others. Today, common configurations of polyamorous relationships include triad or triangle (three persons – regardless of gender – who are romantically involved with one another), V-triad (three persons, two of whom are not romantically involved with each other, quad (four persons who may or may not be involved romantically with one another), and W (a fivesome or two connected Vs).[2] The polygynous relationships in contemporary America are but a subset of the wide range of plural marriages that would probably exist if states were to legalize polygamy and expand their respective legal definitions of marriage to make them more inclusive. To identify the problems associated with some or perhaps many traditional polygynous relationships under certain conditions is not to prove that all multiperson intimate relationships should remain criminalized or are undeserving of legal recognition.

In this chapter and the next one, I reconstruct the case against plural marriage and elaborate on why it is not persuasive. I proceed in this manner because most Americans who have given little or no thought to the topic most

[1] The term is found in Maura I. Strassberg, "The Challenge of Postmodern Polygamy: Considering Polyamory," *Capital University Law Review*, 31 (2003), 439–563.

[2] Tristan Taormino, *Opening Up: A Guide to Creating and Sustaining Open Relationships* (San Francisco: Cleis Press, 2008), 99.

likely assume that the state's not providing such an option is constitutionally unproblematic. At present, no state is required to treat any kind of multiperson intimate relationship as a marriage.[3] In terms of organization, then, it makes more sense to begin with the various arguments against plural marriage, which turn out to be flawed, before developing the positive case on its behalf. As I shall argue, the particular arguments against plural marriage involving the promotion of gender equality and the prevention of coercion fail to justify a numerical limitation.

This chapter will be divided into the following sections. First, I give a brief overview of Mormon polygyny. I do so because most Americans continue to associate plural marriage with Mormonism. Second, I discuss the state's alleged interest in fostering gender equality in personal relationships, articulate why it trades on an ambiguity about the meaning of such equality, and conclude that the extent to which the state can promote such equality during the marriage is constitutionally circumscribed. The state's interest in fostering internal equality while the marriage lasts is weaker than its interest in ensuring such equality if the marriage ends and the community property must be divided, spousal support has to be awarded, custody and visitation of children (if there are any) must be arranged, and so on. Third, I address common concerns about different sorts of coercion and investigate what it would mean for the women involved in plural relationships to have consented, legally speaking. Fourth, I examine paternalistic rationales for not allowing women the option of a plural marriage and find them to be unsatisfactory.

I. THE LONG SHADOW OF MORMON POLYGYNY

Part of the widespread unease concerning plural marriage in the United States can be traced to its historical association with Mormonism. As Elizabeth Emens states, "when Americans hear the term 'polygamy,' or try to picture relationships of more than two, they typically think of traditional polygyny."[4] Unfortunately, some popular television programs confirm this association and perpetuate negative stereotypes about polygamists by inducing viewers into thinking that plural marriage is synonymous with polygyny. Additionally, the judiciary has done little to encourage Americans to view plural marriage as more than a mere opportunity to exploit women and abuse children. In *Reynolds v. United States*, the U.S. Supreme Court ruled

[3] See 28 U.S.C. Section 1783C (2006).

[4] Elizabeth F. Emens, "Monogamy's Law: Compulsory Monogamy and Polyamorous Existence," *New York University Review of Law and Social Change*, 29 (2004), 282.

that the First Amendment does not protect the practice of plural marriage even when such marriage is a genuine religious duty for some persons.[5] As Sarah Song observes: "The *Reynolds* court both drew upon and reinforced ... [a] discourse of racial and cultural superiority of whites over others, casting the American-born Mormon religion as foreign and other."[6] For Kent Greenawalt: "The Court left no doubt that it regarded polygamy as a despicable practice condemned by all civilized nations. ..."[7] In 2004, the Utah Supreme Court used the decision as precedent to uphold Tom Green's conviction for bigamy.[8] Until quite recently, federal courts have not entertained the possibility that polygynous cohabitation is constitutionally protected.[9] None of them ever has endorsed the even more radical view that plural marriage is required on fundamental rights, equal protection, freedom of association, free exercise of religion, or other constitutional grounds. According to one historian, "the opinion in *Reynolds* immediately and irrevocably raised the pitch of antipolygamy activism."[10] Despite its dubious rationale – at least by contemporary constitutional standards – *Reynolds* rarely makes the anticanon (the list of unarguably wrongly decided cases), which includes *Dred Scott*, *Plessy v. Ferguson*, and *Korematsu* and used to include *Lochner*.[11]

As noted, present-day FLDS polygyny is only one of the many forms a plural marriage could take.[12] First, in the nineteenth century, few Mormons actually followed what they referred to as "the principle."[13] Second, today, only a small number of FLDS practice polygyny.[14] Third, the typical FLDS polygynous marriage does not facilitate other crimes, such as sexual assault and child abuse.[15] The vast majority of them are probably no better or no

[5] *Reynolds v. United States*, 98 U.S. 145 (1878).

[6] Sarah Song, *Justice, Gender, and the Politics of Multiculturalism* (New York: Cambridge University Press, 2007), 148–49.

[7] Kent Greenawalt, *Religion and the Constitution: Fairness and Free Exercise* (Princeton, NJ: Princeton University Press, 2006), 28.

[8] *Utah v. Arthur*, 2004 UT 76; 99 P. 3d 820 (2004).

[9] *Brown v. Buhman* (2013) (Case No. 2:11-cv-0652).

[10] Sarah Barringer Gordon, *The Mormon Question: Polygamy and Constitutional Conflict in Nineteenth-Century America* (Chapel Hill: University of North Carolina Press, 2002), 121.

[11] I borrow the term "anticanon" from Jack M. Balkin, *Constitutional Redemption: Political Faith in an Unjust World* (Cambridge, MA: Harvard University Press, 2011), 14.

[12] FLDS polygyny is also diverse. Bennion, *Polygamy in Primetime*, xvii.

[13] Jessie L. Embry, "Effects of Polygamy on Mormon Women," *Frontiers: A Journal of Women Studies*, 7 (1984), 57.

[14] Unlike mainstream Mormons, FLDS continue to believe that polygyny is a religious duty. Bennion, *Polygamy in Primetime*, 7.

[15] See Bennion, *Polygamy in Primetime*, xvi; Turley Report, p. 6.

worse than the monogamous ones that many Americans too often romanticize. This double standard – where the law treats monogamous marriages so much more favorably – continues to lie at the heart of opposition to plural marriage. However, its correctness is far from self-evident. When the legal system does not make room for such marriage, it restricts the freedom of those who are denied the option of the kind of marriage they believe would best suit them and the flexibility they may need to adapt to their particular circumstances. At minimum, this restriction should raise eyebrows, especially when its justification may be in doubt. As Martha Nussbaum writes: "The best way of summarizing the tradition [of the right to marry] seems to be that all adults have a right to choose whom to marry."[16] Apart from the likely wrong of their being denied choice in an undeniably and deeply personal matter, polygamists may not be able to flourish as much as they could if the state were to recognize their unions and treat them equally. Furthermore, it may follow from a commitment to equal protection – understood as external equality – that the state must treat all marriages equally irrespective of their gender and numerical composition. The Supreme Court has never said a couple must promise to have at least a minimally egalitarian marriage before it is eligible for a marriage license or remain above a certain equality threshold as long as the marriage continues to exist.

After *Davis v. Beason*, the Supreme Court has not heard a case involving polygamy.[17] In the coming debate over plural marriage, confining ourselves to the example of FLDS polygyny should not dominate our analysis of the issue to the point where it impairs our thinking about the various forms that such marriage could take in a society that did not marginalize those who are different and force them to conceal their unconventional intimate relationships. For too many commentators, in the ongoing debate about same-sex marriage, the topic of plural marriage only arises when the discussion turns to what the bottom of the slippery slope might be like. Those who advocate same-sex marriage usually take it for granted that the Constitution does not protect the right to plural marriage. Their task is to distinguish same-sex from plural marriage so they can defend a constitutional right to the former (or its equivalent) without proving too much and thereby conceding a right to the latter.

[16] Martha C. Nussbaum, "A Right to Marry?" *California Law Review*, 98 (2010), 689.

[17] *Davis v. Beason*, 133 U.S. 333 (1890). In 2007, the Supreme Court rejected a petition for a *writ of certiorari* in a polygamy case. *Holm v. Utah*, 127 S. Ct. 1371 (2007).

II. GENDER EQUALITY

A. *Feminist Critiques*

All things considered, same-sex marriage is an easier case than its plural counterpart.[18] At present, there are many more gays and lesbians who would like to marry but are still not allowed to do so in a minority of states than plural marriage enthusiasts who seek to do likewise. More importantly, at the end of the day, none of the constitutional arguments against refusing to let same-sex couples marry are compelling. They often contain controversial moral (or religious) and unproven empirical premises that people can (and do) reasonably reject. Indeed, it is becoming increasingly evident that such arguments can no longer do the kinds of justificatory work they once did in defense of an outdated conception of marriage predicated on inequality. If anti-same marriage advocates argue that different-sex marriage is inherently superior, they are probably wrong. Even if they turned out to be right, they would still be advancing a particular conception of marriage that would not be publicly justified under conditions of moral pluralism. After all, being straight is not better than being gay. And lawmakers are not supposed to make legislative classifications on the basis of sexual orientation. Their other option would be to identify other state interests that excluding gays and lesbians from marriage is supposed to serve, which is not promising when the connection between that interest and allowing same-sex couples to marry is so attenuated. Once the debate is framed in terms of freedom of marital choice and marital equality, the game is over for opponents of same-sex marriage. Anyone who tries to cast his or her opposition to same-sex marriage will find it nearly impossible to contend that such different treatment of gays and lesbians satisfies the constitutional requirement of equal treatment.

By contrast, plural marriage raises legitimate concerns about gender equality, the genuineness of the consent, and the treatment of children. Probably the most serious objection to creating a constitutional right to plural marriage would be that to permit such marriage is to subordinate some women and to condemn them to unhappiness or misery. What is implicit in this objection is that such women would have better lives in a different, more equal living arrangement – for example, if they only married one person or did not marry at all. Another serious concern is that too many women have no real choice in the matter.[19] If

[18] For my characterization of same-sex marriage as an easy case, see Den Otter, *Judicial Review in an Age of Moral Pluralism* (New York: Cambridge University Press, 2009), especially 245–61.

[19] Alice Ristroph and Melissa Murray, "Disestablishing the Family," *Yale Law Journal*, 119 (2010), 1261.

their consent is spurious, then they have not really exercised a right but rather have been forced to do something they would not have done but for some kind of pressure or coercion. Recently, in Canada, the Bala Report attempted to document the kinds of harms that traditional polygyny inflicts on women.[20] An extensive nonacademic literature excoriates FLDS polygyny by underscoring the abuse of power by some of its leaders and cult-like behaviors of its members.[21]

The trouble with this one-sided portrayal of such polygyny is that such marriage need not involve such men as David Koresh, Warren Jeffs, Tom Green, or the man who kidnapped Elizabeth Smart.[22] Charles Manson was a polygamist, but it would not be fair to discredit polygamy by using his "family" as an example, as if it were typical. No one uses Tiger Woods, John Edwards, Donald Sterling, or Scott Peterson to vilify all monogamists and their marriages. To equate polygyny more generally with plural marriage is to mistake the part for the whole and rule out the possibility that unconventional marital arrangements may work well for some people in some circumstances. Regrettably, ordinary persons and even scholars frequently reduce plural marriage to the exploitation of women, incest, and the abuse of children. This approach makes it too easy to demonize the other and cuts short the conversation about the merits of unconventional intimate relationships more generally. In making a decisive case against plural marriage, one cannot simply point to its worst manifestations on the assumption that all its possible forms are equally objectionable. A more nuanced analysis would disaggregate multiperson intimate relationships and evaluate each kind separately.

Proponents of the right to plural marriage or at least those who offer limited defenses of it may respond by denying that polygyny causes or exacerbates gender inequality. "Polyfidelity" emphasizes individual choice and equality.[23] As Cheshire Calhoun reminds us, gender inequality is a contingent, not a

[20] Nicholas Bala, "An International Review of Polygamy: Legal and Policy Implications for Canada," in *Polygamy in Canada: Legal and Social Implications for Women and Children – A Collection of Policy Research Reports* (Ottawa: Research Directorate, Status of Women Canada, 2005), 7–17.

[21] See, for example, Jon Krakauer, *Under the Banner of Heaven: A Story of Violent Faith* (New York: Anchor Books, 2004).

[22] After the raid on the Yearning for Zion (YFZ) Ranch in Eldorado, Texas, in 2008 – despite how the media portrayed the event – it would be simplistic to characterize all the women who lived there as "a homogenous crowd of brainwashed girls." Martha Sonntag Bradley, "A Repeat of History: A Comparison of the Short Creek and Eldorado Raids on FLDS," in *Modern Polygamy in the United States: Historical, Cultural, and Legal Issues*, ed. Cardell K. Jacobson and Lara Burton (New York: Oxford University Press, 2011), 27. In 2001, Tom Green was convicted of raping a child (his first wife) when she was thirteen years old and was sentenced to life in prison. His other four "wives" were only fourteen and fifteen years old when he "married" them. Miriam Koktevegaard Zeitzan, *Polygamy: A Cross-Cultural Analysis* (New York: Berg, 2008), 172.

[23] Strassberg, "The Challenge of Post-Modern Polygamy," 452.

conceptual, feature of polygamy.[24] That is a philosopher's way of saying that polygamous intimate relationships can be equal. A plural marriage could be same sex or could be polyandrous, and the participants need not be sexually involved with one another. Thus, many of them may not resemble the kind of polygyny that has raised understandable worries in the past about how women are treated. Most critiques of plural marriage – understood as polygyny – presuppose that the only other option is amorous, usually opposite-sex monogamy. One of the aims of this book is to explain why that assumption is false. Also, it is hard to imagine that any sort of legally recognized polygynous marriage in the United States or Canada, for example, would closely resemble those in underdeveloped countries if they were effectively regulated. Under the right background conditions, such marriage is not always exploitative or bad for women and the law could try to address more directly problems that are unique to multiperson intimate relationships. In other words, regulation – as opposed to criminalization – is worth considering because it may be not only more effective in protecting women but also more humane.

What understandably makes many progressive academics uncomfortable with the idea of a person's marrying more than one person at the same time – probably more than any other single factor – concerns the extent to which women in traditional polygynous relationships rarely would be equals even when such equality is logically possible. That feeling reflects a perfectly reasonable concern about human dignity. In a modern constitutional democracy like our own, gender inequality is supposed to be a relic. According to Simon May: "One of the normative presuppositions of opposite-sex polygamy is that there is some basic and enduring difference between men and women such that asymmetric marriage makes good sense as a way of life."[25] For progressives, that presupposition is unarguably wrong. So-called natural differences, which are often not really natural but a result of socialization, should not limit women's opportunities to cultivate their talents and choose a way of life that best suits them – whatever it happens to be. One way of understanding the moral progress that has taken place in American history is to appreciate how certain minority groups have struggled for the dignity that comes with being treated equally. So far, some of them have achieved more success than others. These days, denying the equality of women is akin to defending slavery or racial segregation. Even if polygynous marriages did not seriously harm women, they are still likely to be unequal in certain important respects, such

[24] Cheshire Calhoun, "Who's Afraid of Polygamy? Lessons for Same-Sex Marriage From the History of Polygamy," *San Diego Law Review*, 42 (2005), 1038.

[25] Simon Cabulea May, "Liberal Feminism and the Ethics of Polygamy," in *Families: Beyond the Nuclear Ideal*, ed. Daniela Cutas and Sarah Chan (London: Bloomsbury, 2014), 155.

as their division of domestic labor, and that likelihood could support the state's not according them legal status.

Alternatively, proponents may concede that even when most plural marriages were more often than not unequal, they are demonstrably worse in this way than monogamous marriages are and consequently should not be on the end of different legal treatment. Even if most plural marriages were much worse in terms of gender equality, such an objection would still not necessarily be decisive. The state's interest in promoting equality in personal relationships – what I call *internal equality* – would have to trump the importance of personal choice. At the very least, this trade-off must be confronted. An individual cannot simply play the gender equality card as if the mere fact that some plural marriages would be inegalitarian justifies denying legal recognition to all its conceivable forms. It would be odd – if not counterintuitive – to ban unequal marriages but permit those that are otherwise dysfunctional, including violent ones, unless all that one cares about is internal equality. A marriage could be sufficiently egalitarian yet still lack love, caring, and other kinds of intimacy. In Nussbaum's words: "But to rule that [opposite-sex] marriage as such should be illegal on the grounds that it reinforces male dominance would be an excessive intrusion upon liberty, even if one should believe marriage irredeemably unequal."[26] One would have to argue convincingly that the promotion of internal equality trumps the importance of protecting personal choice when it comes to the various aspects of marriage. That is easier said than done because all of us want at least some space to shape our intimate relationships to fit our at times idiosyncratic ends. Some of us may care more about internal equality than others and the real issue is how much (and what kinds) of such inequality family law should permit. The other serious difficulty is that it is hard to imagine how the interactions of any couple could be effectively monitored, especially given how variable such patterns of behaviors can be.[27]

Gender inequality is not the only concern that critics of plural marriage have on their list of alleged wrongs. They also tend to believe that monogamy is more conducive to human flourishing. One of the aims in this book is to convince readers not to assume that plural marriage is intrinsically inferior to monogamous marriage. The more open-minded one is with respect to this topic, the more likely one is to appreciate the possible worth of

[26] Martha C. Nussbaum, *Sex and Social Justice* (New York: Oxford University Press, 1999), 295.

[27] Gregg Strauss, "Why the State Cannot 'Abolish Marriage': A Partial Defense of Legal Marriage Based on the Structure of Intimate Duties," *Indiana Law Review*, 38 (forthcoming) http://ssrn.com/abstract=2473182.

unconventional families.[28] For the sake of argument, though, I will work with the worst-case scenario: At least in the near future, if the state were to permit plural marriages, many of them would be polygynous and rooted in traditional religious and cultural beliefs about "proper" gender roles.[29] At least some of them, then, would not only be inegalitarian but also dysfunctional.

For the record, I am not granting the point that the vast majority of plural marriages would be polygynous. Not only would any predictions about the distant future be guesswork, but my rationale for expanding the legal definition of marriage is to make this legal status as nondiscriminatory as possible to achieve the external equality among all types of marriage-like relationships that the Constitution ultimately mandates. In doing so, I hope to induce readers to rethink their assumptions about marriage and the state's involvement with the institution. In this country and abroad, largely as a result of the debate over same-sex marriage, a growing number of Americans are concluding that the meaning of marriage is an open question. Not long ago, many Americans shunned divorce and referred to what today we call "cohabitation" as "living in sin." Obviously, the connotation of the former is much more morally neutral than the latter and exhibits how popular attitudes have changed over time. The public is now more receptive to alternative living arrangements and unconventional families than it used to be.[30]

That is good news to some and bad news to others. For the time being, I shall posit that the state's permitting plural marriage would increase the number of polygynous relationships in the short term, thereby exacerbating gender inequality and perhaps other related harms. Let us also assume that the existence of such marriages would have more than a negligible negative impact on monogamous intimate relationships or marriages. If there is one point I would begrudgingly yield to opponents of same-sex marriage, it is that the existence of such marriage will forever change its meaning. It is hard to imagine that as more and more states allow same-sex couples to marry that the clock ever will be turned back. But as I see it, this change will be for the better by making the institution more inclusive and conveying the message that the lives of sexual minorities are equally worthwhile and deserving of at least tolerance – if not respect. Such a state of affairs would be consistent with what

[28] Before the death of her first husband, John Taylor, and her marriage to John Stuart Mill, Harriet Taylor and Mill had an apparently platonic yet unconventional relationship. Alan Ryan, *J.S. Mill* (London: Routledge and Kegan Paul, 1974), 48–50.

[29] In a majority of cultures in the world, polygamy is an option. See Philip L. Kilbride, *Plural Marriage for Our Times: A Reinvented Option?* (Westport, CT: Bergin & Garvey, 1994), 41.

[30] Andrew J. Cherlin, *The Marriage-Go-Around: The State of Marriage and the Family in America Today* (New York: Vintage Books, 2009), 7.

Bruce Ackerman calls *Brown*'s "anti-humiliation" principle.[31] *Loving* altered the meaning of marriage, but few people openly complain about that decision anymore. Polygamous relationships already exist, their numbers continue to grow, they are becoming increasingly diverse, and the participants are rarely prosecuted for such crimes. Like it or not, multiperson intimate relationships are not going to disappear. In terms of the likely consequences with respect to gender equality, then, the only issues are whether their legal recognition would exacerbate such inequality and, if so, whether such an effect would be so terrible that it might support the view that no adult should ever have the option of marrying more than one other person at the same time under any circumstances.

Again, in the following analysis, my assumption is that to some degree, most plural marriages would be less than equal, even though that is hard to know in advance. After all, it seems improbable that large numbers of American women would select such an arrangement when they would have a long menu of options to choose from in the quasi-contractual marital regime I shall propose in the final chapter. Presumably, in a culture in which marriage is no longer as socially compulsory for women as it once was, this expanded range of marital options would put less social and economic pressure on women to select a more traditional marital relationship that is prone to being unequal. A woman might prefer a same-sex or platonic thruple or quad over an opposite-sex monogamous marriage that incorporates an unequal gendered division of labor and lacks shared decision making. Carrie, Miranda, Samantha, and Charlotte would no longer have to obsess over their romantic lives or subsume them into a monogamous, opposite-sex marriage. Lesbians may have more equal intimate relationships than any other kind of couple.[32] Moreover, it is hard to imagine that the kind of woman who would choose a traditional polygynous marriage over the alternatives would find herself in an egalitarian intimate relationship if she were denied that option and instead then opted for a two-person marriage or polygynous cohabitation. In other words, to deny an adult woman any kind of plural marriage, including a polygynous one, is not necessarily to save her from subordination in her personal life because there is no way to know what she would do if she were denied her first choice and had to settle for something else.

[31] Bruce Ackerman, "Dignity Is a Constitutional Principle," *New York Times*, www.nytimes.com/2014/03/30/opinion/sunday/dignity-is-a-constitutional-principle.html?_r=1.

[32] See Mignon R. Moore, "Independent Women: Equality in African-American Lesbian Relationships," in *Families As They Really Are*, ed. Barbara J. Risman (New York: W. W. Norton, 2010), 214–27.

These concerns about how women are being treated unequally in polygamous relationships have existed in this country since the mid-nineteenth century. As Susan Moller Okin observes, in *Reynolds*, the Supreme Court noticed the state's interest in promoting a more egalitarian family yet overlooked the extent to which the traditional monogamous family undermines gender equality.[33] The Supreme Court uncritically embraced the double standard that many Americans still accept: Monogamous intimate relationships tend to be equal enough, whereas polygamous ones never get over the bar. Even when a traditional polygynous marriage is likely to be less egalitarian than a monogamous one, it does not mean that the former is intrinsically superior to the latter. First, all intimate relationships are probably more equal in some ways than in others. For example, a conventional opposite-sex marriage may be more equal when it comes to domestic labor compared with another marriage but less equal when it comes to, say, familial decision making. Second, equality in personal relationships is not the only value that may be relevant in formulating policy. For the most part, current family law tries to account for what each person wants and in doing so acknowledges the value of personal choice and familial diversity. Some people could be happy in a multiperson relationship or at least happier than they would be in a monogamous one, living with their parents or other relatives, having a roommate, or being alone.[34] Some kinds of plural marriage might even serve as examples of how the more mainstream relationships of opposite-sex monogamous couples could be improved.[35] At minimum, those who oppose plural marriage will have to spell out their objections to expanding the legal definition of marriage in a manner that does not rely so heavily on anti-Mormon prejudices, negative stereotypes, questionable data, or sentimental views about the bliss of monogamous marriage.

One traditional feminist concern about gender equality has been that the state may not use its power to discriminate against women and deny them the rights that men are able to exercise.[36] In explaining how the public–private distinction hides unequal power relations, feminist theorists have illuminated

[33] Susan Moller Okin, *Justice, Gender, and the Family* (New York: Basic Books, 1989), 19.

[34] See Emens, "Monogamy's Law," 284; and David Chambers, "Polygamy and Same-Sex Marriage," *Hofstra Law Review*, 26 (1997), 81.

[35] For example, advocates of polyamory call attention to the social importance of its five main principles: self-knowledge, radical honesty, consent, self-possession, and the avoidance of such emotions as jealousy. See Emens, "Monogamy's Law," 320–31.

[36] The (failed) Equal Rights Amendment (ERA) only applied to government, not to private individuals or corporations. Jane J. Mansbridge, *Why We Lost the ERA* (Chicago: University of Chicago Press, 1986), 2.

how patriarchical institutions subordinate women and have made us more mindful of why practices we take to be natural, normal, fair, or universal are flawed and must be altered. They have also shown that difference is a double-edged sword: It can be used to justify unequal legal treatment.[37] In the 1970s, the Supreme Court developed a special standard of review – intermediate scrutiny – for legislative classifications based on gender.[38] For such a classification to survive a challenge to its constitutionality, the state has the burden of proof in demonstrating that it has an important interest and that the classification is substantially related to that interest. The state must establish that its interest is not only more than legitimate but also that the legislative way of achieving that interest is not too underinclusive or overinclusive. Moreover, in *United States v. Virginia*, in her majority opinion, Justice Ruth Bader Ginsburg decided that a legislative classification, which is rooted in invidious discrimination against women, requires "exceedingly persuasive justification."[39] According to Justice Scalia's dissent, "exceedingly persuasive justification" amounts to strict scrutiny.[40]

A related concern is that the state cannot fulfill its responsibility of ensuring gender equality in public life simply by ceasing to discriminate against women or trying to prevent private persons from doing so in the public sphere. Formal equality is a necessary but not a sufficient condition of women's finally being accorded the equality they deserve. Instead, the state must actively try to root out the worst forms of gender equality, including those that are more difficult to detect in the private sphere. When it comes to polygynous marriages, however, the source of the gender equality may not be easy to identify.[41] It may lie in the particular dynamics of the relationship, its structure, or elsewhere. Such relationships are often accompanied by a traditional belief system, hierarchy, geographic isolation, and poverty, which may have more to do with how unequal a given polygynous relationship is than anything else.[42]

In plain English, the main cause of such gender inequality may be hard to discern. From the perspective of a heightened standard of review, the state cannot simply single out one possible cause – the form of a plural

[37] See, for example, Patricia Smith, "Four Themes in Feminist Legal Theory: Difference, Dominance, Domesticity, and Denial," in *The Blackwell Guide to the Philosophy of Law and Legal Theory*, ed. Martin P. Golding and William A. Edmundson (Malden, MA: Blackwell Publishing, 2005), 90–104.

[38] See *Craig v. Boren*, 429 U.S. 190 (1976).

[39] *United States v. Virginia*, 518 U.S. 515 (1996).

[40] *United States v. Virginia*, 518 U.S. 515, 566–602 (1996) (Scalia, J., dissenting).

[41] Strauss, "Is Polygamy Inherently Unequal?" 517.

[42] Janet Bennion, *Polygamy in Primetime: Media, Gender, and Politics in Mormon Fundamentalism* (Waltham, MA: Brandeis University Press, 2012).

marriage – and ignore the others; it doing so would be grossly underinclusive. Even if the state has an important or compelling interest in promoting gender equality, it may not have such an interest in minimizing gender inequality or internal equality more generally in personal relationships. While some kinds of unequal treatment in intimate relationships may be subject to legal remedies, some of them perhaps ought not to be. No legal solution for every human problem exists. Even non-Libertarians are (and should be) wary of excessive state involvement in their personal affairs. Thus, it is possible that the state may not prohibit polygamy or must permit plural marriage even if they cause or worsen gender inequality. Those who will not accept that possibility may ultimately be justified in their refusal, but they owe a clear explanation to the rest of us about why the state may treat plural marriage so differently than its monogamous counterpart. After all, far more numerous traditional two-person marriages frequently do not serve the end of gender equality or the individual happiness of either party. As one scholar writes: "For many, the fantasy of monogamy is different from its reality."[43] When it comes to such equality – and the only choice is opposite-sex monogamy – many women would probably be better off remaining single.

That may sound harsh, but sometimes, the truth is harsh. In the past, numerous feminist thinkers have taken the institution of (monogamous) marriage to task for being patriarchal.[44] The adverse effects of such gender inequality include depriving women of equal opportunity in their professional or personal lives and undermining their self-worth. It is remarkable how some feminists, who are hardly fans of monogamous marriage, minimize how bad it has been and still is for many women when the discussion abruptly turns to polygamy. Some Christian conceptions of marriage are unequivocally and unapologetically inegalitarian by contemporary progressive standards.[45] Any more-than-superficial defense of limiting marriage to couples will necessitate more than a mere appeal to definition, tradition, conventional morality, preconceptions, or public opinion; it will have to single out at least one intolerable feature of plural marriage or at least one of its dire consequences. Opponents of plural marriage must do more than appeal to gender equality or some other important value if they are to assemble a *prima facie* case against offering adults the option of marrying multiple persons simultaneously. They must show that the kind of gender inequality in question is not only

43 Emens, "Monogamy's Law," 287.

44 Carole Pateman, *The Sexual Contract* (Stanford, CA: Stanford University Press, 1988).

45 Judith Stacey, *Brave New Families: Stories of Domestic Upheaval in Late Twentieth-Century America* (Berkeley: University of California Press, 1990), 61–67.

serious but also so serious that the state's interest in preventing or minimizing it overrides the right of adult women to make their own marital choices.

Although that task is challenging, some opponents of plural marriage endeavor to frame the debate in almost exclusively empirical terms. As one commentator observes, "polygamy is linked to an increased likelihood of several harmful psychological effects."[46] If women are often physically harmed or psychologically damaged in such relationships, then those who are still inclined to defend a right to it will have their work cut out for them. Nobody wants to admit that his or her political or legal position is predicated on tolerating serious harms or the risk of them.[47] These days, this sort of opposition to plural marriage is less prevalent than it used to be and that change in strategy may reflect how some scholars realize that a more in-depth conversation about the future of marriage means that traditional polygyny can no longer be the focal point.

Okin likens polygamy to clitoridectomy and forced marriages.[48] Mary Lyndon Shanley asserts: "Vigorous state action is needed to promote spousal equality" and "withdrawing the state from the pursuit of justice from marriage and the family moves us in the wrong direction."[49] For the sake of argument, in what follows, I will also take for granted that the state has some kind of interest in minimizing inequality in personal relationships, especially those that involve one man and multiple women and are therefore more likely to oppress women. Before proceeding, I want to reiterate that this prediction about the higher probability of more widespread gender inequality if the state were to recognize plural marriage may not be accurate – not only because the empirical situation is uncertain but also because the meaning of equality in the context of personal relationships is vague. Equality may mean equal bargaining positions prior to the formation of the marriage, equal treatment during its existence, or equal shares of the marital property if it ends. When it is not specified, many Americans favor such equality, but that does not mean they believe the state can regulate all aspects of their personal lives. A more nuanced treatment of the state's interest in promoting gender equality in marriage is therefore called for.

Progressive academics tend to agree with a commitment to gender equality at an abstract level, but that consensus breaks down when they have to analyze

46 Thom Brooks, "The Problem With Polygamy," *Philosophical Topics*, 37 (2009), 112.

47 The prevention of such harm would count as a sufficiently public reason. John Rawls, "The Idea of Public Reason Revisited," in *The Law of Peoples* (Cambridge, MA: Harvard University Press, 1999), 161.

48 Okin, "Is Multiculturalism Bad for Women?" 14.

49 Shanley, "Just Marriage," 20, 28.

real situations and decide how to proceed. The most difficult normative part of the analysis involves what sort of trade-off between personal choice and gender equality is appropriate. Presumably, such equality means something like power is evenly distributed in the collective decision making, including over finances, and the couple, thruple, quad, or moresome have a more or less equal division of domestic labor and the same right to exit the relationship with an equitable division of the marital property and the same custody and visitation rights if there are any children. In the two-person situation, due to gender, neither person ought to be too badly disadvantaged with respect to the most important aspects of the marriage. The assumption about the state's aforementioned interest in equality in personal relationships underlies feminist critiques of plural marriage and polygynous marriages may undermine gender equality. The risk is real but should not be overstated when such inequality may have other causes the state can address through regulatory schemes without condemning all plural marriages – regardless of their forms and particular dynamics. After states experiment with such marriages, if it turns out they do not further gender inequality or only have a negligible impact, then the case for a constitutional right to plural marriage (or its equivalent) would be even stronger.

Not all feminists are opposed to plural marriage in principle. An increasing number of them are much more open to the idea than they used to be. Calhoun was one of the first feminist theorists to detach polygyny from its background conditions to show that plural marriages are not invariably inegalitarian.[50] According to Nussbaum, polygamy may be acceptable under some circumstances.[51] She concedes that "polygamy is a structurally unequal practice."[52] Her meaning is that in a traditional polygynous relationship, an asymmetry of power exists between the man and his wives, given its hub and wheel structure, where the man is romantically involved with everyone else, but none of the women have that sort of relationship with one another, even though they may bond in other ways. The sole husband can marry other women, divorce his wives at will, and exercise other kinds of control over them with no accountability, creating a situation in which he can too easily abuse his power. For this reason, Nussbaum's defense of polygamy is qualified, as it should be; she ties it to the possibility that plural marriages could also be polyandrous. For her, the best argument against polygamy is that "men

[50] Calhoun, "Who's Afraid of Polygamous Marriage?" 1023–41.

[51] Martha C. Nussbaum, *Women and Human Development: The Capabilities Approach* (New York: Cambridge University Press, 2000), 230.

[52] Martha C. Nussbaum, *Sex and Social Justice* (New York: Oxford University Press, 1999), 98.

are permitted plural marriages, and women are not."[53] That is not to say that all worries about how women are being treated in polygynous relationships would evaporate due to the mere existence of the legal option of a polyandrous marriage. Today, polyandry is uncommon.[54] Nussbaum's point is that much can be said for men and women having the same formal marital rights, thereby giving women the same legal marital options as men. At the very least, formal legal equality is a step in the right direction.

Just as there is not a single feminist position on other important theoretical, political, or legal issues, there is not a single feminist position on plural marriage. Generally, liberal feminists are divided and postmodernist feminists tend to be more sympathetic to experimentation in the name of difference. Resistance to such marriages is rooted not only in concerns about how women would be treated but also in concerns about how children are being prepared for adulthood and for future democratic citizenship. After all, such marriages may exemplify unequal relations and set a bad example that may be emulated in the future. Those who believe that plural marriage is not always harmful continue to claim that such marriages are intrinsically inegalitarian, and as such, they should not receive legal recognition. In Shanley's words: "In order to decide whether plural marriage should be legalized, one must address the question of whether polygamy can be reformed along egalitarian lines."[55]

The first problem with this well-intentioned approach is that it is not evident that monogamous intimate relationships – marital or otherwise – have been reformed in this way, which is to say that some and perhaps many of them are unequal. The second problem is that constitutionally, the state may not have a compelling or important state interest in promoting such internal equality in personal relationships.[56] At present, no state requires a couple – same or opposite sex – to have an egalitarian relationship as a condition of their eligibility for a marriage license. A monogamous couple is allowed to have as much inequality in the interactions with each other as they want to have. In fact, the norm is probably considerable inequality.

It is important to distinguish between the justification for prosecuting people who attempt to have such marriages and the justification for not defining marriage to include plural forms. The former probably calls for considerably more support than the latter. One should not be prosecuted for

[53] Martha C. Nussbaum, *Liberty of Conscience: In Defense of America's Tradition of Religious Equality* (New York: Basic Books, 2008), 197.

[54] Brooks, "The Problem With Polygamy," 114.

[55] Mary Lyndon Shanley, "Just Marriage: On the Public Importance of Private Unions," in *Just Marriage*, ed. Mary Lyndon Shanley (New York: Oxford University Press, 2004), 18.

[56] See Nussbaum, *Liberty of Conscience*, 197–98.

the "crime" of being "married" to two or more consenting adults unless he or she has also violated the penal code in other ways. His or her being incarcerated for such a "crime" might be unconstitutional under the Eight Amendment's prohibition of "cruel and unusual punishments." Polygamy should not serve as a proxy for other felonies or as a means of prosecutors being able to tack on additional charges to improve their bargaining position during plea negotiations. According to Maura Strassberg: "Maintaining a crime of polygyny on the books is in large part a symbolic rejection of both the specific coercion of teenage and adult polygynous wives and the theocratic communities created by and around polygyny."[57] In *Lawrence v. Texas*, the Supreme Court ruled that almost all consensual sexual behaviors between adults is constitutionally protected.[58] In cases involving deeply personal choice more generally, Justice Kennedy has shifted the Supreme Court away from understanding the limits of the power of the state from privacy toward freedom.[59]

The standard legal position against plural marriage presupposes that the state has an important or compelling interest in ensuring decent treatment in intimate relationships. In one sense, this presupposition is true. Unquestionably, the state can enact laws to reduce intimate partner violence and spousal rape. The state may also create a community property regime or equitable divorce laws requiring spousal and child support to reduce the likelihood that women and children are left economically vulnerable upon dissolution of the marriage. The state should intervene when one person is unquestionably harming another, even if they happen to be married or living together, and not ignore the likelihood that the husband takes his earning power with him in the event of divorce.

In another sense, though, this presupposition is far more contentious. While the state may legislate to require employers to grant parental leave, to subsidize child care, or to prevent sexual harassment in the workplace without violating the Constitution, laws that try to force equality on those who would prefer to have an unequal marital relationship raise a related but distinct issue that calls for more subtle treatment. Americans value choice in the most important aspects of their personal lives. That may mean people may choose to have an unequal marital relationship – at least for its duration. The feminist

57 Maura Irene Strassberg, "Distinguishing Polygamy and Polyamory Under the Criminal Law," in *Families: Beyond the Nuclear Ideal*, ed. Daniela Cutas and Sarah Chan (London: Bloomsbury, 2014), 166.

58 *Lawrence v. Texas*, 539 U.S. 558 (2003).

59 Helen J. Knowles, *The Tie Goes to Freedom: Justice Anthony M. Kennedy on Liberty* (Lanham, MD: Rowman & Littlefield, 2009), 17.

challenge to the public–private dichotomy cannot entail that all behaviors are subject to the authority of the state, including every single aspect of how partners relate to each other in their personal lives, because that understanding would leave no room for the personal freedom all of us want to have as we make our lives our own. As Linda McClain writes: "People may accept the idea that sex equality is an appropriate public value, yet believe that its domain does not extend to 'private' life (the family)."[60] Surely, the state can prohibit the most dangerous behaviors that occur inside the home. The previous examples of such serious crimes as intimate partner violence and sexual assault immediately come to mind.

At the same time, as McClain explains, the state cannot do whatever it wants to do to foster gender equality in family life.[61] Even Okin comes close to conceding this crucial point when she writes:: "Public policies must respect people's views and choices. But they must do so only insofar as it can be ensured that these choices do not result, as they do now, in the vulnerability of women and children."[62] In the eyes of the law, their vulnerability while the marriage lasts is one thing; their vulnerability after its dissolution is another. The question that emerges is the extent to which the state can use its power to compel those who are married to have a more egalitarian marriage to minimize the adverse consequences of such inequality. One might embrace the view that the state could require certain kinds of behaviors between husbands and wives beyond refraining from physically injuring each other.

To claim that people may not choose to have an unequal relationship, though, is to undermine the liberal principle that the state should not interfere with people's most intimate decisions unless it has an adequate rationale for such interference.[63] Absent serious harm or the risk of it, the default should be personal choice. As Martha Fineman states: "Because the law governing marriage leaves the day-to-day implementation to individual spouses, it is the conduct of the parties that defines their marriage, giving it content and

[60] Linda C. McClain, *The Place of Families: Fostering Capacity, Equality, and Responsibility* (Cambridge, MA: Harvard University Press, 2006), 75.

[61] Ibid., 76. [62] Okin, *Justice, Gender, and the Family*, 172.

[63] Some feminist positions have undeniably illiberal implications. In criticizing the privacy rationale of *Roe v. Wade*, Catharine MacKinnon writes: "The right of privacy is the right of men 'to be let alone' to oppress women one at a time." MacKinnon, *Feminism Unmodified: Discourses on Life and Law* (Cambridge, MA: Harvard University Press, 1987), 102. More recently, Robin West has argued that those who advocate for reproductive rights ought to rely less on litigation and more on influencing state legislatures. West, "From Choice to Reproductive Justice: De-Constitutionalizing Abortion Rights," in *Philosophy of Law* (9th ed.), ed. Joel Feinberg, Jules Coleman, and Christopher Kutz (Boston, Wadsworth: 2014), 210–29.

meaning, not the mandates of the state."[64] For the most part, people are left alone to have the kind of marriage they want even when it is unequal in some respects. At present, a spouse cannot have his or her right of support enforced until he or she is legally separated or divorced.[65] Nor does a marriage license require any specific conduct from either party.[66] With few exceptions, family law is indifferent toward hierarchy and toward morally questionable behaviors more generally unless they cause demonstrable harm.

Furthermore, the law does not require equality in most other types of human relationships even when some people are vulnerable. Friends do not have to treat other friends as equals. Employers do not have to treat their employees as equals. Parents do not have to treat their children as equals. Senior faculty members do not have to treat junior faculty as equals. Administrators do not have to treat faculty as equals. In most human relationships, some degree of hierarchy is almost to be expected. That is not to say that such treatment is morally desirable or even acceptable, but it is to say that the law usually permits such treatment, and it would be a noticeable departure to allow the state to mandate, for example, an equal division of domestic labor in which each spouse must do an equal share or incur criminal or civil liability. As Nussbaum remarks: "It just seems an intolerable infringement of liberty for the state to get involved in dictating how people do their dishes."[67]

That is a dramatic way to put it, but a good point can stand to be overstated. There are constitutional limits when it comes to how the state may attempt to regulate the behaviors that take place within a marriage or intimate relationship. Nor can the state force women to see themselves in any particular way or desire a particular sort of intimate relationship or marriage after they have been socialized inappropriately from the standpoint of a strong commitment to gender equality. In a liberal society, women are free to adopt whatever identity they want and live accordingly. Likewise, the law cannot force men to have more progressive attitudes. What the state can do, though – with much less controversy – is to legislate against the adverse consequences of such personal decisions when the marriage ends.

Ultimately, neither of the extremes – the pursuit of gender equality whatever the price or a complete refusal to use the power of the state to create a more just family – is attractive. The former would be illiberal, deny legitimate individual differences, thwart familial diversity, and overlook the importance of personal choice. The latter would leave women and children at the mercy

[64] Martha Albertson Fineman, *The Autonomy Myth: A Theory of Dependency* (New York: The New Press, 2004), 98.
[65] Ibid., 98. [66] Ibid. [67] Nussbaum, *Women and Human Development*, 279–80.

of those who could abuse them or throw them into poverty. For McClain, the state has an interest in fostering gender equality within families.[68] On its face, it would seem to be hard to take issue with this claim, but the question becomes more vexed when we consider exactly how the state may advance it without unduly interfering with people's private lives. The typical answer a liberal will give is that the state's interest in preventing harm is not on par with ensuring that marriages are not too unequal. There are multiple ways in which a personal relationship can be inegalitarian. On some equality dimensions, a particular relationship may leave something to be desired, such as how the couple shares domestic labor, while on other dimensions, it may be less troubling, such as collective decision making about finances and the children (if there are any). Almost all actual intimate relationships would fall somewhere in between perfect equality and perfect inequality on the continuum, with most of them being unequal in some respects but not in others. Part of what complicates the evaluation of polygynous arrangements is that women's experiences in them differ.[69] Like those of monogamous relationships, the dynamics of a given multiperson relationship depend on how the participants interact with one another under particular conditions. One does not have to be Foucault to appreciate just how complex the exercise of power can be in monogamous intimate relationships or marriages. Thus, when one refers to its particulars and not only to its structure, it is almost meaningless to speak of a typical monogamous marriage or relationship; they exhibit considerable variance.

As noted, some of those who are critical of polygamous relationships draw upon data that suggest polygyny is bad for women. The trouble with this approach is that the evidence is far from conclusive. Apart from concerns about the underlying methodology, for every study that shows polygyny does not benefit women, another study indicates that some women are more emotionally satisfied in such relationships. If that were not enough to make one pause, it is notoriously philosophically difficult to define happiness. Such philosophers as Aristotle, Bentham, Kant, Mill, and Nietzsche had very different understandings of the concept. Also, happiness as a mental state or feeling is relative to expectations – and expectations differ from couple to couple and person to person. If happiness is mostly subjective and means something like the satisfaction of personal preferences, at least some women in polygynous relationships are probably happy and happier than some or maybe

68 McClain, *The Place of Families*, 77.

69 Jaime M. Gher, "Polygamy and Same-Sex Marriage – Allies or Adversaries Within the Same-Sex Marriage Movement?" *William and Mary Journal of Women and the Law*, 14 (2008), 583.

many women in monogamous relationships. After all, the best polygynous husband or partner is not worse than the worst monogamous one.

B. Structural Inequality

Other critics of polygamy, who advance the view that the state should have more power to foster gender equality in marital relationships, set their sights on the structure of polygamous relationships. According to Thom Brooks, such relationships are structurally inegalitarian in theory and practice.[70] Samuel Rickless states: "Structural problems only arise in the context of the sort of asymmetrical relationship definitive of polygamous marriage."[71] The advantage of this structural approach is that the quality of polygamous relationships is not contingent on the facts, which vary with the circumstances and may be hard to ascertain, but rather is a function of the form of a polygynous relationship, which always contains a morally problematic difference in power that favors the male.

Brooks has a point: Certain marital structures are conducive to reinforcing hierarchical relations among people and providing opportunities for exploitation. My aim is not to dismiss the legitimate concerns that Brooks, Rickless, and others have expressed about how women and children are treated in such relationships but rather to show that an appeal to structure is not as promising as it may initially seem. Brooks may be right that "[t]oday, 'polygamy' almost exclusively takes the form of polygyny."[72] Nevertheless, that does not have to be the case when more people are practicing polyamory and everyone has a long list of marital options to choose from. The dyadic companionate form of marriage does not have to monopolize the social meaning of marriage in the distant future. Also, one could easily imagine a polygynous relationship in which everyone treated everyone else more or less equally in spite of its structure. The beliefs of the participants would impact how they interact with one another and what they want their marriage to be like. Second, Brooks dismisses the possibility of more egalitarian polyamorous relationships.[73] The existence (and growth) of such relationships in this country, however, indicates that an equal multipartner union is not a contradiction.[74] Despite their structure, they can be sufficiently egalitarian in practice. Third, while traditional

70 Brooks, "The Problem With Polygamy," 109–22.

71 Samuel C. Rickless, "The Meaning of Marriage: Polygamy and Same-Sex Marriage," *San Diego Law Review*, 42 (2005), 1048.

72 Brooks, "The Problem With Polygamy," 109. 73 Ibid., 117.

74 Emens, "Monogamy's Law," 282.

monogamous marriages are not structurally problematic, from the standpoint of gender equality, they may still be unequal and even dysfunctional. One cannot simply point to the structure of polygyny and conclude that particular polygynous relationships are always morally objectionable (and perhaps should be against the law) given how bad monogamous intimate relationships can also be for women.

Brooks maintains that when women are not treated as equals, "[p]olygamy should then be forbidden by the state."[75] Whether he believes that such laws should be enforced vigorously or what the penalties for violations ought to be is left unaddressed. For him, the solution lies in criminalization and not in regulation. Due to *Reynolds*, constitutionally, states may criminalize polygamy and almost all of them do.[76] However, prosecutions for such crimes are rare.[77] In Utah, the state does not charge people with religiously motivated bigamy unless the woman is younger than eighteen.[78] That practice suggests that the age of the "wives" and their inability to consent to such an arrangement concerns law enforcement officers and prosecutors more than anything else – and not its structure and the inequality that may result from it. Additionally, a lack of enthusiasm about enforcement on their part indicates that at least some of them have reservations about whether such behaviors among consenting adults should be a crime, which is reminiscent of the general lack of enforcement of antisodomy laws prior to *Lawrence*. Most Americans seem to be satisfied with the "don't ask, don't tell" policy that is currently in place.

The moral concern is that in most polygamous relationships, the existence of gender inequality denies the female participants the same freedom the male enjoys.[79] They may also lack meaningful opportunities to exit (which is affected by individual situations and background conditions, including the applicable family law). Accordingly, women will not have the same quality of life as their husbands or be as satisfied as they otherwise might be under an alternative, more egalitarian arrangement, where power is more evenly distributed. Brooks concedes that "polygamous partners normally do consent to their marriage."[80] This concession is important because opponents of plural marriage often link the purported lack of equality to other wrongs, such as coercion, to hedge their bets.

[75] Brooks, "The Problem With Polygamy," 113.

[76] Samantha Slark, "Are Anti-Polygamy Laws an Unconstitutional Infringement on the Liberty Interests of Consenting Adults?" *Journal of Law and Family Studies*, 6 (2004), 453.

[77] See Irwin Altman and Joseph Ginat, *Polygamous Families in Contemporary Society* (New York: Cambridge University Press, 1996), 48–52.

[78] *Utah v. Holm*, 2006 UT 31; 137 P.3d 726 (2006). [79] Ibid. [80] Ibid., 111.

The claim that polygynous relationships are in practice unequal is a statistical generalization. One could take issue with the studies Brooks relies on and the causal inference he makes, where the structure of a polygynous relationship either causes its inequality or significantly contributes to it. After all, the nature of contemporary polygynous relationships and their effects requires an empirical inquiry. In May's words, "one cannot simply infer inequality from asymmetry."[81] Brooks relies on studies that confirm his view but involve polygamous relationships in a less-than-ideal setting.[82] The problem with this approach is that it is hard to generalize about polygyny due its current illegality in this country and its aforementioned variance; it has taken different forms at different times in different places and continues to do so.[83] Whatever it might be like in Africa or the Middle East, legalized polygyny in this country would differ from what it would be like in a place with a different culture, different levels of wealth, and different political and legal systems. In Calhoun's words: "The quick dismissal of polygamy on grounds that it, unlike monogamy, is distinctly gender-inegalitarian is the result of smuggling a set of unstated assumptions about the background social conditions for women, the social practice of polygamy, and its likely legal form that would render it inegalitarian. . . ."[84] As Emens declares, that "polygyny is oppressive to women is contingent."[85]

By comparison, I doubt too many people think that the kind of prostitution that takes place in an undeveloped country is the equivalent of what it is or could be like in a developed country that has decriminalized the practice and then regulated it to prevent exploitation and promote public health. Just because one has proved that adult prostitution is wrong in some circumstances does not mean it is wrong in all circumstances. Likewise, if it were legal and recognized by the state, then the structure of a polygamous marriage might be less troubling. Second, by "polygamy," for the most part, Brooks has in mind polygyny, not polyamory or group marriage, and he also assumes it will not be same sex.[86] At most, then, he has shown that traditional polygyny deserves more careful scrutiny. It is hard to imagine, I should add, that legal recognition and more effective regulation would exacerbate the situation of women who are already part of such a relationship.

81 May, "Liberalism Feminism and the Ethics of Polygamy," 152.

82 Brooks, "The Problem With Polygamy," 111–12.

83 Gher, "Polygamy and Same-Sex Marriage – Allies or Adversaries Within the Same-Sex Marriage Movement?" 559–603.

84 Cheshire Calhoun, "Who's Afraid of Polygamous Marriage?" 1040.

85 Emens, "Just Monogamy?" 77.

86 Brooks, "The Problem With Polygamy," 116–17.

According to Brooks, the solution offered to this problem of inequality, which he attributes to Nussbaum and Calhoun, is that polyandry is possible; that is, women are allowed to marry more than one man at the same time.[87] As long as women have the choice of marrying multiple men, the existence of polygamous relationships would not necessarily undermine gender equality – not because they would cancel out each other but because an even number of polygynous and polyandrous relationships would reflect more just background conditions in which women's marital choices are more likely to be independent of coercion, duress, the need for financial security, or a lack of viable options. Statistically, it is probably true that most present-day polygynous marriages or intimate relationships around the world are unequal and oppress women to a greater or lesser extent even though such an unfortunate state of affairs may have other causes. While Nussbaum and Calhoun may be overly optimistic about plural marriage's egalitarian prospects, they have an important insight – namely, that what plural marriage is like in 2015 is not the form it must take, particularly when polygamy is not synonymous with polygyny but could in the future also include polyandry, where one woman marries multiple men, and group marriage (four or more persons). There was a time in our past where one should have been pessimistic about the prospects of reforming two-person opposite-sex marriage along egalitarian lines, but today, few people have such doubts.

Not surprisingly, this response has not satisfied the critics. According to Brian Barry: "The whole idea of egalitarian polygamy is manifest nonsense."[88] In his view, the inequality problem with plural marriage would not be solved by permitting women to marry multiple men, even if they exercised this option, no more than the inequality inherent in racial slavery in the antebellum period would have been mitigated by allowing African-Americans to own whites.[89] In light of the brutality of racial slavery in the antebellum period in this country, this analogy is odd; no slave ever consented to being owned, as far as I know, although indentured servants did – but not for their entire lives. As such, I suspect that Barry misses the point. Involuntary servitude is wrong – whatever form it takes – because it is wrong to own another human being against his or her will. That practice is also unconstitutional under the Thirteenth Amendment, with the notable exception of incarceration as punishment for a crime. By contrast, polygamy would not be as morally troubling

[87] Ibid., 114.
[88] Brian Barry, *Culture and Equality* (Cambridge, MA: Harvard University Press, 2001), 370, n. 96.
[89] Ibid., 370.

if it were really a product of a genuine choice or voluntary enough under normal conditions. A less misleading analogy, then, would be the slave contract, in which the slave could breach the contract and the remedy of the owner could not be specific performance. It is not evident that polygamy involving consenting adults, such as the fictional family in HBO's *Big Love* or the real families in TLC's *Sister Wives* or *My Five Wives*, is nearly as bad as slavery. By referring to slavery as a possible analogue, Barry has already stacked the deck against polygamy and plural marriage. Polygamy is not always abusive, especially when the consent is not spurious, and its particulars are not beside the point. I take Nussbaum and Calhoun's point to be that in a society in which polyandry and polygyny are equally common, a woman's decision to enter into a traditional polygynous relationship or marriage is much more likely to be voluntary in the midst of other marital possibilities, including the option of not marrying at all. The social context always shapes the nature of actual polygamous relationships.[90]

Any intellectually honest defense of plural marriage must come to terms with the possibility that its practice, even under the best of conditions, would still fall short of the kind of gender equality in personal relationships that would be preferable. That said, opponents of plural marriage have still not demonstrated that the inequality in such marriages is worse than that of traditional marriages and other manifestations of gender inequality in other personal contexts other than citing some studies, ignoring others, and relying too heavily on their structure. Just because a monogamous marriage is structurally unproblematic hardly means it is sufficiently egalitarian if we care about how the couple interacts with each other. Very few people believe that a man and a woman who wish to have a marriage that incorporates a traditional division of labor and other inegalitarian practices should be forbidden from marrying on that ground alone. Same-sex marriages tend to be more egalitarian than different-sex ones, but that fact does not imply that the state can only license same-sex couples to marry. The public and the media tend to pick on Mormons, but many other religious groups have less-than-progressive attitudes toward women, and the quality their monogamous marriages should not escape scrutiny. Does anyone really think a state can deny an Orthodox Jewish or a Christian Fundamentalist couple a marriage license because their family life will be unapologetically inegalitarian? No American lawmaking body or court has ever conditioned the constitutional right to marriage on its actual or apparent equality. As a result, opponents of plural marriage must show that the

[90] Bennion, *Polygamy in Primetime*, 283–84.

kind of gender inequality that is likely to exist in a plural marriage is not only unique but worse than other kinds that our society already tolerates.

Brooks also identifies an "asymmetrical ability to leave a polygamous marriage."[91] That assertion is probably true in most parts of the world in which polygamy exists, but that same worry can be raised about any kind of marriage (and many other social institutions) in many underdeveloped countries that do not provide reasonable options for women to exit if they so desire. It is not as if a woman in an undeveloped country who is married to only one man (and where males having mistresses is not culturally frowned upon) is much better off than a woman who has sister wives. The same is true in this nation inasmuch as a woman who lacks marketable job skills may not be able to support herself after she leaves her husband and he takes his earning power with him. Nussbaum and Calhoun have a liberal democracy like ours in mind, where divorce would be no-fault and marital property would be divided fairly if the marriage were to end.

The power relations of real polygynous relationships are more complex than their critics appreciate, and their structure can only tell us so much about their dynamics. If the state decided to recognize plural marriages, it could require that all parties consent to the marriage contract to ensure that everyone is as informed as they can be about their rights and responsibilities, prevent the husband from unilaterally adding other wives, and provide default rules to protect the women if the marriage does not last. Brooks's main target is the kind of polygynous relationship that one would find in the midst of deeply unjust background conditions, but such conditions would usually not be present in such a developed country as the United States that regulated such intimate relationships. At least some plural marriages, then, will not be intolerably inegalitarian.

Even if the structure of traditional polygynous relationships renders them inherently unequal, the form of some plural marriages would still be morally acceptable. As one commentator notes, "polyfidelity" (in which everyone is married to everyone else and thus has the same rights and responsibilities) and "molecular polygamy" (in which peripheral spouses may marry their own additional spouses) do not pose the same kinds of structural problems.[92] Each of these alternatives incorporates the reciprocity that Brooks believes cannot occur in a polygynous or polyandrous relationship where one person is the hub and the others are spokes of the wheel.

[91] Brooks, "The Problem With Polygamy," 116.

[92] Gregg Strauss, "Is Polygamy Inherently Unequal?" *Ethics*, 122 (2012), especially 534–44.

Brooks's structural argument against plural marriage, then, fails to establish the more ambitious conclusion establishing the moral unacceptability of all forms of plural marriage. At most, it gives us some reason to worry about traditional polygynous marriages given a certain structure and certain background conditions. As Adrienne Davis points out, structural problems can be mitigated by legal regulation that reduces the likelihood of mistreatment.[93] Default rules cannot eliminate the possibility of such undesirable behavior, but that is equally true of monogamous marriages – regardless of their structure – in which one party controls the resources and uses them to benefit him or herself.

C. *Okin's Liberal Feminist Critique*

True, the structure of a present-day FLDS or Muslim polygynous relationship (as representative of all forms of traditional polygyny) is less than ideal in terms of the lack of power women may have in such relationships. As such, one has to worry about whether a woman has exercised her autonomy not only in becoming part of such a relationship but also in not leaving it. For Joseph Smith, polygamy strengthened the patriarchical nature of Mormon marriage and enhanced the status of the exclusively male priesthood by creating an extended family.[94] Because it usually takes the form of polygyny, polygamy often incorporates the gendered division of labor that Okin identifies as the primary cause of the subordination of women.[95] Although she never goes into much detail about how a plural marriage is more inegalitarian than a traditional monogamous one, her critique of it would call attention to the power that the male almost always has and exercises in such relationships. In any marriage, social goods (such as paid and unpaid labor, power, prestige, and self-esteem), opportunities for self-development, and physical and economic security are essential to the well-being of the participants.[96] Similarly, in a polygynous marriage, the concern would be that the typical distribution of such goods favors the husband and social norms reinforce the notion that women are the "primary caretakers of children" and responsible for the unpaid domestic work in the household.[97]

These expectations are likely to affect the career choices that women make when they realize it will be difficult to be a wife/mother and have a career that

[93] Davis, "Regulating Polygamy," 2023.

[94] Serena Nanda and Jill Norgen, *American Cultural Pluralism and Law* (2nd ed.) (Westport, CT: Praeger, 1996), 98.

[95] Okin, *Justice, Gender, and the Family*.

[96] Ibid., 136.

[97] Ibid., 138–139.

demands a considerable amount of time away from home.[98] Due to this situation, women are rendered vulnerable not only in the marriage itself but also in the event of its dissolution, particularly when they have minor children and no marketable job skills – perhaps due to their raising their children and making other sacrifices.[99] What makes a traditional family unjust, according to Okin, is the gendered division of labor and its adverse effects on women. Exactly the same worry could be raised about polygyny: that the women would be compelled to provide much more than their fair share of domestic labor and they would not be compensated for their contribution. Their doing such labor would limit their life prospects and prevent them from realizing their potentials and could not reasonably be characterized as a genuine choice in the midst of so few alternatives. At minimum, real choice presupposes a range of plausible options.

Not everyone agrees that such a division of labor in a polygynous relationship will always work to the disadvantage of women. Emens uses the example of Elizabeth Joseph, a lawyer in Utah who lives with her husband and his eight other wives, to formulate a "feminist" argument for plural marriage.[100] Polygamous arrangements can promote a more efficient division of labor through specialization and the sharing of child care and other domestic work.[101] As a result, some of the women in such a relationship may be better able to pursue a career. This possibility is depicted in several episodes of *Big Love*. It is conceivable, then, that even polygyny could be reformed along more egalitarian lines.[102] On the other hand, I doubt anyone who is sympathetic to the cause of plural marriage wants to rest his or her case on that remote possibility. After all, Joseph could be an outlier and her sister wives are responsible for maintaining the household. Their lives count as much as hers does.

Okin has a bit more to say about polygamy in later writings, where she criticizes the French government for ignoring "women's views on polygamy for so long" and tolerating the practice.[103] However, most of these women are not being coerced into such marital arrangements. Rather, their deepest beliefs may lead them down that path, and they may be exposed to social pressures that make polygyny more attractive than it otherwise would be. Different women have different views on the topic and the careful polling of French women in certain religious and cultural communities may not yield

[98] Ibid., 142–144. [99] Ibid., 139. [100] Emens, "Monogamy's Law," 314–16.
[101] Song, *Justice, Gender, and the Politics of Multiculturalism*, 159.
[102] See Rosenblum, "Democratic Sex," 80.
[103] Okin, "Is Multiculturalism Bad For Women?" 10.

the results Okin expects or hopes for. The infamous headscarf controversy in France reveals that Muslim women are divided over the correctness of the practice. The point is not that just because they want to do it that they should be allowed to do it – regardless of the consequences. Rather, their personal reasons ought to be assumed to be legitimate – absent sufficient evidence to the contrary. Okin also lumps polygamy in with other antifeminist practices that are sometimes defended on multicultural grounds, such as female circumcision, the marriage of children, and other kinds of forced marriages.[104] Her doing so may pack a rhetorical punch, but each of these practices merits individualized treatment to discern why they may be wrong. For me, forced circumcision of young females is obviously wrong in a way that a competent adult's choosing such a surgical procedure is not. And I certainly believe that states may set a minimal age to ensure that no one is being coerced when it comes to marriage. Too often, those who are understandably concerned about the harms of certain cultural behaviors point to their worst manifestations, assume that all such behaviors are tainted, and then conclude that such behaviors should be banned – as if more nuanced analysis were in collusion with evil.

What is missing from Okin's account is a full-fledged defense of the claim that all forms of polygamy incorporate gender inegalitarian practices (or why they are necessarily more severe in that regard than those of traditional two-person intimate relationships). In the past, many feminists have insisted that as long as polygamy existed, there could be no equality for women.[105] Increasingly, that sounds more like a slogan than anything else and a good point ought not to be overstated to the extent that the conversation ends prematurely. No doubt, the purpose and effect(s) of plural marriage in some places and at some times is to control women. All things being equal, the more economically underdeveloped the region, the more likely one is to see polygyny being practiced. This is one reason why Africa has the highest prevalence of polygamy.[106] It may be true that such marriages contribute to gender inequality by normalizing a traditional gendered division of labor, confirming social roles, and limiting the career options women have.[107]

Alternatively, there is also a danger, which is just as grave, of arguing from the worst possible case scenario or generalizing from populations to individuals when individuals and their intimate relationships are entitled to their own evaluation under existing constitutional doctrine. According to Bonnie Honig,

104 Ibid., 14. 105 Chambers, "Polygamy and Same-Sex Marriage," 65.
106 Zeitzen, *Polygamy: A Cross-Cultural Analysis*, 4.
107 Kilbride, *Plural Marriage for Our Times*, 77–78.

a feminist does not have to think polygamy is worse than monogamy.[108] A structurally equal marriage might be horribly dysfunctional and a structurally unequal marriage may have much better dynamics that makes it not only more egalitarian but healthier in terms of how the participants treat each another on a daily basis. The underlying concern seems to be that in a polygynous relationship, the male will be able to take advantage of the situation, but even in a monogamous relationship, such undesirable behaviors can and does occur frequently. As one commentator writes in the context of polygamy: "The equal power of any one party *cannot* [his emphasis] be assured."[109] On the other hand, such equal power can never be guaranteed in any two-person intimate relationship or marriage – whatever its structure. In a patriarchal society, considerable gender inequality is just as likely to exist in monogamous relationships.[110] In our own society, in the foreseeable future, many more people will have such intimate relationships than plural ones.

At least initially, the advent of plural marriages would probably have the cumulative effect of exacerbating gender inequality if most of them were traditionally polygynous and such marriage may not be compatible with the kind of equality that is supposed to exist in a democracy.[111] That prediction assumes that legal recognition has something to do with making inequality in multi-person intimate relationships even worse than it would be in its absence. As one commentator states: "Since we can rightly insist on the equality of the sexes, we can ban polygyny on that ground alone without having to justify monogamy."[112] In my view, that conclusion does not follow from the premise that a just society is committed to fostering gender equality, especially when regulation is on the table and the state can use public service announcements to counteract "bad" speech by discouraging people from acting in certain ways, even when such behavior is legal. Also, the ongoing existence of traditional monogamous marriage has made many women's situations worse, not better, and the state cannot arbitrarily single out polygamy and perpetuate the double standard when the primary causes of the problem lie elsewhere.

A just liberal democracy is not committed to fostering internal equality at all costs. Exactly the same concern could be raised about any familial relationship that is predicated on a gendered division of labor or other sexist beliefs

[108] Bonnie Honig, "'My Culture Made Me Do It'," in Susan Moller Okin, *Is Multiculturalism Bad for Women?* ed. Joshua Cohen, Matthew Howard, and Martha C. Nussbaum (Princeton, NJ: Princeton University Press, 1999), 38.

[109] Donald Wilson, "Kant and the Marriage Right," *Pacific Philosophical Quarterly*, 85 (2004), 114.

[110] Ibid. [111] Rosenblum, "Democratic Sex," 80.

[112] Bhikhu Parekh, *Rethinking Multiculturalism: Cultural Diversity and Political Theory* (2nd ed.) (New York: Palgrave Macmillan, 2006), 284.

and behaviors – regardless of their ideological origins. In short, such an argument proves too much: It is not evident why most multiperson relationships cannot be reformed along egalitarian lines if their monogamous counterparts can be so reformed unless one is convinced that their structure alone renders them irredeemably inegalitarian. After all, the structure of, say, a three- or four-person same-sex marriage would not raise the same concerns. By Okin's standard of a gendered division of labor, many opposite-sex monogamous marriages would be equally if not more worrisome, particularly compared with more egalitarian polyamorous ones.

The problem with the typical view advanced to discredit multiperson marriage is that not every plural marriage would be so much more inegalitarian than a typical monogamous one that it could be an exception to the rule that the unequal practices that exist in a personal relationship usually do not merit a legislative remedy. In the name of consistency, if the state permits consensual, inegalitarian behaviors in monogamous marriages, then it should also allow them in plural ones. Under the status quo, the law is largely silent on "what should go on inside the marriage."[113] Couples are pretty much free to do as they please as spouses.[114] As one commentator writes: "Once a couple marries, they need conform to no particular model of behavior in order to receive the legal protections of that status."[115] At the very least, I hope the reader considers the possibility that multiperson relationships may have considerable value, even if they are unequal in certain respects, and may meet the needs of the participants. Constitutionally, people are allowed to exercise their own judgment in deciding whether to marry one person – no matter how bad that marriage may turn out to be.

D. *Lack of Real Choice*

The existence of an asymmetry of power between a man and his wives may also indicate that the women could not be exercising their autonomy in such circumstances or may lack meaningful agency. Thus, the existence of inequality in a typical plural marriage may also imply either that women have not really chosen to be a part of such a marital arrangement or that they would not have done so if a wider range of options were available to them. The difficulty with this position is that some women would still choose plural marriage for a variety of personal reasons.[116] One would be hard-pressed

113 Rauch, *Gay Marriage*, 14–15.

114 Fineman, *The Autonomy Myth*, 97–99.

115 Milton C. Regan Jr., *Alone Together: Law and the Meanings of Marriage* (New York: Oxford University Press, 1999), 8.

116 Judith Stacey, *Unhitched: Love, Marriage, and Family Values From Hollywood to Western China* (New York: New York University Press, 2011), 150–51.

to continue to argue that if states were to legally recognize a wide variety of multiperson marital arrangements, such a choice on the part of a typical woman would still be spurious in the midst of so many marital options, including remaining single. A plural marriage need not be polygynous, and it is mistaken to equate such marriage with the rare but widely publicized kinds of polygynous relationships that involve criminality. With the expanded legal definition I put forth in the Introduction, many of them might not be polygynous. Plural marriage and polygyny are not interchangeable. There is an unfortunate tendency on the part of those who oppose plural marriage to treat it as if it could be reduced to something else, such as the exploitation of women. That is unfair because women (and men, for that matter) can also be exploited or treated badly in monogamous intimate relationships despite their egalitarian structure.

In a liberal democracy like our own, women have multiple legal rights, including a right to end the marital relationship in an era of no-fault divorces, to seek an equitable property settlement, and to (usually) have custody and visitation rights if there are any children. In those ways, the state indirectly and legitimately promotes gender equality. By contrast, directly fostering such equality during the marriage does not leave adequate room for difference and individual choice. As Steven Lecce writes: "Aside from clear cases of spousal abuse or the neglectful treatment of children ... the threshold for political interference with a family's internal affairs is normally and rightfully held to be quite high."[117] Some women may prefer a plural union but not necessarily polygyny. Even when women opt for the latter, polygyny could foster female bonding.[118] With respect to gender inequality, then, at least in a polygynous marriage, the state has a stronger interest in promoting gender equality after the marriage is over than while it continues to exist.

III. PROTECTING WOMEN

A. *Polygamy as a Crime*

In this section, I explain why the harms associated with certain kinds of polygyny are not intrinsic to the practice and make the case for an effective as possible regulation of such intimate relationships. I conclude that it should not be illegal for consenting adults to practice any kind of polygamy as long as

117 Steven Lecce, *Against Perfectionism: Defending Liberal Neutrality* (Toronto: University of Toronto Press, 2008), 262.

118 Davis, "Regulating Polygamy," 1972.

adequate safeguards are in place. While the focus of this book is plural marriage, if polygamy should not be against the law, then at least the ground will have been cleared for the growth of a more radical position, such as my own, involving the legal recognition of such marriage. Around the world, the legal status of polygamy varies from place to place. In North America, only the province of Saskatchewan provides some legal protection for polygamous families.[119] In the United States, polygamy is illegal in all fifty states and most of them treat it as a felony.[120] Many of the reasons, which those who support the continued criminalization of polygamy rely on, have some bearing on the coming debate over plural marriage. The temptation for conservatives who continue to oppose same-sex marriage to bring plural marriage into the picture is understandable: The more same-sex marriage resembles plural marriage, the stronger the anti-same-sex marriage position appears to be.

However, the view that a same-sex marriage cannot be a real marriage finally seems to be antiquated as more and more Americans can no longer countenance treating gays and lesbians so unfairly. As aforementioned, recently, part of Utah's antibigamy statute was found to be unconstitutional.[121] In the wake of the decision, Adam Winkler calls into question the constitutionality of bans on polygamy while pointing out that polygamy may differ from same-sex monogamous relations and noting that the judge went out of his way to distance his opinion from pro-gay-rights decisions.[122] For Judge Waddoups, the constitutional problem lies with Utah's preventing cohabitation and not with the part of the statute that made it illegal for an already married person to "marry" another person. If the rationale for banning consensual same-sex sex is weak, as the Supreme Court found in *Lawrence* on privacy grounds, then the rationale for not permitting certain adults to live together may be equally weak. In both cases, it is hard to see what the state's interest could be – other than the maintenance of a particular kind of family or traditional (usually meaning religious) morality. Just because a majority has the power to enact its view into law does not mean it has acted constitutionally. In fact, for some people, that is the equivalent of constitutionalizing prejudice or animus, provided that minors are protected from harm. What remains unclear from Judge Waddoups's opinion is why

[119] www.courthousenews.com/2011/07/14/Bigamy.pdf

[120] Samantha Slark, "Are Anti-Polygamy Laws an Unconstitutional Infringement on the Liberty Interests of Consenting Adults?" *Journal of Law and Family Studies*, 6 (2004), 453.

[121] *Brown v. Buhman* (2013): Case No. 2:11-cv-0652-CW. The decision will most likely be appealed.

[122] Adam Winkler, "Are Polygamy Bans Unconstitutional?" *Huffington Post*, December 16, 2013.

the state may make "marrying" another consenting adult a crime when doing so has no legal consequences.

The obvious constitutional objection to such laws is that they intentionally target FLDS, who believe plural marriage to be a religious duty, and thereby violate the Free Exercise Clause, even under the rule articulated by the Supreme Court in *Smith*, the famous peyote case, which narrows the scope of constitutionally mandated exemptions.[123] *Reynolds* remains good law.[124] However, that does not mean it should not be overturned. After all, no one disputes that the requirement of plural marriage has deep roots in Mormon theology.[125] As the result of a revelation, Joseph Smith covertly introduced the practice to some of his followers in 1840s.[126] In the case that bears his name, George Reynolds contended that his taking a second wife was a religious duty.[127] It is unarguable that the federal legislation aimed at eliminating the practice toward the end of the nineteenth century was intentionally discriminatory in a manner that would violate the Free Exercise Clause today, even post-*Smith*.[128] The animus that engendered such federal legislation does not dissipate over time. Moreover, many legal scholars have criticized the reasoning employed in *Reynolds*, and no thoughtful person today would accept its racist, ethnocentric, and empirically untested claims that plural marriage is contrary to "social duties and good order" and "odious among the northern and western nations of Europe."[129] Nussbaum adds: "He [Chief Justice Morrison Waite] seems eager … to tar polygamy by association with the bad practices of allegedly primitive races."[130]

Unfortunately, too much of the analysis regarding plural unions overlooks the existence of polyamorous relationships, difference-sex or same-sex relationships, or nonromantic but intimate relationships that are conducive to living a good life. A related and more complicated question involves what the state's interest could possibly be when one person (even a minor with parental permission) can marry another without the state's giving a damn about the personal reasons the couple happens to have. This double standard cries out

[123] *Employment Division v. Smith*, 494 U.S. 872 (1990).

[124] *Reynolds v. United States*, 98 U.S. 145 (1878).

[125] See Joseph Bozzuti, "The Constitutionality of Polygamy Prohibitions After Lawrence v. Texas: Is Scalia a Punchline or a Prophet?" *Catholic Lawyer*, 43 (2004), 417–18. See also Irwin Altman, "Polygamous Family Life: The Case of Contemporary Mormon Fundamentalists," *Utah Law Review*, (1996), 367–70.

[126] Richard Lyman Bushman, *Mormonism: A Very Short Introduction* (New York: Oxford University Press, 2008), 86.

[127] *Reynolds v. United States*, 98 U.S. 145, 161–162 (1878).

[128] *Church of the Lukumi Babalu Aye v. City of Hialeah*, 508 U.S. 520 (1993).

[129] *Reynolds v. United States*, 98 U.S. 164 (1878).

[130] Nussbaum, *Liberty of Conscience*, 196.

for a rigorous defense when adults can be punished for behaviors that otherwise would be allowed if they had not "married" in their own eyes or those of their church. Evander Holyfield can have multiple children with multiple women without incurring criminal liability, whereas Kody Brown, of TLC's *Sister Wives*, risks prosecution for being comparatively more responsible as a husband and a father.[131] As Jonathan Turley writes: "The Law already protects the right of individuals to have as many sexual partners as they wish. ... These individuals are allowed to have children with multiple partners so long as they support their offspring."[132] But if polygamists do likewise but privately treat their partners as spouses, then in many states, they are committing crimes.[133]

At the very least, this state of affairs is counterintuitive. It appears that the law is encouraging men to be more like Evander Holyfield and less like Kody Brown. According to Andrew March: "What anti-polygamists have to show is that polygamy is a practice – like clitoridectomy, domestic violence, depriving children of health care, and forced marriage – which is either an *intrinsic* [his emphasis] violation of the equal civil or human rights of those involved or an unreasonable burden on others."[134] Unfortunately, for those who want to keep polygamy illegal, it is not evident that polygamy is intrinsically harmful or directly harms third parties. The mere act of men conspiring to marry, attempting to marry, or marrying a second or third wife and then acting as if they are married would not seem to be the kind of conduct that the penal code usually concerns itself with unless their doing so involves a lack of consent, minors, or misrepresenting their marital status to commit fraud. By definition, a non-state-sanctioned marriage is not a legal status at all. What crime has a man committed if he is already legally married to one person but also lives with another and treats her as if she were a spouse?

Under the Utah statute, a polygynous thruple could express a lifelong commitment to each other as long as they do not represent themselves as spouses to the rest of the world. Imagine if a state that did not permit same-sex marriages were to make it illegal for two men to go through a marriage ceremony or to present themselves as a married couple under any

[131] As of June 19, 2013, Holyfield has eleven children with six different women. Brown has four wives and seventeen children. Holyfield also has not been able to pay all the child support he owes.

[132] Turley Report, 18.

[133] Emens, "Monogamy's Law," 362. Also, polygamists are not legally protected against other kinds of discrimination, such as employment and housing discrimination.

[134] Andrew F. March, "Is There a Right to Polygamy? Marriage, Equality and Subsidizing Families in Liberal Public Justification," *Journal of Moral Philosophy*, 8 (2011), 255.

circumstances (which might be constitutionally protected speech to the extent that even deliberate falsehoods receive some constitutional protection). If a thruple's living together is morally problematic, then it must be due to the actual behaviors that take place in such relationships and not simply because they are cohabitating or consider themselves to be married. Evidently, what remains illegal in Utah is not their being intimately involved with one another or their living together, but rather the act of going through a marriage ritual or taking wedding vows, which can be traced to invidious discrimination against FLDS. At least in Utah, there is a world of legal difference between a thruple that does not consider itself to be married and one that does. At best, that would seem to be a distinction without much of a difference.

B. *The Constitutional Right to Cohabitation*

When it comes to cohabitation, few U.S. Supreme Court decisions deal directly with the extent to which the state can restrict adults from living together.[135] As a result, people can make different inferences in arguing for different constitutional conclusions. Well-known privacy cases have implications for personal decisions, such as with whom one can live. The only sorts of restrictions that would be unquestionably unconstitutional would be those involving race, gender, sexual orientation, religion, and probably marital status. In *Moore v. City of East Cleveland*, the Supreme Court addresses the constitutional question of whether the state could prevent some family members who are genetically related from residing together.[136] In his plurality opinion, Justice Lewis Powell applies a heightened standard of review to the zoning law, which prevented a grandmother from living with her grandson, and concludes that it could not pass constitutional muster. In his words: "East Cleveland ... has chosen to regulate the occupancy of its housing by slicing deeply into the family itself."[137] For at least four of the justices, the ordinance infringes on the right of family members to associate with one another. The broader implication may be that all adults could decide to make whatever living arrangements they want to make with one another unless the state has a very important interest in limiting their options.

On the other hand, *Belle Terre v. Boraas*, decided three years earlier, appears to declare that people who are genetically unrelated to each other

[135] For an excellent discussion of case law, see Cain, "Imagine There's No Marriage," especially 40–43.

[136] *Moore v. City of East Cleveland*, 431 U.S. 494 (1977).

[137] Ibid., 498.

have no constitutional right to live together.[138] In that case, the Supreme Court only applies the rational basis standard of review to a zoning ordinance that restricted certain living arrangements.[139] In his majority opinion, Justice William Douglas simply accepts the narrow definition of a family, which the ordinance incorporates, and does not even touch the constitutional arguments involving privacy and freedom of association put forth by Justice Thurgood Marshall in his dissent. Therefore, the rule seems to be that only family members (those who are genetically related) have a constitutional right to live together as long as the state has a legitimate rationale for restricting the number of residents in a certain dwelling.

In my view, this holding not only conflicts with the principle of autonomy established in other important constitutional precedents, such as *Roe*, *Casey*, and *Lawrence*, but also represents an impoverished view of freedom of intimate association that cannot withstand critical scrutiny. As Justice Marshall writes: "The choice of household companions – of whether a person's 'intellectual or emotional needs' are best met by living with family, friends, professional associates, or others – involves deeply personal considerations as to the kind and quality of intimate relationships within the home."[140] Unlike that of Douglas, Marshall's view captures how such a choice is best left to the individual. Unless a person is imprisoned, surely the state cannot force him or her to live with another person, meaning that people have a constitutional right to choose where they live and with whom they live. Although usually read quite narrowly, the Third Amendment stands for the more general principle that living arrangements are deeply personal matters and ought to be treated as such. There seems to be an important privacy interest at stake that was missed by Justice Douglas's unfortunate framing of the legal issue as the constitutional acceptability of a mere residential zoning ordinance.

A law that prevented consenting adults from cohabitating with each other or one another, then, would be subject to a serious constitutional challenge. Notwithstanding whether they are genetically related, adults should be permitted to cohabitate with whomever they want, provided that the living arrangement is fully voluntary and the state does not have a compelling interest in preventing such an arrangement (and it is hard to conceive of what would count as "compelling" here). Normally, the kind of living arrangement that one wants affects that person more than anyone else. In Powell's words: "This Court has long recognized the freedom of personal choice in matters of marriage and family life is one of the liberties protected by the Due Process

[138] *Belle Terre v. Boraas*, 416 U.S. 1 (1974). [139] Ibid., 7–8. [140] Ibid., 16.

Clause of the Fourteenth Amendment."[141] Other than for reasons based on a narrow interpretation of tradition, it seems arbitrary to limit this right to family members when one could have a very close friendship with another person who is not a member of his or her immediate or extended family. Usually, one is not genetically related to one's spouse, but the right to marriage would imply the right to live together. It is almost inconceivable a state could permit a couple to marry but then deny them the right to live under the same roof. To be genetically related to another is neither a necessary nor a sufficient condition of establishing the kinds of emotional bonds that make a healthy intimate relationship possible.

The alleged problems with polygamy do not concern the living arrangements in and of themselves but rather their likely secondary effects. In the language of Due Process Clause and Equal Protection Clause jurisprudence, the state must offer adequate reasons to support the statute in question. The persuasiveness of this justification turns on whether there is a fundamental right to cohabitate on privacy, equal protection, free exercise of religion, or intimate association grounds. If there is such a right, then strict scrutiny standard of review would be triggered, which means the state must have a compelling (very, very important) interest and that the legislative means must be narrowly tailored (indispensable) to achieve that interest. A law that bans such cohabitation, would probably be unconstitutional.

C. *Legalization*

Here, I explain why decriminalization makes more sense than any of the alternatives. Critics allege that polygamy fosters crimes against women and children.[142] They further claim that polygamy causes, contributes to, or reinforces male supremacy; female subordination; women being treated as property; unhealthy sexual relations; competition among co-wives; family-related stress and mental illness among women; dangers to their mental, physical, sexual, and reproductive health; economic instability and vulnerability; isolation and alienation; low socioeconomic status; low academic achievement; and low self-esteem for children.[143] Polygamy also purportedly leads to inbreeding, dependence on welfare, and extreme fertility.[144]

[141] Ibid., 49.

[142] Bennion, *Polygamy in Primetime*, 236. See also Julia Chamberlin and Amos N. Guiora, "Polygamy: Not 'Big Love' but Significant Harm," http://ssrn.com/abstract=2395370 (focusing on particular kinds of FLDS polygyny).

[143] Bennion, *Polygamy in Primetime*, 237.

[144] Ibid., 238.

The pro-criminalization position needs to be examined carefully. One would expect that polygamy would have to be decriminalized or legalized before any state could treat a multiperson intimate union as a marriage-like relationship. Similarly, *Lawrence* had to precede *Windsor*. Above all, following John Stuart Mill, one might concentrate on the crime itself and not on behavior that is only associated with the crime.[145] Doing so would call into question why such an act – "marrying" another person when one is already legally married to another person – or why such behavior where one acts as if that person were his spouse is a crime in the first place. Neither seems to be intrinsically harmful.

First, assuming that the aforementioned data are accurate and almost all plural marriages would be polygynous, the most obvious alternative is the regulation of such intimate relationships. Adult women could then be more informed about the apparent risks of being a part of a polygynous living situation and be rendered less vulnerable if the relationship were to end. Again, for the sake of argument, let us suppose that more often than not, it is a not a good idea for a woman to enter into such an arrangement. In a liberal society, softer forms of paternalism should always be preferred. The state must experiment with less intrusive alternatives before it takes the more extreme measure of banning an activity that is supposed to be bad for people despite their wishes to the contrary.

Second, causality in social science is complicated.[146] It may be hard to prove that the structure or the dynamics of a plural marriage cause the aforementioned problems, even when they are positively correlated. According to Janet Bennion, risk factors that often come with FLDS polygyny include "rural and structural isolation and female circumscription, prolonged absences of the father or husband, the absence of a vibrant female financial and emotional network, overcrowded housing where wives and their children are living 'on top of each other,' economic deprivation of both the wives and their husbands, and the presence of rigid patriarchy or a mandate that males have supreme power."[147] In the language of social science, correlation is not causation. The variables must be disaggregated before one can isolate an independent variable (the primary cause of the effect). To make a much longer story much shorter, how bad the polygynous relationship in question

145 Mill, "On Liberty," 148–49.

146 Alexander Rosenberg, *Philosophy of Social Science* (2nd ed.) (Boulder, CO: Westview Press, 1995).

147 Bennion, *Polygamy in Primetime*, 260–61.

is likely to be is contextual; polygamy itself may not produce the problems that are often associated with it unless it is coupled with certain risk factors.

Third, many countries already have decriminalized polygamy.[148] That does not mean that the United States must follow suit, but it indicates that other countries have addressed the problems associated with polygyny in ways that do not require the enforcement criminal sanctions, which should be a last resort in a free society. Sadly, opponents of polygamy use it as a stand-in for other crimes that can and should be treated separately (and, in practice, are usually treated so by the police and prosecutors). By comparison, it would be unthinkable to outlaw the priesthood just because there has been a higher rate of sexual assault of children in Catholic Churches than in other religious organizations. Serious crimes are serious crimes irrespective of the setting in which they occur and the state must treat them as such.

It is fundamental to any theory of criminalization that making a behavior a crime must be considered with the utmost seriousness because of the economic costs of investigating, arresting, prosecuting, and punishing people; the adverse effects on third parties; and how individual defendants are affected by the ordeal of going through the criminal justice system and then possibly being incarcerated. Not only will they have to disclose their criminal history on employment applications after they have served their time and live with the stigma for the rest of their lives, but to deprive them of their freedom in different ways and to make them susceptible to being brutalized is just about the worst penalty the state can inflict on a person. We already live in a country where overcriminalization is the norm.[149] While I cannot argue this point here, making a particular action or behavior a crime should be much more difficult than it currently is.[150] That is not to say such a punishment as incarceration is never warranted, but it is to say that the state should have to prove that criminalization is necessary when other reasonable alternatives exist that are less expensive and more humane. Usually, there are other less drastic means of deterring undesirable behaviors and preventing recidivism. Above all, it is not obvious that polygamy should be a crime in the first place as long as all the parties are adults who have agreed to the arrangement and may exit when they so desire.

[148] Ibid., 236, 247.

[149] See Douglas Husak, *Overcriminalization: The Limits of the Criminal Law* (New York: Oxford University Press, 2008).

[150] Jeffrie Murphy G. Murphy and Jules Coleman, *Philosophy of Law: An Introduction to Jurisprudence* (revised edition) (New York: Westview Press, 1990), 109.

Fourth, serious crimes can occur in a polygamous relationship, but they can also (and often do) occur in other living arrangements.[151] The kinds of undesirable behaviors we want to deter in polygamous relationships also take place in much more prevalent monogamous ones. If the rate of domestic violence or homicide were much higher in some monogamous living situations than in others, such as those involving couples who live below the poverty line or are members of a particular cultural group, it would still be unreasonable for the state to deny them the right to marry for that reason alone. At most, the state would be able to educate the public so people can make more informed decisions about their intimate relationships and can better appreciate their risks. Even mandatory premarital counseling would be extreme, but at least it would not be as extreme as making a certain kind of relationship illegal. The existence of this double standard is one of the most compelling reasons to rethink criminalizing polygamy, particularly when other less severe, more sensible alternatives could protect women who are at some risk of harm as well as criminalization could.

Fifth, other immoral practices also have bad secondary effects, but they are not crimes – or if they are, they state is often not eager to enforce laws against them. For example, binge drinking among college students and the abuse of alcohol more generally is a very serious social problem, but no one wants to repeal the Twenty-First Amendment. Adultery often has serious adverse consequences for the participants and others – such as severe emotional distress or even trauma – but that fact does not lead most people to conclude that adultery should be illegal and that laws prohibiting such behaviors must be rigorously enforced. Moreover, it is counterintuitive that an FLDS member could be prosecuted for spiritually marrying a second wife and becoming responsible for her well-being when that same man could have an affair with her, take on much less – if any – responsibility, and not be criminally liable.

Sixth, not all polygamy is harmful or abusive.[152] To make such a sweeping claim is to ignore considerable evidence to the contrary, rely too heavily on so-called expert witnesses and their biased testimony in some polygamy trials, and minimize the extent to which people can be emotionally satisfied in such unconventional relationships, even when they are hard to understand when judged against a well-entrenched social norm of monogamy. People have different needs, preferences, desires, and life plans. That is not only a fact about the world, but it also has normative significance. When it comes to

[151] Bennion, *Polygamy in Primetime*, 249. [152] Ibid., 241.

personal choices about how to live, one size does not fit all, which is to say that moral pluralism is a permanent condition of a society like our own and the state must do what it can to accommodate the most important individual differences so people can pursue their respective life plans, provided they respect the equally important right of others to do likewise.

Seventh, the negative effects of rendering polygamy illegal are well documented.[153] The raid on the YFZ Ranch in El Dorado, Texas, several years ago was a disaster. Most Americans would prefer not to see another Short Creek raid, where the Arizona National Guard took 263 children from polygamous families and made them wards of the state.[154] They do not want the state to take away children from their parents, even those of polygamous families, without compelling reasons, such as the prevention of child abuse. At first glance, it may seem as if these raids saved women and children from a horrible fate and more of these sorts of raids would deter others from entering into polygamous relationships more generally. As one commentator states: "Given the highly private nature of sexual abuse and the self-imposed isolation of polygamous communities, prosecution may well prove impossible. For those who seek to keep polygamy illegal, this wall of silence provides a compelling justification for criminalizing the act of polygamy, prosecuting offenders, and effectively breaking down the wall that provides a favorable environment in which crimes of physical and sexual abuse can thrive."[155]

The trouble with this line of reasoning is that it has the unintended effect of making the situation of many women in such relationships even worse. Closeted co-wives lack legal protection.[156] The criminalization of polygamy seems to have made it far more difficult than it otherwise would be to detect the real harms that take place in insular polygamous communities and enforce laws aimed at preventing the worst abuses, such as sexual assault, parent–child incest, and underage marriages.[157] That is the case because family members are often reluctant to testify against one another.[158] Ultimately, the criminalization of polygamy – rather than directly targeting other related crimes – is

[153] Ibid., 247.

[154] "Short Creek" on the Utah–Arizona border is now known as "Colorado City." Krakauer, *Under the Banner of Heaven*, 15–17.

[155] Richard A. Vasquez, "The Practice of Polygamy: Legitimate Free Exercise or Religion or Legitimate Public Menace? Revisiting *Reynolds* in Light of Modern Constitution Jurisprudence," *New York University Journal of Legislation and Public Policy*, 5 (2001), 243.

[156] Judith Stacey, *Unhitched: Love, Marriage, and Family Values From Hollywood to Western China* (New York: New York University Press, 2011), 147–49.

[157] Shayna M. Sigman, "Everything Lawyers Know About Polygamy Is Wrong," *Cornell Journal of Law and Public Policy*, 16 (2006), 101–85.

[158] Ibid., 180.

more likely than not to be counterproductive. As Bennion says: "The illegality of polygamy pushes the practice further and further underground, exactly where potential abuses are likely to occur."[159] Common sense tells us that a typical woman is less likely to leave a dysfunctional or even abusive relationship if she could be prosecuted for aiding and abetting other related crimes or being an accessory before or after the fact.[160] While it is evident why prosecutors would want to have this leverage over her, it is not clear why she would want to leave her legal fate to prosecutorial discretion. On the other hand, if she could report crimes without fear of being arrested, then the odds increase that she will not remain silent.[161] Over time, more victims may come forward. It is not as if it is easy for victims of abuse in monogamous relationships to leave them or implicate someone they love in criminal activity, which may explain why at times people file a police report yet later regret it or want to retract a restraining order. Like it or not, polygamy will be practiced.[162] The real issue is how the state can best respond to its inevitable existence. Very much like drug use, prostitution, gambling, and other human vices, legal prohibitions will not only not solve the problem but will probably also worsen it.

Eighth, to believe that polygamy should not be a crime is not necessarily to believe that the state should grant marriages licenses to those who seek to have a plural marriage. But as Calhoun observes: "Failure to extend civil marriage to plural marriages leaves them unprotected by marriage and divorce law."[163] A second, third, or fourth "wife" does not enjoy the legal protection that the first and, legally speaking, only wife enjoys unless common-law marriage exists in that jurisdiction, which is rare these days, and a court views the *de facto* plural marriage in question as more than mere cohabitation. For example, in California, a second "wife," such as a live-in partner, who decides to leave her "husband" is not entitled to any of the community property in the absence of a valid cohabitation contract. This situation is particularly disconcerting in the midst of a traditional division of labor in the household where the "wife" lacks job skills that would enable her to support herself (and her children) if necessary. It also may be more difficult to collect child support. As far as the law is concerned in most states, she is no different than a woman who is just living with her partner. At the very least, the state's permitting plural marriages would make it easier for women to leave such relationships for whatever personal reasons they happen to have for doing so, thus making such relationships more voluntary.

159 Bennion, *Polygamy in Primetime*, 262. 160 Ibid., 256. 161 Ibid., 263. 162 Ibid., 243.
163 Calhoun, "Who's Afraid of Polygamous Marriage?" 1041.

Ideally, every marriage would be a fully voluntary arrangement in which all parties consent to all its aspects without any pressure whatsoever. In an era of no-fault divorce, the law no longer prohibits people from ending their marriages without good cause, but nonlegal factors, such as one's financial future, can have a similar effect. The state's making this option available to those who want to live in this manner would enable women in polygynous relationships to be legally shielded from financial hardship if the marital relationship were to end. They could receive a fair share of the marital property, spousal support for a certain period, and inheritance rights and social security benefits if their husband dies intestate. By contrast, under the status quo, they have no such rights unless a court finds that a common-law marriage exists and treats the woman in question as if she were a spouse. Their absence would make it much harder for many of them to leave such relationships even when they are dangerous. The cumulative effect, then, of not legalizing polygamy and not recognizing plural marriages is to punish women in polygynous relationships for taking part in them. Legal recognition would allow greater regulation of the practice and probably serve the interests of women who want to leave such intimate relationships and start a new life.[164] When it comes to the pro-criminalization position these days, all roads seem to lead to Warren Jeffs. As I have already explained, Jeffs could have been prosecuted for the serious crimes he committed even if polygamy among adults was legal. No reasonable person thinks what he did should be allowed or that decriminalization would entail that the state would be powerless to prosecute people like him.

Those who continue to believe that all kinds of polygamy (or at least polygyny) should remain illegal must believe that decriminalization or legalization would make the situation even worse, but that belief is speculative. It is hard to see why allowing, say, an FLDS thruple to marry legally would have any direct impact on future Warren Jeffs-like scenarios and make it harder for investigators to determine whether other serious crimes had occurred unless second and third wives invoke their spousal testimonial privileges or refuse to cooperate with law enforcement.

Nothing in the decriminalization view precludes age and consent requirements. Additionally, even if crimes associated with certain kinds of FLDS polygyny cannot be separated from such polygyny, we would still have to decide whether the costs of keeping all polygamy illegal to try to prevent such crimes outweighs the aforementioned benefits. Just because crimes occur in some of these polygynous relationships does not mean they occur in all or

[164] Bennion, *Polygamy in Primetime*, 254.

most of them. Nor does it mean that all polygynous relationships should be banned when only some of them – and perhaps very few – involve criminality. Advocates of keeping polygamy against the law cannot simply make their case by showing that certain kinds of polygyny harm women and children. That is not hard to do when one interviews those who have been victimized by such predators as Jeffs. After all, without question, certain kinds of monogamy also harm women and children. What they would also need to prove is that the harms are so bad and so likely to occur in the absence of the illegality of polygamy that considerable overinclusion is unavoidable; that is, the much larger number of consensual polygamist relationships should also continue to be illegal as a necessary means to that end. It is not apparent why those who are involved in nonharmful multiperson unions should not only have to pay for Jeffs's sins but also have to bear the burden of trying to prevent such behaviors in the future by sacrificing the legal recognition of their own intimate relationships.

IV. SAVING ADULT WOMEN FROM THEMSELVES

A. *Paternalism*

Another concern, which opponents of plural marriage often express, is that an adult woman who wants to enter into a plural relationship is invariably exercising poor judgment. Thus, the state should try to prevent her from making an important decision she will probably regret. From this viewpoint, in such situations, the state may act paternalistically to save her from herself, so to speak, even when no one else is directly harmed. According to Gerald Dworkin: "Paternalism is the interference of a state or individual with another person, against their will, and defended or motivated by a claim that the person interfered with will be better off or protected from harm."[165] For different reasons, Lockean, Millian, and Kantian liberalisms are hostile to paternalistic justifications for using the law to try to prevent certain behaviors when they only or largely affect the person who wants to engage in them. Typically, political paternalism has a negative connotation because a liberal state should not treat a competent adult as if he or she were as a child incapable of choosing how to live. Compared with adults, children have underdeveloped rational capacities, fewer life experiences, worse judgment, and are more susceptible to peer pressure. For these reasons, they are less

[165] Gerald Dworkin, "Paternalism," *Stanford Encyclopedia of Philosophy*, http://plato.stanford.edu/entries/paternalism.

likely to understand what they really want and less able to select the most appropriate means to their ends. The younger the child, the more likely it would be appropriate for a parent or guardian to step in and veto a misguided decision. Mill exempts some adults and children from the presumption that paternalism is wrong.[166]

More often than not, competent adults know themselves well enough to know what ends they want to pursue. True, this is only a generalization; it is underinclusive and overinclusive. Some adults will be more like children and some children or adolescents will be more like adults in terms of their maturity. The point is that absent special circumstances, we let the average adult make his or her own decisions about his or her personal life, even if he or she is not fully informed or rational, and justify doing so not simply because adults have a right to choose but because they are better equipped than anyone else is, including lawmakers, to know what is best for them. While there are some exceptions, in a liberal society, the default is usually personal choice; limitations on autonomy and agency require compelling justification and that implies that the burden of proof falls on the state when it seeks to act on the basis of a paternalistic rationale.

That the state can be likened to a benevolent parent is not a view that too many contemporary political theorists share. If they still teach Sir Richard Filmer's *Patriarchia*, it has more to do with its place in the history of ideas than with its merits in a democratic age. Such a view has authoritarian overtones, and most Americans doubt that the state is either sufficiently institutionally competent or well intentioned to make decisions for them for their own good. Here, I am only concerned with what is called *narrow paternalism* or *state coercion*. When it comes to adult women, the state's not recognizing polygynous marriages is undeniably paternalistic. Their refusal to do so at least partially is designed to save women from their own purportedly poor decisions about the kinds of intimate lives they want to have. Those who defend such bans ought to be candid about their rationale: Opposition to polygamy is rooted in a belief that polygamy is bad for the persons involved, especially for women, whether they realize it or not.[167] Even though that belief is sincere, its sincerity does not entail its truth; it may be bad for some women and not for others.

Even if it is bad for them in some circumstances, which is hard to predict with much accuracy, they may still retain the right to decide for themselves whether the rewards of having such a relationship outweigh the risks instead of having what is purportedly "good" or "better" for them imposed on them. To

[166] Mill, "On Liberty," 102.

[167] See Joel Feinberg, *Harm to Self: The Moral Limits of the Criminal Law* (New York: Oxford University Press, 1986), 24.

deny the option of polygamy is to force them to select monogamy (or remain single). It is not hard to see why someone might opt for the former instead of the latter. There is no guarantee that the latter always will be preferable. In addition to the importance of respecting their autonomy, people have different utility functions, as economists would put it. At the very least, each case deserves its own assessment. Presumably, almost all of us value being able to make our own personal choices even when we are prone to making the same mistakes. Morally, to be given advice differs markedly from being denied options, particularly when one would select one of those options if they were available. If we could predict accurately which monogamous marriages were likely to be dysfunctional or even dangerous, we would still let consenting adults to enter to them – regardless of the probable outcome.

In the last few pages of this chapter, I shall focus on the claim that plural marriage is bad for women because these days, polygyny is much more common than polyandry or group marriage.[168] I proceed in this manner with some trepidation because I suspect that plural marriage – if the state legally recognized it – would become even more pluralistic as more and more people experimented with different forms to see which ones worked best for them. Over time, conjugal two-person marriages might become less widespread as more people learn that unconventional intimate relationships are perfectly acceptable and might work better for some individuals compared with a conventional marriage. By not requiring marriages to have a romantic component, a person could marry one or more persons and openly have consensual sex with others if he or she so desires. That possibility could lead to better marital decisions because one would not have to be physically attracted to one's partner to marry and instead would be encouraged to take into account factors that are more conducive to a long term, healthy intimate relationship, such as the prospective partner's personality, deepest convictions, mental health, character, and intellect.[169] By far the most radical part of my proposal in this book is to remove the appearance of amorous relations from the legal definition of marriage.

In some states, with parental permission, minors as young as sixteen can legally marry one person, including someone much older than he or

[168] Polygamy may also be bad for the man in a polygynous relationship. Mill reminds us that an unequal marriage also negatively affects men in several ways. See Mill, *The Subjection of Women*, 141–43.

[169] When it comes to online dating, in general, men are most interested in the physical appearance of their prospective partners and women are most interested in the wealth of their prospective partners, confirming unfortunate stereotypes. See Steven D. Levitt and Stephen J. Dubner, *Freakonomics: A Rogue Economist Explores the Hidden Side of Everything* (New York: HarperCollins, 2005), 80–84.

she is.[170] Anyone above the legal age of consent can marry one person for just about any personal reason he or she happens to have – other than allowing someone who is a noncitizen to legally stay in this country. A couple could meet via a dating website or in a virtual world found in an online game, and provided that each of them satisfies the minimalist requirements for marriage that most states have in place, they may marry. They would not have to know anything about each other, to love each other, or to even like each other before they enter into such a relationship. The existence of K-1 marriage visas reflects the fact that as far as the state is concerned, two people who may have never met in person beforehand can "fall in love" ninety days if they have not done so already. Women are allowed to correspond with most prisoners in maximum-security institutions and are allowed to marry them if they are single. These examples illuminate the critical point: When it comes to monogamous marriage, the state does not evaluate the quality of her reasons and then act paternalistically to save her from what could be a poor decision. If she wants to marry someone with a history of psychological disorders, intimate partner violence, other serious crimes, infidelity, and financial irresponsibility, she has such a right, even if doing so is foolish and she may later regret her decision. As long as she can exit relatively easily by filing for legal separation or divorce, she may be able to undo any mistake she may have made by marrying in the first place.[171]

It appears that many Americans, though, would view her decision to marry a man who is already married quite differently and assume that paternalism on the part of the state would be appropriate in the second case but not in the first. A hard paternalist would insist that even if her choice to enter into a polygynous marriage is fully voluntary, the state may still deny her that choice on the grounds that a rational person who truly understood what was good for her would not find such a marital arrangement to be attractive. By contrast, a soft paternalist would seek to ensure that her choice was sufficiently voluntary. If it were, then she would be allowed to proceed, no matter how foolish or irrational it might be from the standpoint that most of us happen to share. For those sympathetic to paternalistic rationales, the state must be allowed to save people from themselves inasmuch as they want to do something that is almost incomprehensible. It might be hard to fathom why anyone would want

[170] William Burnham, *Introduction to the Law and Legal System of the United States* (5th ed.) (St. Paul, MN: Thomson Reuters, 2011), 518.

[171] The requirements for dissolving a marriage are minimal. See Burnham, *Introduction to the Law and Legal System of the United States*, 522–24.

to free-climb Half Dome in Yosemite National Park, base-jump from a building, highline, or wing-suit from a cliff thousands of feet above sea level – where one small miscalculation could result in death – or to appreciate why one might want to become an ultimate fighter despite exposing oneself to the possibility of serious bodily injury.[172] It is becoming increasingly evident that because of the risk of not only spinal but brain injury (chronic traumatic encephalopathy [CTE]), American football is not nearly as safe as it was once widely believed to be.[173] We let people gamble, play video games, look at pornography, drink alcohol, smoke and chew tobacco, and use prescription drugs – and often look the other way when they use illegal ones recreationally. All these activities can lead to compulsive and self-destructive behavior, but most Americans are willing to let competent adults take their chances and provide them with resources for recovery.

Morally and legally, just about everyone agrees that children can be treated paternalistically by their parents.[174] Probably one of the most difficult parts of parenting involves deciding when such interference is called for and when it is not as the child grows older, his or her faculties mature, and he or she has more opportunities to make his or her own decisions as he or she moves closer to adulthood. Hopefully, he or she develops into a more or less responsible adult. As a prelaw advisor to undergraduates, most of whom are in their early twenties, I have been tempted to dissuade some of them from applying to law school when it is evident they have given the matter little thought, have less-than-ideal work ethics, lack maturity, have shown little academic promise, and only have the option of attending a fourth-tier law school with no scholarship. Many of them can only barely articulate the reasons they have for wanting to enter the legal profession and for incurring considerable debt to finance their legal education in the midst of a bleak legal job market.[175] When you ask them what they will do if they graduate, have $150,000 or more in student debt, and cannot find permanent employment, they rarely have an answer because for too many of them, such an outcome lies outside the realm of possibility. Perhaps being overly optimistic about the future is a part of being young, is

[172] Nicholas Dixon, "Boxing, Paternalism, and Legal Moralism," *Social Theory and Practice* 27 (2001), 323–44.

[173] See Mark Fainaru-Wada and Steve Fainaru, *League of Denial: The NFL, Concussions, and the Battle for Truth* (New York: Crown Archetype, 2013).

[174] Amy Gutmann, "Children, Paternalism, and Education: A Liberal Argument," *Philosophy and Public Affairs*, 9 (1980), 338–58.

[175] See Brian Tamanaha, *Failing Law Schools* (Chicago: University of Chicago Press, 2012); and Robin L. West, *Teaching Law: Justice, Politics, and the Demands of Professionalism* (New York: Cambridge University Press, 2014), especially 1–42.

characteristically American, or is best left to those who study social psychology or behavioral economics to investigate, but without question, such a mindset can have adverse consequences when it comes to trying to enter a profession that costs so much to be a part of, has uncertain job prospects, and is probably more stressful than many other professions. I always advise prelaw students to read certain books to familiarize themselves with the risks (law schools are already very adept at articulating the apparent rewards) of attending law school when other career options exist. Above all, I want them to at least contemplate the worst-case scenario. That is why I include cautionary tales.

To be antipaternalistic in one's attitude and to favor nonpaternalistic justifications for laws is not to believe that ordinary people always or often make wise choices or to be naive about their capacity to learn from their mistakes. When it comes to older adults and their arguably poor personal choices, most people have mixed feelings about paternalism on the part of the state with respect to means and ends. On the one hand, trying to act in the best interest of the person in question may be called for at times. Most Americans would agree that there is at least something to be said on behalf of the view that in some situations, the state may act paternalistically to save someone who is factually mistaken from taking a route that will not serve his or her end. Being your own lawyer – known as *proceeding pro se* – without any legal training, especially in a criminal case, is normally a terrible idea because you probably lack the necessary expertise to defend yourself competently against criminal charges, even if your only option is to have an overworked and underpaid public defender represent you. Even if you have such expertise, your judgment is likely to be clouded by your emotional involvement in the case.

This sort of lapse in judgment is particularly worrisome with respect to financial decisions. Some people simply do not understand probability, risk, or the wisdom of foregoing short-term benefits in the name of long-term ones. For this reason, not allowing people to invest their retirement funds in high-risk, high-reward stocks or mutual funds may be easier to justify than other nonfinancial regulations. There is nothing wrong with government agencies that regulate the financial industry to address the problems associated with it these days, such as predatory lending practices. No one wants to be below the poverty line, especially as he or she gets older. Government's aim is to prevent banks from taking advantage of ordinary people who may not understand the terms of the contract due to its fine print or salespeople who mislead or simply lie to people to meet their own quotas. For example, anyone who borrows money or purchases a home must be made aware of the risks, including the difference between an adjustable and a fixed mortgage rate. The recent behaviors of many banks in this country have been nothing short of unconscionable. Nothing I say in what follows is opposed to informed consent when it comes to marital decisions. Indeed, as I argue in the last chapter, more needs to be done in the name of such consent.

The harder question is whether people can be mistaken about the desirability of their largely self-regarding ends. Assuming they can be so mistaken, whether the state may intervene and save someone against his or her will from doing something he or she wants to do moves us to decide whether the law should permit people to make flawed decisions. As Andrew Koppelman puts it, "perhaps we are entitled to do this [that the person would be better off with a radical conversion] with respect to people whose lives are manifestly wretched, such as homeless drug addicts, but we do not know most of our fellow citizens well enough to make such judgments with any degree of confidence."[176] The state is a poor judge of what an individual believes to be most important in human life and tends to favor the conventional. People are often idiosyncratic in what they find important and many of them care deeply about things that others are indifferent to or have never contemplated. In most scenarios, people should be left free "to choose and pursue life plans that deviate from maximal rationality or that hamper future prospects of rational choice."[177] It may be inaccurate to speak of life plans that "deviate from maximal rationality" because instrumental or means–end rationality is not synonymous with a more robust and controversial conception of practical rationality in which some ends are to be rationally preferred over others.

One of the most compelling rationales for antipaternalism is that what constitutes a good human life is subjective; there is no objective standard when it comes to evaluating the quality of various lives on their merits. It is not unreasonable to believe that ultimately, moral philosophy has little – if anything – to say about the human good. People have different conceptions of the good life under conditions of moral pluralism and thus will take different paths to different destinations. Even if one resists such an extreme subjective or relativistic understanding of human life plans, one still has to accept that considerable variance characterizes what people desire and believe to be valuable. As noted, economists refer to individuals' having different utility functions or payoffs. The late John Rawls built his entire theory of political liberalism on the claim that moral disagreement about the nature

176 Andrew Koppelman, "How Shall I Praise Thee? Brian Leiter on Respect for Religion," *San Diego Law Review*, 47 (2010), 984.

177 Richard J. Arneson, "Mill versus Paternalism," *Ethics*, 90 (1980), 474.

of the human good is not only sincere but also reasonable and intractable.[178] To prove that one particular life is better than its rivals, according to an objective standard of human flourishing, is a tall order. What one can assert with more confidence is that certain life plans seem to fit the unique talents and aims of particular individuals better than others do. If a good human life really lies in the eye of the beholder, then the state cannot act paternalistically to save people from wrong "ends" because there are no such ends. It follows that the state cannot legitimately coerce or even try to discourage people from pursuing ends that do not affect others because there would be no rational way of determining which ends are better. To favor one end over another would be arbitrary.

More than one hundred and fifty years ago, at a different time and in a different place, Mill grappled with the problem of deciding when the state may prevent a competent adult from behaving in chiefly self-regarding ways.[179] While his well-known highly critical views of paternalism expressed in "On Liberty" are underdeveloped, they are a good starting point because they bring the problem of legal paternalism into sharper relief. For Mill, the state is only justified in restraining people against their will to prevent harm to others; their "own good, either physical or moral, is not a sufficient warrant."[180] According to Richard Arneson: "Mill's argument against paternalism is woven of various strands, not all of which mesh smoothly together."[181] Mill may appear to be inconsistent by allowing for exceptions, such as his famous bridge and slavery examples. [182] True, there may be ends that nobody has or wants to pursue. Like most of us, though, Mill has mixed feelings about how the state may employ its authority when people are using their freedom to live "bad" lives or to harm themselves. In such situations, we may not only disagree about the quality of their lives but also about whether, empirically, they are really being harmed.

Much more recently, in the context of debate over the decriminalization of prostitution, Peter de Marneffe argues that prostitution is usually harmful to those who engage in it.[183] According to him, prostitutes are likely to experience lasting psychological damage and feelings of worthlessness, shame, and self-hatred.[184] As a result, certain kinds of paternalism on the part of the state may be called for.[185] It would be more sensible, I think, as opposed to keeping prostitution illegal and arresting and rearresting prostitutes, to treat such

[178] John Rawls, *Political Liberalism* (New York: Columbia University Press, 1993).
[179] Mill, "On Liberty," 13. [180] Ibid. [181] Arneson, "Mill versus Paternalism," 472.
[182] Mill, "On Liberty," 96, 102.
[183] Peter de Marneffe, *Liberalism and Prostitution* (New York: Oxford University Press, 2010).
[184] Ibid., 13. [185] Ibid.

women as victims who may want to leave those who are exploiting and abusing them. To treat prostitutes as criminals may make some of us feel morally superior and help elected officials score political points, but it is not good public policy. Instead of criminalizing adult prostitution, we should conceive of more humane ways that would make this line of work safer – given that there will always be a demand for sexual services – and help women start what might be a better life if they so desire, which would require, among other things, better educational opportunities, more widespread and affordable counseling services, treatment for addiction and other mental health issues if necessary, and more promising professional options that can help people and their families stay above the poverty line. It is probably a tragedy that anyone would be willing to put him or herself at risk to support him or herself (and perhaps his or her children or others) in the adult entertainment industry more generally, but that does not mean the law should be able to try to prevent him or her from making a living in this manner. Compassion and understanding – and not judgment – are what is called for here.

Let us assume for the sake of argument that the kinds of harms that characterize illegal prostitution also apply in the debate over the proper legal status of plural marriage. If plural marriage were to harm at least some of those who are involved in such relationships – in the kinds of ways de Marneffe describes – then there would be a *prima facie* paternalistic reason for the state to ban such relationships. If an activity tends to cause serious physical or psychological harm to those who partake in it, then the state's position is much stronger than it otherwise would be. But that does not mean it is strong enough to support interference in the most personal decisions that people make, such as choosing a profession or a marital partner.

One response, following such feminists as Catharine MacKinnon, would be to maintain that such consent on the part of women is spurious.[186] Choices are the product of oppressive conditioning and such decision making will consequently perpetuate unequal relations. Just as in a capitalist society a worker's choice of employment cannot be free, in a patriarchal society, one has to be skeptical that a woman truly has consented, particularly in the absence of viable options. As Linda McClain writes: "Feminists also caution that women's preferences and choices or associational life may reflect not their exercise of autonomy, but the effects of sex inequality, gender socialization, and constraint."[187]

[186] See, for example, Catharine A. MacKinnon, *Feminism Unmodified: Discourses on Life and Law* (Cambridge, MA: Harvard University Press, 1978).

[187] Linda McClain, *The Place of Families: Fostering Capacity, Equality, and Responsibility* (Cambridge, MA: Harvard University Press, 2006), 26.

Thus, their consent may not be genuine under such conditions. To object to this view is probably to be insensitive to the extent to which women – and not men – are still relatively disadvantaged, but this argument proves too much: The same concern can be raised with respect to the "choice" of the straight woman who marries only one man in a society where she is told over and over again that she should be married by a certain age and have a family, as if there is something wrong with her when she takes a different path. Why is her consent necessarily more genuine than that of a woman who decides to be a part of polygamous arrangement?

Feminist thinkers have long argued that various kinds of socialization predispose women to make their traditionally female traits the focus of their lives to the detriment of other capacities that they may fail to develop. The problem of spurious consent, then, described in various ways, is hardly new. Mill was concerned that women do not really choose marriage or family life given their limited options. Under the nonideal conditions that will always exist in the real world, though, one cannot put off indefinitely letting people make their own choices simply because conditions in the distant future could be more conducive to bona fide consent. The priority should be creating those conditions as soon as possible. As Onora O'Neill explains, real, not abstract, persons either consent or refuse to consent.[188] This fact complicates any analysis inasmuch as we have to take real persons as they are – warts and all – and examine their individual circumstances. Legally, the meaning of consent cannot be choice measured against an ideal standard that never has and never will exist in a society inhabited by real human beings. Female consent or choice presents a special problem and deserves a more thorough analysis than I have presented. If nearly every choice a woman makes is suspect, however, it would be far too easy for the state to forbid women from making certain personal choices that have to be left to them – even when they are not fully autonomous – in a liberal society like our own, such as whether to marry, use birth control, terminate a pregnancy, divorce, or enter a particular profession or how to raise their children.

When it comes to abortion, the only people who seem to be sympathetic to the possible existence of false consciousness are social conservatives who believe abortion to be immoral and therefore should be recriminalized. In his majority opinion in *Gonzales v. Carhart*, Justice Kennedy caught flack for saying that women may regret the decision to terminate the life of a fetus.[189] One way to understand the constitutional right granted in *Roe* is that the state must accept the personal reasons a woman has for terminating

[188] See Onora O'Neill, "Between Consenting Adults," in *Constructions of Reason: Explorations of Kant's Practical Philosophy* (Cambridge, UK: Cambridge University Press, 1989), 105–25.

[189] *Gonzales v. Carhart*, 550 U.S. 124 (2007).

her pregnancy. One way to understand the willingness of those who are otherwise adamantly pro-life to make an exception for rape is to see that as far as they are concerned, that is a good reason, whereas the others are not. Her personal reasons are not subject to further evaluation prior to the viability of the fetus. Likewise, I doubt anyone would take seriously the view that the state may ban monogamous marriage on the grounds that some or most women do not really consent to the arrangement because their life and professional opportunities are more limited than those of men or that they have been enculturated to be wives and mothers. To believe that women ought to be permitted to enter into a plural marriage is not to insist that they should do so or even to take a position on the matter. To advocate a right to such marriage is not to advocate plural marriage in the sense that everyone should try it. It is simply to let her decide – for better or for worse – the kind of personal life she wants to have. In Mill's view, a Mormon wife lived autonomously (enough) to be free to enter into such marital relationships.[190]

In the end, there is no such thing as a perfectly voluntary choice.[191] In between the two extremes of "perfectly voluntary" and "involuntary" lie different degrees of voluntariness. For legal purposes, the issue is how voluntary is voluntary enough?[192] As a practical matter, no legal standard of consent can be premised on an overly robust conception of what it really means to make a choice. According to H. L. A. Hart: "Choices may be made or consent may be given without adequate reflection or appreciation of the consequences; or in pursuit of merely transitory desires; or in various predicaments when the judgment is likely to be clouded; or under inner psychological compulsion; or under pressure by others of a kind too subtle to be susceptible of proof in a court of law."[193]

Just as it is a mistake to employ an almost perfect monogamous marriage as the basis of comparison, it is a mistake to work from an idealized version of consent. Almost all women who were not socialized in a traditional religious environment would not see polygynous marriage as a religious duty, but that does not imply that the woman in question has not consented to the arrangement in the legal sense of the word. This distinction between consent in a perfect world without asymmetries of power and the kind of consent that is good enough in the real world is crucial when opponents of plural marriage claim that coercion characterizes the decision-making process. In determining how the power of the state may be employed, the standard of consent cannot be what her "real self" would have chosen if she had been

190 Arneson, "Mill versus Paternalism," 476–77.

191 Feinberg, *Harm to Self*, 104.

192 Ibid., 113.

193 H. L. A Hart, *Law, Liberty, and Morality* (Stanford, CA: Stanford University Press, 1963), 33.

raised in a more egalitarian environment without traditional preconceptions about the proper place of women.

In this context, then, the question is whether an adult woman's decision to be a part of a plural relationship is free enough under the imperfect conditions of the real world. Probably most FLDS and at least some Muslim women have sincere and deep religious personal reasons for wanting to have such a marital relationship. One cannot simply rest assured that such women are brainwashed because the same could be said about anyone who has had a traditional Christian upbringing. Indeed, it is unlikely that most American children are brought up to be free thinkers; their parents often do little to develop their autonomous capacities and these children often care more about superficial things, such as clothes, electronic devices, popular culture, and physical appearance. As such, the argument "from coercion" does not work with respect to adult women either – unless one defines "coercion" so broadly that just about anything counts as coercion. Historically, few Mormon women were coerced into polygynous marriages.[194] Instead, it is more accurate to describe that what occurs when people are raised in a particular religious tradition makes plural marriage more attractive than it otherwise would be.

In one sense, *de facto* plural relationships already exist – when people have more than one sexual partner at the same time – and the existence of marital infidelity and divorce in our society indicates that some Americans may be more in tune with *de facto* and serial polygamy than they may realize or admit. In the zeal to call attention to what is wrong with plural marriage, they succumb to the temptation to romanticize monogamous marriage (and praise those who opt for it) by minimizing its shortcomings and then presenting it in its ideal form as a contrast to the worst kinds of plural marriages. Nevertheless, a more apt comparison is either the ideal form of both kinds of marriages or their real forms. As noted, the trouble with the latter is that the dynamics of plural marriages are bound to be distorted by their illegality (and the consequent secrecy that surrounds them) or by unjust background conditions.

The reality is that if the state fails to recognize plural marriages, marriage-like relationships involving more than two persons will continue to exist but without the legal rights and duties associated with marriage. A woman who wants to leave a plural marriage but is not a wife in the eyes of the law is not entitled to a fair division of the "marital" property or any spousal support – even when she has performed unpaid domestic labor for years – unless a court

[194] Rosenblum, "Democratic Sex," 78.

finds that a common-law marriage exists.[195] That prospect should bother those who do not believe that any woman should be pressured to remain in an unhealthy intimate relationship out of economic necessity. The most pressing practical legal question relates to how to protect those who are involved in such relationships from being exploited, abused, or forced to remain in them in the absence of a viable option to exit.

CONCLUSION

As I have tried to establish, upon closer inspection, the common justifications examined in this chapter for not allowing plural marriage – promoting gender equality in personal relationships, preventing coercion, and saving adult women from misguided marital choices – are flawed. Surely, in a liberal society, it should not be illegal for a man to live with multiple women, for a woman to live with multiple men, or for more than one woman to live with more than one man after all of them have reached adulthood. A law that infringes on something as personal as living arrangements with little justification would be ripe for a challenge to its constitutionality.[196] True, that does not necessarily mean the state has to recognize every relationship between or among adults that they want to form as a civil marriage and create the same legal rights and duties for them. For a right as important as the right to marry, even for someone who wants to marry someone who is already married, the expectation would be for the state to produce reasons that reasonable persons would accept or at least not reject if the state refuses to permit equal access to the institution.

At the very least, the state needs to articulate why the inequality or another harm, which is supposed to be present in plural marriages, is worse than that of much more common traditional patriarchal marriages with rigid, gendered divisions of labor that disadvantage females. One of the premises of the argument from gender equality is that toleration of different forms of gender equality equates to approval or at least indifference to the oppression of women. Therefore, the state reinforces gender inequality by failing to attack it. Nonetheless, this argument is not nearly as sound as its proponents have made it out to be. That is not to say that such an argument cannot be made, but it is to say that it has not been made yet, especially in a society where there is a strong presumption in favor of letting people make their own choices

[195] Less than one-fourth of the states recognize such marriages. Burnham, *Introduction to the Law and Legal System of the United States*, 519.

[196] Cain, "Imagine There's No Marriage," 27–60.

about how they are going to live. That presumption exists for a number of reasons, not least of which is that it is far too easy for society to look at the "other" with contempt and to use such contempt as an excuse not to accommodate his or her unconventional life plan.

As Martha Nussbaum writes: "But to rule that marriage as such should be illegal on the grounds that it reinforced male dominance would be an excessive intrusion upon liberty, even if one should believe marriage irredeemably unequal."[197] If anything is the identifiable cause of women's subordination in multiperson relationships, it is not the marriage per se but the traditional religious and cultural beliefs that motivate them to adopt a polygynous marriage at the outset and subsequently play certain gender roles that work to their disadvantage. A child who has been brought up in such an environment is less likely to make fully autonomous choices with respect to marriage, career, and the decision as to whether to have children. As one commentator claims, "the use of religious indoctrination undermines the free will that the consenting part of consenting adults presupposes."[198]

At the same time, for consent to be legitimate only when asymmetries of power are completely absent is to set the bar too high. In individual cases, the lack of real options may undermine consent and how a person is raised is bound to affect how he or she understands his or her identity, what is most important to him or her, and what ends he or she wants to pursue. I cannot imagine how it could be otherwise in any diverse human society. One of the consequences of living in a free society is that many people will make less than fully autonomous choices because of the beliefs they have acquired – notwithstanding their rationality. Accordingly, some women will choose an inegalitarian intimate relationship or marriage. We are not justified in only concerning ourselves with polygamous unions when monogamous ones are more widespread and equally morally troubling.

[197] Martha C. Nussbaum, "Taking Money for Bodily Services," in *Sex and Social Justice* (New York: Oxford University Press, 2009), 295.

[198] Cassiah M. Ward, "I Now Pronounce You Husband and Wives: *Lawrence v. Texas* and the Practice of Polygamy in Modern America," *William and Mary Journal of Women and the Law*, 11 (2004), 145–47.

3

Judging the Case Against Plural Marriage (Part II)

In Chapter 2, I explained why on closer inspection the argument from gender inequality is not as compelling as it initially may appear to be. The admirable goal of preventing the subordination of women does not necessarily extend to ensuring their equal treatment in marriage-like relationships against their will while the marriage lasts. Although the law can justifiably prevent women from being discriminated against in education, employment, and housing, people sincerely and reasonably disagree about how the state can use its authority to make such intimate relationships more egalitarian, especially prior to their dissolution. Lawmakers can only go so far in using their power to influence how couples interact with each other, including how they make collective decisions, interact with each other, arrange their finances, take care of their children and other dependents, and divide their respective workloads. From a liberal perspective that emphasizes the primacy of personal choice, the state has no business in promoting such equality in marriage-like relationships even though it may legitimately intervene to shield the participants from serious harms and may protect them from being economically vulnerable if the relationship ends. At present, family law respects such choice by letting the couple decide how egalitarian its intimate relationship or marriage is going to be.

The view that equality can be promoted at all costs is illiberal. That fact alone might persuade those who are on the fence to have second thoughts about precluding plural marriage out of a concern for gender equality – understood as how a thruple or a moresome interacts with one another on a daily basis. Even if it did not have this effect, to deny that option on such grounds is unacceptably paternalistic. The troubling implication of the argument from gender equality is that even when the female adults in question are fully informed about the possible risks and have considered the alternatives, they would still not be allowed to marry multiple persons. The rationale would be they could not possibly be justified in doing so. As I argued, that line of reasoning is suspect. Not only would legally mandating such equality be unworkable due to the kinds of intrusions and administrative resources it would require, but equally importantly, such a law would intrude on the personal space that most couples understandably believe to be their own.

That said, of all the arguments against plural marriage, I believe the strongest one to be the argument for gender equality. When it comes to same-sex marriage, no one is concerned that the legal recognition of such marriage can be objected to on such grounds. Inasmuch as same-sex couples do not as easily fall into traditional gender roles and therefore are less likely to have a gendered division of labor, one might defend same-sex marriage as a means of providing a more egalitarian example, which ought to be emulated, of how opposite-sex couples might relate to each other. In the name of gender equality, then, the state might consider stopping opposite-sex couples from marrying until they can prove that their marital relationship will be sufficiently egalitarian. They could even be asked to take and pass an equality examination before they are eligible to marry, be subject to continuing education requirements, and be put on probation after a second offense. I say that facetiously to drive home the main point: The constitutional right to marriage never has and never will be conditioned on a commitment to gender equality or behaviors consistent with this ideal in personal relationships.

In this chapter, I begin by saying a bit more about paternalism and its dangers in the context of selecting marital partners, underscoring the challenge of understanding various kinds of difference, and explaining why typical cultural defenses fail. I then address other less prominent arguments that purport to cut against the right to choose a plural marriage: the welfare of adolescents and children, administrative considerations, the value of tradition, and the new natural law. I conclude by elaborating on why none of them succeed. In the next chapter, I go on the offensive by beginning to make the case for allowing adults the option of various kinds of plural marriage based on substantive due process grounds – with an emphasis on the importance of marital choice.

I. MORE ON THE PATERNALISTIC TREATMENT OF ADULTS

A. *Pro-Choice*

With respect to something as important as marriage, the more options, the better, even when some of us have understandable reservations about how free the choice is in individual situations or whether it is wise – all things considered. The pro-choice position I later develop and defend does not imply that plural marriage is for all people or even for many of them. In fact, polyamorists are vocal about just how challenging it is to sustain such relationships.[1] At the same time, one might wonder how voluntary the choice of a monogamous intimate relationship or marriage is in a society that endorses the myth of "supermonogamy," where "only one 'right' partner exists for each person."[2] Even in an age of growing familial diversity, many people feel considerable social and economic pressure to marry by a certain age. As Nancy Polikoff observes, marriage would be more of a real choice if the legal status were detached from numerous entitlements that could come from elsewhere.[3]

Those who refuse to accept the option of plural marriage must keep in mind that ultimately, they reject personal choice by telling knowledgeable adults who want a plural marriage that they cannot have one – irrespective of the quality of their personal reasons for wanting such a relationship, which do not have to stem from religious or cultural beliefs. Ultimately, that view is hard to defend; to think that one's personal reasons for selecting a monogamous marriage would always be adequate – whereas one's personal reasons for opting for a plural marriage never would cross the threshold – flies in the face of common sense. Opponents of plural marriage need to come up with a better explanation for this double standard or begin to look more critically at the personal reasons couples have before they are granted a marriage license. What at first seems to be a principled position against the option of plural marriage begins to look more and more like prejudice against those who want to deviate from marital norms. After all, they could have serious reasons for wanting to experiment with marital multiplicity; those reasons may be better than the standard reasons many couples would offer on behalf of their decision to marry. No doubt it can be quite tempting to protect people from their own apparent foolishness and ignorance, but it is a serious mistake for the state to do so when it is institutionally ill-equipped to understand why some persons have unconventional beliefs and want the freedom to live according to them.

While most laws and policies can be based on statistical generalizations, marriage is special in the sense of calling for individualized treatment so

[1] See, for example, Tristan Taormino, *Opening Up: A Guide to Creating and Sustaining Open Relationships* (San Francisco: Cleis Press, 2008).

[2] Elizabeth F. Emens, "Monogamy's Law: Compulsory Monogamy and Polyamorous Existence," *New York University Review of Law and Social Change*, 29 (2004), 291.

[3] Nancy D. Polikoff, *Beyond (Straight and Gay) Marriage: Valuing All Families Under the Law* (Boston: Beacon Press, 2008), 133.

legitimate personal differences can be accommodated. Misunderstanding due to incomplete information or preconceptions is more the rule than the exception with respect to plural marriage because its existence seems to threaten the traditional dyadic form of marriage and the shared understandings that come with it, including a commitment to sexual exclusivity. In the future, hopefully a larger number of Americans will become more aware of the reality of its different forms and possible merits. Normally, consent is a moral trump card; it renders acceptable what would otherwise be morally objectionable behaviors by overriding competing considerations. Most academic critics of plural marriage already concede that most polygamous relationships are sufficiently consensual from a legal viewpoint. For the most part, contract, family, and constitutional law reflect the conviction that each competent adult is entitled to be treated as if he or she possesses a rational capacity to evaluate the reasons he or she has for making the personal choices that directly affect him or her more than anyone else, including whom to marry.

As explained in Chapter 2, to deny an adult female (or any other adult for that matter) the right to select a marital option that the public disapproves of morally – and perhaps even with some justification in some circumstances – is to treat her paternalistically. While this treatment may be well intentioned, it still amounts to dictating to her that she is not qualified to make such a decision on her own because she does not know what is best for her. According to this view, her personal reasons could not possibly rise to the level where they deserve to be seen as *prima facie* good enough. Such an attitude may produce bad or less-than-optimal outcomes in individual cases. It is also insensitive insofar as the person making the decision for her, such as a lawmaker, believes her judgment to be superior to that of the woman who is being saved from her own ostensibly poor judgment. Moral suasion is one thing; making personal choices for others because you think you know best more often than not reveals the kind of arrogance that characterizes an intolerant attitude toward difference. Whatever else might be said on behalf of such paternalism in terms of its overall consequences, it is certainly not treating her with the respect she deserves as an autonomous being who should be allowed to form, revise, and pursue her conception of the good without unnecessary interference by the state. In a liberal society, her marital decisions, like her other personal decisions, are her own. Her choosing to marry more than one person or be part of a triad is not the equivalent of her wanting to walk across a bridge that is going to collapse or allowing herself to be enslaved. It may be the best decision she ever makes or the worst one; it is hard to know in advance how her life will turn out. I suspect it would be much easier to take this paternalistic stance toward an abstract woman or the postmodernist other rather than toward a real woman who is fully committed to having a polygynous relationship and can eloquently articulate her personal reasons for preferring that option.

It would be nearly impossible to find someone who opposes polygamy or plural marriage on feminist grounds yet would deny choice to a woman who wants to procure an abortion. Of course, the rejoinder would be that the two situations are so different that it is offensive to even compare them. Still, one has to wonder why states are constitutionally compelled to respect personal choice in the latter but not in the former when having a child may worsen the quality of the woman's life in some respects. Moreover, in some cases, the decision to end a pregnancy may turn out to be wrong – at least in the sense that the woman subsequently regrets her decision and wishes she had acted differently. That is probably the exception, but the frequency of that reaction is not my concern. For those on the pro-choice side of the debate, that possibility cannot warrant the denial of reproductive choice. In fact, recently, pro-life advocates have appropriated the language of reproductive autonomy to justify certain requirements designed to discourage women from exercising their constitutional right.[4] For me, *Roe* stands for the proposition that the state may not evaluate the quality of her personal reasons for deciding to have her child or to terminate her pregnancy.[5] They may be good or bad or somewhere in between the two extremes. Regardless, the state must defer to her decision during what used to be called the first two trimesters. This requirement may explain why recent attempts to ground the constitutional right to abortion in a commitment to women's equality and equal protection jurisprudence will never fully succeed.[6] The personal choice aspect cannot be severed from its rationale. One can conceptualize a possible world in which the existence of legal and safe abortion did not advance the cause of gender equality but had the opposite effect. Even if this world existed, the decision to have a child (or not) would remain morally serious and the defense of such a constitutional right would have to appeal in one way or another to the value of letting women assess their own situation by leaving the decision to them prior to the viability of the fetus. One could respond that to choose a polygynous relationship is always wrong, whereas to choose an abortion is always right in terms of their respective outcomes, yet this response would overlook the extent to

4 See Jennifer M. Denbow, *Governed Through Choice: Autonomy, Technology, and the Politics of Reproduction* (New York University Press, forthcoming).

5 *Roe v. Wade*, 410 U.S. 113 (1973).

6 For alternative ways of writing the opinion in *Roe*, see Jack M. Balkin, What *Roe v. Wade* Should Have Said: The Nation's Top Legal Experts Rewrite America's Most Controversial Legal Decision, ed. Jack M. Balkin (New York: New York University Press, 2005).

which the consequences of such personal decisions are unpredictable. A woman could have good or bad personal reasons for making either decision. Constitutionally, the state should let her decide for herself what she wants to do – for better or for worse.

B. *The Challenge of Understanding Difference*

Such a paternalistic attitude toward abortion or plural marriage should not fly under the radar in such a liberal society as our own in which majorities often do not appreciate difference, understand the lives of others, or even make the effort to do so. The lives of many different kinds of persons, such as prisoners, felons, veterans, addicts, the elderly, the obese, the undocumented, the homeless, the intellectually disabled and the mentally ill, are not well understood unless a person has some kind of personal experience in which he or she begins to see how they actually live and comprehend the challenges that they regularly face. All of us have blind spots. This is one of the reasons why white persons have such a hard time grasping what it might be like to be victimized by racial discrimination. The problem is not just our obtuseness but our failure to acknowledge it and therefore plow ahead even when we fail to see what we need to see to understand the complexity of the situation. Too often, we pass judgment almost reflexively, miss the underlying causes of what transpires, and do not try to adopt the standpoint of others. Our unjustified confidence in the correctness of our judgment can be our worst enemy. A man who can only go through a pregnancy vicariously is probably not in an ideal position to make abortion policy and a straight person will often fail to grasp what it is like to be a sexual minority. The point is not that we can never identify with others who are different from us due to a lack of empathy but rather that we should be more reluctant to assess the quality of their lives and the attractiveness of their life plans when we have not walked a mile in their shoes, so to speak, and as a result, we lack the vision that would enable us to reach a more informed conclusion with sensitivity to the details. Some polyamorists refer to this care in making such judgments as being "nonjudgmental," which "means being willing to judge an activity or relationship on the basis of how well it works for the participants. . . ."[7]

That is not to say that people can never behave immorally simply because they believe what they are doing or plan to do is right. Rather, it is to say that those who are passing judgment on them and their choices must be mindful that they may not comprehend the importance of the difference in

[7] Dossie Easton and Janet W. Hardy, *The Ethical Slut: A Practical Guide to Polyamory and Open Relationships and Other Adventures* (2nd ed.) (New York: Celestial Arts, 2009), 274.

question nearly as well as they think they do. More often than not, the phenomenon in question may be morally and factually complex. Perhaps when it comes to the proper treatment of some minorities, it is more accurate to say that in this country right now, the glass is now half full (and not half empty) when more Americans seem to be more skeptical of their own supposed moral superiority. Ultimately, as they are trying to understand the lives of others, they are also trying to understand themselves. Particularly under conditions of moral pluralism, there is no virtue in being dogmatic or close-minded, and there is nothing wrong with admitting you might have been mistaken in your assessment of any situation when you become more knowledgeable about it and can develop a more sophisticated view.

Sadly, American history remains full of examples of the worst sorts of intolerance of different religious and cultural practices. That fact by itself should move us to be more careful as we venture into new territory. In the past, Mormons were the victims of such persecution.[8] Even today, FLDS members continue to find themselves on the end of hostility that typically would be considered inappropriate under conditions of moral pluralism. It should not come as a surprise, then, that they tend to react with suspicion toward a government that has a record of treating them with less than the dignity they deserve. This intolerance or unfair treatment may not be as blatant as that of *Reynolds*, where Chief Justice Waite disparages polygamy as a non-Western practice, but with respect to plural marriage, the double standard survives.[9] Polyamorists may be able to avoid such persecution better than FLDS by keeping their heads down, but they are not legally protected from employment or housing discrimination, and they could lose their children in a custody dispute because of their lifestyle.[10]

In a monogamous intimate relationship or marriage, adults can choose just about any arrangement with their partner that they want and treat each other well, decently, or terribly. Each of them has a legal right to stay in a physically or emotionally abusive relationship and that right has nothing to do with the merits of such a decision. Legally, people can have restraining orders rescinded if they subsequently change their minds and stay with or remarry those who have abused them. No one thinks that if the state could prove such abuse that it could divorce a couple without its consent. This hypothetical reveals how in monogamy, the law leaves almost all couples well enough

[8] See Sarah Barringer Gordon, *The Mormon Question: Polygamy and Constitutional Conflict in Nineteenth Century America* (Chapel Hill: University of North Carolina Press, 2002).

[9] *Reynolds v. United States*, 98 U.S. 145 (1878).

[10] Emens, "Monogamy's Law," 277, 310–12, 362.

alone until they want to end their marital relationship, even when they have the most dysfunctional of dysfunctional relationships. No doubt it is a tragedy for anyone to continue to go through such an ordeal, but that does not mean the state can do anything about it unless a crime has been committed. And even then, the state cannot force the couple to leave each other to save them from the unarguably poor choice of staying in an unhealthy or dangerous living situation. Adults are not children who can be taken away from their live-in partner or spouse by the state due to abuse, neglect, or other kinds of mistreatment.

True, the choice to stay may not be fully autonomous, but that can be said about many personal choices that ordinary people make in the imperfect circumstances that characterize the real world. For the person in question, that "choice" may make him or her happier than he or she otherwise would be and is probably autonomous enough. Even if Maura Strassberg is right, then, that "Mormon fundamentalist polygyny is about reproduction and patriarchy,"[11] adult FLDS women still have the right to choose it. They may value a certain way of life more than any of the alternatives and that choice is morally permissible. All of us have some ends that are similar but some that are different, and a person does not have to be Henry David Thoreau and be committed to an uncompromising individualism before he or she defers to how others want to live. In my view, there has to be a very strong presumption in favor of accepting what the adult woman in question ultimately decides and her decision has to be tolerated as long as she is free to end the relationship in the future. At some point, we have to take people as they are, not as we wish they would be or how we wish they had been raised. The implication is that all competent adults, including polygamists, ought to be free to choose inegalitarian intimate relationships, which is already the status quo for same and opposite-sex monogamous marriages. Furthermore, those who oppose plural marriage have not proven that plural marriages are demonstrably worse than their monogamous counterparts. Part of their failure has to do with the fact that data are unreliable. The other problem is that marital quality is difficult to measure.[12] For the double standard to be maintained, they would have to be able to support their rejection of plural marriage with more compelling evidence than they have assembled so far. As Brake observes: "Evidence of

[11] Maura Irene Strassberg, "Distinguishing Polygamy and Polyamory Under the Criminal Law," in *Families: Beyond the Nuclear Ideal*, ed. Daniela Cutas and Sarah Chan (London: Bloomsbury, 2014), 172.

[12] See Paul R. Amato et al., *Alone Together: How Marriage in America Is Changing* (Cambridge, MA: Harvard University Press, 2007), 37–38.

harm must be strong enough to override equality rights, and the simple absence of evidence does not meet this high bar."[13]

II. PROTECTING ADOLESCENTS AND CHILDREN

A. *Protecting Younger Women*

Many opponents of polygamy do not only concern themselves with adult women and their making ostensibly foolish decisions to enter inegalitarian or otherwise undesirable marriage-like relationships. A related concern is that most plural marriages will be traditional polygynous marriages, involving girls or young women – with little or no choice – in the setting of traditional patriarchal religious views about how men and women are supposed to interact. An underage girl who is pressured by her parents, relatives, or her community to marry a man who is twice her age and subsequently fathers his children over and over again is not the kind of difference that most multiculturalists have in mind when they seek to extend the boundaries of tolerance and resist cultural imperialism. An arranged monogamous marriage involving at least one person under the age of consent is equally troubling and persists in some cultures.[14] Usually, it is not young men who are being socially pressured or coerced into marriages they would not choose if the decision were left up to them.[15] For these reasons, it is hard not to be sympathetic to this "protecting young women" rationale. As Susan Moller Okin observes, polygamy (polygyny) involves controlling the sexuality of young girls and enhancing the power of older males by creating a significant age gap between husbands and wives.[16]

The flaw in this line of reasoning is that many of these problems are not about plural marriage among adults per se but about permitting girls or young women to be married to anyone when they lack the capacity to consent due to their age. While that problem may be hard to police, it is not evident that the legalization of polygamy, as discussed in the previous chapter, would make it any more difficult for the state to investigate and prosecute people for such crimes.[17] Such legalization could have the opposite effect if the polygamous

[13] Elizabeth Brake, "Recognizing Care: The Case for Friendship and Polyamory," *Syracuse Law and Civic Engagement Forum*, (2014), 14.

[14] Hegel thought arranged marriages were the most ethical form because they were not based on such a passion as love. On this point, see Brake, *Minimizing Marriage*, 10.

[15] However, the "lost boys" phenomenon shows how young men can be indirectly adversely affected by certain polygynous practices.

[16] See Okin, "Is Multiculturalism Bad for Women?" 15.

[17] Bennion, *Polygamy in Primetime*, 6.

arrangements of consenting adults were not a crime. The occurrence of these abuses in some polygamous communities is inevitable – after all, homes more generally can be dangerous places – but the issue involves what to do about them. Just about everyone agrees that such behaviors should not be tolerated. At times, opponents of decriminalization seem to believe the trouble lies in the failure of law enforcement agencies to enforce preexisting laws against sexual assault and child endangerment. At others, they seem to believe that decriminalization will make a bad situation even worse.

However, these abuses occur much more frequently in monogamous relationships and those who behave in such a manner should be criminally liable for what they have done. Opponents of polygamy have not proved that the legalization and concurrent recognition of plural marriage is at odds with the objective of protecting minors from sexual predators and others who would exploit them. It would seem to be easier to accomplish this important objective if plural marriages were not driven underground, thereby making it less difficult for victims to report such mistreatment and even escape from the community when necessary. Legalization may better protect the women and children in polygamous families, prevent coerced and underage marriages, and reduce welfare fraud.[18] Whether it has this effect can only be determined empirically. The current "don't ask, don't tell" policy with respect to the enforcement of antibigamy laws vis-à-vis FLDS communities may have the unintended and unfortunate ramification of protecting sexual predators who commit heinous crimes – which would remain illegal even if polygamy were decriminalized – by assisting them in avoiding detection. Their doing so is more likely to occur when most members of their community feel persecuted and do not trust outsiders. If one cares about protecting women, young adults, and children in polygamous communities from such crimes, then one should not be in favor of either overzealous enforcement or nonenforcement. The former has awful consequences for families that are not committing crimes by forcing them to live in fear as if they were criminals even when they have done nothing wrong. The majority of those who consider themselves to be FLDS do not live in such communities as those of Warren Jeffs and Winston Blackmore. Nonenforcement may be preferable compared with indiscriminate enforcement, but it still has serious difficulties of its own inasmuch as "don't ask, don't tell" facilitates such crimes as underage arranged marriages, incest, and

[18] See, for example, Emily J. Duncan, "The Positive Effects of Legalizing Polygamy: 'Love Is a Many Splendored Thing,'" *Duke Journal of Gender Law and Policy*, 15 (2008), 315–37. Martha Bailey et al., "Expanding Recognition of Foreign Polygamous Marriages: Policy Implications for Canada," in *Queens University Legal Studies Research Paper No. 7–12*. Prepared for Status of Women Canada, http://papers.ssrn.com/sol3/papers.cfm?abstract_id=1023896.

molestation by creating a culture in which victims fail to report them and witnesses are less willing to cooperate.

B. Cultural Defenses

In this section, let me briefly explain why cultural defenses of polygamy or plural marriage are not promising and why those who wish to defend the practice are better off looking elsewhere for support. Under contemporary conditions of multiculturalism, it is almost instinctual to point to the existence of any cultural practice and derive a rationale for tolerating it from its important place in a particular cultural tradition. This impulse may even be stronger in such a country as our own that has frequently been too eager to assimilate minorities and has not been terribly sensitive to the imperative of allowing such groups to practice their way of life as much as possible. In Jeremy Waldron's words, "there might be something particularly significant about *cultural* [his emphasis] resistance to a paternalistic or regulatory provision, which goes beyond a mere desire for liberty."[19]

In American constitutional law, probably the most famous case involving respect for religious difference is *Wisconsin v. Yoder*.[20] One way to construe the majority opinion is to elaborate on why the Supreme Court concludes that different ways of life cannot be condemned simply because of their differences. Although in the political science subfield of political theory multiculturalism has passed from the scene, it has left its mark. The fundamental normative insight, which such multiculturalists as Will Kymlicka and Charles Taylor drove home, is as relevant now as it was then: that some cultural practices – despite of how wrongheaded or strange they may appear to you and me – are an essential component of some people's way of life.[21] As such, a liberal state must resist the temptation to force cultural minorities to adopt practices they find to be foreign in the absence of a compelling justification for doing so. As John Gray writes, "it is hard to see how we can do without the practice of toleration."[22] A liberal

[19] Jeremy Waldron, "One Law for All? The Logic of Cultural Accommodation," *Washington and Lee Law Review*, 59 (2002), 15.

[20] *Wisconsin v. Yoder*, 406 U.S. 205 (1972).

[21] See, for example, Will Kymlicka, *Multicultural Citizenship: A Liberal Theory of Minority Rights* (Oxford, UK: Clarendon Press, 1995); and Charles Taylor, "The Politics of Recognition," in *Multiculturalism: Examining the Politics of Recognition*, ed. Amy Gutmann (Princeton, NJ: Princeton University Press, 1994), 25–73.

[22] John Gray, "Most of Our Beliefs Are Unwarranted, Even Absurd," Review of Brian Leiter, *Why Tolerate Religion?* www.newstatesman.com/print/culture/culture/2012/11/giant-leaps-mankind.

state must put up with some and perhaps many behaviors it would like to condemn. In some instances, that commitment entails protecting the freedom of those who would never return the favor if they were to constitute a political majority and therefore had political power to make the rules that would govern everyone.

Alternatively, to ask the majority to respect their way of life on its merits is probably asking too much. Invariably, most of us tend to judge such practices from the less-than-objective standpoint of our own system of values, which may be more parochial and less certain than we realize. Some cultures simply do not have liberal understandings of what makes a human life worthwhile and that reality poses a challenge to liberal states to decide how much freedom they will have to practice their way of life.[23] Those who adhere to such illiberal beliefs will not be bothered by behaviors, which some liberals might want to prohibit, and may even aggressively defend them when they are convinced their way of life is being threatened. The challenge of toleration in modern liberal democracies concerns deciding when interference would be appropriate and when the state should leave illiberal practices well enough alone.[24]

Bernard Williams refers to tolerance as an impossible virtue because he thinks it demands something like schizophrenia.[25] On the one hand, tolerance requires moral disapproval of the practice in question, such as polygamy. For him, by definition, one cannot tolerate what one morally approves of or finds to be morally acceptable. Herein lies what appears to be an intractable psychological difficulty: Tolerance asks us to permit what we believe to be morally erroneous.[26] According to Williams, the only way out of this dilemma is for the person who is asked to tolerate the behaviors in question to respect the autonomy of the person who requests what he or she does or plans to do be tolerated. To be tolerant, then, is to care much more about the process of letting the person in question choose and much less about its outcome. Even if Williams overstates the extent to which tolerance is a nearly impossible virtue, he identifies an attitude that will be excruciatingly difficult for most people to adopt: In some situations, others have a right to do what appears to

[23] Erin Kelly and Lionel McPherson, "On Tolerating the Unreasonable," *Journal of Political Philosophy*, 9 (2001), 38–55.

[24] One of the best theoretical treatments of this problem, in the context of civic education, is Stephen Macedo, *Diversity and Distrust: Civic Education in Multicultural Democracy* (Cambridge, MA: Harvard University Press, 2003).

[25] Bernard Williams, "Toleration: Impossible Virtue?" in *Toleration: An Elusive Virtue*, ed. David Heyd (Princeton, NJ: Princeton University Press, 1996), 18–27.

[26] This dilemma – a moral obligation to put up with what you morally disapprove of – is sometimes called the *paradox of toleration*.

be undeniably wrong. While few people still believe that consensual same-sex sex between consenting adults should be a crime, many Americans are convinced that such relations are sinful, and for some of them, that belief alone constitutes adequate justification for resisting the extension of the right of marriage to same-sex couples.

Any society that can tolerate most cultural differences is headed in the right direction, but the rationale for such treatment remains disputed. For most liberals, the best defense of any illiberal cultural practice has something to do with an attempt to tolerate it because it more or less has been chosen. As Williams points out, this approach may not be as effective as alternatives that rely on an attitude of indifference, but at least it is consistent with the liberal value of autonomy or personal choice. To try to defend any cultural practice simply because it happens to exist or has existed for a long time is not nearly as fruitful. Its continuing existence could have a number of causes, including the power that one group of persons, such as men, has exercised over another group of persons, such as women, to make it seem as if certain practices are fair to everyone, when in actuality, they serve the interests of the dominant group in that community and reinforce a morally disturbing hierarchy. One cannot infer from the mere existence of any practice that the practice is good, just, or should be continued. For example, no one today continues to believe that racial slavery in America was justified merely because it was central to the way of life in the antebellum South. Few people think that Michael Vick's lawyer's cultural defense of dog fighting during Vick's sentencing hearing – that the practice is widespread in the rural South where Vick grew up – was persuasive. A cultural defense of cockfighting, intimate partner violence, or honor killings would not (and should not) be taken seriously in the sense of permitting an exception to a rule that governs everyone else. According to Okin, certain cultural practices are bad for women.[27] Brian Barry maintains that certain cultural practices undermine equality.[28]

The trouble with cultural defenses more generally is that they cannot stand on their own; they must be supplemented by normative argumentation that tries to establish that the cultural practice in question is at least morally permissible beyond the brute fact it is a norm that many people in that culture

[27] Susan Moller Okin, "Is Multiculturalism Bad for Women?" in Susan Moller Okin, *Is Multiculturalism Bad for Women?* ed. Joshua Cohen, Matthew Howard, and Martha C. Nussbaum (Princeton, NJ: Princeton University Press, 1999), 9–24.

[28] Brian Barry, *Culture and Equality: An Egalitarian Critique of Multiculturalism* (Cambridge, MA: Harvard University Press, 2001).

accept and follow. That is why Muslim defenders of the practice of polygyny have advanced several normative reasons in its defense, including reducing the number of divorces and extramarital affairs, providing for illegitimate children, and protecting women from "spinsterhood" and prostitution.[29] Whether any of these reasons resonate in contemporary America is neither here nor there. Each reason must be assessed on its own strengths and weaknesses independent of its being rooted in a particular interpretation of the cultural tradition in question.

Multicultural critiques of liberal theory and practice were driven by legitimate concerns about cultural aggression and the extent to which the dominant culture made it too difficult for members of minority cultures to follow their own norms and pass on their respective ways of life to the next generation. In many cases, the state's trying to force such persons to assimilate as quickly as possible was not necessary or even desirable. In addition to outright persecution, cultural majorities can be indifferent to, insensitive to, and intolerant of cultural practices they do not comprehend or whose value they fail to appreciate. Even today, most Americans would probably fail a multicultural literacy test. However, one can endorse the concerns that multiculturalists have expressed without subscribing to the indefensible viewpoint that any culture may continue a practice simply because it has done so in the past and in spite of the harm it may cause. Justice cannot be sacrificed at the altar of respect for cultural difference. At most, an important cultural practice should enjoy a presumption in its favor depending on the situation, which can be overridden by compelling or important state interests. In a liberal society, those who defend any practice and maintain it ought to be legally protected have to make their case beyond a mere appeal to the degree to which members of a cultural minority have engaged in the practice being examined for a long time and want to continue to do so.

C. *Protecting Children*

The normative question of how children can be treated by their families, then, cannot simply be inquiry into how they are raised according to particular cultural practices – some of which may have aspects that fail to be morally tolerable. No doubt, as the future debate over plural marriage unfolds, critics

[29] Bhikhu Parekh, *Rethinking Multiculturalism: Cultural Diversity and Political Theory* (2nd ed.) (New York: Palgrave Macmillan, 2006), 282–83.

will insist that such marriage is bad for children. At present, the emerging consensus among almost all social scientists is that opposite-sex parents are not intrinsically better than same-sex parents.[30] Factors other than the gender of the couple seem to have a much more significant impact on child development. As I shall show in this section, the view that plural marriage will undermine the welfare of children will be hard to defend because (a) children can be protected more directly from harm[31]; (b) all things being equal, multiparent arrangements could be a superior parenting framework compared with the two-parent model; and (c) even if all things are not equal, in the real world, the alternatives may be worse.[32] In what follows, drawing on the kinds of arguments that opponents of same-sex marriage have put forth concerning the welfare of children, my aim is to anticipate the forms they will take in the coming debate over plural marriage.

Beginning in the 1990s, it became increasingly common – even for some of those to the left of the center of the political spectrum – to join the family values crusade and link the alleged breakdown of the family to the decline of traditional marriage. This project involved not only defining "the family" but also defending a distinct version of it by emphasizing the welfare of children. As President Bill Clinton moved the Democratic Party to the center, William Galston, a prominent political theorist and member of the Clinton administration, insisted that such conservatives as Dan Quayle had been correct all along: that strengthening the traditional two-parent family was indispensable to raising children who were more likely to be well-adjusted, responsible adults.[33] In a widely read *Atlantic Monthly* article in 1993, Barbara Whitehead wrote that many children do not respond well to divorce or remarriage and that these disruptions make it harder for them as adults to have their own stable marriages or to hold steady jobs.[34] Some studies indicate that two-parent families benefit children more than single-parents ones.[35] Positions like this

30 But see Mark Regnerus, "How Different Are the Adult Children of Parents Who Have Same-Sex Relationships? Findings From the New Family Structures Study," *Social Science Research*, 41 (2012), 752–70.

31 See Cass R. Sunstein and Richard H. Thaler, "Privatizing Marriage," *Monist*, 91 (2008), 385.

32 On this point, See Goldfeder and Sheff, "Children of Polyamorous Families," 169–70.

33 William A. Galston, *Liberal Purposes: Goods, Virtues, and Diversity in the Liberal State* (Cambridge, UK: Cambridge University Press, 1991), 283–89. His basis of comparison, though, was single-parent households.

34 www.theatlantic.com/magazine/print/1993/04/dan-quayle-was-right/7015

35 See, for example, Amy Wax, "The Two-Parent Family in the Liberal State: The Case for Selective Subsidies," *Michigan Journal of Race and Law*, 1 (1996), 491–550.

one have had a considerable impact on family policy and continue to be used to rationalize limiting marriage to different-sex couples.

While it lasted, this trend was unfortunate not only because it gave conservatives ammunition in the battle over same-sex marriage, but it also made it seem as if unconventional families were less worthy of support. These days, a common tactic of those who continue to oppose same-sex marriage is to downplay moral disapproval of being gay or lesbian and instead to call attention to how two-person opposite-sex marriages are better for children than any of the alternatives. This tactic is rhetorically effective to the extent that the debate about the meaning of marriage can be cast in terms of child development, which minimizes how laws that do not permit same-sex couples to marry discriminates against them. For example, David Blankenhorn believes that marriage is "fundamentally about the needs of children."[36] In his view, having a father (male) and mother (female) who are married – both of whom are the biological parents of the child – defeats any of the alternatives, such as having two same-sex parents; a single biological father or mother; a biological father or mother and a stepparent; unmarried biological parents; or a caregiver who is not a parent, such as a grandparent, or another relative or nonrelative who has adopted the child. Unlike earlier critiques, which attacked cohabitation, out-of-wedlock reproduction, and divorce, Blankenhorn connects the problem of the family to same-sex marriage. For him, the purpose of marriage is to raise well-adjusted children and same-sex marriage does not serve that end because it undermines "the basic idea of a mother and father for every child."[37]

As Blankenhorn reveals, he would support same-sex marriage if it turned out to benefit children.[38] But as he interprets the existing data, that is not the case. Thus, the expansion of the definition of marriage, even if it also had some positive externalities, would change the culture of marriage, leading more people to conclude that marriage does not have to be between a man and a woman. It is important to keep in mind that Blankenhorn's view is not that same-sex marriages directly undermine the welfare of children. Rather, because they shape how the public thinks about the institution, they indirectly and ultimately cause even more children to be brought up in less-than-ideal situations – namely, those where the primary caregivers are not married and are not their biological parents.

[36] Blankenhorn, *The Future of Marriage*, 2. [37] Ibid., 3.

[38] Ibid., 19–20. It is worth noting he subsequently switched sides. See Jo Becker, *Forcing the Spring: Inside the Fight for Marriage Equality* (New York: Penguin Press, 2014), 313–19. Better late than never.

D. Critique

Although Blankenhorn and Okin do not have much in common, both of them see the family as central to the proper raising of children. For the latter, the family serves as "an important locus for the development of a sense of justice."[39] In her words, "if the relationship between a child's parents does not conform to basic standards of justice, how can we expect that child to grow up with a sense of justice?"[40] In a different time and place, Mill made the same observation in his *The Subjection of Women*.[41] For most political theorists, he is the only male member of the canon who has anything close to a modern-day feminist sensibility.[42] Nonetheless, according to Okin, even Mill does not seriously question the traditional division of labor within the family.[43] As she points out, in the history of political thought, theorists are fond of using an idealized concept of the family in rationalizing why it falls outside the scope of justice.

If one wants to take a slightly different tack and contend that plural marriages set a bad example for children, one immediately runs into further obstacles. Unfortunately, parents set bad examples for their own children (and for other children) all the time – through such behaviors as alcohol and drug abuse, violence, manipulation, racism, sexism, homophobia, intolerance, out-of-control gambling, irresponsible spending, infidelity, callousness, excessive attention to physical appearance, and crass consumerism. The list of human vices and psychological disorders is as long as it is disheartening. Less dramatically, parents can push their children too hard to accomplish what they could not accomplish themselves and live vicariously through them. For every John Stuart Mill or Tiger Woods, there are probably thousands of children who did not turn out so well due to unrealistic parental expectations

39 Okin, *Justice, Gender, and the Family*, 135. 40 Ibid.

41 John Stuart Mill, *The Subjection of Women*, ed. Susan Moller Okin (Indianapolis: Hackett, 1988), 86–88.

42 The earliest and most famous argument in favor of the abolition of the family – if it can be taken at face value – is found in Plato's *Republic* in the section following the discussion of the equality of women. Plato argues that for the guardian class to be sufficiently unified, the common sources of political conflict, such as private interest, must be removed. Thus, guardians may not have traditional families. Rather, like other kinds of property, women and children must be held in common. With communal living arrangements, parents and children will not know each other's identities, and the philosopher kings control sexual relations at festivals for eugenic purposes. The aim is to turn what would be loyalty to one's family into loyalty to the city-state. *The Republic of Plato*, trans. Francis MacDonald Cornford (New York: Oxford University Press, 1945), 155–68.

43 Susan Moller Okin, *Women in Western Political Thought* (Princeton, NJ: Princeton University Press, 1979), 226.

and excessive pressure. Parents are not under a legal duty to follow their children's wishes, respect their autonomy, identify their talents, reinforce their self-esteem, or even care about what they want to do with their lives. They are free to impose their visions of the good life on them, provided they do not abuse or neglect them.

Some opponents of plural marriage maintain that we should not be eager to permit practices that encourage the subordination of women, put the apparent imprimatur of the state on them, place those practices entirely beyond the reach of the law, and teach children that such an arrangement is morally permissible. Granted, children may acquire beliefs and learn behaviors that a liberal society probably wants to discourage. On the other hand, exposure to gender injustice may have the opposite effect.[44] A child of an alcoholic may not repeat such behavior but after witnessing the detrimental effects might decide not to drink or might at least monitor his or her thought processes and actions more closely to avoid compulsivity. As Elizabeth Brake writes: "What matters greatly to child psychological development is continuity of care, which is available in polygamous, same-sex, single-parent, and extended families."[45] Marriage sometimes benefits but sometimes harms children.[46] In high-conflict marriages, women and children may be much better off outside of marriage.[47]

One of the conspicuous advantages of an extended family lies in the availability of multiple persons to share domestic labor, including child care, without having to incur the additional expense of paying someone else to do it and also leaving the safety and well-being of your child in the hands of a stranger. Children may benefit from the existence of multiple caregivers.[48] By comparison, two parents may have less time and energy to provide the supervision and care their children need. Also, parental multiplicity may be more conducive to enabling each child to develop his or her potential to its fullest. The existence of multiple caregivers increases the odds that each child will have a parent who has different talents and interests. It is not hard to imagine that a child who has musical, artistic, academic, or athletic talent, for example, would benefit greatly from a parent who also has such ability and is willing to mentor him or her.

[44] Linda C. McClain, *The Place of Families: Fostering Capacity, Equality, and Responsibility* (Cambridge, MA: Harvard University Press, 2006), 83.

[45] Elizabeth Brake, "Minimal Marriage: What Political Liberalism Implies for Marriage Law," *Ethics* 120 (2010), 318.

[46] Ibid., 317. [47] Stacey, *In the Name of the Family*, 60.

[48] Sanford Levinson, "The Meaning of Marriage: Thinking About Polygamy," *San Diego Law Review*, 42 (2005), 1056.

That is not to say that Blankenhorn is entirely wrong. One can appreciate why Americans must be concerned about the welfare of their children and the kinds of adults they will become someday. Because marriage is closely related to such development, they might be expected to take some interest in the health of the institution as a means to that end. Family law incorporates a legal standard that considers what legal disposition will serve the best interests of the children.[49] They should not only be protected from sexual, physical, and emotional abuse and neglect but should be raised in environments that help them cultivate their talents, develop their identities, and prepare them for adulthood.[50] Without question, alternative parenting structures – even if not optimal according to the traditional criteria – may still meet the needs of children well enough in an imperfect world. Inevitably, many children will not be raised by their biological parents. As a result, even Blankenhorn would have to concede that policymakers can consider "less than ideal" options in some cases.[51]

A state that refuses to let same-sex couples adopt children is not only invidiously discriminating against gays and lesbians, but it is also depriving children who would otherwise be adopted of the kind of care they are entitled to, especially when foster care in most places leaves so much to be desired. Even when one believes same-sex relations to be sinful and same-sex couples to be inferior parents, it does not follow that such couples should not be allowed to adopt children when the alternatives often are inferior. Unless one also thinks that children should be punished to send a message of moral disapproval to sexual minorities or that the worst foster care is better than the best same-sex parenting, any reasonable person would have to conclude that such adoptions must be permitted.

Rhetorically, it is not hard to imagine why framing the issue in such a manner – saving the children – has been so effective. Who is opposed in principle to doing what is best for children when it is obvious that children are vulnerable and poor parenting has serious social costs? However, once we look beyond sound bites, it becomes evident that Blankenhorn may be wrong on two counts: (1) that marriage should be thought of as a child-centered institution and (2) that traditional marriage usually serves the best interests of children. On (1), as Martha Fineman observes, if the interest of the state in

49 William Burnham, *Introduction to the Law and the Legal System of the United States* (5th ed.) (St. Paul, MN: Thomson Reuters, 2011), 527–32.

50 There are, of course, very different parenting styles – some of which are bound to generate controversy. See, for example, Amy Chua, *Battle Hymn of the Tiger Mother* (New York: Penguin Group, 2011).

51 Brake, "Minimal Marriage," 316.

marriage is the caretaking of children due to their dependency, then the state could pursue this interest through policies that directly promote their welfare.[52] The parenting framework and the legal duties parents have toward their children can be detached from the marital relationship. On (2), many biological parents fall short of the ideal and some of them fall so far short that the state takes their children from them and places those children in foster care – either temporarily or permanently. As a statistical generalization, even if married biological parents constituted the best parenting arrangement, individualized assessment would still be called for. It would be cold comfort for a child who grows up in a two-parent but dysfunctional household to be told that statistically, the odds are in his or her favor. In some cases, reinforcing a high-conflict marriage can worsen the living situation for children.[53]

No one thinks these bad parents should be automatically divorced if they are married and prohibited from marrying and having children ever again. Blankenhorn cares more about the form of a marriage than its quality – like many of those who reject plural marriage – and refuses to examine the particulars of each kind more closely. The problems associated with his child-centered view do not end there. Not only do Americans disagree profoundly over what "best" means in this context – just think about the wide range of opinions about the meaning of being a good parent – but also over the most appropriate route to that destination. As an example, it is far from obvious that making divorce more difficult to obtain – for example, moving away from a no-fault regime – would serve the best interests of all children. Even from a consequentialist standpoint, more sophisticated analysis would contain an itemization of the costs of preserving marriages that are likely to be characterized by conflict and for that reason detrimental to the well-being of the children.[54] According to Fineman, the burdens that women (and children) may bear if divorce were made more difficult to obtain cannot be wished away.[55] A thoughtful person has to worry that "saving the children" does not account for the drawbacks of inducing couples to stay together who have unhealthy or abusive relationships. As Linda McClain observes: "Overemphasis on family form as such obscures the importance of variables

[52] Martha Albertson Fineman, *The Autonomy Myth: A Theory of Dependency* (New York: The New Press, 2004), 108.

[53] Eric M. Cave, "Marital Pluralism: Making Marriage Safer for Love," *Journal of Social Philosophy*, 34 (2003), 236.

[54] Judith Stacey, *In the Name of the Family: Rethinking Family Values in the Postmodern Age* (Boston: Beacon Press, 1996), 78–80.

[55] Fineman, *The Autonomy Myth*, 87.

such as the emotional tenor of families and the quality of both the parent–child and parent–parent relationships."[56]

In this age, most people concede that children of divorced parents are likely to be relatively disadvantaged, but that state of affairs often results from how divorce renders children susceptible to poverty when the male takes his earning power with him when he leaves the household, the challenges of collecting child support payments, and the emotional turmoil that custody and visitation arrangements may cause, not to mention the inevitable trials and tribulations of life. A society that is truly committed to the welfare of children does not have to rely as heavily as it does on parents or relatives to provide them with basic goods and services.[57] Here, I am not saying anything that has not been said more eloquently before by other scholars. More generous child support and child allowances would soften the financial blow of divorce on children. Marriage does not have to function as an antipoverty program.[58] The economic vulnerability of children need not be contingent on their good or bad luck of being born into certain conditions.[59] Overreliance on marriage as an antipoverty program may impede the formulation of other more promising solutions.[60] When it comes to children, the deeper question concerns the proper balance between personal and public responsibility for their care.

The narrow focus on the husband–wife dyad, then, fails to pay sufficient attention to the inner dynamics of each family and the possibility that socioeconomic benefits – many of which are currently filtered through marriage – could come from elsewhere in a more just society. The main advantages of the two parents, compared with a single parent, lie in higher income and more thorough supervision.[61] On average, children of parents who have remarried may do worse than children who live with single parents.[62] To reduce the debate about the meaning of marriage to the welfare of children, as Blankenhorn does, has further weaknesses. First, many married couples do not have children and that is often by choice. One of the most morally important decisions that anyone can make is whether to bring a new human being into

56 McClain, *The Place of Families*, 127.

57 In its current form, marriage privatizes dependency. See Martha Albertson Fineman, "Why Marriage?" in *Just Marriage*, ed. Mary Lyndon Shanley (New York: Oxford University Press, 2004), 46–51.

58 On this point, see Fineman, *The Autonomy Myth*, 89.

59 McClain, *The Place of Families*, 21.

60 Fineman, *The Autonomy Myth*, 122.

61 Nancy D. Polikoff, *Beyond (Straight and Gay) Marriage: Valuing All Families Under the Law* (Boston: Beacon Press, 2008), 74.

62 Andrew J. Cherlin, *The Marriage-Go-Round: The State of Marriage and the Family in America Today* (New York: Vintage Books, 2009), 22.

the world, particularly in conditions that are not conducive to the child's well-being. I doubt most parents treat this decision with the care it deserves and that may be a tragedy, but I do not see what the law can do about it. That is the price of the privatization of the upbringing of children in a liberal society like our own.

Nor is there an inevitable conflict between the rights of children and the rights of same-sex couples, as some opponents of same-sex marriage have led us to believe. Under no scenario will the state enthusiastically take children from their married biological parents and hand them over to same-sex couples. For Blankenhorn, an increase in the number of same-sex marriages will ultimately lead to fewer married biological two-parent couples, which in turn will lead to fewer children growing up in what he thinks of as an ideal environment. Over and over again, he chants the mantra of "for every child, a mother and father."[63] Too often, however, "Do it for the children" amounts to emotional blackmail. In many instances, the actual choice is not between two biological parents and an obviously inferior alternative but among a number of suboptimal possibilities according to the traditional criteria of the well-being of children. There is a tendency on the part of those who are critical of traditional families to concede far too much to traditionalists in the name of trying to be charitable. It is not empirically beyond dispute, though, that the two-parent heterosexual family is the best arrangement for children when other family structures may achieve the same or even better results. The key to their normal development is financial and emotional support that need not come from a married opposite-sex couple. The quality of the upbringing of children depends on the ability and willingness of their care-giver(s) – whomever they happen to be – to provide them with what they need.

In the real world, the relevant basis of comparison is not between an ideal nuclear family and every other allegedly second-best option but among various imperfect options. Some two-parent nuclear families will be inferior to what Blankenhorn sees as nonideal arrangements. Is an exceptional mother really worse than two mediocre or bad parents? At times, Blankenhorn's nostalgia for the traditional family is hard to put up with. It is true that the traditional justification for state regulation of marriage is child welfare, but the legal benefits and obligations of marriage are not directly about children.[64] In all states, biological but unmarried parents are equally responsible for child support.[65] In some cases, parents who stay together purportedly for the good

[63] Blankenhorn, *The Future of Marriage*, 101.
[64] Eskridge, *The Case for Same-Sex Marriage*, 117.
[65] Burnham, *Introduction to the Law and the Legal System of the United States*, 519.

of the children are making a terrible mistake. Marriages that are characterized by physical, emotional, or substance abuse are usually beyond repair and hardly provide the kind of environment where children will grow up to be well-adjusted adults. At minimum, policymakers should avoid sentimentality and resist the temptation to endorse the belief that biology magically transforms people into better parents than they otherwise would be. As long as raising children remains more of a private than a public matter, as it always will be in a free society, the quality of the marriage and family environment will depend on a wide variety of factors, including socioeconomic and cultural ones. A single parent might turn out to be better at parenting if he or she has the resources many two-parent households have. Single-parenthood is positively correlated with low income and society continues to stigmatize such parents (and their children).

Not everyone is cut out to be a parent, and the physical ability to procreate has nothing to do with parenting in the sense of raising a child that is adequately prepared for the challenges of adulthood. Regrettably, it is far too common for people to conflate the biological ability to reproduce with what is supposed to occur afterward, which is the much harder part. My point is not just about abuse and neglect but also other kinds of undesirable behaviors, such as manipulation, thoughtlessness, selfishness, irresponsibility, stupidity, laziness, deceit, and dishonesty. In marriage, we cannot hide from ourselves, and sooner or later, our weaknesses as human beings come to the surface, as painful as that process may be. This is common sense, and therefore it is unnecessary for me to elaborate on why children are sometimes better off when their biological parents do not stay together, even if we did not give a damn about allowing the parents to make their own decisions. At present, every state has no-fault divorce laws.[66] Such laws would not have the widespread appeal they do if the public did not share this sentiment. The availability of no-fault divorce is not simply a matter of letting people be selfish by putting their own desires ahead of those of their children, as some critics continue to portray it. The decision to end the marriage may be the best decision for everyone, including the children. Blankenhorn is silent about the high costs of preserving some high-conflict or miserable marriages, particularly those that have serious detrimental effects on children.

In *The Future of Marriage*, he devotes much of his energy to documenting the history of marriage to prove that over time, a shared understanding of the meaning of marriage across time and culture has come into being.[67]

[66] Ibid., 509. [67] Blankenhorn, *The Future of Marriage*, 23–89.

Unfortunately, Blankenhorn papers over cultural differences and some of its most unpalatable aspects. As Stephanie Coontz has shown, the complexity of the history of the family has been obscured by recent political rhetoric.[68] Marriage has always had multiple purposes and effects – some positive and some negative – including the reinforcement of gender, racial, and even religious hierarchies.[69]

The historical record is complicated but should not substantiate the claim that the institution of marriage and its evolution can be reduced to procreation and the welfare of children. In the end, Blankenhorn's opposition to same-sex marriage is predicated on his prediction that the legal recognition of same-sex marriage will inevitably further the decline of traditional marriage, which will then negatively affect how a substantial number of children are raised. His defense of the state's limiting marriage to opposite-sex couples is contingent on the facts. If it turns out empirically that same-sex couples parent as well or better than their opposite-sex counterparts on average, then his defense collapses, assuming we can agree on what counts as better parenting in the first place. The risk of such an empirical defense is that the facts – when they become available – may ultimately support the contrary position. Blankenhorn does not have a crystal ball and the conclusion regarding the superiority of opposite-sex parents he reaches turns on a number of questionable predictions – none of which are certain or even likely to occur.

The legal recognition of same-sex marriage may have a negligible effect on the traditional institution of marriage. Or it may strengthen it in that such recognition will encourage more people over time to think through their marital commitments, to take them more seriously, and to encourage flexibility and experimentation in a rapidly changing world. Only time will tell. In any event, marriage could be more a product of genuine choice and less a product of norms that are supposed to be followed because they are norms. My intention is not to indulge in my own equally speculative judgments about the future of marriage or how well comparatively same-sex couples parent (if they choose to raise children) in general but to note that it is nearly impossible to ascertain at this moment what effects the legal recognition of same-sex or plural marriage will have over time. What is evident is that the effects of such recognition will depend on the surrounding social, political, and economic structures, including more tolerant attitudes toward sexual minorities and less conventional families. If one really cares about the future

[68] Stephanie Coontz, *The Way We Never Were: America's Families and the Nostalgia Trap* (New York: Basic Books, 1992).

[69] Cott, *Public Vows*, 4–5.

of American families, there are many more sensible ways to strengthen them without attacking or undermining unconventional ones, as if their existence made an enormous difference.[70]

III. CHILDREN AND POLYGAMOUS FAMILIES

This child–welfare rationale for not permitting same-sex marriage may extend to polygamy; that is, if multiperson relationships are bad for children, then that is another argument against legal recognition of such relationships. Blankenhorn refers to "poly parenting" in passing.[71] What children must have, as he puts it, are (biological) mothers and fathers.[72] Oddly enough, from Blankenhorn's standpoint, having more than one "father" or "mother" as caregivers would not necessarily undermine the welfare of children. Children may be loved and nurtured in unconventional families, provided that their caregivers have the necessary skills and the motivation to use them. They may benefit from having more than two adults to talk to about their lives and receive advice. It is probably fair to say that most children are more inclined to discuss important issues with one parent rather than the other, and some of them may not feel comfortable sharing any aspects of their personal lives, such as their problems and self-doubts, with either parent. Several states already allow children to have more than two legal parents, including California.[73] The presence of multiple parental figures would probably benefit children more often than not due to the presence of multiple caregivers who could better coordinate their efforts in nurturing their children and providing for their material needs; it is not hard to see how three or four parental figures could be advantageous in most situations.

The sample size of polygamous and polyamorous families is probably too small to generate any reliable results about how well poly-parents parent.[74] Even such a vocal critic of polygamy as Strassberg admits that more data on contemporary polygamous families is needed before how they impact children can be evaluated.[75] This much is for certain: The empirical case against plural marriage on child welfare grounds needs considerably more evidence. At present, it is far from compelling. It may not take an entire village to raise a child, but it stands to reason that all things being

70 See Martha C. Nussbaum, *From Disgust to Humanity: Sexual Orientation and Constitutional Law* (New York: Oxford University Press, 2010), 98.

71 Blankenhorn, *The Future of Marriage*, 258. 72 Ibid., 3.

73 https://verdict.justicia.com/2013/10/15/california-allows-children-two-legal-parents.

74 However, some recent qualitative research shows that concerns about poly-parenting may be exaggerated. See Goldfeder and Sheff, "Children of Polygamous Families," 150–243.

75 Strassberg, "The Challenge of Post-Modern Polygamy," 560.

equal, parental multiplicity may be even more conducive to meeting children's needs. Indeed, it may turn out that on average, the existence of more than two caregivers is the superior parenting arrangement.

A. *Child Abuse*

As mentioned, some critics of polygamy maintain that the practice facilitates child abuse and that the state should be able to ban it to shield children from such harm. The trouble with this view is that (1) parenting can easily be separated from marriage or marriage-like relationships[76], and (2) almost all people can practice polygamy without abusing or neglecting the children. Even in Utah, which has a history of persecuting polygynous families, such families are legally permitted. Under Utah's penal code, criminal liability can be incurred only when the participants try to marry in a private ceremony or represent themselves as being married. Furthermore, nationally, the overwhelming majority of abused and neglected children do not grow up in polygamous households.[77]

For the sake of argument, though, let us once again assume the worst: Children who grow up in polygamous households are more at risk of being abused or neglected than those who grow up in a more traditional family, controlling for other factors. First, it is not acceptable to proscribe an otherwise legitimate practice merely because it "tends to encourage" other kinds of crimes.[78] In Elizabeth Emens's view, the penal code can directly address the worst problems associated with traditional religiously motivated polygyny, such as underage girls being coerced into marriages and being physically abused.[79] Those who act in this manner should be prosecuted for what they have done – just like anyone else who commits the same serious crime.[80]

The argument about secondary effects reminds me of American television programs that used to depict the dangers of dealing drugs, engaging in prostitution, and smuggling illegal immigrants across the border in graphic detail but fail to contextualize them. One does not have to be a Libertarian to see that many of the bad secondary effects of such lines of work stem from

76 On this point, see Brake, *Minimizing Marriage*, 149–51.

77 Turley Report, 29–30.

78 Slark, "Are Anti-Polygamy Laws an Unconstitutional Infringement on the Liberty Interests of Consenting Adults?" 458.

79 Elizabeth F. Emens, "Just Monogamy?" in *Just Marriage*, ed. Mary Lyndon Shanley (New York: Oxford University Press, 2004), 76.

80 Steve Chapman, "Two's Company; Three's a Marriage," *Slate*, June 4, 2001.

their illegality.[81] A more enlightened national policy with respect to controlled substances, sexual services, and immigration would address the exploitation and violence that surrounds them due to the conditions under which they exist. Similarly, the decriminalization of polygamous relationships may reduce problems associated with some of them, such as incest, child abuse, statutory rape, and underage "marriage."[82] While understandable, the disposition to criminalize them to prevent other crimes "evades the real issue of how best to protect the women who either choose or accept a polygamous lifestyle."[83] Additionally, no state currently criminalizes polygynous cohabitation.[84]

B. *Child Welfare*

Blankenhorn concedes that "polygynous marriage conforms to the principal [sic] that each marriage unites one woman with one man" and he also remarks that much rarer polyandry "is a similar case."[85] For him, a monogamous, opposite-sex marriage more closely resembles a polygynous or polyandrous marriage than a monogamous same-sex marriage does when it comes to children and their well-being. As the basis of a legal restriction, then, sexual orientation is more relevant than numbers. Those who oppose plural marriage can still play the child welfare card by insisting that plural marriage is bad for children even if it does not increase the likelihood they will be abused or neglected. As Bhikhu Parekh writes: "Since the polygamous marriage is likely to be marked by jealousy, unhealthy competition for affection, insecurity, intrigue and mutual manipulation, it is also unlikely to create an environment conducive to the balanced growth of children."[86]

First, Parekh has particular Muslim polygynous marriages in mind, and as I have reminded readers repeatedly, polygyny is only one possible kind of plural marriage. Second, even if Parekh is correct that the dynamics of a typical polygynous marriage set a poor example for children and, for this reason they are less likely to become well-adjusted adults or good citizens, that statistical generalization alone is not conclusive. In a monogamous

[81] See, for example, Randy E. Barnett, "Curing the Drug-Law Addiction: The Harmful Side Effects of Legal Prohibition," in *Drugs: Should We Legalize, Decriminalize or Deregulate?* ed. Jeffrey A. Schaler (Amherst, NY: Prometheus Books, 1998), 155–80.

[82] Brake, *Minimizing Marriage*, 199.

[83] Michele Alexandre, "Big Love: Is Feminist Polygamy an Oxymoron or a True Possibility?" *Hastings Women's Law Journal*, 18 (2007), 5.

[84] Brake, *Minimizing Marriage*, 200.

[85] Blankenhorn, *The Future of Marriage*, 255.

[86] Bhikhu Parekh, *Rethinking Multiculturalism: Cultural Diversity and Political Theory* (2nd ed.) (New York: Palgrave Macmillan, 2006), 290.

relationship, a couple is legally allowed to engage in all sorts of inappropriate behaviors for their children to emulate someday, but no one seems to think that such a couple should be denied the right of marriage or to have children. Parekh intimates that the chance of such behaviors occurring in monogamous households is considerably lower. His doing so is to commit the fallacy of comparing the worst polygamous relationships with the best monogamous ones. Because many monogamous relationships or marriages damage children, it is not evident that plural forms are or would be worse.[87] A plural marriage could be more conducive to the raising of children when there are multiple caregivers and multiple incomes and thus greater familial stability. Polygamous parents could more easily institute a more efficient division of labor with respect to parenting responsibilities, which can cause trouble for single parents and even couples, especially when both of them work outside the home to earn two incomes. Also, a plural marriage may turn out to be good for children because one person's leaving the marriage or a death probably would not be as disruptive.[88]

C. *Parenting*

Remember that in this country, parents can pretty much bring up their children however they please. One concern in the context of FLDS or Muslim polygyny is that children will be taught traditional gender roles, never critically evaluate them, and then live according to them. The most important personal decisions they ever make will be based on beliefs they might reject if they were more autonomous or at least had been brought up differently. Morally, this a legitimate concern, but politically and legally, the issue is more complicated. By definition, to be an antiperfectionist liberal is to be hesitant to use the coercive power of the state to endorse a particular way of life as being the best kind of human life. It is regrettable that people who grow up in such environments are much less autonomous than those who are raised by parents who encourage them to partake in Millian experiments in living, but it is not evident that the state can (or should) do anything about this problem by legislating against it. The same could be said of how most people are socialized – regardless of the configurations of their families.

87 Will Kymlicka, "Rethinking the Family," Review Susan Moller Okin, *Justice, Gender, and the Family Philosophy and Public Affairs*, 20 (1991), 92 and n. 17.

88 See Philip L. Kilbride, *Plural Marriage for Our Times: A Reinvented Option?* (Westport, CT: Bergin & Garvey, 1994), especially 10–11, 18–22.

As I see it, this lack of being taught critical reflection is a shame and this world would be a better place if this did not happen as often as it does. Obviously, my view reflects a distinct moral theory that many people would not share. Also, short of draconian measures, I do not see how the law can address such concerns. We are understandably disturbed by how some or even many parents bring up their children. The legal line is drawn at serious physical or emotional abuse or neglect and the state may not remove children from such homes in the absence of such occurrences. The consequence is that parents may inculcate in their children whatever beliefs or values they believe to be most important. They may name their children after leaders of the Third Reich, raise them to believe white people are superior to black people (or vice versa), let them shoot automatic weapons at some guns ranges even when they are too young to use them safely, tell them AIDS is a plague from God, convince them the Antichrist is on his way, inform them Earth is at the center of the solar system, teach them homosexuality causes earthquakes, let them believe African slavery in the antebellum period did not exist or insinuate that it benefitted slaves, and/or indoctrinate them into believing abstinence-only sex education is more effective than any of the alternatives. That is the price of living in a society that not only takes the free exercise of religion seriously but also respects the almost absolute rights of parents to control the upbringing of their children.

In what I wrote here, I may have conceded too much to those who insist that polygamous living arrangements do not serve the interests of children. A strong theoretical case can be made that such arrangements might work better for them more often than not given the numerous advantages of having multiple caregivers. Even though empirically the jury is still out, some recent research indicates that all things being equal, the more, the merrier when it comes to parenting.[89] Polyamorists maintain that having multiple parents is superior to the two-parent model or a single parent. Here, my aim is not to settle this dispute but instead to point out that opponents cannot simply assert that polygamy is always bad for children and leave it at that, as if there were nothing to be said on behalf of the advantages of the presence of more than two caregivers. At the end of the day, so much ultimately depends on the particulars of each situation. The most obvious and perhaps compelling rationale for preferring a polygamous structure over the traditional dyad parallels the advantages of having an extended family. Family members can

[89] See Elisabeth Sheff, *The Polyamorists Next Door: Inside Multi-Partner Relationships and Families* (Lanham, MD: Rowman & Littlefield, 2014).

pool their resources, enjoy greater financial security, and implement a more efficient division of domestic labor, even when the arrangement in question is far from ideally egalitarian. A bad father or mother (or absent one in either case) cannot cause nearly as much trouble or damage when another, more competent parent can step in if need be, like a player coming off the bench. This point can be extended to caretaking involving not only children but also the elderly and disabled adults. That is not to say that everyone should prefer polygamy or plural marriage, but in some circumstances, it may be advantageous in terms of the amount and quality of the caregiving.

When it comes to same-sex marriage and the capacity of same-sex couples to raise children, the empirical child welfare argument is weak.[90] Same-sex couples may raise children who are more tolerant, which is a virtue in such a society as our own characterized by moral disagreement and various kinds of diversity. Usually, this belief – that children can become better citizens or better people when raised in such an environment – is premised on the likelihood that living in an unconventional family will help expand their moral imagination by showing them how a much wider variety of familial structures is not only possible but also desirable. Some commentators maintain that the state may subsidize the two-parent family at the expense of other kinds, but the implicit basis of comparison is a single parent or an unmarried couple.[91] True, a family that has what seems to be too many children may not be able to expend the necessary resources on all those children so each one of them develops into the best person he or she can be. But no one believes there should be a cap on the number of children a two-parent family can have even if they cannot afford them or give them the love and attention they deserve.

For polyamorists, children are more likely to flourish in the midst of more than two committed caregivers.[92] There is an old Woody Allen joke that "most people do not survive one mother." However, it would seem that multiple caregivers – who have the parenting skills and the willingness to care for the children – would be a superior arrangement – all things being equal. Normally, we have no problems with close friends or relatives' assisting in providing child care. This is one of the reasons why – compared with single-person and even two-person households – extended families can provide better child care; additional persons can do whatever needs to be done. In this

90 See Courtney G. Joslin, "Searching for Harm: Same-Sex Marriage and the Well-Being of Children," *Harvard Civil Rights – Civil Liberties Law Review*, 46 (2011), 81–101.

91 See, for example, Wax, "The Two-Parent Family in the Liberal State," 491–550.

92 See, for example, Deborah Anapol, *Polyamory in the Twenty-First Century: Love and Intimacy with Multiple Partners* (Lanham, MD: Rowman & Littlefield, 2010).

country, it is common for couples who work outside the home and can afford to hire help for child care do so. Moreover, the effect of a bad or mediocre parent might be offset when a better parent could do what either the bad parent does not want to do or cannot do competently. In the end, it would seem that the quality of parenting would come down to the parents – however many there happen to be – and whether they have the motivation, parenting skills, economic and social resources, and time to devote to raising their children. In this regard, a single parent may be much better than two indifferent or selfish parents and a household with three or more parents may turn out to be superior.

IV. ADMINISTRATIVE CONSIDERATIONS

The purpose of this section is not to detail how family law could be reformed to accommodate multiperson marital relationships but only to explain why such objection is not decisive. Unlike a monogamous marriage, unique complications may arise when an individual either seeks to enter or exit an extant plural marriage due to its multiperson form. Even if women are not disadvantaged, in terms of their typical bargaining power before the formation of the marriage, they may be after its beginning, which is called the "paradox of polygamy" in the literature.[93] As such, any regulatory scheme will have to take into account how women could be exploited by the male when a plural marriage is polygynous.

It is important to not forget that polygyny is not the only form a plural marriage could take. In this section, I use it as an example because no one is too worried about one gay man taking advantage of his two other spouses or a sister exploiting her three other sisters, as if such behavior is unlikely to be present in multiperson but nonpolygynous arrangements. The underlying assumptions are probably false. Friends can take advantage of friends, siblings can take advantage of siblings and other family members, and husbands can take advantage of wives (and vice versa) in monogamous relationships. The presence of a thruple or a moresome changes how the persons would bargain with one another.[94] When it comes to plural marriage, then, the question that has to be addressed is how multiplicity renders its participants uniquely vulnerable to be exploited, calling for regulations more like those of business partnerships.[95] As Adrienne Davis writes: "Regulation can only do so much to

[93] See, for example, Adrienne D. Davis, "Regulating Polygamy: Intimacy, Default Rules, and Bargaining for Equality," *Columbia Law Review*, 110 (2010), 1995–97.

[94] Ibid., 2043. [95] Ibid., 1999.

alleviate vulnerability and opportunism."[96] As much as possible, then, the aim is to reduce the kind of strategic behavior that is more likely to occur in a plural marriage and produce unfair outcomes.

At this stage, research on the topic is preliminary. Among the few family law scholars who have devoted their time to it, the consensus seems to be that family law could be restructured in the event of the state's recognizing different types of plural marriage without too much difficulty.[97] Over time, as the topic of plural marriage becomes less taboo and the popular discourse more sophisticated, I expect more academics will come up with promising ideas about how family law could be altered in the face of marital multiplicity as they learn from experience. In what follows, I plow ahead by showing how legal scholars, who have been doing such research, have made impressive progress on how family law could be revised to address the unique challenges that plural marriages would present. At least for the time being, the tentative conclusion should be that they would be so difficult to administrate that they cannot be permitted. Although many ordinary people seem to think that family law could not possibly accommodate plural marriages, there is not a single academic article or book that shares that view. At most, family law scholars argue for the necessity of creating safeguards for those who would enter or leave such a marriage.

Thus, one cannot reflexively conclude that the state cannot or does not have to recognize plural marriages because it would be administratively out of the question to do so.[98] So far, those who are skeptical about such reform have not defended their skepticism in any depth. Rather, they make quick points about administrative difficulties – as if they are obvious and need no defense – and encourage their readers to surmise that the difficulties cannot be overcome. But as Diane Klein states: "Whatever political or social barriers to the legalization of plural marriage – and they may be insurmountable – it cannot be fairly said that it would be impossible to adjust our laws to take account of it."[99] Here, my goal is to take some of the sting out of the objection that family law could not possibly be reformed to cover different kinds of multiperson marital relationships and to offer some tentative suggestions based on the growing body of family law scholarship that focuses on

96 Ibid., 2020. 97 See Mark Goldfeder, *Legalizing Plural Marriage*, especially 147–86.

98 March refers to administrative considerations as "unforeseeable legal-administrative complications." Andrew F. March, "Is There a Right to Polygamy? Marriage, Equality and Subsidizing Families in Liberal Public Justification," *Journal of Moral Philosophy*, 8 (2011), 246.

99 Diane J. Klein, "Plural Marriage and Community Property Law," *Golden Gate University Law Review*, 41 (2010), 81.

their administrative aspects. If the past is the best predictor of the future, family law has proved to be remarkably resilient in responding to fundamental societal changes. The claim that plural marriage would be administratively untenable needs more support than it has received so far.[100]

That is not to say that all skepticism will evaporate. For example, William Eskridge claims that such marriage would threaten the social safety net and create confusion over custody decisions, who would make medical decisions for the husband or wife if he or she were unable to do so for him or herself, and so on.[101] The practical challenge of extending marital entitlements to more persons is not to be dismissed but neither is it to be overstated, as if the state could not reform marriage law to address the most serious problems. If it really were impossible for the law to accommodate such relationships, then that fact could be used to contend that the legal definition of marriage should not be changed. Normally, something done exclusively for administrative convenience will not count as an important state interest and thereby serve as a reason to deny equal treatment.[102]

That said, there may be exceptions to this general rule when it comes to what Brake refers to as "ludicrously large marriages."[103] For such a consideration to be decisive, though, it would have to be the case that plural marriage would cause such administrative havoc with respect to marital property, immigration, custody and visitation of children, and taxation that it would be unworkable. As it turns out, that is not an easy hill to climb. If a marriage were to become so large and complicated that it would be administratively unmanageable, then the state could properly limit its size, as opposed to disallowing all such marriages because some of them are problematic. The state could not restrict marriage to couples only because some marriages potentially could be so large that they could present serious administrative challenges. Keep in mind that their alleged seriousness would have to be proved and not merely speculated about by those who are looking for an excuse to deny adults the right to plural marriage. The same could be said about the concern that the existence of plural marriage would invite immigration fraud by allowing American citizens to marry more than one noncitizen at the same time to sponsor him or her for permanent residency. The government could continue to do what it already does: Use marriage fraud

[100] Phone conversation, Mark Goldfeder, May 13, 2014.

[101] Eskridge, *The Case for Same-Sex Marriage*, 148–49.

[102] *Craig v. Boren*, 429 U.S. 190 (1976).

[103] Brake, "Minimal Marriage," 310. http://slace.syr.edu/slace-journal-vol-1/recognizing-care-the-case-for-friendship-and-polyamory. In the *Old Testament*, King Solomon had seven hundred wives and three hundred concubines. 2 Samuel 5:13.

tests and investigate such cases more carefully to determine whether the second, third, or fourth marriage in question is fraudulent. Also, as Brake points out, immigration policy already recognizes multiple family members.[104] No one seems particularly concerned that a parent can sponsor all of his or her minor children for citizenship, even when the number is in double digits. After all, it is not as if minimizing fraud is only a state interest when it comes to marriage or that short of a complete ban, the state is powerless to do anything about the problem. According to Mark Goldfeder, regulation would probably decrease fraud.[105] If the state could not effectively prevent marital fraud, which would be hard to believe if it devoted enough resources to this public policy goal, it could simply limit the number of spouses concerning immigration benefits to three or four.

Martha Ertman was the first legal scholar to propose that the certain commercial partnerships could serve as models for how family law could be modified to take into account marital multiplicity.[106] The basic (and promising) idea is that some business models are analogous to some intimate relationships and can be used to regulate entrance into and exit from them, as if the plural marriage were a business association. That may not be romantic, but overly sentimental views about traditional marriage and nostalgia about the past impair our thinking by preventing us from seeing what can go wrong in a marriage (and what to do about it). Unlike family law, business law "recognizes a range of valid arrangements."[107] The legal resources for such modification, then, can already be found in business law, which provides much greater flexibility than current family law.[108] For example, a partnership can be likened to two-person cohabitation and a close corporation to a two-person marriage.[109] A plural marriage can be analogized to a limited liability corporation – that is, a hybrid of a partnership and a corporation.[110] Done properly, the incorporation of business models into family law could counteract inequality.[111]

Additionally, several other law professors have begun to address how polygamous relationships might be regulated given the main purposes of

[104] Elizabeth Brake, "Recognizing Care: The Case for Friendship and Polyamory," *Syracuse Law and Civic Engagement Forum* (2014), 2.

[105] Mark Goldfeder, *Legalizing Plural Marriage*, 174.

[106] Martha M. Ertman, "Marriage as Trade: Bridging the Private/Private Distinction," *Harvard Civil Rights – Civil Liberties Law Review*, 36 (2001), 123–31; Martha M. Ertman, "The Business of Intimacy," in *Feminism Confronts Homo Economicus: Gender, Law, and Society*, ed. Martha Fineman and Terrance Dougherty (Ithaca, NY: Cornell University Press, 2005), 467–500.

[107] Ertman, "The Business of Intimacy," 492. [108] Ibid., 468. [109] Ibid., 491–92.

[110] Ibid., 489. [111] Ibid., 493.

family law.[112] Davis also draws upon commercial partnership law to explain what could happen when one of the participants wants to leave the marriage or someone else seeks to enter it.[113] Both possibilities raise questions about how marital property would be affected. This concern may necessitate granting veto power to everyone in the marriage because his or her share of the marital property might be diminished with the addition of new spouses, not to mention other ways in which he or she might be impacted. When a new member enters or an old member leaves – voluntarily or via death – either a new marriage would be formed (after the old one had been dissolved) or the currently existing one would be transformed. That is probably the most fundamental practical issue. In either case, as Klein puts it, "new marital property concepts" would be required.[114]

But they would not have to do "violence to any of the basic principles of the marital property system."[115] The resulting task in the future would involve moving family law beyond dyads and regulating marital multiplicity in a manner that captures the unique problems that are likely to arise in such relationships and does not give up without exploring possible analogues. One worry is how bargaining power is distributed in marriage.[116] For Davis: "Multiplicity can generate additional chances for opportunistic and exploitative behavior that runs counter to contemporary family law's investment in formal equality and fair treatment."[117] In this respect, dyadic marriage – opposite or same sex – differs from its plural counterpart. Specifically, the addition of spouses during the marriage may shift power in the marital relationship.[118] A unanimity rule – in which everyone in the marriage must consent to a new person's becoming a part of it – could be an immutable rule (not subject to contract or negotiation).[119] Such a rule would protect those who would otherwise be vulnerable as the marriage expanded and might be an exception to the general rule that competent adults can form whatever kind of marriage they want to form. Or before another person marries a person you are already married to, the law could require you to receive legal advice before you consent to the new arrangement so you are aware of how the change affects you financially.

The law already accommodates *de facto* or serial polygamy.[120] The impressive progress that such scholars have made so far indicates that the claim that

[112] See, for example, Diane J. Klein, "Plural Marriage and Community Property Law," 39–57; and Davis, "Regulating Polygamy," 1955–2046.

[113] Ibid., 2002–04. [114] Klein, "Plural Marriage and Community Property Law," 2.

[115] Ibid., 6. [116] Davis, "Regulating Polygamy," 1962. [117] Ibid., 1955, 1995.

[118] Ibid., 1991–97. [119] Goldfeder, *Legalizing Plural Marriage*, 166.

[120] Davis, "Regulating Polygamy," 1964.

family law could never be reformed to accommodate thruples and groups is exaggerated. It should not be too easy for opponents of plural marriage to play such a card when family law could be altered to accommodate multi-person intimate relationships. The historical solution to the problems for women associated with patriarchal monogamous difference-sex marriage was not abolition but regulation.[121] According to Goldfeder, for multiperson unions, a dyadic network model – where people are free to be married to more than one person concurrently – is better than the group model, where everyone is married to everyone else and thus constitutes a single marital unit.[122] If there really is a good argument against the legal recognition of plural intimate relationships, it is probably not to be found in alleged administrative impossibility.

V. THE ARGUMENT FROM TRADITION

A. *American Conservatism*

Like some of those who oppose same-sex marriage, those who oppose plural marriage can be expected to fall back on "tradition" to justify their opposition. Here, I shall explain why even nuanced forms of this line of reasoning will not work. What counts as "tradition," of course, is subject to controversy. When we let same-sex couples marry, are we departing from our tradition and discounting its purported wisdom or honoring our commitment to the fair treatment of all persons? Ultimately, the most jarring change with respect to marriage would be its abolition – understood as complete state withdrawal from the institution, with the exception of the enforcement of private contracts. The advent of same-sex marriage in this country still strikes many Americans as a dangerous break from the past, but that belief does not necessarily make it so. After all, what counts as a departure from tradition turns on how one understands that tradition.

Traditionalists also frequently gloss over past marital diversity in this country and abroad.[123] As Brake writes: "So-called traditional marriage is historically variable."[124] For traditionalists who consider themselves to be Burkean conservatives, what is supposed to be conserved is relative to time and place and each society has its own distinct traditions that are worth conserving. In this respect,

[121] Ibid., 2037. [122] Goldfeder, *Revisiting Polygamy*, 187–90.

[123] In China, for example, the Na had no marriage practice. Brake, *Minimizing Marriage*, 2. Furthermore, multiperson marriages, especially polygynous ones, have been common in many societies.

[124] Brake, *Minimizing Marriage*, 2.

Burke was a proto-multiculturalist. American conservatism is "deeply and unmistakably liberal in inspiration."[125] American Burkean conservatives, then, try to conserve a particular political tradition, which is distinctly liberal in character and thus values individual freedom to some extent and may include the right to choose different kinds of marriages.

Another problem is that appeals to tradition can take different forms. According to Brake, the "love revolution" did not come about until the eighteenth century.[126] The problem I believe has to be taken most seriously stems from the value of not breaking too quickly from past practices and unsettling people's expectations and ways of living. Constitutionally, for some judges, constitutional rights are only those that are "deeply rooted in this Nation's history and tradition."[127] Two constitutional law scholars characterize Justice Samuel Alito's jurisprudence as Burkean.[128] The more radical the change, the more disruptive and disorienting it can be, but change can and does occur. At particular historical moments, the ideas of interracial and same-sex marriage probably seemed disruptive to the "proper" social order. The most serious flaw in the well-known "Argument From Tradition" – where we continue to define civil marriage in a particular way because we have always defined it in that way – is that it cannot stand on its own. Just because a behavior or social institution has existed over time does not mean it should continue to exist, especially when it is unjust or troubling in other ways. Otherwise, the status quo would always be at least morally tolerable and reformers would never have reason to tinker with it. Therefore, those who want to rely on "tradition" must put together a separate normative defense that elaborates on why past practices must be assigned so much moral weight. In *The Conservative Mind*, as Russell Kirk makes clear, Burkean conservatives are not opposed to change – after all, it is inevitable – but rather prefer such change to take place slowly to avoid the disruption that ensues following sharp departures from the past.[129] It is more accurate, then, to characterize the conservative mind that Kirk valorizes as an attitude of risk aversion. The more sudden the change, the more likely it is to have bad unintended consequences and that likelihood should not be minimized.

[125] Peter Berger, "Ideologies, Myths and Moralities," in *The Americans: 1976 (Critical Choices for Americans)* vol. II, ed. Irving Kristol and Paul Weaver (Lexington, KY: Lexington Books, 1976), 347.

[126] Brake, *Minimizing Marriage*, 10.

[127] *Moore v. East Cleveland*, 431 U.S. 494, 503 (1977).

[128] Tribe and Matz, *Uncertain Justice*, 142.

[129] Russell Kirk, *The Conservative Mind: From Burke to Eliot* (7th revised ed.) (Washington, DC: Regnery Publishing, 2001), especially 3–70.

There are a number of powerful, probably decisive objections to Burkean conservatism, even in a more sophisticated form, and I will not list all of them here. Instead, I want to focus on one of them – namely, what I call the vagueness objection.[130] It has never been sufficiently clear, in Burkean accounts, when change is too large or so radical that it ought to be resisted. For example, during the Civil Rights movement, many conservatives were willing to continue to put up with racial discrimination.[131] An important passage of Martin Luther's King Jr.'s famous "Letter From Birmingham Jail" involves urging moderates to reject the view that political activism or non-violent resistance can wait. Any Burkean conservative will respond that the right course of action requires prudence or judgment in which the decision-maker is not supposed to apply abstract principles mechanically but rather pays close attention to the particulars of the situation. It is hard to take issue with that approach unless one believes that principles can apply themselves or should be applied without sensitivity to the context. A Burkean conservative has to presume that change is more likely than not to be unfavorable, and if it has to occur at all, then it ought to be managed as carefully as possible. Ultimately, that preference for gradualism is rooted in a consequentialist rationale. It is not a coincidence that Cass Sunstein's Burkean-inspired judicial minimalism is preoccupied with adverse consequences.[132]

Perhaps the most infamous reliance on tradition in a modern constitutional case is found in Justice Byron White's majority decision in *Bowers v. Hardwick*, where the Supreme Court upheld a Georgia statute that made it a crime for consenting adults to perform certain kinds of sex acts.[133] In *Washington v. Glucksberg*, Chief Justice William Rehnquist appeals to tradition to deny a constitutional right to suicide.[134] In a number of well-known cases, Justice Scalia takes a similar tack by bringing up the levels of abstraction problem when it comes to defining constitutional rights and insists that tradition can limit judicial discretion.[135] For example, in his dissent in *Lawrence*, he cites

130 See Anthony Quinton, "Conservatism," in *A Companion to Contemporary Political Philosophy*, ed. Robert E. Goodin and Philip Pettit (Cambridge, MA: Blackwell Publishers, 1995), 244, 261.

131 See, for example, Barry Goldwater, *Conscience of a Conservative* (Shepherdsville, KY: Victor Publishing, 1960), 41–47.

132 Cass R. Sunstein, *One Case at a Time: Judicial Minimalism on the Supreme Court* (Cambridge, MA: Harvard University Press, 1999); Cass R. Sunstein, *A Constitution of Many Minds: Why the Founding Document Doesn't Mean What It Meant Before* (Princeton, NJ: Princeton University Press, 2009).

133 *Bowers v. Hardwick*, 478 U.S. 186 (1986).

134 *Washington v. Glucksberg*, 521 U.S. 702 (1997)

135 See, for example, *Michael H. v. Gerald D.*, 491 U.S. 110, 122 (1989).

Washington v. Glucksberg – "which held that fundamental rights are 'deeply rooted in this Nation's history and tradition'" – to deny that the right to same-sex consensual sex is fundamental.[136]

At the very least, it is strange to fall back on tradition to determine whether a right is truly fundamental when one would expect that if such a right were fundamental, a lawmaking body would not have infringed on it in the first place. That approach would seem to be superfluous. The very fact that a lawmaking body does not recognize the concrete right in question indicates it probably cannot be easily found in the relevant tradition. Not all judges, of course, are so willing to defer to the purported wisdom of tradition. In *Lawrence*, Justice Kennedy elaborates on why the "tradition" the majority had relied on in *Bowers* should not be followed.[137] It would seem as if mere reliance on tradition – because it is tradition – will not work without an additional normative argument that establishes that it makes more sense not to change course. Scalia can respond to this worry in several ways – all of which involve a defense of reliance on tradition – at least with respect to determining which constitutional rights are fundamental. According to one scholar, Scalia's original meaning approach to constitutional interpretation reflects a commitment to text and tradition.[138] When constitutional language is more open textured, Scalia believes that the judge must apply "the specific legal tradition flowing from that text" and investigate how the society that adopted those words would have understood them.[139]

That is easier said than done because as noted, tradition cannot speak for itself; it calls for interpretation and application. In the United States and most other places, something like licensing parents would qualify as being too radical, but most of our political choices lie in between the two extremes of too radical and perfectly acceptable, as in gradual enough for even a Burkean conservative. Sixty years ago, many Americans did not tolerate cohabitation, interracial marriage, divorce, children being born out of wedlock, same-sex romantic relations, and gender equality and would have equated marriage with procreation.[140] The advent of same-sex marriage no longer seems to be a dramatic departure from our "tradition," especially when national public

[136] *Lawrence v. Texas*, 539 U.S. 558, 589 (2003).

[137] *Lawrence v. Texas*, 539 U.S. 558, 568–72 (2003).

[138] Ralph A. Rossum, *Antonin Scalia's Jurisprudence: Text and Tradition* (Lawrence: University Press of Kansas, 2006).

[139] Ibid. 2.

[140] Pamela Haag, *Marriage Confidential: The Post-Romantic Age of Workhorse Wives, Royal Children, Undersexed Spouses and Rebel Couples Who Are Rewriting the Rules* (New York: HarperCollins, 2011), xv.

opinion polls reveal that American attitudes are rapidly changing. The extension of the right to marriage to same-sex couples is not only long overdue but also reflects a longstanding commitment to equal treatment under the law. It is not so much that we are abandoning tradition, then, but that our interpretation of the meaning of equality has changed over time – whatever its past referents – and for the better in the name of respecting human dignity. By finally extending the right of marriage to gays and lesbians, we are honoring the principles of our constitutional tradition that make it worthy of such reverence.

That said, a "damn the consequences, full speed ahead" approach may not be practical if it leads to a backlash. If the Supreme Court in *Hollingsworth* had decided that the Constitution requires same-sex marriage – known as the *fifty-state solution* – those who continue to oppose such marriage might have pushed a constitutional amendment, such as the one President George W. Bush proposed, that would limit marriage to one man and one woman. Such an amendment would be very difficult to repeal if it were ratified by three-fourths of the states. That caution may explain why three liberals – justices Stephen Breyer, Elena Kagan, and Ginsburg – did not want to reach the merits, even if with Kennedy and Sonia Sotomayor, they would have had the five votes necessary to nationalize same-sex marriage. In Peter Berkowitz's view, a commitment to what he calls "constitutional conservatism" dictates that the question of same sex-marriage should be left to the states.[141] This remains the current position of moderates who fear that the country may be moving too fast in a direction that too many Americans find disorienting. Sunstein also believes that Americans should tread cautiously and permit states to experiment with same-sex marriage without national intervention.[142] More or less, that is what the Supreme Court has done so far, but that trend may change in the near future.

Political conservatives purport to follow tradition by insisting that marriage must be between one man and one woman.[143] In the past, this strategy has had considerable success in the ongoing debate over same-sex marriage, but a cursory examination of the literature on the history of marriage reveals they are defending a particular interpretation of that tradition where they pick the aspects of so-called traditional marriage they like and discard the rest. When conservatives maintain that the meaning of marriage in this nation and

[141] Peter Berkowitz, *Constitutional Conservatism: Liberty, Self-Government, and Political Moderation* (Stanford, CA: Hoover Institution Press, 2013), 120.

[142] Cass R. Sunstein, "Of Federalism and Caste," in *Just Marriage*, ed. Mary Lyndon Shanley (New York: Oxford University Press, 2004), 41–45.

[143] See, for example, Blankenhorn, *The Future of Marriage*, 91.

elsewhere has always been the same, they are wrong.[144] Historically, marriage has had different functions and different meanings to different people at different times in different places.[145] Only relatively recently has marriage in the United States, for example, been companionate or about self-fulfillment.[146] The meaning of marriage continues to evolve.[147] Consequently, it is disingenuous to pretend that what marriage is like today has much resemblance to what it was like more than two hundred years ago or, for that matter, even fifty years ago. Even the most conservative of contemporary conservatives would reject certain aspects of the so-called traditional marriage they claim to be championing. Presumably, they would not want to return the country to the kind of marital regime portrayed in a Jane Austen novel. Under coverture, wives could not own property, make a will, earn a living, form a valid contract, leave their husbands, sue their spouse for a personal injury, or protect themselves against intimate partner violence and sexual assault. John Stuart Mill famously compared their condition to that of slaves.[148] Morally, tradition may leave something to be desired and it cannot speak for itself to solve any important political or legal problem for us. That is why the debate over the meaning of marriage cannot be exclusively historical or anthropological.

In the ongoing debate over the meaning of marriage, even someone as sympathetic to same-sex marriage as Andrew Koppelman acknowledges that perhaps states should be able to decide for themselves – if only to avoid antagonizing social conservatives.[149] Surely, consequences matter. Only the most extreme forms of deontological ethics would incorporate the contrary view. On the other hand, the unintended consequences of not acting can be serious too. This may be more obvious when it comes to foreign policy, but I believe it is equally true with respect to domestic issues. For example, during the Civil Rights movement, inaction on the part of the federal government may have fostered the subsequent massive resistance in the Deep South by sending a message of appeasement to white Southerners that they were welcome to resist the mandate of the

[144] Nancy F. Cott, *Public Vows: A History of Marriage and the Nation* (Cambridge, MA: Harvard University Press, 2000).

[145] Coontz, *Marriage, A History*, 1.

[146] Paul Amato et al., *Alone Together: How Marriage in America Is Changing* (Cambridge, MA: Harvard University Press, 2007), especially 11–18.

[147] See Fineman, *The Autonomy Myth*, 99.

[148] John Stuart Mill, "The Subjection of Women," in *On Liberty and Other Writings*, ed. Stefan Collini (Cambridge, UK: Cambridge University Press, 1989), 123.

[149] Andrew Koppelman, *The Gay Rights Question in Contemporary American Law* (Chicago: University of Chicago Press, 2002), 141–54.

Brown opinion.[150] Not to mention that putting off the racial desegregation of public facilities meant continuing to sacrifice the constitutional rights of African-Americans. I shall not discuss the philosophically complicated distinction between acts and omissions, but I simply want to point out that the refusal to protect same-sex couples from discrimination may also have bad consequences depending on the situation and on what counts as "bad." It should not be so easy, therefore, for those who are uneasy with change to play the bad consequences card when the consequences are usually so uncertain, and on balance, they may turn out be good.

Some recent national polls indicate that a majority of Americans already favor same-sex marriage.[151] Popular attitudes toward such marriage are changing rapidly and younger persons are more likely not to object to it. Koppelman remains agnostic about the existence of a slippery slope between the legal recognition of same-sex marriage and that of plural marriage.[152] As I shall show in the next two chapters, the same kinds of reasons that support a constitutional right to same-sex marriage – respect for freedom of choice and A commitment to external equality – also lead to such a right to plural marriage. I want to emphasize that even if there is (or should be) a constitutional right to plural marriage, it does not follow that the judiciary should impose such a right on the states without considering the likely adverse consequences. If compelling reluctant states to create only civil unions for such people for the time being would be prudent, then surely there is something to be said for a more cautious approach until the winning of more hearts and minds makes the timing more fortuitous. As we have learned from the ongoing debate over same-sex marriage, the "m" word is special for both sides. One who opposes plural marriage, then, cannot simply rely on the claim that marriage has always been between two people in this country. At the end of the day, "tradition" will not do much work; the real normative work must come from elsewhere.

VI. ARGUMENTS FROM NATURE

A. *Nature*

Last but not least, in this section, my aim is to deconstruct arguments against plural marriage that appeal to nature, including the new natural law (NNL),

[150] Michael J. Klarman, *Brown v. Board of Education* and the Civil Rights Movement, abridged ed. (New York: Oxford University Press, 2007), especially 79–104.

[151] www.gallup.com/poll/147662/first-time-majority-americans-favor-legal-gay-marriage.aspx (May 20, 2011)

[152] Andrew Koppelman, "Judging the Case Against Same-Sex Marriage," *University of Illinois Law Review*, 447–48, n. 94 (forthcoming). Available at http://ssrn.com/abstract=2257557.

which has not yet passed from the scene.[153] The initial complication is that those who make such arguments usually have same-sex marriage in mind. They only use the possibility of marrying multiple persons simultaneously to discredit same sex-marriage by trying to establish that if marriage is not defined exclusively as being between a man and a woman, then it can be defined however one pleases. That is a non sequitur; that the law permits two women to marry does not imply that a man may marry his cat, his armchair, or his favorite golf club. Still, they are correct in their assertion that the legal recognition of same-sex marriage invites us to consider unconventional definitions of marriage. Like other progressives, I just do not believe that our doing so is mistaken. Conservatives who oppose same-sex marriage claim that marriage will be deinstitutionalized if same-sex couples are allowed to marry, but it is probably more accurate to describe the change as "re-institutionalization" inasmuch as the institution will continue to exist but will be more inclusive. One could have – and some did – made the same argument with respect to any change in how marriage is defined at any point in American history, including invalidating bans on interracial marriage.

In the history of political thought, theorists have often appealed to nature to argue for or against certain political arrangements, particularly hierarchical ones where some people are supposed to be by nature better suited to exercise political power than others are.[154] For this alone reason, in a democratic age, such appeals to nature are suspect. Furthermore, some people were believed to be naturally incapable of engaging in the kinds of thinking and virtuous behaviors that are essential to political life, making them less than fully human. Aristotle used nature to distinguish between different sorts of slaves and to differentiate men from women.[155] Ancient and medieval political thinkers assumed that some persons were naturally or divinely ordained to rule others. A question about the legitimacy of political rule for them would only come about when those who were "inferior" by nature held political power. By contrast, early modern political thinkers who appealed to natural rights and social contracts were convinced that the basis of political legitimacy had to be located in another source – namely, some sort of consent. In a democratic age, where there seems to be no better government than some form of democracy, it is much harder than it used to be to rely on nature to

[153] For objections to new natural law views with respect to marriage, see Brake, *Minimizing Marriage*, 71–80.

[154] Burke also made references to nature. See, for example, Edmund Burke, *Reflections on the Revolution in France* (Garden City, NY: Anchor Books, 1973), 61.

[155] Aristotle, *The Politics*, trans. Stephen Everson (Cambridge, UK: Cambridge University Press, 1996), 11–15.

produce political justifications for various sorts of unequal treatment. When it comes to present-day gender discrimination, fewer persons would take seriously the claim that women are not naturally suited to practice law, to work as bartenders, or to serve as military or correctional officers because experience has proved they are fully capable of doing so. In 1996, Justice Ginsburg emphatically rejected this kind of thinking in rendering the Virginia Military Institute's (VMI) all-male admissions policy unconstitutional.[156]

However, our widespread commitment to equality has not stopped some Straussians from appealing to nature in developing and defending what might be called an elitist or aristocratic liberalism.[157] Allan Bloom is well known for introducing a vulgar form of Straussianism that attacks egalitarian thinking and behavior in higher education and insists that some kinds of inequality are natural.[158] Such antifeminists as Bloom insist that feminists do not acknowledge the "reality" of natural differences between men and women. These antifeminists claim that natural differences based on gender do not imply the inferiority of women but rather that these differences set the limits of what is socially possible and that laws and policies that ignore them are doomed to failure. Along similar lines, Harvey Mansfield develops an antifeminist argument that underscores how men and women possess different natural capacities and thus can be expected to have different virtues.[159] For Mansfield, feminism has a target on its back because most of its variations attempt to alter what cannot be altered; nature limits what men and women can be, even if outliers may sometimes exist. The rhetorical advantage of appealing to nature is that if the appeal is successful, it is hard to refute because it would be akin to arguing that German Shepherds should be able to vote. What is natural should not be tinkered with and institutions that are not premised on natural differences cannot possibly work. In his concurrence in *Bowers*, Chief Justice Warren Burger quoted Blackstone's remark that same-sex sex acts are an "infamous crime against nature."[160]

[156] *United States v. Virginia*, 518 U.S 515 (1996).

[157] See Shadia B. Drury, *The Political Ideas of Leo Strauss*, updated edition (New York: Palgrave Macmillan, 2005); and Ann Norton, *Leo Strauss and the Politics of American Empire* (New Haven, CT: Yale University Press, 2004). For a defense of Strauss, see Catharine and Michael Zuckert, *The Truth About Leo Strauss: Political Philosophy and American Democracy* (Chicago: University of Chicago Press, 2006).

[158] Allan Bloom, *The Closing of the American Mind* (New York: Simon and Schuster, 1987).

[159] See, for example, Harvey C. Mansfield, *Manliness* (New Haven, CT: Yale University Press, 2007).

[160] *Bowers v. Hardwick*, 478 U.S. 186, 197 (1986) (Burger, J., concurring).

Appeals to nature more generally are tricky because those who employ the term often exploit its vagueness. The first problem with appeals to nature is that some natural (as in statistically common) behaviors should be discouraged or even criminalized. It may be natural to blame others and not take any responsibility for one's wrongful actions or for men to be aggressive or even violent, but that does not mean it is a virtue or even morally acceptable to behave in such a manner, as if one could not act differently. Plenty of scientific evidence indicates that nonmonogamy is more natural in the sense that many mammals, including humans, are hardwired to prefer multiple sexual partners.[161] Around the world, polygamy is common.[162] The second problem is that it is hard to know what is natural and what is not, as Mill once astutely observed in *The Subjection of Women*.[163] Thus, even if such natural differences did exist, it may be nearly impossible to discern what is really natural when it comes to human beings because we only observe those who have already been socialized. Nevertheless, Hadley Arkes contends that marriage is rooted in nature.[164] At the outset, this claim is peculiar because marriage is a social institution and a legal status and the debate is typically about which intimate relationships should be recognized by the state. If, say, it were unnatural for men to marry men but they are permitted to form such a legal relationship where they live and decide to do so, they would still be married in the eyes of the law and would be treated as such. It would be incoherent to insist they are not really married when they have fulfilled all the legal requirements. The third problem is that the term *natural*, as John Corvino states, "has normative force, as well as strong emotive connotation."[165] As he continues, "to call something 'unnatural' is not to *describe* [his emphasis] its infrequency but to *prescribe* [his emphasis] its avoidance."[166] For example, when someone says same-sex sex acts are unnatural, he or she usually does not mean they rarely occur or are biologically impossible. What they really intend to say is that they are normatively inappropriate.

161 See, for example, David P. Barash and Judith Eve Lipton, *The Myth of Monogamy: Fidelity and Infidelity in Animals and People* (New York: Henry Holt, 2001), 1–2.

162 See Miriam Koktevedgaard Zeitzan, *Polygamy: A Cross-Cultural Analysis* (Oxford, UK: Berg, 2008); Philip L. Kilbride, *Plural Marriage for Our Times: A Reinvented Option?* (Westport: Bergin & Garvey, 1994).

163 John Stuart Mill, "The Subjection of Women," in *On Liberty and Other Writings*, ed. Stefan Collini (Cambridge, UK: Cambridge University Press, 1989), 119–217.

164 See Hadley Arkes, "The Role of Nature," in *Same-Sex Marriage: Pro and Con*, ed. Andrew Sullivan (New York: Vintage Books, 1997), 276–77.

165 John Corvino, *What's Wrong With Homosexuality?* (New York: Oxford University Press, 2013), 78.

166 Ibid., 81.

B. Natural Law

One argument from nature, though, about marriage continues to thrive – at least among those who identify with Catholicism and other Christian views. In a scientific world, it can be hard to embrace the idea that animate and inanimate objections have natural functions or essences or that anything has intrinsic value, including marriage. Nevertheless, a more sophisticated use of nature can be found in the writings of the NNL theorists, including Mary Geach, Germaine Grisez, Roger Scruton, John Finnis, and Robert George, who deliberately attempt to avoid appeals to any sort of theology. Even though their views have been subject to withering criticisms and probably would not appeal to anyone who is not already theistically inclined, they have not exited the stage and often appear in much less nuanced forms in the ongoing debate over same-sex marriage when opponents of same-sex marriage maintain that same-sex relations or marriage is contrary to nature. To modern ethical sensibilities, what makes a sexual act wrong involves the lack of consent on the part of one of the persons due to age, coercion, duress, manipulation, or deception or the bad consequences that it produces. Legally, there is a world of difference between sex acts that are consensual and those that are not. It is not a brute moral fact that an open or a plural marriage is intrinsically wrong in the way that it is virtually self-evident that rape, genocide, slavery, and child molestation are wrong. Even Finnis does not believe that a "corrupt" sexual act between two consenting adults should be a crime.[167]

According to NNL thinking, there are basic goods that all human beings should have in their lives to make them more worthwhile than they otherwise would be. For Finnis, marriage is such a good, "with two constitutive and mutually supportive aspects, friendship and procreation."[168] As Andrew Lister writes: "The fundamental idea is that sexual intercourse within marriage can actualize, express, and allow the couple to experience the reality of their union as spouses."[169] "It must involve both mutual affection ('the generosity of acts of friendship')," Lister continues, "and openness to procreation."[170] Finnis's position on the nature of marriage has been elaborated on by George

167 John Finnis, "Natural Law: The Classical Tradition," in *The Oxford Handbook of Jurisprudence and Philosophy of Law* (Oxford, UK: Oxford University Press, 2002), 42.

168 Ibid., 43. However, as Corvino notes, marriage was not on the list of basic goods until relatively recently, suggesting its inclusion may have been motivated by the beginning of the debate over same-sex marriage. See Corvino, *What's Wrong With Homosexuality?* 93.

169 Andrew Lister, *Public Reason and Political Community* (London: Bloomsbury Publishing, 2013), 143.

170 Ibid.

and his co-authors (hereinafter, "George") quite recently in a legal journal article and book-length treatment. They characterize their thoughts on marriage as the "conjugal view," where "[m]arriage is a union of a man and a woman who make a permanent and exclusive commitment to each other of the type that is naturally (inherently) fulfilled by bearing and rearing children together. The spouses seal (consummate) and renew their union by conjugal acts – acts that constitute the behavioral part of the process of reproduction, thus uniting them as a reproductive unit."[171]

This definition of marriage is cryptic. At the core of George's view is the belief that marriage has an essence: by nature, it is heterosexual or sexually complementary, meaning that only a man and a woman could have a real marriage, and it also requires permanence and exclusivity. At most, even in a state that permits same-sex marriage, two men or two women who are faithful to each other would have an ontologically defective marriage, which is a convoluted way of saying they are not really married. According to this definition, plural marriage is ruled out only by the adjective "exclusive."[172] George does not have a lot to say about the topic, which may be attributed to his understandable preference for fighting only one war at a time and his rhetorical tactic of inducing those who favor same-sex marriage to explain why the slope is not slippery. Or else, just like a monogamous marriage, if a plural marriage were opposite sex, sexual, and took the form of a V, for example, it could meet the other criteria. For NNL theorists, the concern about same-sex acts is that they are akin to masturbation.[173] It is worth noting that from George's standpoint, an opposite-sex polygynous/polyandrous marriage appears to be closer to being a genuine marriage than a monogamous same-sex marriage due to the possibility of reproductive acts. Even if both of them fall short of being basic goods, one may come closer than the other to realizing that good; it could be less defective, so to speak.

By contrast, what George calls the "revisionist view" of marriage covers a much wider range of intimate relationships and its rationale is rooted in beliefs about the importance of freedom of choice or equal treatment.[174] He puts forth a number of distinct arguments against same-sex marriage, such as those that deny the similarity between interracial and same-sex relationships, appeal to the welfare children, and honor religious freedom – none of which break new ground. As such, my analysis will be limited to his claim that a same-sex

[171] Sherif Girgis, Robert P. George, and Ryan T. Anderson, "What Is Marriage?" *Harvard Journal of Law and Public Policy*, 34 (2010), 245–46.

[172] Ibid., 253. [173] Corvino, *What's Wrong With Homosexuality?* 80.

[174] George et al., "What Is Marriage?" 246–47.

marriage cannot be a genuine marriage insofar as same-sex couples cannot possibly perform the sexual acts with the appropriate mindset that such a marriage requires. I then elaborate on the shortcomings of this view and spell out its implications with respect to plural marriage.

For George, marriage is an "organic bodily union" or of "one flesh."[175] Only a certain kind of sexual intercourse, then, makes such a union possible – namely, an act of the "reproductive type." As Corvino writes: "On the physical level, it requires that the partners unite biologically in conjugal acts."[176] Stephen Macedo advances what might be called the "infertile couples" or "firing blanks" objection in explaining why George must exclude a couple who cannot reproduce on its own from real marriage.[177] If Macedo is right, then George will have to concede that an opposite-sex couple who is biologically incapable of reproduction cannot really be married – a conclusion he would not want to embrace. George slips this jab, responding that an infertile opposite-sex couple, which can engage in such acts even when conception cannot occur, still can be married. This response is supposed to address the objection that infertile opposite-sex couples are not really married because they are incapable of reproducing; furthermore, it enables opponents of same-sex marriage to differentiate same-sex couples from their infertile counterparts. As long as an infertile difference-sex couple engages in coitus for the right reasons, they have satisfied at least part of the criteria. It is unclear what NNL theorists would say about a couple who engaged exclusively in noncoital sexual behavior with the appropriate attitude or who loved each other, showed physical affection, but never performed any kind of sex act with each other. For the former, such sex acts obviously would not be of a "reproductive type," but they could not simply be reduced to sex acts for mutual pleasure. By contrast, two men or two women could never achieve bodily union.[178] For the latter, it would seem that the couple is still married despite their not being sexual. Imagine a couple that is legally married but one of the persons has no desire to have sex due to past sexual trauma and the other has a diminished sex drive due to the antidepressant that he takes. An appeal to natural biological functions, seems to perform most of the labor in this argument. Nature is what makes the act a procreative-type union by being oriented toward producing children.[179]

175 Ibid., 253. 176 Corvino, *What's Wrong With Homosexuality?* 89.

177 Stephen Macedo, "Against the Old Sexual Morality of the New Natural Law," in *Natural Law, Liberalism, and Morality: Contemporary Essays*, ed. Robert George (New York: Oxford University Press, 2002), especially 36–43.

178 George et al., "What Is Marriage?" 255. 179 Ibid., 256.

Additionally, mentally, the act of sexual intercourse has to be "a free and loving expression of the spouses' permanent and exclusive commitment."[180] This requirement, I believe, is the key to rendering the NNL view of marriage less obscure, but it has difficulties of its own. As it turns out, George says little about exactly what "permanent" and "exclusive" mean in this context and why they are part of the criteria that define a genuine marriage. The "exclusive" part would explain why a polygynous marriage would be contrary to natural law. For George, everything hinges on the critical difference between a series of procreative or procreative-like acts that are permanent and exclusive and those that are not.[181] Permanence and exclusivity must refer to the intentions or expectations of the participants in the sense that coitus symbolizes their lasting commitment to each other and only to each other. These criteria cannot be reduced only to a matter of biological or natural function but instead implicates the mental states of the two people engaged in the sexual act. "Permanence" cannot mean forever because all of us will die someday and many of us will divorce – and more than once in many instances. I doubt George wants to acquiesce to the conclusion that in one's second (opposite-sex, monogamous) marriage, the couple never can achieve bodily unity. "Exclusive" seems to mean only one marital partner at a time and would imply that an open marriage is not a real marriage or a marriage in which one or both of the participants are unfaithful does not fulfill the criteria. The latter is implausible, especially after the affair has ended. When infidelity exists, though, according to George's criteria, it seems that the couple does not have a real marriage inasmuch as it is not exclusive.[182]

The aforementioned example of marital infidelity connects to plural marriage in the following way. As George sees it, a real marriage "is possible only between two people."[183] It would appear that for him, the implication is that such a marriage between a man and a woman can cease to be a real marriage – at least for the time being – when at least one of the partners is cheating on the other. It can become a real marriage again, however, when the infidelity ends because the couple returns to exclusivity. He could accept this strange conclusion or try to distinguish a couple where one partner is unfaithful to the other. He opts for the latter and retains the option of characterizing sex acts between, say, a man and his wife differently than those between a man and his mistress. For him, not all acts of coitus within a marriage are "marital," such as

180 Ibid., 255. 181 Ibid., 266, n. 55.

182 There are many different kinds of infidelity – not all of which involve sexual intercourse – conventionally defined.

183 George et al., "What Is Marriage?" 272.

unloving coitus.[184] A married couple, then, who ceases to have sex or always has unloving sex would not seem to be really married.

In his view, the marital commitment has to be undivided.[185] Presumably, that means one person commits to being sexually exclusive and the other reciprocates. More is packed into the notion of exclusivity than meets the eye. What George must mean is that just as it is physically impossible for two men or two women to engage in a procreative act, a triad also cannot do so. As he puts it, "no single act can organically unite three or more people at the bodily level. . . ."[186] But it is not evident why this is a criterion when this is not how those involved in a polygamous relationship have to be physically intimate. Even if it were the only way, as Koppelman observes, "one person can coordinate bodily with multiple others."[187] First, a plural relationship with at least one member of the opposite sex could be characterized by loving procreative or procreative-like acts, accompanied by the desire to maintain the relationship forever, provided it was one-on-one. Polyamorists do not have to have an ongoing open intimate relationship. Just as a multipartner relationship is not sexually exclusive, neither is a dyadic marriage if one or both of the participants has an affair. Presumably, George does not want to concede that Bill and Hillary Clinton were not married when Bill was having an affair with Gennifer Flowers before he became president or with Monica Lewinsky during his second term – unless he is unconcerned with the legal definition. Normally, "exclusive" is synonymous with an ideal monogamous relationship; not seeing other people covers not being romantically involved with others at the same time or even thinking about the possibility. By this definition, at that time, Bill and Hillary were nonexclusive and thus did not have a real marriage. For the aforementioned reasons, this conclusion does not seem to follow. But if George describes their marriage at that time as a real marriage, albeit inferior to the best kind of marriage, he will have conceded that same-sex marriages are real but of a lesser kind.[188]

In his more recent co-authored book, George continues to defend the conjugal view of marriage and openly challenge those he calls "revisionists" to distinguish between (monogamous) same-sex marriage and its plural counterpart(s) on the assumption that revisionists will be eager to deny the slope is so slippery.[189] As I have tried to show, it is not evident that George himself has

[184] Ibid., 282, n. 11. [185] Ibid., 272. [186] Ibid.

[187] Andrew Koppelman, "More Intuition Than Argument," Review of Robert George, *What Is Marriage?* In *Commonweal*, March 2013.

[188] On this point, see Andrew Lister, *Public Reason and Political Community* (London: Bloomsbury Publishing, 2013), 147.

[189] Sherif Girgis, Ryan T. Anderson, and Robert P. George, *What Is Marriage? Man and Woman: A Defense* (New York: Encounter Books, 2012), 18–19, 51.

or could make this distinction. Increasingly, so-called revisionists are willing to slide down the slope until the conversation turns to marrying pets and rocks. The best rejoinder is to concede that to leave the meaning of marriage in the eye of the beholder implies that marriage does not have to be predicated on gender, numbers, sexual exclusivity, or even sexual intimacy, which is the view I unapologetically defend in this book. It is an implication that should not be eschewed because it reflects a better understanding of marriage in a society committed to the freedom and equality of all its members.

In fairness, plural marriage is not George's main concern, but I doubt George and his co-authors can adequately differentiate a plural marriage or a polygamous relationship from a monogamous opposite-sex marriage in which one or both of the partners are regularly unfaithful or have an understanding. As I pointed out, the unfaithful couple can still engage in procreative sex acts. The problem seems to be their lack of exclusivity. The same is true of the polygamous partners. This leaves George with two unpalatable options. He can acquiesce to the view that Bill and Hillary were not really married at times during their legally recognized marriage. That would mean that some present-day opposite-sex couples are not really married either because they are not exclusive due to infidelity, open marriages, and swinging. Or he can include opposite-sex polygamous units, such as a three-person polygynous or a polyandrous relationship, because the man with each woman or the woman with each man can engage in heterosexual sex acts that may end in reproduction.

It is worth calling attention to the strange preoccupation with sex and sexual exclusivity that underlies the NNL view of marriage. If asked, few of us would describe the meaning of our marriages by fixating on its physical aspects – with or without a particular mindset. Intimacy can incorporate sexual acts, but it does not have to. Indeed, the most worthwhile relationships may be platonic. As Koppelman astutely remarks, George provides us with "a lucid window into a dying worldview."[190] Of course, George is not interested in what real people think but rather in explicating the ontological nature of marriage, which, I should underscore, may not be relevant to the legal status of marriage. When one is married, legally speaking, one is married irrespective of the nature of one's marriage. Unless one believes the state cannot possibly legally recognize a same-sex or plural marriage, then his or her position is not that the state cannot do so but rather that it should not do so, which is normative. In California, for example, married same-sex couples really are married under

[190] Koppelman, "Judging the Case Against Same-Sex Marriage," 465.

existing family law. They just should not be permitted to have such a legal status according to NNL theorists. Some opposite-sex marriages meet all three criteria: complementarity, exclusivity, and permanence (but perhaps many of them do not). No same-sex marriages can meet the first criterion, whereas they can meet the last two criteria. Some multiperson units can meet the first and the third criteria (or at least it needs to be argued more forcefully why they do not meet the first criterion).[191] Exclusivity implies that one cannot love or be emotionally close to more than one person at the same time, but that belief may not be warranted if we examine human behavior. A father or mother usually loves all his or her children and most of us have more than one close friend.

CONCLUSION

In this chapter, I tried to take some of the sting out of a second set of less well-known objections to plural marriage, including the welfare of children, administrative considerations, the value of tradition, and appeals to nature. Constitutionally, what would matter is how reasons that derive from this set of concerns would be translated by the state into interests in which during litigation, lawyers would develop and judges would determine their strength. If under fundamental rights or equal protection analysis the state's limiting marriage to couples triggers a heightened standard of review, then the burden of proof would fall on the state to show it has either an important or compelling interest in treating couples differently (more favorably) than thruples or groups when it comes to the legal status of marriage. Even if such a legislative classification only triggers rational basis, the state would still have to enunciate a legitimate interest for such unequal legal treatment.

[191] Even if George can defend his position against this objection and even if his position is not rooted in a religious view, he is still offering nonpublic or perfectionist reasons in support of limiting marriage to opposite sex-couples, which runs afoul of a commitment to public justification in constitutional essentials and matters of basic justice.

4

The Importance of Marital Choice

In the last two chapters, I spelled out why the kinds of arguments that opponents of plural marriage typically put forward are much weaker than they initially appear to be. As a result, the state's interests in not permitting plural marriage may not be important or compelling, which a heightened standard of review would require. These interests may not even be legitimate if they are rooted in moral disapproval or animus.[1] Just as the state must have an adequate constitutional rationale not to grant marriage licenses to same-sex couples, it also must have such a rationale for limiting marriages to couples. As I have tried to show, none of the reasons offered against plural marriage so far have crossed the threshold of a heightened standard of review. In this chapter, I go on the offensive and develop a "pro choice" position by articulating the significance of being able to select multiple marital partners.

When it comes to marriage, there ought to be no restrictions on numbers unless a multiperson marriage-like relationship is so complex that it becomes administratively unmanageable. In the last chapter, I explained why this objection is far from decisive. Every competent adult should be able to marry whomever he or she wants for whatever personal reasons he or she happens to have. When it comes to your own life, you are the expert. I show that marital choice is just as important as other kinds of personal choices the Supreme Court already protects from legislative encroachment, such as whether to use birth control, to have a child, to have consensual sex with another adult, or to end one's life.[2] All these matters tend to have a significant

[1] *Romer* and *Lawrence* make clear that such a justification is suspect. *Romer v. Evans*, 517 U.S. 620 (1996); *Lawrence v. Texas*, 539 U.S. 558 (2003). For a recent and interesting take on animus, see Dale Carpenter, "'*Windsor* Products': Equal Protection for Animus," http://ssrn.com/abstract=2424743.

[2] I stick with fundamental rights analysis and do not use venture into the territory of fundamental rights under equal protection because if a right is fundamental, strict scrutiny applies. On this

impact on the quality of human lives. True, not everyone would care about all of them all the time. Some rare individuals may not care about any of them. But the point is that most people would not be indifferent to being able to make such personal decisions and normally would prefer to have as much control over them as possible. As irrational or misguided as any personal decision may be, including the decision to marry, under existing constitutional doctrine, a strong presumption in favor of letting competent adults decide for themselves how they want to live exists. As Martha Nussbaum states: "Articulating and protecting ... spheres of personal liberty has been a crucial task of our tradition of constitutional law."[3] The more personal the decision is, the higher the likelihood the state cannot interfere with it. As I shall argue, that right of personal choice or autonomy includes the right to marry multiple persons simultaneously.

This chapter will be divided into four sections. First, in providing background, I shall discuss the fundamental rights of privacy and marriage. Second, I shall elaborate on the value of personal choice more generally and not limit myself to the ideas found in the American constitutional tradition. Third, I will articulate the idea of Millian experiments in living and defend the view that plural marriages can be seen as such experiments. Fourth, I will explicate the possible virtues of plural relationships. As much as possible, I try to avoid appealing to equal protection, which is a related but separate line of analysis, so I can explain how a constitutional argument for a right to plural marriage can stand on its own.

I. FUNDAMENTAL RIGHTS ANALYSIS

A. *Privacy*

Because the concept of privacy is philosophically complex, I will restrict my discussion to what constitutional law scholars typically mean by "privacy." Privacy includes information secrecy, modesty, seclusion, and decisional autonomy.[4] In what follows, I mean decisional autonomy or the ability to form, revise, and pursue one's conception of the good human life (and then act accordingly, which some philosophers would see as agency). In the 1980s, Robert Bork was probably

point, see Erwin Chemerinsky, *Constitutional Law: Principles and Policies* (4th ed.) (New York: Wolters Kluwer 2011), 691–92.

3 Martha C. Nussbaum, *From Disgust to Humanity: Sexual Orientation and Constitutional Law* (New York: Oxford University Press, 2010), xvi.

4 Ibid., 74.

the most vocal of the conservative critics of the constitutional right of privacy – laid down in *Griswold* – and used it as a prime example of what was supposed to be the most repugnant kind of liberal judicial lawmaking.[5] The U.S. Senate's rejection of his Supreme Court nomination more than twenty-five years ago indicates that many and perhaps most Americans then and now do not share his aversion to the judicially created right to privacy.[6] It is probably not uncommon for people to reject a constitutional right in the abstract but then be in favor of it in particular situations when they see its implications. During the hearings, Bork himself retreated from some of his more extreme constitutional positions in what was later dubbed a "confirmation conversion" to enhance his chances of being confirmed.[7] Bork's unsuccessful effort at distancing himself from views that most Americans still refuse to embrace is an aspect of the more general problem that haunts originalists who have the courage of their convictions: Many well-established constitutional rights we take for granted are not enumerated cannot be easily found in the original public meaning of the constitutional text.

The right to privacy is one of them. For example, a law that bans the sale, distribution, or use of contraceptives would be more than "uncommonly silly"; it would force sexually active couples who do not want children to risk a pregnancy or practice abstinence. As Nussbaum observes, one can acknowledge flaws in Justice Douglas's opinion yet still embrace the conclusion.[8] A constitution that permits the state to force a couple into this dilemma might not be a constitution that deserves our allegiance. After all, most of the time, couples have sex for reasons that are independent of procreation and many of them want to plan a pregnancy so they can raise their children when they are best prepared to do so financially, professionally, and emotionally. Americans always have and always will disagree about the scope of such a right in real cases, but that disagreement does not mean they completely reject the right and its rationale.

One has to wonder how controversial this right to privacy would be – whatever it is called – if it had not been the basis of *Roe v. Wade*. Even today, forty years after this decision, when most Americans think of the right to privacy, they immediately visualize abortion and all the controversy that comes with it. However, that does not have to be so, given that the Supreme Court articulated something like a right to privacy decades earlier when the

5 Robert Bork, *The Tempting of America: The Political Seduction of the Law* (New York: Simon and Schuster, 1990).

6 David J. Garrow, *Liberty and Sexuality: The Right to Privacy and the Making of* Roe v. Wade (Berkeley, CA: University of California Press, 1998), 671.

7 See Benjamin Wittes, *Confirmation Wars: Preserving Independent Courts in Angry Times* (Lanham, MD: Rowman & Littlefield, 2006), 123.

8 Nussbaum, *From Disgust to Humanity*, 74–76.

unconstitutionality of laws banning abortion was not imminent. As early as 1928, Justice Louis Brandeis alludes to "the right to be let alone."[9] In his famous dissent in *Poe v. Ullman*, Justice John Harlan writes "there is a realm of personal liberty which the government may not enter."[10] In *Casey*, Justice Kennedy states: "At the heart of liberty is the right to define one's own concept of existence, of meaning, of the universe, and of the mystery of life."[11]

Despite Justice Scalia's ridiculing these words as the "sweet mystery of life" passage, Kennedy's point cannot be ignored: The right to privacy encompasses far more than the right not to have the government violate the sanctity of one's home or to eavesdrop on one's private conversations. While the term *privacy* may be more trouble than it is worth these days, we are stuck with it; privacy captures the widely shared intuition that an essential part of human flourishing necessitates the freedom to try to achieve one's most important ends without unjustified interference by the state. A society like ours that is committed to protecting such freedom cannot be unconcerned with the reasoning for restricting such choice or simply defer to legislative judgments in such situations, as if it were self-evident that lawmakers can do whatever they like irrespective of its adverse effects on personal liberty. American constitutionalism will always be predicated on the belief that legislative majorities have a tendency to exceed their authority. While a commitment to constitutionalism does not have to take the form of American-style judicial review, Americans have become accustomed over time to delegating the power to determine constitutional limits in real cases to judges. Judicial restraint or deference should not be praised when the alternative – namely, judicial abdication – is worse. There is no point to giving the power of judicial review to judges if they rarely use it to check lawmakers who are hostile or indifferent to individual rights and refuse to protect discrete and insular minorities.

In the past, many legal academics equated the right to privacy with the right to personal choice or autonomy. As early as 1975, philosopher Judith Thomson contended that the constitutional right to privacy is more accurately described as a right to personal liberty.[12] In this section, then, in associating privacy with the broader concept of personal liberty, I am not breaking new ground.[13] Even though what I plan to say about its place in American constitutional law with respect to marital choice is bound to engender disagreement,

[9] *Olmstead v. United States*, 277 U.S. 438 (1928).
[10] *Poe v. Ullman*, 367 U.S. 497 (1961) (Brandeis, J., dissenting).
[11] Garrow, *Liberty and Sexuality*, 694.
[12] Judith Jarvis Thomson, "The Right to Privacy," *Philosophy and Public Affairs*, 4 (1975), 295–314.
[13] See Garrow, *Liberty and Sexuality*, 659; 916, n. 25; 939, n. 92.

nothing remotely interesting can be said about constitutional law or theory that is not subject to some controversy. At present, the vast majority of constitutional law scholars deny that the state must provide the option of a plural marriage on any constitutional ground. In the first chapter, I explained why my pro-choice position – despite its radical appearance – could someday become a new constitutional construction as public opinion evolves and lawmakers and judges become more receptive to new constitutional meanings. All constitutional positions, even the most familiar ones, were conceived at a particular time and place and gestated before they assumed their present-day form.

The trouble with constitutional law is that too often, people do not know what counts as a *good* constitutional argument.[14] For some experts, a particular constitutional position is untenable, whereas for others, that same position is more than tenable because it has adequate support. It is remarkable how often legal commentators assume the Constitution either did or did not dictate the result, as if it could not have been otherwise, especially when they do not see eye to eye on which sources advocates and judges may properly rely on and which interpretive methodology should be employed. These difficulties would continue to exist even if Americans did not care about outcomes in important cases. Moreover, no constitutional right is absolute and the question of its proper scope can cause not only sincere but also reasonable disagreement with respect to its application in particular cases. As a result, knowledgeable people can be expected to disagree about how certain constitutional principles ought to be understood under what John Rawls called "the burdens of judgment," which are the sources of the intractable disagreement that exist in matters of political morality.[15]

These burdens also affect constitutional cases, particularly hard ones, and the implication is that judges must exercise their own judgment when they must reach a decision by applying an abstract constitutional principle, such as freedom or equality, to a unique fact pattern. In this respect, judging in hard constitutional cases resembles applied ethics. The harder the case, the more likely such reasonable disagreement is to occur along a number of axes. Not all the cases as possible precedents in any area of constitutional law will be consistent with one another, which is one of the drawbacks of a common-law system. For example, it is hard to reconcile such decisions as *Roe*, *Casey*, and *Lawrence*, which underscore the role of personal choice in human

[14] See Michael J. Gerhardt et al., *Constitutional Theory: Arguments and Perspectives* (4th ed.) (Albany, NY: Matthew Bender, 2013), 3.

[15] John Rawls, *Political Liberalism* (New York: Columbia University Press, 1996), 54–58.

flourishing, with a case like *Glucksberg*, where the Supreme Court denied that even a terminally ill person in excruciating pain has the constitutional right to physician-assisted suicide.[16]

My impression is that almost everyone appreciates the importance of such choice to some degree and is hesitant to let legislative majorities make such decisions for him or her when the state's interest in denying choice is comparatively weak. Even some religious and cultural minorities that do not value autonomy still want the state to leave them alone so they can practice and preserve their nonautonomous way of life. While they do not describe themselves as liberals or admit to caring about the rights of others to be left alone, they have their own reasons for wanting freedom. When necessary, they will appeal to group autonomy and ask for exemptions, which is akin to saying they would prefer to follow a different set of rules than those the state has enacted for everyone else. They are demanding the right to live differently. In opposing personal choice in other situations, they will be disputing its limits because they believe that autonomy does not trump other countervailing values.

How one uses the term *autonomy* must be specified. As Thomas Hill writes: "Autonomy . . . is not the name of one single thing; it means quite different things to different people."[17] A commitment to autonomy – or something like it – is not just found in the philosophical writings of Immanuel Kant, John Stuart Mill, John Rawls, and Joseph Raz. In my view, it is also a significant part of American constitutional doctrine and puts the onus on the state to establish that such choice, which should be the default, will not be allowed. Competent adults are supposed to be able to make up their own minds with respect to their most crucial personal decisions, including whom to marry and what their marriage is going to be like. More or less, that is already the status quo with respect to two-person marriages. This right to select a marital partner is imperative when it comes to intimate relationships because people do not converge on what they want the particulars of such relationships to be. They will have different expectations, different ideas about how they are supposed to interact, different understandings of how they will divide their respective workloads, and different views of how they will spend (or invest) their money and leisure time. I take it that apart from the obvious – discriminating against

16 *Roe v. Wade*, 410 U.S. 113 (1973); *Planned Parenthood of Southeastern Pennsylvania v. Casey*, 505 U.S. 833 (1992); *Lawrence v. Texas*, 539 U.S. 558 (2003); *Washington v. Glucksberg*, 521 U.S. 702 (1997).

17 Thomas E. Hill Jr., *Autonomy and Self-Respect* (New York: Cambridge University Press, 1991), 44.

gays and lesbians and demeaning their relationships and lives – the trouble with the family values movement is that it is premised on the idea that a certain kind of family is most appropriate for everyone.

The principle of autonomy found in our constitutional tradition is also connected to the idea of liberal neutrality in which the state is not supposed to act on perfectionist reasons in advancing particular conceptions of the good. A neutral state can provide only a framework of social justice in which political and legal equals are left to choose their morally permissible ends. As Jonathan Quong writes, "... the government should remain *neutral* [his emphasis] on the issue of the good life, and restrict itself to establishing the fair terms within which citizens can pursue their own beliefs about what gives value to their lives."[18] This approach is recognizably Rawlsian and reflects the belief that the American constitutional tradition – properly understood – is antiperfectionist in some important respects. As a result, the state must let competent adults decide for themselves how they want to live when their decisions are sufficiently self-regarding.

The point is not only that our constitutional practice incorporates a commitment to autonomy but also that such an understanding makes the best normative sense of that practice, even though some scholars would dispute that claim. People should be the authors of their own lives and pursue the ends they most value – whatever they happen to be – and be able to experiment to see what works best for them. At present, Americans have little marital choice. If they had more choice, they might think and act more unconventionally and have different priorities. They might begin to be more realistic about what they can expect from other people, to learn that love never is unconditional, and to appreciate other kinds of intimacy and activities. Historically, marital norms have been oppressive. Today, they are less likely to foster patriarchy and heterosexism, but they are still easily internalized and therefore shape people's thinking, sometimes for the worse, about what they want their lives to be like. In a society characterized by "compulsory monogamy," one might wonder how voluntary the choice to marry only one person at a time really is.[19]

In the name of marital freedom, then, the state should not be enacting laws that reinforce already well-established marital norms that push people in a particular normative direction when they should be able to choose the kind of marriage they want to have because even if we did not care about respecting

[18] Quong, *Liberalism Without Perfection*, 2.

[19] I borrow the term "compulsory monogamy" from Elizabeth F. Emens, "Monogamy's Law: Compulsory Monogamy and Polyamorous Existence," *New York University Review of Law and Social Change*, 29 (2004), 277–363.

their autonomy, the individual outcomes – namely, personal happiness or satisfaction – may be superior. Their personal reasons are their own and should not be subject to further examination. A constitutional right, can be seen in the following manner: Whatever your personal reasons are for wanting to have an abortion, end your life, worship god(s), speak your mind on political topics, raise your children in a particular manner, or be sexually intimate with another consenting adult, they are legally irrelevant. The state cannot second-guess whatever decision you make – no matter how poorly informed or poorly reasoned it was; its (de)merits are beside the point. The state can only step in to limit that right when its exercise harms others or unreasonably puts them at risk.

That freedom enables competent adults to formulate and then pursue their respective life plans, with personal risks and rewards. There is something characteristically American about not wanting to be told what to do and being able to choose, even when exercising such judgment leads to worse outcomes. While antigovernment Libertarians work with an impoverished conception of personal liberty – they tend to be too preoccupied with the government's power to take away choices and do not fully appreciate how other sources of power, such as market mechanisms, can have the same effect – classical and egalitarian liberals share a commitment to helping people have as much control as possible over their own lives. Without that kind of control, they are less likely to flourish or even have a decent life.

True, it may be hard to fathom why anyone would choose a plural marriage. Samuel Rickless worries about how much emotional intimacy could exist among multiple persons.[20] I would be interested in knowing (and trying to measure) how much of such intimacy actually exists in real monogamous marriages given the inherent difficulties of trying to share your life with someone else and making yourself emotionally vulnerable. Almost every episode of *Big Love* and *Sister Wives* contains scenes that display the trials and tribulations of a four-person polygynous "marriage." Many married couples do not have the time or the energy to work through their own problems to achieve the intimacy that makes a higher-quality marriage possible. But that point about why anyone would do this or that is equally applicable to many of the most important personal choices all of us make every day. Some people may believe a plural marriage to be a religious duty. Others may find such a marriage to be more emotionally fulfilling or sexually exciting. Others may see such marriage as a vehicle of self-development.

20 Samuel C. Rickless, "Polygamy and Same-Sex Marriage: A Response to Calhoun," *San Diego Law Review*, 42 (2005), 1047–48.

Others may believe such marriage to enable taking better care of children, the elderly, or other dependents. Whether such personal reasons are compelling depends on the ends the individuals in question happen to share and find worthwhile. Respecting personal choice in this context is imperative; marriage is not just a means to an end but may be an end in itself or at least a key component of a particular life plan. The more modular marriage is, the more people will be able to customize their marital relationship so it meets their unique needs and satisfies their particular desires – no matter how idiosyncratic they may be. They will also have more flexibility to adapt to new circumstances. At bottom, the meaning of marriage ought to be left to those most directly affected by it.

For intimate relationships, then, one size does not fit all and it is unlikely that such relationships can ever be closely regulated without the state's unreasonably interfering with the personal freedom of those who think and act differently and may want to experiment. That is one of the points I tried to drive home in the second chapter by deconstructing the argument from gender inequality. We can generalize about human beings and why they need certain basic primary goods, such as education, health care, and adequate income, to have decent lives. For such a political philosopher as John Rawls, the purpose of the state's providing such goods is to ensure that all persons – regardless of their luck – have the resources they need to increase the chances they will flourish – whatever their conception of the good happens to be. Beyond having at least the minimum resources, they often have very different needs, desires, and expectations in what they are looking for in intimate partners and what they want their intimate relationships to be like. Their feelings about them change over time and each marriage will have different dynamics because people have different personalities and behavioral dispositions. Some couples will complement each other perfectly, whereas other couples will bring out the worst in each other and make their lives miserable. The point is not only that some marriages will be much happier and much healthier than others but also that each marriage tends to have highs and lows and it is nearly impossible to predict its quality in the midst of so many variables. Even when people are compatible, no one can know with anything resembling certainty that circumstances will not change how they interact with and feel about each other.

B. Arranged Marriages

Most Americans have such a hard time grasping the very idea of an arranged marriage between adults, which is common in some cultures, because they cannot fathom not going through the process of selecting a partner themselves. In their eyes, the problem with such a marriage is not so much that two people in question could not possibly come to love each other when they live together and act as spouses. Rather, the process of getting to know each other and determining whether they are compatible seems rushed, impersonal, and too important to leave in the hands of third parties,. Even eHarmony lets its members make their own decisions; its matchmaking ends at introducing people who are supposed to be best suited for each other based on its own compatibility criteria. The Internet dating industry has grown dramatically and at least part of its appeal has to do with the extent to which members can specify what they are looking for in a prospective partner: wealth, physical appearance, personality, religion, age, sexual orientation, lifestyles, values, political beliefs, goals, hobbies, and interests. I suspect the concern about arranged marriages is less about the likely outcome – after all, an experienced matchmaker or computer software might be more proficient – and more about the couple's not being nearly as actively involved as they should be in the process. One never finds everything one is looking for in a significant other – trade-offs are unavoidable – but at least when one can select one's own partner, one has directly participated, which in itself should not be undervalued. Additionally, the likelihood increases that one has found someone who shares some of one's eccentricities and aspirations – that is, the things that make us the people we are. Understood in this manner, it is hard to imagine anything that could be more personal than the decision to become involved in an intimate relationship or to marry. It may be hard to fit Harold and Maude's fictional intimate relationship into one's view of how the world is supposed to be, but that does not excuse those in more socially accepted relationships from being close-minded and acting intolerantly on the (false) assumption that what they happen to value is universal.

In the past, states have imposed few restrictions on marriage. Under their police powers – with rare exceptions – states can do just about whatever they want to do with marriage, including (probably) abolishing it.[21] As noted, some of those restrictions, such as those based on race, are no longer morally or constitutionally acceptable. Typically, the state suspends judgment about the personal reasons competent adults (or, in some states, minors with parental permission) have to marry only one person. The decision is simply left up to the individuals to decide whether they want to enter into such a legal relationship with its accompanying benefits and burdens. As one

[21] But see Pamela S. Karlan, "Let's Call the Whole Thing Off: Can States Abolish the Institution of Marriage?" *California Law Review*, 98 (2010), 697–707.

commentator observes: "The law determines who is eligible for marriage ... but it says almost nothing about what marriage itself consists in; it is a contract without content. The law prescribes no behaviors, not even sexual consummation, that must be exhibited in order to marry or stay married. It dictates no requirements for the living arrangements of married people."[22]

The double standard, in which the law treats monogamy so much more favorably, is increasingly hard to defend in the wake of the increased marital freedom that legal recognition of same-sex marriage in a growing number of states has produced. If the standard justification for denying the option of polygynous marriage is that a woman could not possibly have an intelligible reason for selecting it, then what about the long and disheartening list of poor reasons that some and perhaps many or even most couples have for marrying? Why are those reasons not also subject to such skepticism? That is not to say that the decision to marry or enter into an intimate relationship is to ever be taken lightly. Anyone who rushes into matrimony can expect criticism from his or her family and friends because the expectation is that (a) the couple has taken enough time to get to know each other well enough to determine whether they are sufficiently compatible and (b) each of them has given the matter much more than a moment's thought. Normally, the decision to wed is not simply another lifestyle choice for those who believe their lives would go better if they were married or want the state and society to acknowledge their intimate relationship.

In contemporary America, without question, marriage is not just another social institution and it is unlikely that this state of affairs is going to change anytime soon given the extent to which most Americans continue to put marriage on a pedestal. Despite all the talk about the breakdown of marriage in America, the push for same-sex marriage or marriage equality seems to reaffirm why most Americans value the institution and want the state to remain involved with it even in the midst of decreasing marriage rates. The existence of a menu of marital options would make marriage more voluntary, encourage people to be more thoughtful, and may ultimately strengthen the institution. It is hard to imagine that Americans will ever be antimarriage in the sense they would not marry under any circumstances. As Susan Moller Okin once observed: "Marriage has a long history, and we live in its shadow."[23] If you do not think marital choice is important, imagine a society where at a certain age, men and women have to register for the marriage draft

[22] Brook J. Sadler, "Re-Thinking Civil Unions and Same-Sex Marriage," *Monist*, 91 (2008), 580–81.

[23] Okin, *Justice, Gender, and the Family*, 140.

and the state arranges marriages based on eHarmony or Match.com compatibility criteria. There are at least a few serious reasons to oppose such a proposal, but one of them regards how almost all of us would prefer to make such marital choices for ourselves, even if we know we would not choose wisely based on poor personal choices in the past and even if such paternalism on the part of the state would produce better consequences, such as creating higher-quality marriages and decreasing the rate of divorce (assuming that is a good consequence).

C. *Against Autonomy*

Not everyone believes that autonomy is all it is cracked up to be. Different kinds of utilitarians are notorious for finding room for the values of autonomy or agency but only as a means to the end of producing good consequences, which can be defined differently. Recently, Sarah Conly offers a qualified defense of coercive paternalism on the part of the state with respect to people's means and not their ends.[24] Her position is consequentialist – she asks whether the benefits of state involvement outweigh the costs – and is premised on the probably accurate assumption (based on recent research in social psychology and behavioral economics) that almost all people make cognitive errors that impair their instrumental reasoning. This is not the time nor the place to go into any detail about objections to her provocative position, but even someone as sympathetic to paternalist justifications of the exercise of political power as Conly is still distinguishes between means and ends. When it comes to ultimate ends, she is as subjectivist as the most antiperfectionist liberals because people have different payoffs.

This belief in leaving well enough alone when possible is a standard liberal response to the kind of moral pluralism that characterizes contemporary liberal democracies. Under such conditions, reasonable people will have different conceptions of what is most valuable in human life, will want to act in accordance with these conceptions, and will understandably demand the right to do so. That presupposes, following Mill, that they are in a much better position than lawmakers are to know what is best for them. They may not have expertise, but they are better qualified to exercise the judgment that the situation calls for. Later, some of them may have regrets, but under conditions of uncertainty, that possibility is unavoidable. At least they cannot say they were forced to do something they did not really want to do; that may induce

[24] Sarah Conly, *Against Autonomy: Justifying Coercive Paternalism* (New York: Cambridge University Press, 2013).

them to take more responsibility, as they are "experts" when it comes to their own lives. Although this presupposition about their expertise with respect to their own lives may be false, as Conly argues, it underlies some of the Supreme Court's most important fundamental rights decisions. As a result, unlike moral philosophers, constitutional law scholars are not free to overlook the extent to which people have a constitutional right to make personal decisions, even if they do so incompetently. Adults are assumed to have the right to not only choose their ends but to also decide the means to those ends without undue involvement by the state, leaving aside the potentially vexing issue of when the particular behavior in question counts as a means to an end and not an end in itself. It is hard to read the American constitutional tradition in any other way without distorting it beyond recognition.

D. Abortion Revisited

Whatever one thinks about the legitimacy of *Roe v. Wade* or the privacy rationale that underlies Justice Harry Blackmun's majority opinion, it would be disingenuous to deny that the decision to have a child is not one of the most personal of personal decisions a woman could possibly make.[25] In his plurality opinion in *Casey*, Justice Kennedy emphasizes that abortion is not simply about terminating the life of a fetus.[26] Even if the constitutional right to terminate the life of a fetus prior to its viability had nothing to do with gender equality – envision a world in which child care did not actually disproportionately impact women – some people would continue to believe it would be imperative to protect such a choice. Unlike, say, feeding stray cats or deciding to plant tomatoes in the backyard, having a child invariably has serious consequences; it can never be a trivial decision for a human being.

These comments are not designed to settle the abortion controversy or even take sides but instead to call attention to why many people believe that ultimately, the decision is the individual woman's and not the state's. Justice Ginsburg criticizes the rationale of *Roe*, favoring equal protection grounds.[27] Regardless of its constitutional justification and whether the privacy rationale caused a backlash, which is debatable, what makes the abortion question so complicated concerns the moral status of the nonviable fetus. In one way or another, one's view of that status will reflect how one understands the moral

25 *Roe v. Wade*, 410 U.S. 113 (1973).

26 *Planned Parenthood of Southeastern Pennsylvania v. Casey*, 505 U.S. 833 (1992).

27 See, for example, Ruth Bader Ginsburg, "Some Thoughts on Autonomy and Equality in Relation to *Roe v. Wade*," *North Carolina Law Review*, 63 (1985), 375–86.

criteria of personhood. If abortion really is infanticide or the killing of the innocent, then those who are pro-choice would have to reconsider their position.[28]

E. Same-Sex Sex and the Right to Die

Although I doubt most opponents of abortion really believe that nonviable fetuses are persons with a *prima facie* right not to be killed in the sense of unconditionally approving of the prosecution of women for homicide, the message I am trying to get across is that the importance of such personal freedom is not confined to the context of abortion. The vast majority of Americans do not think that consensual same sex between adults should be a crime.[29] This fact reflects their willingness to permit such sexual conduct even when many of them continue to believe that such behavior is sinful. This kind of tolerance is remarkable in a society that has discriminated against sexual minorities in so many ways for so long. Almost thirty years ago, in *Bowers v. Hardwick*, the Supreme Court not only allowed states to criminalize consensual same-sex sex between adults, but it also permitted them to impose harsh sentences.[30] This growing tolerance comes from greater familiarity with sexual minorities and a Libertarian spirit of "live and let live" in which more and more people do not believe that mere moral disapproval is a sufficient reason to make a particular activity illegal.[31]

In the context of end-of-life decisions, in *Cruzan*, the Supreme Court recognized a right to refuse medical care.[32] In 1996, two U.S. Courts of Appeal extended this right to physician-assisted suicide.[33] By contrast, in *Washington v. Glucksberg*, the Supreme Court rejected the extension of this right beyond refusing artificial nutrition and hydration.[34] As Erwin Chemerinsky notes, this decision still "left open doors to future legal protection of a right to physician-assisted death."[35] In the future, the Supreme Court may change its mind or state legislatures may jump into the fray, as that of Oregon did, and protect this

28 Unless they want to adopt some sort of utilitarian view that the killing of innocent infants before a certain age may be justifiable in some circumstances depending on the likely overall consequences.

29 Klarman, *From the Altar to the Closet*, 156.

30 *Bowers v. Hardwick*, 478 U.S. 186 (1986).

31 Klarman, *From the Closet to the Altar*, 156.

32 *Cruzan v. Director, Missouri Department of Health*, 497 U.S. 261 (1990).

33 *Compassion in Dying v. Washington*, 79 F. 3d 790 (9th Circuit 1996) (en banc); *Quill v. Vacco*, 80 F. 3d 716 (2d Cir. 1996).

34 *Washington v. Glucksberg*, 521 U.S. 702 (1997) (due process grounds).

35 Chemerinsky, *Constitutional Law*, 875.

right. To defend such a right is to take the view that one's personal reasons trump other considerations; that is, if one really wants to die, then as long as safeguards are in place to ensure the decision is informed and fully voluntary, it would seem to follow that he or she should be able to proceed accordingly. If someone were in chronic, unbearable pain and had a terminal illness, was paralyzed from the neck down, or was in a coma with no chance of recovery, his or her reasons for wanting to end his or her life would be intelligible. Unless one believes that life is sacred, which usually reflects a religious viewpoint, and that suicide is never morally acceptable, most of us can imagine a person's having good reasons in some circumstances to want to die. The only remaining issue would be what kinds of safeguards ought to be in place.

II. AUTONOMY

A. *The Exercise of Autonomy*

Constitutionally, then, it is a mistake to conceptualize the right of privacy too narrowly, seeing it only as a right to engage in sexual activities or other behaviors that occur in a particular space, such as that of one's home. In protecting alternative lifestyles, one does not have to be worried only about sexual freedom or reproductive autonomy inasmuch as most human beings also value other kinds of intimacy. To reduce a marriage to sex acts or procreation is to leave out everything else that remains so important to most Americans and makes us the individuals we are. Even NNL thinkers, as noted in the last chapter, do not crudely reduce marriage to something merely biological. Many people already have premarital sex and reproduce without being married. One of the main reasons for being concerned with sexuality or reproduction is that just about everyone cares about these aspects of their lives. The aim is not to protect difference per se – after all, not all difference is morally unobjectionable, especially when others are being harmed or unreasonably being put at risk of such harm – but to acknowledge how much all of us want the ability to make the most personal of personal choices, even when our exercising of our autonomous capacities does not result in a better state of affairs.

There is vast philosophical literature on the concept of autonomy and I shall not attempt to survey it here. Still, I would like to point out before proceeding that philosophers are not in agreement when it comes to specifying autonomy's meaning or its role in human flourishing. Unlike Joseph Raz, I do not believe that autonomy only has value when intrinsic goods are chosen.[36] Unlike Robert Paul Wolff, I do not believe that an autonomous choice always includes almost full information, deep contemplation, and careful review of the arguments for and against each possible course of action.[37] For constitutional purposes, what I mean by "autonomy" is the freedom to make personal choices – regardless of how informed or thoughtful the person making the decision is, which I believe is consistent with the definition that emerges from a defensible interpretation of the relevant constitutional doctrine. By this standard, almost all personal decisions are at least minimally autonomous and must be respected. Presumably, measured against an ideal standard, most real human choices fall far short. As Steven Lecce puts it: "Personal autonomy is not all of nothing . . . but rather a matter of degree."[38]

Ideally, most people would desire to be well above the threshold. Such a right involves being given as much discretion as possible to make one's own decisions with respect to how one forms and revises a conception of the good – whatever it happens to be – and to live accordingly, provided that the resulting behavior does not unreasonably interfere with the equally important right of others to do likewise. After all, their lives count equally. The more important the choice is in terms of that life plan, the more the state should be inclined to defer to that individual's judgment. Philosophically, then, when it comes to defining autonomy, I prefer as minimalist a conception as possible in the midst of moral pluralism, where people in a free society will not only sincerely and reasonably disagree about the nature of a good human life but perhaps also about the fundamentals of social justice. However, what they can agree on – at least in the abstract – is that for the most part, people should be able to decide for themselves about the kinds of lives they want to have without unnecessary interference by the state. For Joel Feinberg, "the life that a person threatens by his own rashness is after all *his* [his emphasis] life; it belongs to *him* [his emphasis] and to no one else. For that reason alone, he must be the one to decide – for better or for worse – what is to be done with it. . . ."[39]

Like Laurence Tribe, one can read *Lawrence v. Texas* as creating a broad constitutional right of autonomy.[40] What follows from this commitment to

36 Joseph Raz, *The Morality of Freedom* (New York: Oxford University Press, 1986).

37 Robert Paul Wolff, *In Defense of Anarchism* (Berkeley: University of California Press, 1970), 12–18.

38 Steven Lecce, *Against Perfectionism: Defending Liberal Neutrality* (Toronto: University of Toronto Press, 2008), 105.

39 Feinberg, *Harm to Self*, 59.

40 Laurence Tribe, "*Lawrence v. Texas*: The 'Fundamental Right' That Dare Not Speak Its Name," *Harvard Law Review* , 117 (2004), 1893–1955.

personal autonomy is a constitutional version of antiperfectionism or neutrality on the part of the state. I am not going to defend such neutrality here, which would take an entire book and already has been defended effectively (in my view) by Steven Lecce and Jonathan Quong.[41] I take up the constitutional implications of such neutrality with respect to marriage in the last chapter. Alternatively, my assumption is that something like a neutrality requirement exists in the American constitutional tradition when it comes to fundamental rights, equal protection, free speech, and religion.[42] The conception of autonomy that such a perfectionist liberal as Raz develops and defends in *The Morality of Freedom* does not accurately (nor is meant to) reflect what the Supreme Court has said about autonomy in many important constitutional cases. In other words, the constitutional right to autonomy – what one can believe, say, or do – has never been and never should be contingent on choosing wisely.

Furthermore, Raz's conception is not practical inasmuch as no real state could promote such a rich conception of autonomy in the midst of the kind of deep moral pluralism that characterizes contemporary America. Rawls has come under fire from those believe his political liberalism is unfair to those who are religious and it is hard to fathom what they would have to say about Raz's liberal perfectionism, which would not leave nearly as much room for difference when the state is supposed to encourage valid and discourage invalid conceptions of the good.[43] Indeed, Raz himself expresses a similar reservation about the realization of more ideal forms of freedom at the very end of his famous book.[44] Ideal Theory has its place, no doubt, but I have never understood how more ambitious liberal perfectionist theories, which want the state to promote autonomous lives, are supposed to be implemented in the nonideal conditions that characterize morally pluralistic liberal democracies. At the center of constitutional theory lies the intersection of normative political theory and constitutional practice.

In Rawlsian terminology, many unquestionably unreasonable people are members of our society and their lives cannot be dismissed. As such, they must be treated fairly, which means that as much as possible, their personal decisions should not be infringed on. I believe it is a grave error to overlook unreasonable people and what is owed to them, as if they only exist on the

[41] Lecce, *Against Perfectionism*; Jonathan Quong, *Liberalism Without Perfection* (New York: Oxford University Press, 2011).

[42] With respect to religion, see Andrew Koppelman, *Defending American Religious Neutrality* (Cambridge, MA: Harvard University Press, 2013).

[43] Raz, *The Morality of Freedom*, 133. [44] Ibid., 429.

periphery. After all, most people are probably unreasonable in one way or another. Also, there are unreasonable people (those who seek to harm others or interfere in their lives without sufficient justification) and there are unreasonable people who have lives that are not particularly autonomous – no matter how expansively "autonomous" is defined. Their way of life will often be rooted in particular religious and cultural traditions that may not have freedom and equality at their cores. To try to force a richly autonomous life on them is to invite serious and unnecessary conflict. It is also mistaken to overestimate how autonomous many Americans really are just because they live in a liberal society. At the end of the day, the greatest advantage of antiperfectionist political liberalism as a political theory is that it can accommodate a much wider range of ways of life than any of the alternatives and thereby allow us to live together in peace and aspire to something like a well-ordered society even when we will never come close to converging on a shared conception of the good life.

Theoretically, much can be said in favor of thicker conceptions of autonomy and the liberal perfectionism that follows from it. The truth is that I am sympathetic to the project that such perfectionist liberals as Raz have engaged in but doubt its practically under conditions of moral pluralism, worry about how we could ever know what would constitute the human good with any degree of confidence, and call into question its constitutional relevance at least for the time being. It would seem to follow from the premise that an autonomous life really is the best form of human life that the state should not only be able to promote that form of life but also discourage other less worthwhile kinds of lives in the process. Perhaps the simplest and most compelling way of conceptualizing American constitutionalism from a normative standpoint is to see that its overarching purpose as creating space for individual decisions and the behaviors that follow from them do not need to be left to legislative majorities. In practice, though, conditions of moral pluralism render such perfectionist liberalism ill-suited for a society that is so diverse, still is quite religious, and remains so deeply divided over so many questions of political morality. Even if it were more practical, for constitutional purposes, the bar cannot be set too high for real persons. At some point, political and legal theorists have to take them as they are (and what they value) and not as they would like them to be (and what perfectionist liberals wish they would value). One does not have to be cynical about human nature to appreciate that any normative political or constitutional theory worthy of serious consideration cannot make unrealistic assumptions about human beings and their inherent limitations even under the best of conditions.

Allowing the exercise of such autonomy may lead to personal choices that are foolish, self-destructive, or bizarre, but their having such unfortunate qualities does not mean the state may deny such personal choice on that ground alone. For example, as evidenced by the high divorce rate, for many persons – particularly younger ones – the decision to marry is probably flawed – unless one sees it as a learning experience and thus an opportunity for personal growth. It would probably not be a terrible idea to regulate childbearing and childrearing more strictly if one is mainly concerned about outcomes. It might even be defensible to set the minimum age for a marriage license at thirty, when more people are financially stable and mature enough to undertake the responsibilities that marriage demands. Even if the state could identify proven risk factors as part of its criteria in determining whether to issue a marriage license, it would be constitutionally unthinkable. The Constitution does not require the decision to have a child or marry to be wise or minimally informed. With respect to monogamous marriage, neither person has to reflect carefully about forming a marital relationship. In fact, they do not have to put any serious time or effort into the decision and may later regret it. At most, the state could probably encourage them to do so by providing financial incentives, such as tax credits, to take a course. Constitutionally, it remains unclear when a regulation is so strict – such as mandatory, extensive premarital counseling – that it amounts to an infringement on the right to marry.

A deeply personal choice, then, is normally considered to be at least minimally autonomous, even if it were easier somehow than it normally is for the state to evaluate the quality of the decision making. Under the law, competent adults are treated as if what they decide to do is to be permitted and that does not involve a judgment by the state about the merits of their decision. Even if it were possible for philosophers to come up with a robust conception of autonomy and agree on its essentials, it still would be nearly impossible for the state to ascertain how autonomous each decision to marry actually is. Legal theorists cannot overlook such practical considerations. And if that were not enough, to trust the state to do so competently and fairly would be an exercise in wishful thinking. If personal choice were not so important, then the state might be able to compel women to have abortions or force fathers to marry the mothers of their children to avoid the possible disadvantages of single motherhood. The state may not interfere with their private lives even with the best of intentions. Nor would such interference be warranted even in situations where such interference would produce overall good consequences (say, fewer unwanted children and fewer unhappy marriages and nasty divorces).

B. Neutrality Revisited

Why, then, should marital choice be restricted to only one partner at a time? After all, under the status quo, we let people choose whom they want to marry, even if such a marriage is probably doomed to failure, as if it were part of the plot of a Shakespearean tragedy. The decision to marry is probably one of the most important decisions many people will ever make – about half of them more than once – because their marital arrangement affects all aspects of their lives – from their living arrangements to their career decisions. In terms of constitutional neutrality, the state should not promote a particular view of marriage on the grounds that such an intimate relationship is better than the alternatives because (a) people are different and consequently flourish in different ways; (b) flexibility can be beneficial when circumstances and personal feelings change; and (c) they have a right to make such choices – for better or for worse. One of the lessons from the debate over the constitutionality of laws that limit the right to marriage to opposite-sex couples is that the state may not do so to foster a particular conception of marriage at the expense of other potentially valuable conceptions. That is why those who have vociferously opposed same-sex marriage have gone out of their way to fall back on rationales that ostensibly do not implicate judgments about which lives are best, such as the state's purported (and almost silly) interest in promoting responsible procreation. Those who oppose same-sex marriage continue to conceal their real reasons for their opposition, which are often linked to their moral disapproval of homosexuality, which in turn can usually be traced to their religious convictions. The other less obvious and more controversial implication is that the state should leave the marriage business.[45]

One way to understand a constitutional requirement of neutrality more generally is that the state must respect the freedom and equality of all adults and sincere and reasonable disagreement in important constitutional cases frequently stems from what these values are supposed to mean in the twenty-first century. In my view, the decision to marry implicates both of these values. *Lawrence v. Texas* can be read as standing for a *prima facie* right of freedom of choice in personal matters.[46] As Sunstein notes, this decision means that in discerning which rights are fundamental, tradition is not always determinative.[47] Ultimately, *Lawrence* may serve as precedent for a constitutional right

[45] See Bedi, *Beyond Race, Sex, and Sexual Orientation*, 208–47.
[46] *Lawrence v. Texas*, 539 U.S. 558 (2003).
[47] Cass R. Sunstein, "The Right to Marry," *Cardozo Law Review*, 26 (2005), 2107.

to plural marriage.[48] American constitutional practice strongly suggests that when the timing is right, judges have little trouble reinterpreting past judicial decisions to find support for the constitutional conclusion that they want to reach. The line of argumentation would be that competent adults are better equipped than anyone else is to decide what is best for them in selecting marital partners. Without this assumption more generally, it is hard to make sense of the constitutional doctrine of substantive due process that engendered so many cherished U.S. Supreme Court decisions.

That is not to say that everyone would subscribe to that bold claim. Even when one disputes the constitutional concept of autonomy I advance and prefers letting the state act for paternalistic reasons, that preference still has to be articulated and defended. Judicially, such a preference is usually considered to be a conservative position, as expressed in *Washington v. Glucksberg*, where the Supreme Court rejected the right to physician-assisted suicide.[49] This constitutional principle of respecting personal choice is sufficiently well established to be used as the basis of a constitutional right to plural marriage. As such, the state may have a *prima facie* obligation to respect each person's decision to marry one or more persons for whatever personal reasons he or she happens to have. At the very least, that view is more plausible than it may initially seem. Here, let me remind readers that constitutional understandings are not static; all of them can and some of them do change dramatically over time. Even though the structural parts of our Constitution seem impervious to social forces, so much of the Constitution-in-practice lies outside of the constitutional text and original public meanings.

C. The Status Quo

Constitutionally, that people exercise their autonomy or freedom of choice poorly with respect to their means and ends is neither here nor there; it may be sad they make the personal choices they do, but that possibility or even likelihood does not warrant the state's interfering with the most important aspects of people's private lives unless compelling reasons for such interference exist – and "compelling" does not mean any reason the state happens to come up with. The rationale for intervention cannot be the poor quality of the decision-making process or the likely outcome of the choice, as I have explained earlier. Under the status quo, even when many individuals

48 See Michael G. Myers, "Polygamist Eye for the Monogamist Guy: Homosexual Sodomy ... Gay Marriage ... Is Polygamy Next?" *Houston Law Review*, 42 (2006), 1471–76.

49 One notable exception is *Washington v. Glucksberg*, 521 U.S. 702 (1997).

make bad choices regarding whom to marry and later have second thoughts, the state does not intervene. The mere possibility of future regrets does not warrant the infringement of the right to choose to marry even the worst possible partner for that person. The state could not subject those who want to marry to background checks or psychological evaluations, as if they were purchasing a handgun, to identify marriages that are more likely to be dysfunctional or are at a greater risk of failing. Nor is there a legal limit on how many times people can marry or divorce or how many children they may have, even when they have criminal records, diagnosed psychological disorders, substance abuse problems or other addictions, have anger management issues or a history of violence, are insolvent, or are delinquent on child or spousal support payments. They are free to make the same bad choices over and over again.

A high divorce rate indicates that many couples eventually realize they cannot continue to live together and would prefer to be single or look for another partner. Even if they do not divorce, a married couple may stay together for the wrong reasons and be anything but happy. Being together fifty years does not necessarily reflect marital bliss. Like it or not, with respect to monogamous marriage, as far as the state is concerned, adults are left to reap the benefits or to suffer the consequences. These days, marriage law for couples is laissez-faire with respect to their "internal marriage."[50] It tells the couple very little about how they are supposed to interact with each other. They do not have to live together, pool their finances, cooperate, treat each other nicely, or love each other; basically, they only must refrain from harming each other. Within such a minimally regulated monogamous marriage, "individuals are free to create a variety of meanings of marriage for themselves."[51] For the most part, the state is indifferent to its quality. Why, then, is marital choice so limited when it comes to marrying more than one person at the same time or marrying someone who is already married to someone else? The decision to enter into such a marital relationship may turn out to be wonderful, terrible, or somewhere in between the two extremes, but the likely outcome is hard to predict without a crystal ball.

D. *Lawrence*

In this section, I want to highlight the importance of *Lawrence* in the coming debate over plural marriage and explain why this decision stands for a lot more

[50] I borrow the term "internal marriage," which covers the personal interactions of the couple, from Regan, *Alone Together*, 5.

[51] Martha Albertson Fineman, *The Autonomy Myth: A Theory of Dependency* (New York: The New Press, 2004), 97.

than the narrow constitutional right to have sex with a consenting adult in the privacy of one's home. The holding of this case transcends its particular fact pattern and can be construed more broadly to establish the constitutional right of marital choice. As Kennedy writes, this "case involves liberty of the person in both its spatial and more transcendent dimensions."[52] Prior to *Lawrence*, the Supreme Court laid the groundwork for a more expansive conception of personal liberty in *Casey*:

> These matters, involving the most intimate and personal choices a person may make in a lifetime, choices central to personal dignity and autonomy, are central to the liberty protected by the Fourteenth Amendment. At the heart of liberty is the right to define one's own conception of existence, of meaning, of the universe, and of the mystery of human life. Beliefs about these matters could not define the attributes of personhood were they formed under compulsion of the State.[53]

In *Lawrence*, Kennedy cites this passage to support his belief that the Constitution protects a fundamental right to not only make deeply personal decisions but to also live according to them. To view *Lawrence* as a case merely about same-sex sex or sexual activity more generally is to miss its deeper meaning: why we value the freedom to select our intimate partners in forming the kinds of personal relationships we find most worthwhile. If Texas had made friendships between gay persons illegal, then even if such friendships were platonic, many of us would still conclude that such a law violates the constitutional principle of individual autonomy without adequate justification.

From this perspective, *Bowers* is wrongly decided not so much because a state could criminalize certain kinds of consensual sex acts but because it denies a competent adult sovereignty over crucial aspects of his or her life. As I mentioned earlier, it is important to distinguish between criminalizing the practice of plural marriage and the state's refusal to include such relationships in its definition of civil marriage. Kennedy draws this distinction in *Lawrence*.[54] The former would seem to require even more justification than the latter because before the Supreme Court's decision, a person could be prosecuted for violating the Texas statute and deprived of his or her freedom. Even if criminalization did not require additional justification, though, in his dissent in *Lawrence*, Justice Scalia fails to distinguish between them. Additionally, he insinuates that the right to autonomy articulated by Justice Kennedy in

[52] *Lawrence v. Texas*, 539 U.S. 562 (2003).
[53] *Planned Parenthood of Southeastern Pennsylvania v. Casey*, 505 U.S. 833, 851 (1992).
[54] *Lawrence v. Texas*, 539 U.S. 567 (2003).

his majority opinion might force the state to recognize bigamy. The failure on Scalia's part to recognize such a distinction weakens the slippery slope argument that the judicial invalidation of laws that ban consensual same-sex sex between adults will invariably lead to a constitutional right to plural marriage. Because there may be relevant differences between the two situations, one may be able to draw a principled distinction between them.

A closer examination of *Lawrence* reveals that the Supreme Court did not explicitly equate a privacy right to engage in same-sex sexual intercourse with same-sex or plural marriage. For Kennedy, this case "does not involve whether government must give formal recognition to any relationship that homosexual persons seek to enter."[55] As he later explains, the constitutional concern that arises in this case is that in the eyes of the law, those who engaged in such sex acts were criminals.[56] For Justice Sandra O'Connor, a rational basis for prohibiting same-sex marriage still may exist.[57] On the other hand, Scalia has a point: It is not unreasonable to identify the implications that the justices themselves may not have seen (or may not have said out loud to avoid provoking controversy). After all, when it comes to public opinion about same-sex marriage, 2003 is not 2015. At the end of the day, Scalia may be right – for the wrong reasons – in linking what the Supreme Court said in *Lawrence* to the future meaning of marriage. Kennedy begins his majority opinion in *Lawrence* by writing that "[f]reedom extends beyond spatial bounds" and speaking of the "transcendent dimensions" of liberty.[58] That is language that invites interpreters to expand the constitutional right of autonomy and it is hard to believe that Kennedy was unaware that what he had said could be taken in different directions under different circumstances. Shortly thereafter, he refers to such well-known substantive due process cases as *Pierce*, *Meyer*, *Griswold*, *Eisenstadt*, and *Roe*.[59] In fairness, then, Scalia cannot be labeled an alarmist, particularly when Kennedy may have intimated a much broader right to autonomy and judges will have to construe the holding of the case and apply it to unforeseeable fact patterns. No one can know with any certainty what a precedent may come to mean in the future or what outcome in a new case it may ultimately support.

That said, Scalia's view could be more nuanced. The first step to distinguishing the privacy right recognized in *Lawrence* from a right to plural marriage would be to see that there may be plausible or even compelling reasons to justify a ban on plural marriages that simply do not support keeping same-sex sex acts illegal. *Lawrence* can be reasonably construed as standing for

[55] Ibid., 578. [56] Ibid., 567. [57] Ibid., 585 (O'Connor, J., concurring). [58] Ibid., 562.
[59] Ibid., 562–65.

a presumption in favor of freedom of choice in the most important aspects of people's private lives.[60] The state can no longer rely on its purported interest in preserving public morality without providing additional (and better) reasons for prohibition, but the Supreme Court does not specify which reasons would suffice.[61] As one commentator writes, *Lawrence* not only "remove[d] one huge roadblock" to same-sex marriage, but it also may have laid the groundwork for a more Libertarian understanding of the extent to which the state may not restrict options when it comes to deeply personal decisions.[62]

Today, a law that made interracial marriage a crime would be undeniably unconstitutional.[63] A law that made interracial cohabitation a crime would also be characterized as such and banning other sorts of cohabitation between consenting adults would be – at the very least – constitutionally suspect.[64] Those constitutional facts imply that it may not be as easy as it used to be to interfere with people's private lives by limiting their choice of marriage partners. True, one could believe a state could not criminalize a consensual living arrangement without recognizing it as a marriage-like status. Whether states may make polygamy illegal is a separate (but related) question from whether states must treat a plural marriage as if it were a monogamous marriage; the sorts of reasons the state would adduce to defend such a law are also relevant in the second situation.

At the same time, we now live in a post-*Lawrence* world, and in terms of human psychology at least, it seems that as time passes, more people will become more accustomed to defining marriage less narrowly when the Supreme Court refuses to permit the state to restrict freedom on the basis of traditional morality. Mere moral disapproval of same-sex consensual sex no longer suffices to make that act a crime from the standpoint of the Constitution and in the eyes of most Americans. Instead, the rationale for such a law will have to be more compelling than the purported sinfulness of the behavior in question or the moral distress that that behavior may cause others when nobody is being directly harmed.[65] The privacy rationale of *Lawrence* is less

60 Ibid., 558. 61 Sanford Levinson, "The Meaning of Marriage," 1052.

62 Dale Carpenter, *Flagrant Conduct: The Story of* Lawrence v. Texas (New York: Norton, 2012), 283.

63 *Loving v. Virginia*, 388 U.S. 1 (1967).

64 *McLaughlin v. Florida*, 379 U.S. 184 (1964) (invalidating a Florida law that banned interracial cohabitation).

65 Plural marriage advocates are increasingly using privacy-based arguments, as opposed to religious freedom ones, to argue in favor of decriminalization. Jeffrey Michael Hayes, "Polygamy Comes Out of the Closet: The New Strategy of Polygamy Activists," *Stanford Journal of Civil Rights and Civil Liberties*, 3 (2007), 109.

controversial than it used to be and the notion that the state should not interfere in people's most important personal choices is no longer limited to the question of whether the state may criminalize certain sorts of activities.

E. The Right to Marriage

The constitutional right to marriage does not appear in the constitutional text, but it is well established in case law and only the most fanatical of originalists would take the opposite view. As the Supreme Court stated in 1974: "This Court has long recognized that freedom of personal choice in matters of marriage and family life is one of the liberties protected by the Due Process Clause of the Fourteenth Amendment."[66] However, knowledgeable people sincerely and reasonably disagree about its scope; they do not always converge on the rationale for the constitutionality of certain restrictions.[67] The constitutional right to marriage – unlike most other fundamental rights – is a positive right; it does not ask the state to refrain from doing something but rather places an affirmative duty on the state to provide a status.[68] States can decide some of its eligibility requirements and which material benefits or legal privileges – if any – to attach to it.[69]

F. Utah Cases

Although the U.S. Supreme Court refused to hear this case on appeal, the Utah Supreme Court directly addressed the issue in *Holm* of whether polygamy can be a crime. Rodney Holm was convicted of violating an antibigamy statute despite raising a number of claims under the U.S. Constitution, including free exercise of religion, substantive due process, overbreadth, freedom of association, and equal protection.[70] The Utah Supreme Court ruled that "Holm misconstrues the breadth of the *Lawrence* opinion" and concluded that it is "actually quite narrow."[71] According to its opinion, that court had no other choice but to read the decision as narrowly as possible and in doing so distinguish the fact pattern of Holm's case. Unlike *Lawrence*, this case involves "marriage" and a minor.[72]

[66] *Cleveland Board of Education v. LaFleur*, 414 U.S. 632, 639–40 (1974).

[67] In discussing the constitutional right to marry, Cass Sunstein draws a useful distinction between its content and its scope. See Sunstein, "The Right to Marry," *Cardozo Law Review*, 26 (2005), 2082.

[68] Patricia A. Cain, "Imagine There's No Marriage," *Quinnipiac Law Review*, 16 (1996), 32.

[69] *Maynard v. Hill*, 125 U.S. 190, 205 (1888).

[70] *Utah v. Holm*, 2006 UT 131; 137 P.3d 726 (2006). [71] Ibid., 54. [72] Ibid., 56.

To be in favor of the decriminalization of polygamy is certainly not to be in favor of a brave new marital world in which anything goes and the state condones child brides, lost boys, or other serious crimes. At the outset, we would be equally concerned if Holm had only "married" one minor. The harm, which the Utah penal code covers, concerns the state's interest in preventing minors from making decisions they are not sufficiently prepared to make and subsequently being exploited or harmed. The rationale of *Holm* parallels that of statutory rape laws that take into account differences in power and the greater likelihood of immaturity on the part of the person who is too young to consent legally (and also too young to form a valid marital contract). If a minor had not been involved, then Holm would probably not have been prosecuted in the first place. Even if he had been prosecuted, the result on appeal would probably have been different because a minor's involvement was a material fact of the holding. It is not terribly difficult to see why the state's interest in protecting minors is much stronger than its interest in saving competent adults from themselves. *Lawrence* is about consenting adults and not minors. This kind of narrow reading is not obviously wrong, but it fails to capture the spirit of the opinion, which as I explained earlier is about having the right to make the most personal of personal choices without undue interference by the state.

In *Green*, another case from Utah involving a criminal conviction for polygamy, in his concurrence, Justice Matthew Durrant claims that the state has a compelling interest in prohibiting polygamy because it threatens monogamous marriage.[73] This is a remarkable admission on the part of one of the justices that the state's rationale is perfectionist; it is advancing a particular conception of marriage on the ground it is superior to the alternatives. Unlike in the past, that rationale is increasingly problematic. The more recent lower federal court decisions regarding same-sex marriage indicate that the state may no longer use the alleged superiority of monogamy to justify the unequal treatment of certain marriages. By contrast, in her dissent, Chief Justice Christine Durham maintains that Utah lacks the authority to criminalize "the privacy of intimate, personal relationships between consenting adults" and adds that if Holm's intimate partner had not been a minor, his conviction would have to be overturned.[74] While she stops short of recognizing a constitutional right to plural marriage, she points out that Utah has not adduced evidence that supports its position that polygamy causes incest, sexual assault, statutory rape, and/or failure to pay child support.[75] She then concludes that Utah lacks an important state interest in criminalizing bigamy.[76]

[73] *Green*, 2004, UT 276. [74] *Utah v. Holm*, 2006 UT 131–34. [75] Ibid., 175.
[76] Ibid., 179.

G. Personal Choice Revisited

Those who oppose plural marriage – if they want their view to have the force of law – must do a better job of elucidating why the legal definition of marriage should exclude marital relationships that contain more than two adults and must address why an exclusion of that kind is consistent with treating everyone fairly. My point is not that they could not possibly do so but that they have not come close to doing so when their constitutional position cannot be based on legal moralism, tradition, or on utilitarian reasoning that relies so heavily on the empirically questionable secondary effects of only one type of plural marriage – namely, traditional polygyny. Their only real option is to reject the value of autonomy or personal choice and maintain that paternalism on the part of the state would be appropriate because some women will make the decision, which they will later regret, to enter a multiperson marriage.

Even if this option were more plausible, it does not cohere with the American constitutional tradition, which can be construed as requiring exceedingly persuasive justification when a statute infringes on the fundamental right to marry. My defense of plural marriage does not stem from a crude moral relativism or subjectivism but from a basic moral insight: What is good for human beings varies significantly with particular facts about them and their circumstances. Respecting their right to choose – notwithstanding the potentially adverse consequences – reflects the constitutional importance of their participating in the decision-making process and the likelihood that they are more knowledgeable about themselves than anyone else could be. That is why I defend the constitutional right to marry more than one person at the same time and remain agnostic about whether it would be better for more people to have multipartner relationships. A plural marriage is not for everyone and probably not for most of us, given the time, patience, and effort that having a decent intimate relationship with only one partner requires.

On the other hand, marriages not based on any sort of romance or sexual intimacy might turn out to be not only more stable and fulfilling for more people but also invite them to reconsider their priorities and figure out what is most important to them. Just because two people are mutually sexually attracted hardly means that they will be compatible in the most important ways, enjoy each other's company, and live happily ever after. In the end, whether a particular person should make such a choice – like other profoundly personal choices – is best left up to him or her. Premarital agreements already permit couples to contract around most of the default rules that would otherwise govern the end of their marital relationship, allowing them to customize their marital relationship to a great degree. Still, courts can invalidate such agreements in situations where the party that is disadvantaged had no legal representation or the terms are egregiously unfair. Whether it ultimately works better than the alternatives is contingent on the particulars. This is why everyone should care about whether such a right ought to exist; it is wrong to frame the issue too narrowly and not see it as a matter of whether the state has the authority to restrict people's freedom of choice in highly personal matters.

If traditional monogamous marriages were inherently unequal, frequently involved less than fully autonomous choices, or were unarguably dysfunctional, to ban them on those bases alone would amount to a serious violation of the liberty of the two persons who want to marry each other.[77] Critics of plural marriage have not yet adequately defended this double standard. I doubt they will be able to do so if what they have produced so far is any indication of the quality of arguments they shall offer at a later date. At bottom, the state's not extending the constitutional right of marriage to those who would marry more than one person at the same time is unjustified discrimination. That conclusion follows from the premise that all of us are free and equal under the Constitution and must be treated as such.

In the last century, family law in the United States changed dramatically, offering "adults a lot more choices" than they used to have.[78] One way to understand the aim of this book is to see it as an attempt to defend the continuation of this trend to maximize marital choice. In 1993, in *Baehr v. Lewin*, the Hawaii Supreme Court decided that the denial of marriage to same-sex couples constitutes gender discrimination and thus violates the Equal Protection Clause of the Hawaii Constitution.[79] That was the first time a court created something like a constitutional right to same-sex marriage.[80] The U.S. Supreme Court has declared that the right to marriage is "one of the vital personal rights essential to the orderly pursuit of happiness."[81] That declaration alone suggests that the denial of such a right to those – male or female – who want to marry multiple persons must be based on more than mere moral disapproval, visceral dislike of the people or conduct in question, or negative stereotypes. The rationale behind the use of strict scrutiny in

77 See Cheshire Calhoun, "Who's Afraid of Polygamous Marriage? Lessons for Same-Sex Marriage Advocacy From the History of Polygamy," *San Diego Law Review*, 42 (2005), 1040–41.

78 William N. Eskridge Jr., "A Liberal Vision of U.S. Family Law in 2020," in *The Constitution in 2020*, ed. Jack M. Balkin and Reva B. Siegel (New York: Oxford University Press, 2009).

79 *Baehr v. Lewin*, 852 P. 2d. 44 (Haw. 1993).

80 Daniel R. Pinello, *America's Struggle for Same-Sex Marriage* (New York: Cambridge University Press, 2006), 25.

81 *Loving v. Virginia*, 388 U.S. 12 (1967).

fundamental rights and some equal protection cases is that the state may not deprive people of their personal freedom or treat them unequally without very good reasons for doing so.[82]

In the past, though, most judges have not been receptive to arguments that support a right to plural marriage and that fact probably stems from the extent to which the thinking of most judges on novel constitutional questions does not stray too far from public opinion. All things being equal, the more unconventional the legal thinking on the part of the attorney, legal scholar, or judge, the less likely he or she will ever serve on an appellate court. Not surprisingly, the vast majority of judges have been much less critical than they ought to have been toward the strength of the state's interests in not allowing the option of plural marriage. In upholding the Mann Act, Justice Douglas writes, "the establishment or maintenance of polygamous households is a notorious example of promiscuity."[83] Today, I suspect no justice could get away with such an inaccurate statement and frame the putative right to plural marriage as simply being about having multiple sexual partners. That said, no state permits plural marriage and no state is likely in the near future to create such a right. Nor do any domestic partnership or civil union laws in this country allow multiple partners to register.[84] In almost all states, polygamy is illegal, with the exception of Hawaii, where the second marriage is merely annulled.[85] These states criminalize remarrying, attempting to remarry, purporting to remarry, or cohabitating as man and wife when a former marriage has not been terminated and the former spouse is still alive.[86]

On the other hand, antipolygamy laws are usually not enforced.[87] In *Lawrence*, for Kennedy, the nonenforcement of statutes prohibiting same-sex sex acts meant that the state did not have a particularly strong interest.[88] In *Meyer v. Nebraska*, the Supreme Court first announced that marriage must be treated as a fundamental right.[89] The Supreme Court has extended this right by ensuring that states may not restrict that right without adequate justification and rejected the following reasons for limiting the choice of one's marital

[82] See Sonu Bedi, *Rejecting Rights* (New York: Cambridge University Press, 2009).

[83] *Cleveland v. United States*, 329 U.S. 14, 19 (1946). [84] Emens, "Monogamy's Law," 361.

[85] Samantha Slark, "Are Anti-Polygamy Laws an Unconstitutional Infringement on the Liberty Interests of Consenting Adults?" *Journal of Law and Family Studies*, 6 (2004), 453.

[86] Ibid.

[87] Jaime M. Gher, "Polygamy and Same-Sex Marriage–Allies or Adversaries Within the Same-Sex Marriage Movement?" *William and Mary Journal of Women and the Law*, 14 (2008), 579.

[88] *Lawrence v. Texas*, 539 U.S. 562 (2003). [89] *Meyer v. Nebraska*, 262 U.S. 390, 399 (1923).

partner: being a member of a particular race, being incarcerated, and being behind on child support payments.[90] More recently, a growing number of state and federal judges have also found sexual orientation as a basis of marital discrimination to be constitutionally unacceptable. In sum, there is a constitutional right to marry for just about any competent adult who wants to marry another competent adult of the opposite gender.

G. *Interracial Marriage*

In *Loving v. Virginia*, Chief Justice Earl Warren articulated the importance of a person's being able to choose his or her spouse.[91] In the context of the debate over same-sex marriage, however, each side disagrees about what the holding is. One may read Warren's majority opinion narrowly and conclude there is only a fundamental right to interracial marriage. According to this view, *Loving* stands for the principle that the state may not deny the right to marry to someone who seeks to marry a person of a different racial or ethnic group. The only reason the state could have for such a prohibition is racist and thus illegitimate.[92] In *Loving*, Warren did not find that the infamous "equal application theory" – where under state law white and black persons are "punished to the same degree" – could be separated from invidious racial discrimination against African-Americans.[93] Throughout his majority opinion, Warren's focal point was race which not surprising in the context of the struggle for civil rights. In a relatively short opinion, he mentioned "race" or "racial" numerous times in explaining why the legislative classification in question is not subject to the rational basis standard of review Virginia had asked for.[94] That is why such a narrow reading of this well-known decision is at least defensible.

Alternatively, one could construe the principle of nondiscrimination that underlies *Loving* more broadly and not reduce its scope to restrictions on marriage that involve race but stretch it to cover all classifications where the state does not have an adequate rationale to treat particular persons differently. Therefore, all laws restricting marriage ought to be subject to strict scrutiny, which is a fancy way of saying the state must have very good reasons for

[90] See *Loving v. Virginia*, 388 U.S. 1 (1967); *Zablocki v. Redhail*, 434 U.S. 374 (1978); *Boddie v. Connecticut*, 401 U.S. 371 (1971); and *Turner v. Safley*, 428 U.S. 78 (1987).

[91] *Loving v. Virginia*, 388 U.S. 1 (1967).

[92] The Virginia Supreme Court had found that the state's purposes of preserving "the racial integrity of its citizens" and preventing "the corruption of blood" were legitimate. As Warren points out, these reasons are an "endorsement of the doctrine of White Supremacy." *Loving v. Virginia*, 388 U.S. 1, 7 (1967).

[93] Ibid., 8. [94] Ibid., 8–9.

treating some persons differently than others when it denies only some persons the right to marry. No constitutional right is absolute, and even when strict scrutiny is not always fatal in fact, a very strong presumption against restricting any constitutional right is present unless the state can justify such a restriction. The implication of the use of this analytical framework is that the alleged immorality, strangeness, or offensiveness of certain kinds of marriages – even as far as most people are concerned – cannot perform the necessary justificatory work. As Evan Gerstmann observes: "If the fundamental right to marry did not protect some things that shock and repulse most people, it would be a uniquely narrow right."[95] At present, that a particular kind of behavior allegedly corrupts public morals or causes others distress but does not directly harm them is unlikely to rise to the level of an important or compelling interest.[96]

III. MILLIAN EXPERIMENTS IN LIVING

A. *Overview*

In this section, I want to shift gears by focusing on the possible individual and collective benefits that legal recognition of plural marriage could produce. For the most part, those who defend the legal recognition of plural marriage rely on one or more of the following justifications: equal treatment, freedom of association, tolerance, respect for personal choice in private matters, acknowledgment of cultural difference, and free exercise of religion. Their strategy is recognizably liberal in incorporating a presumption in favor of allowing behavior that is largely self-regarding, putting the burden of proof on those who oppose plural marriage, and then explaining why these opponents have not met this burden. That is my basic strategy in this book. That someone has chosen to have such a marital relationship – for whatever personal reason(s) he or she happens to have – is supposed to trump any countervailing considerations – unless they are compelling. The critical point is that those reasons are his or hers. Their quality is neither here nor there because it is his or her life and no one else's. As I have argued, it is reasonable to assume that (a) most people do not try to know other people very well, (b) are not privy to the details of their lives, and (c) are not well equipped to

95 Evan Gerstmann, *Same-Sex Marriage and the Constitution* (New York: Cambridge University Press, 2004), 109.

96 On the weaknesses of arguments that purport to justify the legal enforcement of morality, see H. L. A. Hart, *Law, Liberty and Morality* (Stanford, CA: Stanford University Press, 1963).

know what is best for them. As a result, the state should defer to his or her marital choices. At most, it can try to ensure that those choices are as well informed and as voluntary as possible, which can be consistent with empowering him or her to exercise his or her autonomy as effectively as possible.

Proponents of the right to plural marriage pay much less attention to the possibly good consequences of expanding the legal definition of marriage to include multiperson relationships. In constitutional theory, the defense of the importance of personal choice in many contexts, ranging from abortion to freedom of religion, is rarely consequentialist. Furthermore, rhetorically, silence about the good consequences that might follow from such marriage is understandable when beginning a conversation about the possible merits of plural marriage may involve more risk than reward in a society that continues to privilege monogamy, has not yet fully accepted same-sex marriage, and tends to be prejudiced against sexual minorities.

However, the disadvantage of the standard liberal approach, which relies so heavily on the intrinsic value of the exercise of autonomy, is that those who employ it must remain reticent about the benefits that might flow from the advent of plural marriage. While asking for or demanding tolerance is a prudent strategy, it may amount to conceding the superiority of monogamous marriages and acknowledging that the state is justified in privileging them.[97] By comparison, in the context of the debate over same-sex marriage, to settle for civil unions is to signal that (real) marriage is only for straight persons. Unconventional marriages may move others to think more critically about the nature of their own intimate relationships and how they might improve them. As Elizabeth Emens observes: "The frequent failure of supermonogamy – the idea of one partner forever – is reflected in our high divorce rates."[98] Even if monogamous marriages work better for most people most of the time, it does not follow that they work better for all people all the time. Because individuals and their differences matter, nothing less than individualized treatment by the state is called for. As time goes by, social acceptance of thruples or group or two-person nonromantic marriages may change the institution for the better in the sense that more people are more actively involved in making their marital relationship their own because they have a much longer list of options to choose from and have given more thought to what they ultimately want.

97 See Michael Sandel, "Moral Argument and Liberal Toleration: Abortion and Homosexuality," *California Law Review*, 77 (1989), 521.

98 Elizabeth F. Emens, "Monogamy's Law: Compulsory Monogamy and Polyamorous Existence," *New York University Review of Law and Social Change*, 29 (2004), 297.

The typical liberal strategy of avoidance of the possible merits also reinforces what is supposed to be "normal" by obscuring how the state's privileging certain intimate relationships marginalizes others that may be equally or more valuable.[99] The state's creating the possibility of plural marriage would let Americans know that at least for some people, a nonmonogamous or nonsexual marital relationship fits in with their way of life better than the alternatives. The measure of a successful marriage, then, could be less about its form – whether it is two-person or opposite sex – and more about the quality of the relationship and what the individuals in that relationship happen to value, need, or desire.[100]

We live in a society in which the superiority of monogamy goes virtually unchallenged and social pressures and legal incentives nudge most of us in a monogamous direction.[101] In a new marital regime, some people might not choose monogamy if other options are available. Politically, one might go even further by taking John Stuart Mill's position that the state should promote unconventional behaviors because such a policy creates opportunities for experimentation.[102] In what follows, I put forth an affirmative case for plural marriage – rooted in Mill's well-known idea of experiments of living – by calling attention to the value of the unconventional to the individual and the society in which he or she lives.

My position is premised on the importance of enabling people to develop into the kinds of people they aspire to be. For some of them, a plural marriage could be a vehicle of self-development. There may be a lot more to be said on behalf of the experiment of plural marriage and its possible benefits than most people realize when so little is known about what such marriages might be like in a society that did not reduce all of them to the worst manifestations of polygyny or demonize those who partake in them. Most Americans have little familiarity with plural marriage because the media tend to focus on FLDS polygyny – at the expense of all its other forms – and to be preoccupied with its

[99] See Elizabeth Brake, *Minimizing Marriage: Marriage, Morality, and the Law* (New York: Oxford University Press, 2012), 4–5.

[100] It is notoriously difficult to measure marital quality. See Paul R. Amato et al., *Alone Together: How Marriage in America Is Changing* (Cambridge, MA: Harvard University Press, 2007), 37–38.

[101] Emens, "Monogamy's Law," 284.

[102] See Jeremy Waldron, "Mill and the Value of Moral Distress," in *Liberal Rights: Collected Papers 1981–1991* (Cambridge, UK: Cambridge University Press, 1993), 115–33. One of the prominent themes in some of Thoreau's writings involves the necessity of personal experience, attention to the most minute details, and experimentation in learning how to live well. See, for example, Henry David Thoreau, "Walden," in *Walden and Other Writings by Henry David Thoreau*, ed. Joseph Wood Krutch (New York: Bantam Books, 1982).

salacious aspects. [103] Moreover, those who practice nonmonogamy more generally are not inclined to out themselves to their colleagues, friends, neighbors, and family members. Like many gays and lesbians in the past and some of them today, most polygamists do not feel comfortable disclosing their identities to the rest of the world.

B. Mill's "On Liberty"

The vast literature on Mill's political thought is daunting and I shall not attempt to take sides in debates over what Mill really meant or believed. Instead, I will try to reconstruct his idea of experiments of living in the present-day setting of the question of how our society should view plural marriage and treat those who want to have such a marital relationship. Plural marriage was not what Mill had in mind when he spoke of experiments of living in the nineteenth century, but at present, we would not embrace a number of Mill's views, such as those involving nonwhite societies, which Mill thought to be uncivilized. Moreover, in some respects, Mill is far from a twenty-first-century feminist. That is not to say that Millian insights about the value of the unconventional are no longer relevant. If anything, they are even more crucial in a society that normally prides itself on its tolerance of difference and therefore tends to be too complacent. The greatest danger is that we sincerely think we are open to the unconventional when we are not because we have internalized the correctness of the conventional. Our moral judgment about nonmonogamous intimate relationships is more likely to reflect our love of the familiar and our fear of difference than its possible merits.

My primary purpose, then, is not exegetical, which is why I will refer to "Millian" experiments of living as I attempt to put together a Millian argument in favor of unconventional personal relationships and marriages while giving credit where credit is due.[104] Mill puts his finger on a problem that still characterizes a liberal democracy like our own: The real threat to individuality is not only to be found in coercive laws but also in the tyranny of public opinion, which too often confirms the status quo and pressures people to conform to widely accepted social norms that threaten individuality and

[103] See Janet Bennion, *Polygamy in Primetime: Media, Gender, and Politics in Mormon Fundamentalism* (Waltham, MA: Brandies University Press, 2012), especially 163–94.

[104] Mill is not the only thinker who emphasizes the importance of personal experience (and its emotional dimensions) in human flourishing. Such experience is also central to Buddhism. Damien Keown, *Buddhism: A Very Short Introduction* (2013), 8.

impede self-cultivation. Most Americans sincerely believe themselves to be open-minded, but they are too often prone to be afraid of the other, to make rash judgments, to be self-righteousness, and to make themselves feel morally superior by condemning what they do not know or understand.[105] Even when they make the effort, they still may not appreciate what is unfamiliar when it has no place in their conceptual framework about how people are supposed to live.

This all-too-human practice of distrusting the unconventional continues to occur – even in liberal societies that are supposed to be open to difference – and remains troubling because it unnecessarily interferes with some persons' lives and detracts from their quality. It is never easy for anyone to adopt a different way of life in the midst of well-entrenched social norms that most people take for granted. Being misunderstood is particularly painful. That Mill was opposed to social conformity goes without saying; to follow custom uncritically is to avoid the duty of developing one's own individuality. Failing to do so reveals a character flaw on the part of the person who cares more about how others perceive him or her than what he or she ought to care deeply about – namely, becoming the kind of person who does not fear the unconventional and acts accordingly. The trouble lies not in the fact that public opinion tends to converge on certain beliefs and behaviors but that ordinary people care too much about what others think, thereby deterring them from what they would otherwise do.

For Mill, unconventional ways of life must be tolerated because they may illuminate the nature of human flourishing and yield examples that can be emulated, making social progress possible.[106] As David Heyd writes: "Tolerance is a philosophically elusive concept."[107] As it is usually understood, toleration involves noninterference so people are free to choose how they want to live. The trouble that results from intolerance is not just political conflict and even violence but also that intolerance leads to interference with how that person is living his or her life when the state could simply leave him or her alone to allow him or her to have the life he or she desires. The wrong stems from the unnecessary restriction of personal liberty when others are not being harmed or at risk of being harmed. In terms of autonomy or freedom of conscience, what matters is the extent to which that way of life was freely

[105] For an insightful critique of how such liberal feminists as Susan Okin implicitly assume such a posture by disparaging non-Western cultural practices, see Wendy Brown, "Tolerance as/in Civilization Discourse," in *Toleration and Its Limits*, ed. Melissa S. Williams and Jeremy Waldron (New York: New York University Press, 2008), 406–41.

[106] Mill, "On Liberty," 57.

[107] David Heyd, "Introduction," in *Toleration: An Elusive Virtue*, ed. David Heyd (Princeton, NJ: Princeton University Press, 1996), 3.

chosen.[108] It does not mean acceptance in the sense of respect for that way of life due to its quality. To ask someone to value or respect my particular way of life on its merits is to ask too much. It may be unreasonable to criticize others for not respecting a life they sincerely believe to be frivolous or mistaken. That is why, at the end of the day, widespread tolerance is a substantial achievement in any human society – whatever its basis happens to be.

Mill did not have a lot so say about tolerance per se, but he opposed coercive interference and left room for noncoercive interference, even in cases of self-regarding conduct for people to convince others that their way of life is misguided. In his words:

> As it is useful that while mankind are imperfect there should be different opinions, there should be different experiments of living; that free scope should be given to varieties of character, short of injuries to others; and that the worth of different modes of life, should be proved practically, when anyone thinks fit to try them.[109]

In this passage, Mill makes several points that need to be disaggregated. First, human agents have to do it themselves. As John Skorupski writes: "People then have to do their own work of self-development, because human potentialities are diverse and best known to the individual person, and because only by working out their own plans of life, do they develop more freedom."[110] Second, Mill assumes that people have not perfected themselves. They cannot continue to cultivate their capacities and learn from the process of trial and error unless they retain the imagination and courage to take advantage of opportunities for such growth. Third, people must have space to cultivate their own individuality, provided they do not harm others. Fourth, what a good human life consists of is to be determined by experience. The "experiments" part of "experiments of living" suggests that for Mill, personal growth or self-improvement is always possible, provided that one is continually willing to experiment. A life is not best because it is "the best in itself, but because it is his own mode [of living]."[111]

Other than the previous passage, Mill has a bit more to say about the character of such experiments and why they are worthwhile. As he remarks: "People should be eccentric."[112] A conception of the good is supposed to yield a perspective of self-understanding, which is personally compelling (has normative force for the agent) and guides him or her in deciding how to live in a

[108] See Bernard Williams, "Toleration: An Impossible Virtue?" in *Toleration: An Elusive Virtue*, ed. David Heyd (Princeton, NJ: Princeton University Press, 1996), 18–27.

[109] Mill, "On Liberty," 57.

[110] John Skorupski, *Why Read Mill Today?* (New York: Routledge, 2007), 25.

[111] Mill, "On Liberty," 67. [112] Ibid.

manner that reflects the kind of individual that he or she aspires to be. The implication is not that a particular conception of the good that meets this test is superior to all its rivals. Rather, each person must test his or her theoretical conception against his or her personal experiences and adjust his or her conception accordingly.[113] In this respect, one's life is always a work in progress.

Above all, people must be open to having new experiences, learn from them, and scrutinize their most cherished beliefs. Otherwise, they will not only fail to appreciate the lives of others who are different from them but will also lack self-awareness. It is not enough for an individual to reject conventional wisdom, to display contempt for tradition, to be different just for the sake of being different (like teenagers), or to contemplate theoretical possibilities from a distance. They also must "acknowledge the contingency of their inherited commitments."[114] Put another way, nobody should ever forget that had they been born at a different time in a different place into different circumstances, their lives would be very different. As John Gray states, "an autonomous agent must have distanced himself in some measure from the conventions of his social environment and from the influence of the persons surrounding him."[115] This statement may mean that at least some people will adopt nonliberal ways of life. In Alan Ryan's view, "The moment of truth for a pluralist comes when he is asked whether he is happy to see a great variety of non-liberal ways of life flourish for the sake of variety. . . ."[116] According to Ryan, Mill ducks this normative question by insisting we simply do not know enough about nonliberal ways of life to render an informed judgment about their merits.[117]

Unlike Ryan, I think that Mill may be more right than he is wrong about how well, even today, we understand how people in other cultures understand themselves and what makes life worth living. Mill's way of thinking about the nature of a good human life has political and legal implications. The trouble is that in a democracy, Mill believes that citizens are likely to misuse their power by suppressing dissent and difference.[118] Public opinion more often than not turns out to be uninformed oppressive. In the end, Mill seems to be mostly pessimistic about the prospects of most people's successfully resisting conformity in thought and action. The forces of individuality do not stand much of a

[113] Elizabeth S. Anderson, "John Stuart Mill and Experiments in Living," *Ethics*, 102 (1991), 26.

[114] Alex Zakaras, *Individuality and Mass Democracy: Mill, Emerson, and the Burdens of Citizenship* (New York: Oxford University Press, 2009), 128.

[115] John Gray, *Mill on Liberty: A Defence* (2nd ed.) (London: Routledge, 1996), 74.

[116] Alan Ryan, "Mill in a Liberal Landscape," in *The Cambridge Companion to Mill*, ed. John Skorupski (Cambridge, UK: Cambridge University Press, 1998), 534.

[117] Ibid. [118] Zakaras, *Individuality and Mass Democracy*, 127.

chance against them. Majorities tend to marginalize minorities – and not just religious and cultural ones – and people do not want to be treated in that way if they can avoid it. The problem is not force or the threat of force but what Mill refers to as "prevailing opinion and feeling."[119] Thus, democratic societies tend to produce a certain type of person – namely, one who is inclined to accept norms uncritically, look skeptically at difference, not be introspective, and not be willing to consider the possibility that how things are done may not be the best way of doing them – at least not for everyone. Nonetheless, some hope remains. In Mill's words: "In this age, the mere example of nonconformity, the mere refusal to bend the knee to custom, is itself a service."[120]

As aforementioned, my aim is not to reconstruct what Mill had in mind with respect to experiments of living or to suggest we should be proud we have met his low expectations. Instead we should think about how all of us can use the concept today in a world that differs from that of Mill but is not too far removed from it. What should count as such an experiment, then, should not be confined to what was considered experimental in the past when circumstances change. Some people will probably be more emotionally satisfied in plural marriages, but they will also develop into better human beings insofar as they become more open, self-aware, emotionally mature, thoughtful, and better at communicating and resolving conflicts.[121] The jury is out until we have sufficient data – and that means Americans must be willing to countenance plural marriages at least until they learn more about them.[122] As Justice William Brennan writes in his dissent in *Michael H.*, "we must be willing to abide someone else's unfamiliar or even repellant practice because the same tolerant impulse protects our own idiosyncrasies."[123]

VI. THE VIRTUES OF POLYAMORY

A. *Monogamy*

I suspect that some plural marriages will turn out to be more like traditional monogamous marriages than many people anticipate – with the good and the bad – because no one who shares social space with others escapes adopting many of the common beliefs in circulation about how people are supposed to interact with one another. The success of any given plural marriage is

[119] Mill, "On Liberty," 8. [120] Ibid., 67.

[121] Ryam Nearing, *Loving More: The Polyfidelity Primer* (Captain Cook, HI: PEP Publishing, 1992), 24–27.

[122] Stanley Kurtz, "Here Come the Brides," *The Weekly Standard*, vol. 11, issue 15, (2005), p. 3, www.weeklystandard.com/Content/Public/Articles/000/000/006/494pqobc.asp.

[123] *Michael H. v. Gerald D.*, 491 U.S. 110, 141 (1989).

contingent on its specifics.[124] In that sense, it does not differ from its monogamous counterpart. In other respects, though, plural marriages are bound to present unique challenges for those involved in them due to the presence of multiple persons and their special dynamics. Ultimately, there is much to be said for monogamy inasmuch as a closer companionate relationship probably requires emotional and sexual exclusivity for the vast majority of people. There are only so many hours in a day and only so many days in a week. The more time each person has to spend with the other, the more emotionally close they can become. The same can be said about friendship. Most people do not have six or seven best friends, but they may have more than one or two. They may have many "Facebook friends" but to call a "Facebook friend" a real friend is like saying that an honorary degree is the equivalent of a real one. The development of such intimacy is more likely to take place if one does not have multiple partners and lacks the time it usually takes to get to know someone more than superficially. Along similar lines, for a parent with multiple children, it will be harder to discover what the child cares about, to meet his or her particular emotional needs, and to help him or her cope with hardships. The larger the family, the harder this task becomes, which is not to say a father or mother in a large family could not be a better parent than a father or mother with only one child.

B. *Overview of Polyamory Movement*

Unfortunately, from an early age, most Americans are taught that being married is part of a good human life.[125] I say "unfortunately" because such socialization may preclude them from seriously considering the upside of remaining single or encourage them to sacrifice other equally worthwhile personal relationships or goals. My impression is that most women suffer more than most men do from such social expectations when they have internalized certain beliefs about marriage and its importance but fail to meet what society expects of them. By contrast, few men dream about their wedding day. Today, the belief that marriage has to be opposite sex is changing slowly but surely, which means marriage is more diverse than it once was. Despite more diversity, most people continue to assume marriage has to involve two – and only two – persons at the same time. As noted, part of the trouble is that for most Americans, plural marriage is synonymous with the worst aspects of FLDS polygyny and thus it is likely to consist of one man married to multiple wives. In this country, people continue to associate polyamory with promiscuity and continue to believe that

[124] See Jon Mahoney, "Liberalism and the Polygamy Question," *Social Philosophy Today*, 23 (2008), 161–74.

[125] Sadler, "Rethinking Civil Unions and Same-Sex Marriage," 585.

unconventional sexual behavior is shameful.[126] While they can no longer have their legislators make certain consensual sex acts a crime, they can make nonconformists feel guilty about their personal choices. In a polygynous marriage, the wives would not be romantically involved with each other or one another, as they would be in a polyamorous triad. This assumption about plural marriage is understandable, given the link between it and traditional polygyny in our culture, but at least several multiperson intimate relationships, which already exist, could constitute a plural marriage. Almost any combination of numbers and sexual orientation is possible in a polyamorous arrangement. If any new form of marriage threatens to undermine traditional marriage, I suspect it would not be plural unions but rather nonsexual ones – regardless of the number of persons involved. Most Americans cannot imagine a "marriage" between two very close friends – regardless of their gender. Nor can they wrap their minds around the possibility that someone's life may be complete without her being romantically entangled with anyone.

Although the legal recognition of plural marriage would probably increase the number of people who practice nonmonogamy over time, it is difficult to predict the magnitude of such an increase or the forms it would take. Notwithstanding what the law permitted, for the foreseeable future, American society would not stop sending very strong messages about the superiority of monogamy. On the other hand, such recognition also would open the door to a woman's marrying multiple men, multiple women, or multiple men and multiple women simultaneously. A plural marriage would not always be polygynous and therefore would not always reinforce traditional gender roles. The existing polyamory community in the United States is diverse.[127] At present, those who partake in such relationships tend to be mostly white, older, straight, and middle class.[128] Also, polyamory is not the equivalent of an open marriage, which requires emotional monogamy but not sexual exclusivity.[129] Some situations may not have bright lines and polygamists may describe their unconventional lifestyles differently. The point is that any polyamorous relationship – whatever form it takes – is oriented toward emotional and sexual nonexclusivity.

For the most part, the literature on polyamory is not theoretical. Thus, there is a real need for more scholarship on this topic. The extant literature is not written for an academic audience and rarely offers a sophisticated defense of

126 Michael Warner, *The Trouble With Normal: Sex, Politics, and the Ethics of Queer Life* (Cambridge, MA: Harvard University Press, 1999), 21.

127 See Anthony D. Ravenscroft, *Polyamory: Roadmaps for the Clueless and Hopeful* (Santa Fe, NM: Fenris Brothers, 2004), 1.

128 Deborah Anapol, *Polyamory in the Twenty-First Century: Love and Intimacy With Multiple Partners* (Lanham, MD: Rowman & Littlefield, 2010), 43.

129 Ibid., 13–16.

the practice. When it does, though, writers highlight the benefits to the individual in terms of self-growth. Mostly, it contains practical advice about courting, living arrangements, parenting, and legal issues.[130] That focus is understandable due to the continuing marginalization of polyamory and its analogues and the risk of being discriminated against for being different. One of the primary assumptions in the literature is that one partner will never meet all the other partner's needs and that one of them is likely to want intimate interactions with others.[131] People who are intimate are likely to be compatible in some ways but not in all ways. No single person can meet all of his or her partner's needs, which dooms many monogamous relationships from their inception. It is natural, moreover, to want to spend quality time with more than one partner – just as it is natural to want to have multiple friends. But that does not necessarily mean he or she wants the current relationship to end. Polyamorists insist that polyamory is not only about sex but also about emotional intimacy and self-realization. It cannot be reduced to swinging or sexual experimentation but rather is a way of life.[132]

C. *Benefits to Society*

According to Judith Stacey, many same-sex relationships cross such social boundaries as race, gender, age, and socioeconomic status and facilitate more democratic social interactions.[133] One of the somewhat underappreciated arguments in favor of same-sex relationships relies on the claim that such relationships indirectly undermine traditional patriarchal relationships by providing a counterexample of how two people can live together as equals. These days, such an argument – while perhaps sound – would play right into the hands of those who oppose same-sex marriage on the ground that its legal recognition will forever change what marriage means in this country (for the worse). The mere existence of same-sex marriage may prompt people to realize that marriage could be much more diverse than it currently is. Quite frankly, those who draw the line at traditional opposite-sex marriage do not want Americans to take seriously its other possible forms because they may adopt those forms someday, which amounts to saying that competent adults are better kept in ignorance for their own good. Otherwise,

130 See, for example, Ryam Nearing, *Loving More*.

131 Tristan Taormino, *Opening Up: A Guide to Creating and Sustaining Open Relationships* (San Francisco: Cleis Press, Inc., 2008), xix.

132 Ibid., 71.

133 Judith Stacey, *Unhitched: Love, Marriage, and Family Values From West Hollywood to Western China* (New York: New York University Press, 2011), especially 42–46.

they (or their children) may end up preferring other marital forms that better suit their unique circumstances.

The existence of same-sex marriage may encourage people to be more introspective and to reflect on the choices they have made and are going to make in the future with respect to their own intimate relationships or marriages. If that turns out to be true, it is not to be regretted. More and more people would think more deeply about what they want their intimate relationships and families to be like, which would make such serious choices more autonomous and probably improve the quality of their lives. People's perspectives are often limited because their personal experiences are limited. They need to have their emotions engaged before they can see others less judgmentally, which demands more than mere exposure to unconventional ideas and practices. Without such experiences, it will be much harder for them to become more enlightened. The truth is that most of us are afraid to leave our comfort zones. The worst kind of intellectual arrogance is the refusal to appreciate the fact that we normally do not understand others and their lives very well, but we act as if we do and have nothing more to learn. After all, straight persons may learn from gay and lesbian persons about how to have healthier intimate relationships. Indeed, it would be hard to find anyone who believes that his or her intimate relationship does not contain considerable room for improvement when he or she has a moment of clarity. The existence of a variety of plural marriages would be the next logical step in inducing Americans to think and act beyond what is socially approved at a particular historical moment.

In the spirit of Mill, real examples of unconventional ways of life have no substitutes. People learn most from their own experiences and some of these experiences cause them to question whether the life they are leading is the right life for them when they begin to see the world in a different light. Under the First Amendment, it is often said there are no false ideas. The marketplace of ideas (and not the government) is supposed to determine which ideas are most likely to be true. People are legally permitted to say just about whatever they want to say about opposite or same-sex marriage or alternative lifestyles. A person is as free to defend a traditional conception of marriage as he or she is to claim it is a racist, patriarchal, or heterosexist institution that should be abolished. In a society such as ours that is committed to free speech, we will not have to worry too much about a shortage of unconventional ideas, especially in an Internet age in which it is so much easier than it used to be for like-minded people to discuss issues they care about. In such circumstances, people have access to a wide range of ideas. However, such possible exposure may be inadequate when it is so much more instructive to see real examples, to be given the opportunity to experiment and learn from the experience, and to develop empathy for those who are different and curiosity about what could be.

There is an enormous difference between reading about something or watching a documentary about it and meeting real people and interacting with them to discover what their lives are like. The latter tends to be so much more emotionally powerful. Some personal experiences, I believe, are necessary for people to see themselves and others with less distortion and to develop the compassion that can help them understand all forms human suffering. I take Mill's point to be that personal growth only takes place when we are no longer so intimidated by the unfamiliar. I doubt anyone who has not been married or cohabitated with a romantic partner could give very useful marital advice. Personal experience (and failure) and trigger introspection in a manner that cannot easily be duplicated. Part of the explanation why younger people are so much more tolerant of gays and lesbians and their intimate relationships is that they are much more likely to know nonstraight persons as colleagues or friends.[134] The point is not only that some people will be happier in nonmonogamous marriages but also that those who directly experience it are more likely to be tolerant of other differences and look at their own lives more critically. Also, they may come to have less unrealistic expectations about themselves and their partners. Eventually, the mere presence of such marriages is likely to make others less fearful about the unconventional more generally, even if that way of life is not for them.

D. Benefits to the Individual

One of the profound insights in Mill's political writings is that people are different, and as a result, what may make one person happy is not necessarily what would make another happy. Such a legal status as marriage can serve multiple purposes: to foster companionship, friendship, sexual gratification, caregiving, intellectual stimulation, and financial security. Under the status quo, every state cares about how a marriage is configured; it has to be between two and only two persons. In all fifty states, as long as a person meets the age, mental competence, and consanguinity requirements and is not already married, he or she may marry another person of the opposite gender.[135] As one cultural anthropologist puts it, "our national American culture, in its narrowly focused absolutist vision as the *only* [his emphasis] proper martial form, has

[134] Michael J. Klarman, *From the Closet to the Altar: Courts, Backlash, and the Struggle for Same-Sex Marriage* (New York: Oxford University Press, 2013), 199.

[135] William Burnham, *Introduction to the Law and Legal System of the United States* (5th ed.) (St. Paul, MN: Thomson West, 2011), 518–19.

caused much suffering to many, if not most, Americans."[136] For some or even most persons, monogamy has some well-known advantages. On the other hand, it may cause frustration, boredom, despair, and misery. One of the prominent themes in the growing nonacademic literature on polyamory is that of personal fallibility (or what Mill would have referred to as our imperfection). Because all humans are deeply flawed, they ought to take advantage of the opportunities that life gives them to identify their shortcomings in the name of self-improvement. Above all, this process includes being more honest with yourself and others.[137] The vast majority of intimate relationships are probably not as honest as they could be. For a variety of reasons, partners do not share everything with each other and will rationalize their dishonesty and conceal the kind of person they really are because they fear their partner will no longer love them or stay with them when he or she learns the truth.

For polyamorists, though, this typical way of being in a monogamous relationship is misguided. Expectations of sexual and emotional monogamy cause misery by forcing people to be more dishonest than they otherwise would be and precipitating feelings of guilt and shame. By contrast, being radically honest with oneself and with one's intimate partner(s) enhances communication.[138] If you think it would be easy to be radically honest, then trying being that way for more than a few days. Do not rationalize white lies, correct misunderstandings instead of letting them slide by, and avoid misleading people by taking things out of context or one sharing your side of the story. If you think that such honesty is not important when all is said and done, then imagine how much better your life might be is you were more honest with yourself, your colleagues, your friends, your neighbors, and your family members. The reasons to aspire to an ideal plural marriage are recognizably Millian. The aim is to become a better person by being more honest with yourself and with others, including your intimate partner(s). Part of this commitment to radical honesty requires seeing sex, love, and human relationships through a new pair of eyes and behaving accordingly. If a man or woman wants to have other sexual partners, then he or she does not have to hide that fact from his or her partner(s), creating a more authentic relationship in which neither person has to lie to or deceive the other about what he or she really wants, thereby minimizing hypocrisy and making a genuine commitment (and intimacy) possible.

[136] Philip L. Kilbride, *Plural Marriage for Our Times: A Reinvented Option?* (Westport, CT: Bergin & Garvey, 1994), x.

[137] Dossie Easton and Janet W. Hardy, *The Ethical Slut: A Practical Guide to Polyamory, Open Relationships, and Other Adventures* (2nd ed.) (Berkeley, CA: Celestial Arts, 2009), 21.

[138] Anapol, *Polyamory in the Twenty-First Century*, 76–81.

Long before the word *polyamory* came into being, Bertrand Russell described jealousy as being a creature of convention.[139] These days, many polyamorists stress the importance of overcoming jealousy.[140] For polyamorists, jealousy is a vice. Polyamorists do not see it as an inevitable reaction rooted in evolutionary biology. Instead, it is a barrier to developing healthier relationships with others. For most adults, to be jealous of a friend's other friends is to be immature or petty. Having multiple friends is not only normal but desirable because each of them has different admirable qualities we appreciate. Having multiple husbands or wives, by contrast, seems to be fundamentally different in the minds of most Americans. When one examines why one feels jealous, one can begin to overcome certain fears, such as not being everything to one's partner, feeling inadequate, and being abandoned. Polyamorists have coined a term for overcoming jealousy – "compersion" – which involves taking joy in your partner(s)' pleasure or happiness with another partner.[141] As Stacey observes, gay men seem to manage jealousy better than most opposite-sex couples do.[142] While doing so is easier said than done, its possibility indicates people can work against what appears to be natural human limitations.

Another related theme in the literature is the importance of escaping the tyranny of socialization, where many people are forced to conform to norms that do not suit them, may frustrate them, and may make them miserable. We still live in a society in which, for the most part, alternative lifestyles are discouraged, even if most of them are no longer illegal. Those who are unconventional are the target of emotional blackmail. Society tells them they are "morally deficient, psychologically disturbed, and going against nature."[143] In the past, these same kinds of accusations were leveled against gays and lesbians. Consequently, most of us internalize a norm of monogamy and believe that the only choice is monogamy or infidelity.[144] As one writer puts it: "But there I was, thinking that maybe I wanted to stay in my marriage *and* [her emphasis] see other people."[145]

Surely, this desire could be selfish or driven by one's libido. My aim is not to romanticize polygamous relationships, which are surely difficult to maintain

[139] Bertrand Russell, "Our Sexual Ethics," in *Why I Am Not a Christian* (New York: Simon and Schuster, 1957), 170.

[140] Anapol, *Polyamory in the Twenty-First Century*, 105–26; Easton and Hardy, *The Ethical Slut*, 108–30; Taormino, *Opening Up*, 153–81.

[141] Anapol, *Polyamory in the Twenty-First Century*, 22.

[142] Stacey, *Unhitched*, 46–47.

[143] Easton and Hardy, *The Ethical Slut*, 9.

[144] Deborah Anapol, *Polyamory in the Twenty-First Century*, x.

[145] Jenny Block, *Open: Love, Sex, and Life in an Open Marriage* (Berkeley, CA: Seal Press, 2008), 91.

and probably as flawed as their monogamous counterparts. One could have good or bad personal reasons for wanting to have or experiment with some sort of a multiperson relationship. Nor is there a guarantee that a person in such a relationship will develop into a more enlightened human being. His or her experience could have the opposite effect. Be that as it may, that personal choice – freely made – is his or her own and must be treated as such; it may serve as a path toward self-knowledge by providing opportunities to come to terms with his or her flaws, insecurities, and unhealthy desire to control others. As much as possible, as the pro-polygamy argument goes, people should be able to opt for such a relationship without being condemned as immoral, immature, deviant, or weird. Legal recognition of such relationships would reduce the stigma associated with them. For these reasons, we could view a polygamist relationship as a present-day Millian experiment of living and the state could foster it by allowing plural marriage to be a marital status. That reform would not only help normalize polygamist relationships and families, but it would also send a more general message to society that unconventional families are *prima facie* morally acceptable. This change in the law would allow those who partake in them to have the opportunity to have more fulfilling lives because they would have different opportunities to learn about themselves and others, to face their fears, to be honest with themselves, to decide what kind of life best suits them, and to be willing to change when necessary.

As Mill reminds us, what a good life consists of is always subject to experience and revision; it is not the kind of question that can be answered *a priori* but rather demands imagination and the courage to defy convention. The refusal to recognize the truth of this statement has a high cost, such as depriving those who would adopt that way of life under conditions of greater tolerance of the opportunity of leading what may be a better life for them. That is a Millian argument in favor of plural marriage that urges us to guard against our unfortunate tendency to assume that the conventional is correct when it comes to how people should arrange their personal lives. More than 150 years ago, Mill warned us against the tyranny of public opinion. In a modern democracy, the real threat to freedom is not the coercive power of the state but the power of others to marginalize those who are different by making them feel as if they are not only different but inferior.

We seem to have come a long way from the kind of conformity that existed in Victorian England at the time Mill penned "On Liberty." When it comes to marriage, though, our congratulating ourselves is premature. After all, three or more may not be a crowd; whether it is depends on the participants and what kind of intimate lives they want to have together. As I have tried to show in this section, the legal recognition of plural marriage could not only help normalize polygamist relationships and families – whatever forms they take – but it would also communicate to society that unconventional relationships, provided they are consensual and involve adults, are not to be ruled out without serious consideration about their possible merits. That is another way of saying the state must respect the lives of marital nonconformists.

CONCLUSION

In this chapter, I have tried to lay the groundwork for a constitutional right to plural marriage by first showing that such a right is a logical extension of the more abstract constitutional right of autonomy. Nonrecognition of plural marriage amounts to an unconstitutional denial of marital choice. I then explained, using Mill's famous idea of experiments of living, why plural marriages present opportunities for introspection and self-growth that may not exist in a society that continues to revere monogamous marriages. A real plural marriage could be morally problematic for the same reasons a monogamous relationship could be morally problematic: It could be characterized by selfishness, insensitivity, laziness, manipulation, jealousy, exploitation, and physical and emotional abuse. But that sort of dysfunctional behavior can be and too often is present in much more widespread monogamous intimate relationships and marriages.

That is not to say, of course, that people should seek out plural marriages if they prefer a two-person sexually and emotionally exclusive arrangement. It may be true that today, for most individuals, having multiple partners at the same time is unworkable. As Oscar Wilde might have put it, the trouble with plural marriage is it might take up too many evenings. However, advocates of the constitutional right to plural marriage need not argue for the more ambitious conclusion that such marriage is superior to its monogamous alternative. They only have to show it is possible that plural marriage may work for the people who participate in such unconventional arrangements. Such a marriage may also serve as an example of a way of life that enables others to see (a) there are other options that may better fit their circumstances and (b) to enable those who will never opt for plural marriage to be more reflective about their own intimate lives to improve them. "Respecting one's fellow citizens as equals," Nussbaum writes, "doesn't mean approving of their choices, but it does mean respecting their right to make certain choices consistent with the principles of equal dignity and equal entitlement."[146]

[146] Martha C. Nussbaum, *From Disgust to Humanity: Sexual Orientation and Constitutional Law* (New York: Oxford University Press, 2010), 34.

The question of whether (unqualified) monogamous marriage is better than (unqualified) plural marriage obscures what is really at issue: whether unconventional intimate relationships have enough potential value to receive legal recognition. The route toward more understanding and subsequently more acceptance requires depicting such relationships more accurately, appreciating their diversity, and reflecting on why someone – gay, straight, bisexual, transgender, or asexual – would want to have such a marriage. Sooner or later, as a society, we need to have this conversation. Just as Americans must resist caricatures and see sexual minorities as they are, they also need to recognize the possibility that the love different kinds of polygamists may express for each other is as real as that of any gay or straight couple.

5

Marriage Equality

Like it or not, the ongoing debate in America over same-sex marriage has set the stage for the coming debate over plural marriage. In the last thirty years or so, what was once an almost unimaginable constitutional view – that people have a right to marry someone of the same sex – not only reflects more progressive thoughts and egalitarian sentiments but is becoming a widely accepted constitutional understanding. How Americans eventually decide the fate of same-sex marriage is bound to influence how they discuss and evaluate numerical limitations in the perhaps not-so-distant future. The increasingly apparent unconstitutionality of laws that limit marriage to opposite-sex couples does not bode well for states' continuing to treat groups of three or more persons unequally when it comes to eligibility for a marriage license. After all, laws that treat different groups differently cannot be rooted in animus against politically unpopular groups.[1] According to Bruce Ackerman, the principle of antihumiliation, announced in *Brown*, can be extended far beyond racial discrimination.[2]

If the reasons the state relies on to support a numerical restriction are insufficient, then under the Equal Protection Clause, the state would be required to extend the right of marriage to all kinds of polygamists or cease legally recognizing any marriages. As I shall show, the state's real reasons for not permitting same-sex marriages too closely resemble those for not permitting plural marriage. In both instances, the rationale for employing a perniciously narrow definition of marriage is constitutionally unacceptable. As it turns out,

[1] *Romer* is a case that can be construed to stand for the view that the state cannot enact a legislative classification with an illegitimate purpose. See Martha C. Nussbaum, *From Disgust to Humanity: Sexual Orientation and Constitutional Law* (New York: Oxford University Press, 2010), 113.

[2] Bruce Ackerman, *We the People: The Civil Rights Revolution* (Cambridge, MA: Belknap Press of Harvard University Press, 2014), 335.

restricting the legal status of marriage to a man and a woman is no more constitutional on equal protection grounds than limiting the size of a marriage. Indeed, some of the arguments made against plural marriage bear a striking resemblance to those that were made against same-sex marriage; that is not good news for opponents of plural marriage.

This chapter shall be divided into the following sections. First, I discuss the implications of the same-sex marriage debate with respect to plural marriage and explain why the slope may be slippery. Second, I explore the analogy between them and conclude they are sufficiently similar to warrant the same treatment. Third, I give an overview of constitutional standards of review and argue that a heightened standard of review applies to laws that deny people the option of marrying more than one person simultaneously. Fourth, I finish with some thoughts on the symbolic significance of limiting marriage to couples and elaborate on why the message being conveyed is constitutionally objectionable.

I. EQUAL PROTECTION JURISPRUDENCE

A. *Background*

The current preoccupation with same-sex marriage in America is perfectly understandable in a society that has discriminated severely against gay, lesbian, bisexual, and transgendered persons and continues to do so.[3] Not so long ago, during the AIDS crisis, fringe political figures, such as Lyndon LaRouche, called for quarantines.[4] In 1978, the Briggs Initiative (Proposition 6) attempted to ban gays and lesbians from teaching in California public schools.[5] The same year the Federal Marriage Amendment failed (in 2006), thirteen states passed their own versions of it.[6] In 1986, in *Bowers v. Hardwick*, the U.S. Supreme Court stated it was "at best facetious" to maintain that the Constitution precludes states from making same-sex sex acts a crime.[7] In doing so, it constitutionalized a horrific form of invidious discrimination. As of this

[3] For an excellent discussion of past discrimination against gays and lesbians, see William N. Eskridge Jr., *Dishonorable Passions: Sodomy Laws in America, 1861–2003* (New York: Viking Books, 2008).

[4] Dennis King, *Lyndon LaRouche and the New American Fascism* (New York: Doubleday, 1989), 140–42.

[5] Randy Shilts, *The Mayor of Castro Street* (New York: St. Martin's Press, 1982), 238–50.

[6] Daniel R. Pinello, *America's Struggle for Same-Sex Marriage* (New York: Cambridge University Press, 2006), 20.

[7] *Bowers v. Hardwick*, 478 U.S. 186 (1986).

writing, certain sexual minorities, including gays and lesbians, remain unprotected from discrimination in housing and employment under federal law and only receive such legal protection in less than half the states. Many Americans continue to believe homosexuality to be a sin and are less accepting of gays and lesbians than other Westerners are.[8] In those Americans' eyes, at least with respect to marriage, unequal legal treatment remains permissible. Sexual minorities can only hope for tolerance from them. The good news for those who support marriage equality is that such tolerance is more prevalent than it used to be and seems to be spreading. Some opponents of same-sex marriage are willing to entertain the possibility that marriage may improve same-sex intimate relationships. Others are willing to countenance civil unions as long as the state does not use the "m" word.[9] While such a "separate but equal" marital regime is not what gay and lesbian rights activists have in mind, the situation could be worse.

On the other hand, *Lawrence* moved constitutional meaning much closer to the view that the state cannot target people due to their sexual orientation.[10] *Romer* took seriously the invidious motives that voters might have for denying legal protection to gays and lesbians that racial minorities already receive.[11] Much more recently, *Windsor* came even closer to adopting the view that no meaningful difference exists between straight and gay people in terms of legal treatment.[12] Now it could be just a matter of time before the inappropriateness of using sexual orientation as the basis of a legislative classification would shape constitutional thinking about marriage more generally and change the idea that numerical restrictions are acceptable. The recent lower federal court decision from Utah, finding the denial of same-sex marriage to be unconstitutional, simply connects the dots between the equal dignity of gays and lesbians and the right to marriage.[13] Most lower federal courts are reading *Windsor* in the same manner.[14]

Recently, some legal scholars have gone out of their way – in the name of tolerance, I suppose – to defend those who continue to oppose same-sex marriage and their right to speak out against it and contribute money to the

8 www.pewresearch.org/fact-tank/2013/06/12/americans-are-less-accepting-of-homosexuality-than-canadians-western-europeans-and-religion-may-be-one-explanation

9 Michael J. Klarman, *From the Closet to the Altar: Courts, Backlash, and the Struggle for Same-Sex Marriage* (New York: Oxford University Press, 2013), 179–80.

10 *Lawrence v. Texas*, 539 U.S. 558 (2003).

11 *Romer v. Evans*, 517 U.S. 620 (1996).

12 *United States v. Windsor*, 570 U.S. __ (2013).

13 *Kitchen v. Herbert* (2013) (case no. 2:13-cv-217)

14 http://blogs.findlaw.com/strategist/2014/06/one-year-after-windsor-the-state-of-same-sex-marriage.html

anti-same-sex marriage cause, as if somehow they are also the victims of unjustified discrimination. Of course, they have a First Amendment right to do so, but I cannot help wondering what kind of verdict future Americans will render. If in fifty years just about everyone will probably see discrimination against sexual minorities as the equivalent of racial discrimination and will equate not allowing same-sex marriage with not allowing interracial ones, then they will not only be on the wrong side of history, but they will also have been a part of defending what will be come to be seen as almost evil beliefs and practices.

Although Justice Oliver Wendell Holmes once derisively quipped that the Equal Protection Clause is "the usual last resort of constitutional arguments,"[15] it has served as the source of some of the most important constitutional decisions in American history and is poised to continue to do so in certain constitutional controversies. In Cass Sunstein's view, the Equal Protection Clause can shield even minorities who have not traditionally received constitutional protection from discrimination.[16] I am not unsympathetic to Martha Nussbaum's belief that in a constitutional sense, liberties precede equal treatment, which captures why such unequal legal treatment is problematic.[17] When judges strike down a particular legislative classification on equal protection grounds, they do not simply believe one group is being discriminated against. By their very nature, legislative classifications treat different people differently. No one believes that the Equal Protection Clause requires identical treatment in all situations. If that were the case, then the state could never make any legal classifications – no matter how warranted. Instead, judges also think the reasons the state has offered on behalf of the law are inadequate in the following sense: Those reasons do not justify the unequal treatment in question.[18]

A number of legal scholars, including myself, have referred to this requirement as a *public justification requirement*, borrowing the term from political philosophy and theory literature.[19] Unlike fundamental rights analysis, the

[15] *Buck v. Bell*, 274 U.S. 200 (1927).

[16] Cass R. Sunstein, "Sexual Orientation and the Constitution: A Note on the Relationship Between Due Process and Equal Protection," *University of Chicago Law Review*, 55 (1988), 1161, 1163.

[17] Nussbaum, *From Disgust to Humanity*, 87.

[18] One of the most recent, impressive, and innovative approaches to understanding equal protection jurisprudence in terms of public reasons is Sonu Bedi, *Beyond Race, Sex, and Sexual Orientation* (New York: Cambridge University Press, 2013).

[19] In *Political Liberalism*, Rawls referred to the U.S. Supreme Court as "exemplar of public reason" (231). Lawrence Solum was the first legal scholars to connect the concept of public

inquiry is not into why the state may prohibit everyone from engaging in a certain behavior. Rather, in equal protection cases, it involves whether the state may treat one group of people more or less favorably and therefore prevent only some people from behaving in a certain way or denying them a right or benefit. A law that allows only persons over a certain age to consume alcohol, for example, would only survive a challenge to its constitutionality if a court finds the reasons that underlie it to be sufficient under the appropriate standard of review. In other words, some kind of public justification requirement is already in place, where judges must assess the quality of the state's reasons. The higher the standard of review triggered, the stronger those reasons must be for the state to prevail.

In equal protection cases, then, the state may not treat certain groups differently unless it can successfully defend such treatment. According to Erwin Chemerinsky, the basic question in all equal protection cases centers on whether the legislative classification in question is "justified by a sufficient purpose."[20] When it comes to heightened standards of review, such as strict and intermediate scrutiny, judges vet the reasons the state offers in support of the legislative classification in question with a presumption they are inadequate. At times, even when rational basis applies, that presumption may also exist. While *Lawrence* is not technically an equal protection case, it implicates the rationale for allowing the state to treat sexual minorities differently.[21] Texas was not only trying to control the personal lives of gays and lesbians, but it was also reinforcing their status as second-class citizens. Laws that do not treat same-sex couples equally imply their inferiority.[22]

Before *Lawrence*, activists had begun to move away from privacy-based arguments toward equality-based ones to shield gays and lesbians from discrimination in housing and employment.[23] The application of a heightened standard of review more generally in some equal protection cases reflects the worry that the state is probably acting on the basis of the wrong kinds of reasons.[24] Even if only rational basis is triggered, the legislative classification cannot be rooted in prejudice or animus against a politically unpopular

reason to law and legal reasoning. See, for example, Lawrence B. Solum, "Pluralism and Public Legal Reason," *William and Mary Bill of Rights Journal*, 15 (2006), 7–23.

20 Erwin Chemerinsky, *Constitutional Law: Principles and Policies* (4th ed.) (New York: Wolters Kluwer 2011), 685.

21 *Lawrence v. Texas*, 539 U.S. 558 (2003).

22 See John Corvino, "Homosexuality and the PIB Argument," *Ethics*, 115 (2005), 509.

23 Carlos A. Ball, *The Morality of Gay Rights: An Exploration in Political Philosophy* (New York: Routledge, 2003), 3.

24 Tribe, *American Constitutional Law*, 1364–65.

group.[25] True, most legislative classifications do not have such implications. An affirmative action plan does not convey to white persons they are racially inferior and separate-sex public restrooms do not inform women they are unequal to men. Rather, whether a law has such meaning depends on its underlying purpose, which is not independent of its context. In sum, the state may not make distinctions under the Equal Protection Clause in the absence of an adequate justification for doing so and what counts as adequate is connected to the nature of the legal classification in question.

B. The Same-Sex Marriage Debate

As noted, less than thirty years ago, the Supreme Court allowed the criminalization of consensual same-sex sex between adults in a decision that most people would no longer defend.[26] While some of the justices in the majority in *Bowers*, such as Lewis Powell, acquiesced, others (such as Warren Burger and Byron White) seemed strangely enthusiastic about empowering states to continue to discriminate against gay men.[27] One commentator once described the decision as the "Dred Scott" of the gay community.[28] Less than ten years ago, then-president George W. Bush endorsed the Federal Marriage Amendment, which would have forced even states sympathetic to same-sex marriage to define marriage as being only between a man and a woman.[29] At that time, a number of prominent conservatives also subscribed to the same position.[30] By 2005, forty states had passed statutes or constitutional amendments limiting marriage to opposite-sex couples.[31] As a result, one should not overestimate how much public opinion is changing with respect to gays, lesbians, and same-sex couples and conclude that the battle is over; in some states, it is just beginning.

As of this writing, more than half of the states perform same-sex marriages and that change feels like it has happened overnight perform same-sex marriages. However, even same-sex couples who were validly married in one state are not married when they travel through or vacation in a state that does not

[25] See *Romer v. Evans*, 517 U.S. 620 (1996); *Cleburne v. Cleburne Living Center*, 473 U.S. 472 (1985); *Plyer v. Doe*, 457 U.S. 202 (1982); and *U.S. Department of Agriculture v. Moreno*, 413 U.S. 528 (1973).

[26] See David A.J. Richards, *The Case for Gay Rights: From* Bowers *to* Lawrence *and Beyond* (Lawrence: University of Kansas Press, 2005), 73–87.

[27] *Bowers v. Hardwick*, 478 U.S. 186 (1986).

[28] Klarman, *From the Closet to the Altar*, 37.

[29] Pinello, *America's Struggle for Same-Sex Marriage*, 20.

[30] William N. Eskridge Jr. and Darren R. Spedale, *Gay Marriage: For Better or For Worse? What We've Learned From the Evidence* (New York: Oxford University Press, 2006), 204.

[31] Pinello, *America's Struggle for Same-Sex Marriage*, 29.

recognize such marriages, which is permitted by the Defense of Marriage Act (DOMA). Some liberals believe that same-sex marriage in the whole country is a fait accompli, but that overconfidence may partially explain why Proposition 8, which was losing so badly in the polls a few months prior to California voters' casting their ballots on November 4, 2008, ultimately succeeded. Until *Windsor*, DOMA prohibited federal recognition of same-sex marriage and denied same-sex couples numerous federal benefits, even those who were legally married in the state where they resided.[32] It does not appear that all states on their own will extend the right of marriage to same-sex couples anytime soon. Because of state-by-state differences, if the timing is fortuitous, the U.S. Supreme Court may step in and nationalize the right to same-sex marriage. According to Nate Silver's regression model, by 2024, Mississippi will be the last state in the country to recognize same-sex marriage.[33]

All that said, for those who favor marriage equality in America, the future looks a lot brighter than it did a few years ago. It is becoming increasingly evident that fears of backlash are no longer as warranted as they once were. In 2003, the Massachusetts Supreme Court became the first state supreme court to recognize the right of marriage for same-sex couples.[34] Before the passage of Proposition 8, the California Supreme Court had created such a right under its own constitution. In *Perry v. Schwarzenegger*, Judge Vaughn Walker ruled that this proposition violates the U.S. Constitution.[35] Subsequently, a three-judge panel of the Ninth Circuit affirmed his decision.[36] Several state supreme courts have also moved in this direction.[37] Before the *Windsor* decision, a few lower federal courts found certain parts of DOMA to be unconstitutional.[38] *Romer v. Evans* established that animus is an insufficient reason for unequal treatment.[39] *Lawrence* intimated that mere moral disapproval does not count as a constitutionally admissible rationale for such treatment. In *Windsor*, Justice Kennedy goes out of his way to underscore how Section 3 of DOMA demeans and the valid marriages of gays and lesbians.[40] According to Justice Scalia's dissent,

[32] Defense of Marriage Act, Pub. L. No. 104–199, 110 Stat. 2419 (Sep. 21, 1996) (codified as 28 U.S.C. Sect. 1738 (1996) (codified at 1 U.S.C. Section 7 (2006)).

[33] See Klarman, *From the Closet to the Altar*, 202.

[34] *Goodridge v. Department of Public Health*, 798 N.E. 2d 407 (Mass. 2003).

[35] *Perry v. Schwarzenegger*, 704 F. Supp. 2d 921(N.D. Cal. 2010).

[36] *Perry v. Brown*, 671 F. 3d 1052 (9th Cir. 2012).

[37] See, for example, *Baehr v. Lewin*, 852 P. 2d 44 (Haw. 1993); *Baker v. Vermont*, 744 A. 2d 864 (Vt. 1999); *Goodridge v. Department of Health*, 798 N.E. 2d 941 (Mass. 2003); *In re Marriage Cases*, 43 Cal. 4d 757, 183 P. 3d 384, 76 Cal. Rptr. 3d 683 (2008); and *Kerrigan v. Commissioner of Public Health*, 289 Cnn. 135, 957 A. 2d 407 (2008).

[38] Defense of Marriage Act (1996), Title 1 U.S.C. Section 7, 28 U.S.C. Section 1738C (2000).

[39] *Romer v. Evans*, 517 U.S. 620 (1996).

[40] *United States v. Windsor*, 570 U.S. __ (2013) (pp. 20–25).

Kennedy's majority opinion lays the foundation for a constitutional right to same-sex marriage on equal protection grounds.[41]

There is no shortage of academic writing on the topic of same-sex marriage.[42] Here, I will only summarize some of the main points and articulate their relevance to the coming debate over plural marriage. Obviously, the future of same-sex marriage in all states is much more promising than that of plural marriage. By now, most of the traditional arguments offered against same-sex marriage have been found to be flawed in one way or another and those who still oppose it are on the ropes, covering up, and occasionally throw a counter punch. Their most recent rhetorical strategy has been to try to link legal recognition of such marriage with the decline of the traditional family and the welfare of children.[43] No longer do they overtly claim that gay men are pedophiles who want to seduce children or recruit them to the "homosexual lifestyle," which is not to say they never make such insinuations. The days of Anita Bryant's vitriol may be over, but the rhetoric of "saving the traditional family" still resonates with many Americans.[44]

Moreover, constitutionally, the state is more likely to have a stronger interest in limiting marriage to opposite-sex couples if it can establish that including same-sex couples in the new, expanded definition will have bad consequences. As I have already explained, the future is uncertain, reasonable people do not agree on what qualifies as "bad" in this context, and even if some of the consequences are bad, they still have to be weighed against the costs imposed on same-sex couples. Hypothetically, by comparison, if not permitting interracial marriage would somehow strengthen the institution – say, by stabilizing

[41] Ibid. (Scalia, J., dissenting).

[42] See, for example, Evan Gerstmann, *Same-Sex Marriage and the Constitution* (New York: Cambridge University Press, 2008); Andrew Koppelman, *The Gay Rights Question in Contemporary American Law* (Chicago: University of Chicago Press, 2002); Jonathan Rauch, *Gay Marriage: Why It Is Good for Gays, Good for Straights, and Good for America* (New York: Henry Holt, 2004); Evan Wolfson, *Why Marriage Matters: America, Equality, and Gay People's Right to Marry* (New York: Simon and Schuster, 2004); and William N. Eskridge Jr., *The Case for Same-Sex Marriage: From Sexual Liberty to Civilized Commitment* (New York: The Free Press, 1996).

[43] In his last writing on public reason, John Rawls referred to child welfare as a public reason, which suggests that such a rationale could be thin enough (sufficiently removed from any particular conception of the good) to count as a neutral reason for treating same-sex marriage differently. John Rawls, "The Idea of Public Reason Revisited," in *The Law of Peoples* (Cambridge, MA: Harvard University Press, 1999), 147. In a footnote, he then makes clear he is not trying to settle any question of law or public policy but merely to expand on the kinds of reasons that might be public reasons depending on the circumstances (147, n. 38). Whether such a reason is sufficiently public would be contingent on the particulars – and those particulars, in turn, would be contingent on a number of controversial causal inferences.

[44] See, for example, David Blankenhorn, *The Future of Marriage* (New York: Encounter Books, 2007).

it – we still would not deny the right to marriage to interracial couples. Recall that opponents of same-sex marriage are fond of lauding the merits of two-person opposite sex marriage. Marriage is supposed to benefit those who are married in the sense of making them happy, healthier, and wealthier. In denying gays and lesbians access to the institution, then, they are trying to make the lives of sexual minorities worse or at least do not mind this side effect. After all, if being married generally improves the lives of its members, then one could conclude that gays and lesbians should also be able to marry so the quality of their lives improves. No one seems to think that their marrying would be bad for them. These days, those who are against the legal recognition have been put on the defensive. At one time, the burden of proof was not theirs; that no longer appears to be the case.

Constitutionally, they need to find another rationale for their position and have recently insisted that letting same-sex couples marry has something to do with how straight people behave sexually. In *Perry v. Schwarzenegger*, the defendants claimed that the main interest of the state was to promote "responsible procreation."[45] In the absence of any empirical evidence, it is hard to know what the connection between them is supposed to be. Thus, one should be skeptical that "bad consequences" are the real reasons for their opposition.[46] Opponents of same-sex marriage have eschewed openly religious reasons about the wrongfulness of homosexuality in favor of speculative consequentialist ones, but this way of proceeding undermines their sincerity. Sincerity is not too much to ask for and "responsible procreation" seems disingenuous when Charles Cooper – the attorney defending Proposition 8 – was asked by Judge Walker during oral arguments to state the state's reasons for supporting the proposition but could not even begin to verbalize the alleged link between not legally recognizing same-sex marriage and protecting opposite-sex couples from harm.[47] The ostensible reasons for different legal treatment have changed more than once, which suggests that the state's interests are offered in bad faith.[48] Thus, it is not obvious how the existence of same-sex marriage or relationships would directly affect the sexual behavior and childrearing practices of straight persons. In *Perry*, Judge Walker doubted that this interest was the state's real interest.[49]

[45] *Perry v. Schwarzenegger*, 704 F. Supp. 2d 921 (N.D. Cal. 2010).

[46] See Courtney G. Joslin, "Searching for Harm: Same-Sex Marriage and the Well-Being of Children," *Harvard Civil Rights – Civil Liberties Law Review*, 46 (2011), 81–101.

[47] Jo Becker, *Forcing the Spring: Inside the Fight for Marriage Equality* (New York: Penguin Press, 2014), 62–63.

[48] Bedi, *Beyond Race, Sex, and Sexual Orientation*, 97–103.

[49] *Perry v. Schwarzenegger*, 704 F. Supp. 2d 921, 999 (N.D. Cal. 2010).

Normally, this sort of skepticism is reserved for the application of a heightened standard of review. Even under rational basis, surely the state cannot merely create figments of imagination and then insist that no one knows what will happen in the future if marriage were made less discriminatory. If the state were permitted to do so, then it could discriminate against any minority that is not treated as a suspect class or quasi-suspect class for whatever lousy reasons it happens to have. Moreover, it could conceal animus anytime it wanted to do so by appealing to the mere possibility of the occurence of some kind of harm to someone somewhere sometime in the future. Such a view almost refutes itself.

At most, one could try to argue that altering the definition of marriage to encompass same-sex couples would be the final nail in the coffin of a uniquely valuable conception of marriage.[50] The other nails would be such social changes as widespread acceptance of premarital sex, cohabitation, single motherhood, infidelity, and no-fault divorce. The legal recognition of same-sex marriage, coupled with the aforementioned changes, might irreparably damage the institution and forever change its meaning for the worse. This approach is somewhat more credible than the others, but it proves too much: It concedes that the decline of traditional marriage is mostly due to socio-economic forces and the choices of straight persons.[51] By itself, that concession might not be fatal. It would be strange, though, for the state to try to protect the family only by targeting same-sex couples, whose numbers are comparatively small, and not even bothering to address the other more serious underlying causes of the so-called decline-of-marriage problem. After all, the state could adopt many policies to promote responsible procreation more directly – if it cared to do so – that would be even more promising than limiting marriage to opposite-sex couples.[52] That way, same-sex couples would not be asked to bear the burden of saving traditional marriage by themselves.

In terms of standards of review used in equal protection analysis, then, it is not apparent how not permitting same-sex marriage is even rationally related to the state's ostensible interest of promoting such procreation, which presumably means having children grow up in a household with two parents of the opposite sex. A law that limits marriage to opposite-sex couples in the name of responsible procreation would be grossly underinclusive. That opposing the

[50] See, for example, Stanley Kurtz, "The End of Marriage in Scandinavia," *Weekly Standard*, February 2, 2004.

[51] Eskridge and Spedale, *Gay Marriage: For Better or for Worse?* 208.

[52] For a radical reform, see Hugh Lafollette, "Licensing Parents," *Philosophy and Public Affairs*, 9 (1980), 182–97.

legal recognition of same-sex marriage is the last chance to preserve traditional opposite-sex marriage in the minds of some conservatives does not magically transform laws that discriminate against same-sex couples into constitutional ones.[53] The trouble is not only that those who oppose same-sex marriage are relying on controversial empirical and, less charitably, specious claims about the possible negative consequences that cannot pass constitutional muster unless one's view is that the state can do whatever it wants to do for any reason whatsoever. It is only safe to assert that the costs and benefits of marriage (and its dissolution) are hard to measure and vary according to the social structures in which marriage exists. For example, divorce would not have the devastating financial impact on children it too often does today if our society were to do more to help children in poverty and not use marriage as an antipoverty program.

The position of those who oppose same-sex marriage also assumes that the "welfare" of children is more important than treating all people fairly. Thus, they are not just citing the alleged bad social consequences, but they are also objecting to the morality of same-sex marriage.[54] The reliance on different sorts of consequentialist arguments is misguided when considerations of fairness (usually seen as a demand for individualized treatment) characterize equal protection cases. When the sky has not fallen in other places where same-sex marriage has been legally recognized, those who continue to resist it have put themselves in a precarious position. At the same time, resorting to such empirical claims is strategically understandable. The state can no longer simply rely on moral disapproval as its interest without risking that a judge will find that animus underlies the legislative classification in question and conclude that it is unconstitutional even under a rational basis standard of review.[55]

[53] In other countries, the legal recognition of same-sex marriage has not directly undermined tradition marriage. See Eskridge and Spedale, *Gay Marriage: For Better or for Worse?* 131–67.

[54] Ibid., 221.

[55] *Romer v. Evans*, 517 U.S. 620 (1996). The distinction between moral disapproval and animus or prejudice against sexual minorities is contested. For an enlightening discussion of the role that disgust plays in opposition to homosexuality and same-sex marriage, see Nussbaum, *From Disgust to Humanity*. For a discussion of the practical difficulties of discerning invidious legislative intent in this context, see Koppelman, *The Gay Rights Question in Contemporary American Law*, 6–34. Legally, it may be easier for judges not to draw any such bright line or any line at all and simply do what Justice Kennedy did in *Lawrence v. Texas*, 539 U.S. 558 (2003) and assume that sincere moral disapproval is not a strong enough state interest to be important or compelling when a fundamental right is at stake. The rationale of such an approach would be something like tolerance.

II. THE ANALOGY BETWEEN SAME-SEX AND PLURAL MARRIAGE

A. *Analogy or Disanalogy?*

Despite vast interdisciplinary literature on same-sex marriage and the family more generally, scholars have written little about plural marriage and even less about nonsexual or sexual but incestuous marriage between consenting adults.[56] This neglect probably results from the fact that the same-sex marriage battle is still raging and opponents of same-sex marriage have employed slippery slope arguments indiscriminately to discredit such marriage.[57] As a result, the topic of plural marriage is rarely discussed with the kind of care it deserves. As I have already shown, such marriage cannot be reduced to polygyny or its worst possible manifestations and scholars should not ignore different background conditions that will shape the dynamics of each one. For example, one cannot cite the recent legal recognition of polygynous marriages in an undeveloped country, as if that is the only possible form the legal recognition of plural marriage could take in a country like ours that could regulate such marriage to make it as fair as possible to everyone. In the near future, it is highly improbable that the legal recognition of same-sex marriages by itself will lead to the social acceptance of any kind of plural marriage, even as the public moves closer to adopting the belief that the meaning of marriage lies in the eye of the beholder.

As I have emphasized, this book is not about making predictions or formulating political and legal strategies but about spelling out why the Constitution requires states that legally recognize two-person marriage to also include multipartner relationships – whatever the future holds. The same-sex marriage debate is instructive because it has far-reaching ramifications; it is not only about whether a man should be permitted to marry another man or a woman should be permitted to marry another woman but also about how marriage should be understood under conditions of moral pluralism, how (and even whether) the state ought to be involved in the institution, how Americans

56 For a brief discussion of incestuous marriage, see Eskridge, *The Case for Same-Sex Marriage*, 144. For a nuanced defense of its adult form, see Andrew F. March, "What Lies Beyond Same-Sex Marriage? Marriage, Reproductive Freedom and Future Persons in Liberal Public Justification," *Journal of Applied Philosophy*, 27 (2010), especially 42–45. Different kinds of incestuous relationships among adults raise different concerns. The state might have a stronger interest in banning parent–child incestuous marriages in the name of discouraging child abuse than in banning, for example, sibling incestuous marriages.

57 Stanley Kurtz, "The Libertarian Question: Incest, Homosexuality, and Adultery," in *Same-Sex Marriage: The Moral and Legal Debate* (2nd ed.), ed. Robert M. Baird and Stuart E. Rosenbaum (Amherst, NY: Prometheus Books, 2004), 263–68.

should construe marriage equality, and when – if ever – marital choice ought to be restricted with respect to competent adults.

Ironically, something noticeably conservative emerges in many current defenses of same-sex marriage. Proponents of same-sex marriage go out of their way to deny that legal recognition will forever change the meaning of marriage for the worse. Alternatively, they are determined to establish that such recognition will perpetuate the traditional meaning of marriage in the sense of reinforcing the notion that two persons are committed to each other (and only to each other) in a long-term, loving relationship. The gender composition of the couple is supposed to be beside the point. That approach has the intended and unfortunate effect of reinforcing what Elizabeth Brake calls "amatonormativity" – the unjustified privileging of romantic dyads at the expense of other equally valuable intimate relationships. Amatonormativity is closely related to heteronormativity; both of them involve unjustified discrimination.

Unfortunately, some marriage equality activists do not see both kinds of discrimination as similar. Originally, they insisted that the experiences of sexual minorities differ from those of straight people and some of them rejected the traditional institution of marriage that had been monopolized by opposite-sex couples for so long. As more and more sexual minorities assimilated, though, they warmed up to a more traditional understanding of marriage and began to emphasize its dyadic nature, as if they were now part of the majority, and discrimination against plural marriage enthusiasts was not a wrong that needed to be addressed. Apart from that change in thinking and behavior, this rhetorical strategy is not hard to grasp and is probably shrewd. If the ultimate political objective is to convince straight persons, who compose most of the electorate, that they should cease discriminating against gays and lesbians, it would not behoove them to call attention to difference and remind voters, politicians, and judges of negative stereotypes about gay men. In 2015, it seems like this strategy is finally paying dividends. Unlike their parents and grandparents, younger straight people do not seem to care much about sexual orientation.

But what looks like a victory comes with a hidden cost: The more difference is downplayed, the more difficult it becomes to point out the unique benefits that same-sex and plural marriages may produce. Additionally, it makes it easier for gay and lesbian activists who oppose plural marriage to make common cause with traditionalists – some of whom have accepted the inevitability of defeat in the battle over same-sex marriage – to fight a common enemy in the near future. Under more ideal circumstances, there would be no need to throw polygamists under the bus and recycle the same sorts of bad arguments that no longer have much force when it comes to same-sex marriage. Finally, the arc of justice is bending toward marriage equality. As our political climate changes, gay and lesbian proponents of same-sex marriage no longer have to distance themselves from plural marriage.

B. Common-Law Reasoning

In such a common-law system as our own, radical changes – driven by judicial decisions alone – are infrequent. Those who put all their faith in courts to promote social justice, such as legal equality for sexual minorities, are more likely than not to be disappointed. It is probably accurate to describe the possibility of change as a matter of under what circumstances can judges – through their decisions – help to move constitutional understandings in new directions. When the opportunity arises, that process is facilitated by the fact that our Constitution is not a seamless whole but rather a patchwork of constitutional meanings, not all of which fit together neatly, and that allows lawyers, judges, and others to formulate novel legal arguments and modify constitutional doctrine over time. Some legal academics are convinced that past judicial decisions and practices are more important than the text itself.[58] If they are right, then especially in challenging constitutional cases, judges have considerable discretion in how a case may be decided because they have so much case law and so many other sources to draw from in defending their constitutional conclusions. They not only characterize the legally relevant facts but also decide how the law as they understand it applies to the fact pattern.

Past decisions do not speak for themselves. As Edward Levi writes: "The basic pattern of legal reasoning is reasoning by example. It is reasoning from case to case."[59] If one case has been previously decided one way, then a similar case should be decided in the same manner in the name of consistency. This kind of legal reasoning would be less problematic in terms of consistency or predicting outcomes if it were more deductive. As Frederick Schauer observes: "More commonly, however, it is not nearly so clear which cases are to count as precedent cases, and even more importantly, it is rarely obvious what those cases will be taken to stand for."[60] The trouble, then, is not only that a judge could act in bad faith, ignore precedent, and conceal his or her real reasons for

[58] See, for example, David A. Strauss, *The Living Constitution* (New York: Oxford University Press, 2010), 3.

[59] Edward H. Levi, *An Introduction to Legal Reasoning* (Chicago: University of Chicago Press, 1949), 1.

[60] Frederick Schauer, *Thinking Like a Lawyer: A New Introduction to Legal Reasoning* (Cambridge, MA: Harvard University Press, 2009), 44.

his or her decision just to reach a particular outcome that refelects his or her partisan preferences. Furthermore, even when he or she acts in good faith, he or she has multiple ways of following a precedent because it is often not straightforward whether a case is analogous to another case in the sense of having sufficiently similar material facts. Past judicial decisions may conflict and they have to be interpreted; it is up to the judge to decide what they mean and how they may apply to a new fact pattern. In 1954, few scholars would have anticipated that *Brown* stood for a constitutional principle of color blindness that could be used to protect white persons from so-called reverse discrimination in affirmative action cases. As a consequence of inevitable judicial discretion, some of the most important and well accepted of the Supreme Court's decisions only have an attenuated connection to the constitutional text. It is hard to imagine how it could be otherwise in such a common-law system and such a political system as our own that politicizes its constitutional issues. At the level of the U.S. Supreme Court, the justices can overturn or overlook precedent. In *Romer*, as Justice Scalia angrily points out in his dissent, Justice Kennedy writes his majority opinion as if *Bowers v. Hardwick*, which was supposed to be established law, did not exist.[61] After *Lawrence*, those who oppose same-sex marriage can continue to argue that because sexual orientation is a constitutionally relevant difference, lawmakers may treat same-sex couples differently when it comes to eligibility for marriage licenses. The constitutional text itself certainly does not tell us what would count as such a difference.

C. *Similarities and Differences*

The issue of same-sex marriage implicates plural marriage because Americans are in the process of deciding whether to expand the meaning of marriage beyond its present legal definition.[62] Therefore, they have to address at least two questions: (1) whether the two kinds of marriage are sufficiently similar and (2) what the state's interests are in having the legal status of marriage more generally. Not all scholars believe the analogy between same-sex and plural marriage is good.[63] After all, there is some reason to believe they are not

[61] *Romer v. Evans*, 517 U.S. 620, 636, 640–41 (1996) (Scalia, J., dissenting).

[62] At present, the only country that legally recognizes same-sex and plural marriage (but only for some male members of certain tribes) is South Africa. See Judith Stacey, *Unhitched: Love, Marriage, and Family Values From West Hollywood to Western China* (New York: New York University Press, 2011), 10.

[63] See, for example, Elizabeth M. Glazer, "Sodomy and Polygamy," *Columbia Law Review Sidebar*, 111 (2011), 66, 71.

analogous.[64] First, strategically, associating them may be mistaken.[65] Second, the reasons that fail to justify treating same-sex couples differently than their opposite-sex counterparts may still justify treating thruples or groups differently. As John Corvino describes the slippery slope argument: "The general idea is that there is some connection between same-sex marriage, on the one hand, and various objectionable relationships on the other."[66]

Unfortunately, for many observers, plural marriage is only worthy of consideration as a limit case in theoretical discussions about same-sex marriage. As Michael Dorf states, "they cite polygamy . . . and other taboos precisely because they know that laws prohibiting these practices in fact serve no valid purpose, and they also know that our leading constitutional organs will be unwilling to say so."[67] In such discussions, the assumption is that the Constitution does not protect the right to plural marriage. The only remaining intellectual challenge is how to distinguish same-sex marriage from plural marriage so one can defend a constitutional right to the former without conceding a right to the latter. During the hearings that preceded the passage of DOMA, some members of Congress and some witnesses equated polygamy with same-sex marriage.[68] As early as 1978, Justice Potter Stewart voiced his concern that the Supreme Court's recognizing a fundamental right to marry would impede the states in not having to recognize other kinds of unconventional marriage.[69] From this standpoint, it is not self-evident that same-sex and plural marriage are morally or legally equivalent when the latter is structured differently and could take so many divergent forms. A restriction based on sexual orientation may not be sufficiently similar to a numerical restriction.

D. *The Slippery Slope*

Many proponents of same-sex marriage "go to great lengths" to deny the existence of a slope between same-sex and plural marriage.[70] That is a way

64 On the disanalogy, see Andrew F. March, "Is There a Right to Polygamy? Marriage, Equality and Subsidizing Families in Liberal Public Justification," *Journal of Moral Philosophy*, 8 (2011), 247–48.

65 Jaime M. Gher, "Polygamy and Same-Sex Marriage – Allies or Adversaries Within the Same-Sex Marriage Movement?" *William and Mary Journal of Women and the Law*, 14 (2008), 602.

66 John Corvino, "The Case for Same-Sex Marriage," in *Debating Same-Sex Marriage* (New York: Oxford University Press, 2012), 64.

67 Michael C. Dorf, "God and Man in the Yale Dormitories," *Virginia Law Review*, 84 (1998), 851.

68 David Chambers, "Polygamy and Same-Sex Marriage," *Hofstra Law Review*, 26 (1997), 53.

69 *Zablocki v. Redhail*, 434 U.S. 374, 399 (1978) (Stewart, J., dissenting).

70 March, "Is There a Right to Polygamy?", 245.

of proclaiming that the two kinds of marriage are not analogous. There is very little empirical evidence that shows that the legal recognition of same-sex marriage inexorably leads to the legal recognition of plural marriage, and in this country, the reverse may be true.[71] Let me reiterate before I am misunderstood that I am not trying to establish that we should no longer be concerned with discrimination against gays and lesbians or other sexual minorities. Marriage is just one front on the battlefield. Obviously, there are others. Nor is my aim to show that present-day discrimination is worse for polygamists.[72] One of the themes in this book is we do not have to choose which one is worse or more pressing to remedy. If one cares about addressing racial and gender discrimination, then one should also care about such discrimination against sexual minorities and vice versa. A conscientious person cares and wants to end unjustified legal discrimination – regardless of which minority group happens to be the target.

As I see it, most of the main reasons that work in favor of recognizing same-sex marriages – such as respect for personal choice and equal legal treatment – are also applicable to plural marriages.[73] Pro-Polygamy.com declares that plural marriage is "the next civil rights battle."[74] In the United States, for the few polyamorists who have been politically active, a crucial part of their campaign to win hearts and minds has been to equate same-sex and plural marriage.[75] Initially, this approach may be surprising when members of the LGBT community do not see eye to eye on whether these two kinds of marriage are comparable.[76] Moreover, conservatives have tried to link same-sex and plural marriage to discredit the former on what is supposed to be the unassailable assumption that an individual has a right to marry one person – and only one person – at the same time.[77] Those who have defended plural marriage in this fashion are wagering that eventually, more and more people will come to see same-sex marriages as normal. Some proponents of plural

[71] See Judith Stacey and Tey Meadow, "New Slants on the Slippery Slope: The Politics of Polygamy and Gay Family Rights in South Africa and the United States," *Politics and Society*, 37 (2009), 190–92.

[72] One study concludes that it is easier for polygamists to stay in the closet if need be and to only come out selectively. Goldfeder and Sheff, "Children of Polygamous Families," 198.

[73] March, "Is There a Right to Polygamy?" 246; Brake, *Minimizing Marriage*, 198.

[74] www.Pro-Polygamy.com

[75] Jeffrey Michael Hayes, "Polygamy Comes Out of the Closet: The New Strategy of Polygamy Activists," *Stanford Journal of Civil Rights and Civil Liberties*, 3 (2007), 104–05.

[76] Jaime M. Gher, "Polygamy and Same-Sex Marriage – Allies or Adversaries Within the Same-Sex Marriage Movement?" *William and Mary Journal of Women and the Law*, 14 (2008), 572.

[77] See, for example, Kurtz, "The Libertarian Question: Incest, Homosexuality, and Adultery," 263, 266.

marriage then hope to convince those who accept same-sex marriage that the two kinds of marriage are not so different that the state may treat them unequally. For Corvino, the "polygamy, incest, bestiality" (PIB) argument, which opponents of same-sex marriage often fall back on in a more nuanced form, is not as bad as it appears to be.[78] Scalia's slope, where legal recognition of same-sex marriage will invariably lead to legal recognition of plural marriage, may be somewhat slippery after all.[79]

On the one hand, it does not follow from the expansion of the legal definition of marriage that people may marry children, pets, rocks, or themselves. The slope is not necessarily that slippery. Children are legally incapable of giving consent and forming contracts more generally. For the same reason, nonhuman animals and inanimate objects cannot be married. A numerical restriction may not be justified, whereas one based on age or species is easily justifiable. On the other hand, the slope may be slippery in the following respect: The legal recognition of same-sex marriage – to the extent it redefines marriage – may pave the way for an even more expansive redefinition of marriage in the near or distant future. Slippery slope arguments are probably the most misused arguments in the history of informal fallacies. They often falsely assume that no one can draw a principled distinction between one thing and another thing.

However, that does not mean that all of them are flawed all the time. Such arguments take this form: If A, then B, and if B, then C; C is unacceptable; therefore, A is unacceptable.[80] They are predicated on the claim that no logical stopping point exists, which is related to the above point about the inability of anyone to make principled distinctions. For the most part, slippery slope arguments are psychological.[81] The thought is that even when the two cases can be distinguished logically, at a later date, people will mistakenly end up not distinguishing them when they should do so. That consequence is not certain, or even likely. Its occurrence is contingent on many other factors that may be very difficult to identify and measure. Whether the slope between same-sex and plural marriages is slippery, then, cannot be known with any confidence in advance; it requires a complex probabilistic judgment about the likelihood that the former will contribute to or cause the latter. As Eugene Volokh observes, people have been too dismissive of slippery slope arguments

[78] John Corvino, "Homosexuality and the PIB Argument," *Ethics*, 115 (2005), 502.
[79] *Lawrence v. Texas*, 539 U.S. 558, 599 (Scalia, J., dissenting).
[80] Corvino, "Homosexuality and the PIB Argument," 503–04.
[81] See Eugene Volokh, "Same-Sex Marriage and Slippery Slopes," *Hofstra Law Review*, 33 (2005), 1156.

with respect to privacy because it is hard to predict whether more people might eventually be receptive when circumstances change to a new idea they had previously rejected.[82]

A familiar example of a slippery slope argument is that the decriminalization of marijuana will necessarily lead to the decriminalization of other harder drugs, which are too dangerous to be legally permitted. The obvious problem with this line of reasoning is that perhaps lawmakers should (and will) treat different controlled substances differently when some pose more risks to society than others. Most Americans do not equate marijuana with heroin, cocaine, painkillers, or crystal meth. But if someone contends that the decriminalization of marijuana will lead to an increase in the consumption of that drug and a corresponding reduction in work productivity and a rise in lung cancer, that is not a slippery slope argument; it is an old-fashioned claim about cause and effect. People misuse slippery slope arguments by claiming that one event will eventually cause another when there is (a) no clear causal relationship between them, (b) a much lower probability that A will ultimately cause C, and (c) no good reason to single out one independent variable as the likely primary cause in the midst of so many other independent variables that must be disaggregated. Historically, in this country, same-sex and plural marriage have very little in common. That could change over time when Americans stop reducing all forms of polygamy to traditional religiously inspired polygyny. At present, little popular support for plural marriage exists and the bleak political situation of polygamists is not likely to change anytime soon.

That said, in the case of plural marriage, a right to such marriage may follow from a right to same-sex marriage in the following manner: Same-sex marriage could serve as a precedent for redefining marriage again to make it even more inclusive. For most Americans, the distance between the legal recognition of opposite-sex monogamous and same-sex monogamous marriage is not nearly as great as the distance between opposite-sex monogamous and plural marriage. However, the abstract constitutional principle of nondiscrimination without adequate justification can always be taken in a number of unanticipated directions by skilled political and legal actors when the timing is right. That is what happened in *Baehr v. Lewin* and subsequently in the *In re Marriage Cases* in California.[83] In 1967, few – if any – people ever contemplated the possibility that *Loving v. Virginia* could support a constitutional right to same-sex marriage decades later. The use of an old case in a novel way occurs not because a lawyer or a judge necessarily acts in bad faith.

[82] Ibid., 1158–62.

[83] *Baehr v. Lewin*, 74 Haw. 530, 852 P. 2d 44 (1993); *In re Marriage Cases*, 43 Cal. 4th 757 (2008).

Rather, as public opinion begins to change, new arguments that activists and legal advocates put forth may begin to resonate with the public and members of the legal community. Thus, the meaning of equal protection may transcend its particular context. The more abstract the principle, the more likely this can happen. The application of abstract principles to concrete circumstances is not strictly deductive in the sense that a premise implies a conclusion.[84] As I explained in the first chapter, the necessity of constitutional construction in hard cases forces judges to bridge the gap between highly abstract constitutional language and the actual particulars of the case to render a decision, thereby creating new law.[85]

Judges can do that bridging in a number of ways and they normally try to decide the case in a manner that is more or less consistent with past decisions. In doing so, they often rely on analogical reasoning.[86] Such reasoning is more complicated than it may seem to be.[87] To draw an analogy between two or more entities is to indicate one or more respects in which they are similar.[88] In analogical reasoning, one discerns a particular characteristic in one item and infers the presence of that same characteristic in a different item. An analogical inference proceeds from the similarity of two or more things in one or more respects to the similarity of those things in some further respect.[89] For example, A, B, and C have properties X and Y. A and B also have property Z. Therefore, C probably also has property Z. Analogical arguments, which cannot be deductively valid, can still be more or less cogent depending on the degree to which we are justified in affirming their conclusions.[90] Because the two items compared can be alike or unlike in an almost infinite number of ways, relevance comes in. What is relevant depends on how one characterizes the details of the context of the comparison. To draw an analogy between two or more items, then, is to indicate one or more respects in which they are relevantly similar.[91]

84 See Klaus Gunther, *The Sense of Appropriateness: Application Discourses in Morality and Law*, trans. John Farrell (Albany, NY: State University of New York, 1993), xiii; Ronald Dworkin, *Freedom's Law: The Moral Reading of the American Constitution* (Cambridge, MA: Harvard University Press, 1996), 2–30.

85 See Ronald Dworkin, *Taking Rights Seriously* (Cambridge, MA: Harvard University Press, 1977), 136.

86 See Edward H. Levi, *An Introduction to Legal Reasoning* (Chicago: University of Chicago Press, 1949), 1.

87 See Hilary Putnam, *The Many Faces of Realism* (LaSalle, IL: Open Court Publishing, 1987), 73.

88 Irving M. Copi and Carl Cohen, *Introduction to Logic* (10th ed.) (Upper Saddle River, NJ: Prentice Hall, 1998), 472.

89 Ibid., 473. 90 Ibid., 477. 91 Ibid., 472.

Less formally, such analogical reasoning is no stranger to prelaw students, law students, lawyers, judges, and legal academics, for whom past judicial decisions may serve as precedents in a common-law system. Legally, if in an earlier case one set of reasons had outweighed the other set, then one can argue that consistency dictates the same result in the present case. Because a court had decided one case one way, that is a *prima facie* reason for deciding a case that is not too different in the same way. Still, that conclusion would call for an argument to support the claim that the two cases being compared are sufficiently similar in the relevant respects to be analogous. The harder the case, the more likely there will be at least one plausible counterargument that supports the opposite conclusion – namely, that the two cases in question are not sufficiently similar. New cases will usually differ in some important respects from previous cases and the strength of the relevant reasons will vary according to their context and the extent to which they are stronger or weaker in combination with other reasons. Although consistency demands that like cases be treated alike, lawyers and judges must be mindful of the possible relevant differences. The unique details of new cases may put into doubt whether an earlier case is sufficiently similar to the case in question to be a precedent.

Ultimately, the task is to determine when two cases are close enough in the relevant respects to warrant the same kind of treatment. Judges have a great deal of work to do, then, in figuring out whether two cases are really analogous, and whatever conclusion they reach, it will probably be subject to dispute. In a common-law system, when a judge or lawyer appeals to precedent, he or she is claiming that the previous rationale for treating *Smith v. Jones* in one manner is a good enough reason for treating a subsequent case close enough to *Smith* in the same manner. The relevance of an earlier precedent turns on how the judge characterizes the material facts of the earlier case. No two appellate cases are factually identical down to the last detail, but they may be sufficiently similar in the relevant legal respects for a judge to decide that the holding of a previous case also controls the new case.

E. *As Applied to Plural Marriage*

Many of those who are in favor of same-sex marriage continue to maintain that the legal recognition of same-sex marriage will not inevitably lead to the legal recognition of plural marriage.[92] They assert that certain social dangers, such

[92] See, for example, William N. Eskridge Jr., *The Case for Same-Sex Marriage: From Sexual Liberty to Civilized Commitment* (New York: Free Press, 1996), 8.

as sexual abuse and incest, which are present in polygamous relationships, are not likely to appear in same-sex relationships.[93] For example, Jonathan Rauch insists that no slippery slope between same-sex and incestuous or plural marriages exists.[94] In his words: "People who insist on marrying their mother or several lovers want an additional (and weird) marital option. Homosexuals currently have no marital option at all. A demand for polygamous or incestuous marriage is thus frivolous in a way that the demand for gay marriage is not."[95] According to Evan Gerstmann, polygamy differs from same-sex marriage because the would-be polygamist still can marry the person of his first choice.[96] As he puts it: "There certainly seems to be a difference between a right to marry *who* you want and marrying *however* many people you want."[97] Consequently, the situation a gay or lesbian person confronts is worse than that of any straight person.[98] Along similar lines, Andrew Sullivan claims: "Almost everyone seems to accept, even if they find homosexuality morally troublesome, that it occupies a deeper level of human consciousness than a polygamous impulse."[99] A person – male or female – who seeks to marry more than one person can at least marry one person he or she loves and that is supposed to be an improvement over being denied the right to marry the only person you think you love.

No doubt, in some respects, the two kinds of marriages differ. But are they different enough to warrant such unequal legal treatment? ? On the one hand, two-person same-sex and plural marriage are not identical in this manner: The right to marry someone at all seems to differ from the right to marry multiple persons – at least on the surface. Rauch is right, then, in this claim: "The gay situation is unique."[100] However, he is wrong when he refers to a demand to

93 See, for example, Hema Chatlani, "In Defense of Marriage: Why Same-Sex Marriage Will Not Lead Us Down a Slippery Slope Toward the Legalization of Polygamy," *Appalachian Law Journal*, 6 (2006), 129–32.

94 Jonathan Rauch, *Gay Marriage: Why It Is Good for Gays, Good for Straights, and Good for America* (New York: Henry Holt, 2004), 123–58.

95 Jonathan Rauch, "Marrying Somebody," in *Same-Sex Marriage: Pro and Con*, ed. Andrew Sullivan (New York: Vintage Books, 1997), 286.

96 Gerstmann, *Same-Sex Marriage and the Constitution*, 104.

97 Ibid.

98 Not all gays and lesbians believe the right to same-sex marriage would improve their lives or serve the cause of gay liberation. In fact, some gay and lesbian opponents of same-sex marriage insist the recognition of such a right would have the opposite effect. See, for example, Paula L. Ettelbrick, "Since When Is Marriage a Path to Liberation?" in *Same-Sex Marriage: The Moral and Legal Debate* (2nd ed.), ed. Robert M. Baird and Stuart E. Rosenbaum (Amherst, NY: Prometheus Books, 2004), 257–61.

99 Andrew Sullivan, "Three's a Crowd," in *Same-Sex Marriage: Pro and Con*, ed. Andrew Sullivan (New York: Vintage Books, 1997), 279.

100 Rauch, *Gay Marriage*, 127.

marry more than one person as frivolous. A couple who wants to have more than one child is not necessarily making a frivolous demand; its frivolity would depend on the quality of their underlying personal reasons – something which cannot be known in the abstract. What is allegedly frivolous to one person is not necessarily frivolous to another when it comes to how one wants to arrange one's personal life. As I have tried to show, such reasons tend to be subjective. That is the case because what matters most to us is a function of our uniqueness. And to refer to what someone wants to do as "weird" is surely more than a mere observation. Nor is Sullivan's use of the word "impulse" an accurate way to describe what is really at stake, as if wanting to marry more than one person were akin to a middle-aged man's wanting to buy a sports car or a professor's impulsively purchasing a Diet Mountain Dew as a legal performance-enhancing drug while standing in the checkout line at the local market. One can concede that the situation of gays and lesbians is worse – and perhaps even much worse – than that of plural marriage enthusiasts and still conclude that a right to such marriage exists. One also can believe that there are much better reasons in favor of defining civil marriage to include same-sex couples and still believe that there are sufficient reasons to support plural marriage. This distinction is critical. As one commentator puts it: "The relevant issue is whether there are sufficiently weighty paternalistic reasons to ban polygamy (or certain forms of polygamy), without there being sufficiently weighty paternalistic reasons to ban same-sex marriage."[101]

While I do not blame gay rights activists for distancing themselves from plural marriage for strategic reasons and worry that a book that defends plural marriage may be misappropriated by opponents of same-sex marriage as proof that the slope really is slippery, I do not feel that the rights of all kinds of polygamists ought to be sacrificed in the name of equality for gays and lesbians. Americans do not have to choose between them or make comparative judgments about which kinds of discrimination are worse. The lives of plural marriage enthusiasts also count – whether they are straight, gay, bisexual, or asexual. William Eskridge devotes some space in his otherwise excellent book on same-sex marriage to explain why the slippery slope argument fails and why the state has a compelling interest in promoting gender equality.[102] I have already responded to such points in some depth and will merely remind readers that plural marriage is not synonymous with traditional polygyny and the state can try to foster gender equality through regulatory

[101] Samuel C. Rickless, "Polygamy and Same-Sex Marriage: A Response to Calhoun," *San Diego Law Review*, 42 (2005), 1046.

[102] Eskridge, *The Case for Same-Sex Marriage*, 144–45, 148–49.

schemes without denying competent adults the ability to marry more than one person at the same time.

There are several ways to show that same-sex and plural marriage are sufficiently similar to merit the same legal treatment. For me, the most compelling rationale for having both options involves the importance of allowing people to select their own marital partner(s). Although a ban on interracial marriage can be attacked as illegitimately promoting racial supremacy, it also denies the interracial couple the choice of the person he or she want to marry and ideally spend the rest of his or her life with. To suggest he or she could marry someone of the same race as a substitute is to be obtuse. These days, it would be hard to take seriously a comment along the lines of "Couldn't you just find a nice white girl to marry?" I cannot imagine too many other choices that are so deeply personal. To treat same-sex and plural marriage equally, then, is to acknowledge that just like race, the state may not restrict personal choice on the basis of sexual orientation and numbers. Unlike, say, age, which could support such a marital restriction, "due to legitimate concerns about the genuineness of the consent of someone under a certain age," most reasons the state would offer against the legal recognition of plural marriage are insufficiently public and therefore cannot override each competent adult's right to choose.

III. STANDARDS OF REVIEW

A. *Traditional Standards of Review*

What I just wrote may seem more like a substantive due process or fundamental rights argument than an equal protection one, but the Equal Protection Clause can do indirectly what other constitutional provisions do more directly. Take *Brown*, which is an exemplary equal protection case. After the initial oral argument in 1952, had Chief Justice Fred Vinson lived, the outcome could have been different.[103] His replacement (Earl Warren) tried to make the opinion, which rendered unconstitutional purposefully racially segregated public schools, as innocuous as possible to avoid antagonizing white Southerners who favored segregation. As such, one has to read in between the lines to discern what Warren and the rest of the Supreme Court really meant. The most obvious way to interpret the unanimous opinion is to underscore that, as Justice Harlan once put it in his lone dissent in *Plessy*, "there is no caste system here," meaning the state may not use law to reinforce the belief that one race is superior to

[103] See Bernard Schwartz, A *History of the Supreme Court* (New York: Oxford University Press, 1993), 286.

another. At the same time, racially segregated public schools or passenger cars also do something else: They deny choice. In his majority opinion in *Plessy*, Justice Henry Brown made it seem as if the judicial invalidation of the Jim Crow law in question would unreasonably force racial integration, but as it stood, the reverse was true: The Louisiana statute did not permit anyone to choose with whom to sit in passenger cars if they were of a different race. At the time, *Brown* did not stand for the proposition that African-American parents must send their children to racially integrated public schools but that they should be able to do so, especially when their children are more likely to receive a better education. Likewise, in *United States v. Virginia*, VMI's all-male admissions policy denied women the choice of attending the only public university in the state where they could receive a first-rate military education.[104]

My point is not that every single important equal protection case can be reduced to a different and perhaps more persuasive constitutional rationale but instead that such cases often involve the denial of personal choice. Why should one group of persons receive a benefit or opportunity the state denies to another group in the absence of relevant differences? For example, if marital choice is important for people who are straight, is it not equally important for those who are gay or lesbian? Just as the question of the appropriate standard of review is central to whether states can deny same-sex couples marriage licenses, the same question arises when the state refuses to allow thruples or groups to marry when they would prefer some sort of a multiperson marital arrangement. The Equal Protection Clause requires that legislative classifications be sufficiently justified and the strength of the justification that is called for reflects the nature of legislative classification whose constitutionality is being contested. The implication of a heightened standard of review is that the law in question is most likely unconstitutional. As Gerald Gunther famously put it, strict scrutiny is strict "in theory and fatal in fact," whereas rational basis is "minimal scrutiny in theory and virtually none in fact."[105] According to Sonu Bedi: "Whether a group counts as a suspect class makes all of the constitutional difference in the world."[106] At present, doctrinally, only suspect classes are entitled to extra judicial protection and the vast majority of minority groups do not qualify for such treatment.

However, empirically, when real judges apply standards of review to real cases, the process of application may be less straightforward. Between 1990 and

[104] *United States v. Virginia*, 518 U.S. 515 (1996).

[105] Gerald Gunther, "Foreword: In Search of Evolving Doctrine on a Changing Court: A Model for a Newer Equal Protection," *Harvard Law Review*, 86 (1972), 1, 8.

[106] Bedi, *Beyond Race, Sex, and Sexual Orientation*, 2.

2003, only 73 percent of all race-conscious laws subjected to strict scrutiny were invalidated.[107] That figure not only suggests that the outcome may be harder to predict but that some judges may employ a less strict scrutiny standard of review in certain situations. The rationale for such extra protection, as expressed in Justice Harlan Stone's famous footnote number four in *Carolene Products*, draws upon the imperative of protecting discrete and insular minorities who cannot defend themselves in the legislative process.[108] The traditional criteria for being characterized as a suspect class are an immutable characteristic, a lack of political power, and a history of discrimination.[109] Most legal scholars (and even some judges these days) treat gays and lesbians as a suspect class.[110] It is not hard to see why they do so. As a group, not only do gays and lesbians meet the aforementioned criteria well, but these days, they also seem to meet it at least as well – if not better – than women, who continue to constitute a quasi-suspect class. Consequently, it might be surprising to learn that the Supreme Court continues to refuse to treat gays and lesbians – at least officially – as a suspect class in *Romer*, *Lawrence*, *Hollingsworth*, and *Windsor*.

Constitutionally, if the denial of a right to plural marriage were to trigger a heightened standard of review, such as intermediate or strict scrutiny, then the state has the burden of proof; it must articulate why it has a substantial or a compelling interest in defining marriage so narrowly and why the legislative means it has chosen directly advance that interest. The placement of the burden of proof on the state in such cases could be taken to mean that people are entitled to individualized treatment.[111] That is the interpretation I prefer, meaning the state cannot use statistical generalizations – even if they were more or less accurate – about the harms associated with plural marriages to support their not treating them equally – that is, like two-person marriages. The strength of the main state interests against plural marriage – ensuring gender equality, protecting women's autonomy, preventing other related crimes, and promoting the welfare of children – are much weaker

[107] Adam Winkler, "Fatal in Theory and Strict in Fact: An Empirical Analysis of Strict Scrutiny in Federal Courts," *Vanderbilt Law Review*, 59 (2006), 839.

[108] *United States v. Carolene Products*, 304 U.S. 144, 153 (1938) (153, n. 4).

[109] Erwin Chemerinsky, *Constitutional Law: Principles and Policies* (4th ed.) (New York: Wolters Kluwer 2011), 688–89. For an extended discussion, see Bedi, *Beyond Race, Sex, and Sexual Orientation*, 38, 43–71.

[110] See, for example, Bruce Ackerman, "Beyond *Carolene Products*," *Harvard Law Review*, 98 (1985), 713.

[111] I owe this point to Andrew Lister (e-mail correspondence).

than most people believe on closer inspection. Even when such interests are compelling or substantial, the legislative means may still not be sufficiently narrowly tailored or substantially related.

As I tried to prove in the second chapter, it is not evident that encouraging or preserving internal equality is important or compelling. People are allowed to choose inegalitarian monogamous marriages, friendships, employment relationships, associations, religions, and so on, and may bring up their children to believe that different kinds of inequality are natural or morally correct. Nor is it obvious why the purported lack of such equality in a plural marriage entails the state may deny the right to marry on that basis only in the case of plural marriages while it turns a blind eye to much more prevalent inegalitarian monogamous ones. Surely, in terms of equality along any dimension, the best polyamorous marriage would be much better than the worst opposite-sex monogamous one. I also suspect that many real polygynous marriages would not compare as unfavorably with many real monogamous marriages as opponents of plural marriage would have us believe. If it is to meet its burden and defend the double standard, the state must be able to demonstrate that such marriages are prone to being intolerably inegalitarian and that the harm that results from this inequality is serious enough to justify unequal treatment despite the cost of denying marital choice to competent adults, including even those who prefer a more egalitarian arrangement.

The implicit premise in the argument from gender inequality is that all or at least most legally recognized plural marriages would be polygynous. An all-male or all-female triad or mixed gender, asexual intimate relationship does not raise the same concern about how women will be treated. A society that permitted such marriages and did not stigmatize the participants would probably learn over time that the quality of individual plural marriages would vary widely – like that of monogamous ones. The apparent differences among them might turn out to be less significant than critics of plural marriage have long alleged and that would be a devastating blow to their position. If they are going to be consistent, their only other option is to condemn traditional monogamous marriage on the same grounds, but that change in attitude is not forthcoming.

Part of the problem with the standard views of opponents of plural marriage is that most of them are crudely utilitarian. I say "crudely" because they highlight all the possible negative consequences, conveniently overlook the possible positive ones, and grossly oversimplify complex probabilistic judgments. Normally, in constitutional cases, such justifications for laws that restrict personal freedom or treat groups of people unequally are only appropriate in situations involving a rational basis standard of review in which judges pretty much let lawmakers do whatever they want to do.[112] Those who oppose plural marriage – if they want their view to have the force of law – must do a better job of elucidating why the legal definition of marriage should exclude marital relationships that contain more than two persons and why such discrimination is consistent with treating people fairly. Their constitutional position inaccurately assumes the worst kind of unregulated polygyny and rests on the unsubstantiated dire consequences of all plural marriages – notwithstanding the empirical uncertainty surrounding them. One cannot simply cite the example of Warren Jeffs or Winston Blackmore, as if those cases exemplify all plural relationships, unless one has no objections to people's arguing from irrelevant extremes. Because polygamous relationships already exist – some of which are illegal – opponents must also believe that the legal option of a plural marriage will increase the number of polygynous marriages over time, thereby exacerbating gender inequality and other associated harms.

B. Immutability

Although the Utah Supreme Court read *Lawrence* narrowly and rejected Holm's equal protection argument,[113] in what follows, I want to explain why polygamists could be treated as a suspect class under existing constitutional doctrine. They meet at least two of the three traditional criteria – immutability, a history of discrimination, and political powerlessness – for giving extra judicial protection to a minority group. As Nussbaum reminds us, the criteria "are indicia, not necessary conditions,"[114] meaning that not all three of them have to be satisfied before a judge can conclude that the group in question is a suspect class or quasi-suspect class. It makes sense, then, following Nussbaum, to view any group's meeting some or all of the criteria as evidence that the legislative classification whose constitutionality is being challenged is much more likely than most legislative classifications to reflect animus against that group.

Typically, immutability or unchangeability means that one is not responsible for the trait in question. For example, one cannot choose one's race or sex and it would seem to be unfair to disadvantage anyone for something that

[112] A standard of review is the lens through which a court examines the constitutionality of a law and includes a presumption of un/constitutionality. Rational Basis is a nonheightened standard of review, which means there is a strong presumption in favor of the constitutionality of the law in question.

[113] *Utah v. Holm*, 2006 UT 31; 137 P.3d 726 (2006).

[114] Nussbaum, *From Disgust to Humanity*, 116.

is out of his or her control. The problem with this interpretation is that many things are out of people's control. Some people may be genetically predisposed to being obese or having psychological disorders, but laws that discriminate against such persons would probably only trigger rational basis and thus pass constitutional muster. I believe the importance of immutability as a criterion has outlived its usefulness, even though historically, it was intelligible in the midst of widespread racial injustices. For most of American history, until the Supreme Court dealt with affirmative action, the immutability of race served as a proxy for membership in a racial minority that was being invidiously discriminated against. Even though race is immutable, that fact does not necessarily mean that affirmative action plans, which disadvantage white applicants, are automatically unconstitutional or should trigger strict scrutiny standard of review.

David Richards once took issue with the immutability requirement.[115] These days, it is evident that gays and lesbians do not choose their sexual orientation any more than straight persons do – if by "sexual orientation" one means to whom a person is physically attracted. As Corvino explains, the description of being gay as a "choice" is ambiguous; it could mean what causes it or it could mean whether it can be changed.[116] If one believes that sexual orientation is a choice, then it would seem to follow that all people at some point in their lives choose to whom they are attracted and their four options would be (1) the same sex (gay or lesbian), (2) the opposite sex (straight), (3) both sexes (bisexual), or (4) nobody (asexual).[117] These options do not capture the nuances of sexual identity, but for my purposes, they will suffice. Using this definition, it is false that everyone chooses his or her sexual orientation. One possible response would be to argue that only gays and lesbians choose their sexual orientation and all of them happen to choose to be homosexual, which is logically possible but so statistically improbable that it lacks plausibility as an explanation. The other response would be that they do not choose to whom they are attracted, but they can decide not to act on such feelings and refuse to identify themselves as nonstraight. I believe this is what those who characterize being gay as a choice really mean more often than not these days – that is, even if people is genetically predisposed to preferring members of one gender

[115] David A. J. Richards, *Identity and the Case for Gay Rights: Race, Gender, Religion as Analogies* (Chicago: University of Chicago Press, 1999), 93.

[116] Corvino, *What's Wrong With Homosexuality?* 99–102.

[117] Here, I exclude disorders in which people are sexually attracted to nonhuman animals and inanimate objects.

for romantic intimacy – they does not have to behave accordingly. This response presupposes the state can legitimately ask them to not be gay or lesbian, which means the state may disadvantage them for the "choice" they have made in assuming an identity that a majority of people believe to be inappropriate identity.

However, what if, in fact – in one way or another – they did choose their sexual orientation? Would it matter constitutionally speaking? Sexual orientation could be at least partially socially constructed, even when the vast majority of us are hardwired to be straight, gay, bisexual, or asexual in terms of our sexual desires. Some scholars contend that far too much time and effort has been spent on this not terribly important question regarding immutability.[118] By comparison, it is probably fair to say that most people choose to identify with a particular religious group – after all, some people who are born into such groups leave them – but it would seem almost silly to argue that because someone chose to be a Jehovah's Witness or a Seventh-Day Adventist that the state could discriminate against him or her because he or she could or should have selected a more mainstream Christian denomination if he or she were more enlightened. Even if people ultimately choose their sexual orientation, then, their doing so would not necessarily imply the state could discriminate against them because the choice is theirs and, their situation could be otherwise. Jews could convert to Christianity, but obviously, they should not be required or even asked to do so in a society that values freedom of conscience. When there is nothing wrong with being a religious or racial minority, the state should not be allowed to interfere with the kind of life their members want to have on the ground that there is something wrong with such membership. Anyone who relies on the view that gays and lesbians choose their sexual orientation and could decide not to be homosexual must believe that being gay or lesbian is somehow illegitimate.

Although polygamists are not born that way, they may be inclined toward a multipartner intimate relationship. "Poly" identity for polyamorists is not frivolous, even though it may seem that way to those who do not know or want to know any of them. Being polyamorous cannot be reduced to having sex openly with multiple people. To claim that to want a multiperson intimate relationship is akin to promiscuity is to not only rely on a vicious stereotype, but it is also to be dismissive of the personal reasons people have to want to have a certain kind of life. The average person is idiosyncratic in at least some

[118] Edward Stein, "Law, Sexual Orientation, and Gender," in *The Oxford Handbook of Jurisprudence and Philosophy of Law*, ed. Jules Coleman and Scott Shapiro (Oxford, UK: Oxford University Press, 2002), 1014.

ways but we only become aware of this fact when we come to know that person better. These days, no progressive would tolerate for a moment someone's insinuating that gay identity is really about having sex as often as possible with as many partners as possible. Indeed, the fact that anyone wants to marry anyone suggests he or she sees his or her intimate relationship as something he or she wants to be permanent. If polyamory is as frivolous as its critics maintain, then one has to wonder why polyamorists see themselves so differently. Are all of them obtuse or deluded? One only has to meet some of them or do a little reading with a semi-open mind to get a better sense of just how important their poly identity is to them. There was a time in American history when few straight persons knew anyone who was openly gay or lesbian and bought into stereotypes. Whoever you are, you d not want how you see yourself and your life reduced to demean everything that you care about. All nonstraight persons could hope for from the straight community was that the stereotypes would not be too pernicious. Even if being polygamist were more a function of socialization or individual preference, it still may make legal sense to treat polyamory as a sexual orientation for purposes of antidiscrimination law.[119] Their choosing to be polygamists in a manner that gays and lesbians do not choose their sexual orientation would not mean it would be acceptable for the state to discriminate against them when their having such a relationship is morally permissible or perhaps morally admirable.

C. *Political Powerlessness*

In his dissent in *Romer*, Justice Scalia notoriously exaggerates how much political clout gays and lesbians have.[120] After all, if they have so much influence, then why do some states, even today, reject same-sex marriage and refuse to shield sexual minorities from different sorts of discrimination that racial minorities and women are already protected from at the federal and state levels? At most, in some locales, due to demographics, they may have political power proportional to their numbers. By comparison, polygamists find themselves in an even worse position: They have no political or legal representation and even fewer resources. Today, generally, it may be even easier for a gay or lesbian person in some locales to leave the closet than a straight polygamist or polyamorist. Despite the growing tolerance of sexual minorities and their intimate relationships and the increasingly common view

[119] See Ann Tweedy, "Polyamory as a Sexual Orientation," *University of Cincinnati Law Review*, 79 (2011), 1461–515; Bedi, *Beyond Race, Sex, and Sexual Orientation*, especially 208–47.
[120] *Romer v. Evans*, 517 U.S. 620, 646 (1996).

that marriage does not have to be between a man and a woman, most Americans would not let even competent, fully informed adults marry more than one person at the same time.[121] According to Eugene Volokh, "pro-polygamy forces are in a lousy political position."[122]

D. *History of Discrimination*

The other traditional criterion for treating a minority group as a suspect class is a history of discrimination. Discrimination against gays and lesbians is a sad but undeniable historical fact. More generally, in Nussbaum's words: "Societies have many ways of stigmatizing vulnerable individuals."[123] Mormons in general and FLDS in particular have been repeatedly persecuted for their religious beliefs and practices and their suffering should not be minimized, even if one is convinced that that of gays and lesbians deserves more immediate action. The fact that polygamists can still be prosecuted for being polygamists and having certain living arrangements indicates they are not close to being free from being victimized.

Part of the unease within contemporary political and legal thought with respect to plural marriage in the United States can be traced to the historical association of such marriage with Mormonism.[124] The judiciary has done little to encourage Americans to view plural marriage as more than a mere opportunity to exploit women and abuse children. In 1878, in *Reynolds*, the Supreme Court ruled that the First Amendment does not protect the practice of plural marriage.[125] Since then, federal courts have not taken seriously the claim that an adult may marry more than one person at the same time on fundamental rights, equal protection, free exercise of religion, freedom of association, or other constitutional grounds.

The persecution of Mormons for the practice of polygamy is a tragic episode in American history, and even today, anti-Mormon sentiment has not disappeared. In the nineteenth century, the newly formed Republican Party connected polygamy and slavery, dubbing them the "twin relics of barbarism."[126] The American government was not the only agent of

[121] According to a Gallup poll, 90 percent of them believe the practice of polygamy is immoral. Gallup poll, May 8–11, 2008. N = 1,017 adults nationwide; margin of error: +/– 3 percent. www.gallup.com/poll/108115/americans-evenly-divided-morality-homosexuality.aspx.

[122] Eugene Volokh, "Same-Sex Marriage and Slippery Slopes," *Hofstra Law Review*, 33 (2005), 1177.

[123] Martha C. Nussbaum, *From Disgust to Humanity: Sexual Orientation and Constitutional Law* (New York: Oxford University Press, 2010), 17.

[124] Emens, "Monogamy's Law," 282.

[125] *Reynolds v. United States*, 98 U.S. 145 (1878).

[126] Sarah Barringer Gordon, *The Mormon Question: Polygamy and Constitutional Conflict in Nineteenth-Century America* (Chapel Hill: University of North Carolina Press, 2002), 55–58. In 1852, the same year it officially endorsed polygamy, Utah legalized slavery. James M.

persecution.[127] As Sarah Barringer Gordon writes: "Like other antipolygamists, novelists connected Mormonism to other non-Protestant faiths, drawing on popular prejudices to argue that any radical departure from Protestantism would corrode true liberty."[128] Recently, a number of nonacademic accounts of FLDS fundamentalism have painted a bleak picture of the lives of the women who engage in the practice.[129]

In the contemporary United States, some estimates put the number of FLDS who practice polygamy at approximately 40,000.[130] Other studies indicate that that figure may be as high as 60,000.[131] Some non-Mormon groups also have polygynous living arrangements, including some families in Muslim immigrant communities.[132] Most FLDS do not use the terms *polygamy* or *polygyny* to describe how they live.[133] In Mormon theology, polygamy is also known as the *celestial law of plural marriage* or *patriarchal marriage* or as *the principle* and those who are sealed are supposed to be sealed for eternity.[134] Polygyny was not one of the original tenets of the Mormon faith found in *The Book of Mormon* but was promulgated in Joseph Smith's "Revelation on Celestial Marriage" in 1843.[135] In 1883, the Edmunds Act banned polygamy and unlawful cohabitation and set up a federal commission to administer test oaths to compel voters to swear they were neither bigamists nor polygamists and Mormons who refused to take these oaths were barred from public service and voting.[136] During the 1880s, the federal government prosecuted more than 1,300 Mormons for the religious practice of polygyny.[137] In 1887, the Edmunds-Tucker Act disinherited the children of plural marriages and disenfranchised Mormons who advocated polygamy, even when they did not practice it.[138] In 1890, due to intense pressure from the federal

McPherson, *Battle Cry of Freedom: The Civil War Era* (New York: Oxford University Press, 1988), 76.

127 For a concise description of anti-Mormon legislation, see Nancy F. Cott, *Public Vows: A History of Marriage and the Nation* (Cambridge, MA: Harvard University Press, 2000), 112–20.

128 See Gordon, *The Mormon Question*, 33.

129 See, for example, Jon Krakauer, *Under the Banner of Heaven: A Story of Violent Faith* (New York: Anchor Books, 2004).

130 Jill Norgren and Serena Nanda, *American Cultural Pluralism* (2nd ed.) (Westport, CT: Praeger Publishers, 1996), 110.

131 Miriam Koktvedgaard Zeitzan, *Polygamy: A Cross-Cultural Analysis* (New York: Berg, 2008), 89.

132 Janet Bennion, *Polygamy in Primetime: Media, Gender, and Politics in Mormon Fundamentalism* (Waltham, MA: Brandies University Press, 2012), 7.

133 Ibid., xvi. 134 Gordon, *The Mormon Question*, 1. 135 Ibid., 22–23.

136 Norgren and Nanda, *American Cultural Pluralism*, 100. 137 Ibid. 138 Ibid., 101.

government, as a condition of statehood for Utah, the Mormon Church formally repudiated polygamy.[139]

E. *Reynolds*

According to early Mormon constitutional theory, the principles of federalism and the religion clauses of the First Amendment protect plural marriage.[140] In *Reynolds*, Chief Justice Morrsion Waite conceded that the practice of plural marriage was rooted in sincere religious convictions yet distinguished between beliefs and actions based on those beliefs. The former fell within the protection of the Free Exercise Clause, but the latter did not.[141] The belief-action distinction, which Waite relied on, remains problematic when such a narrow understanding of the Free Exercise Clause nearly eviscerates its meaning.[142] After all, most people do not simply want the right to hold certain beliefs; they also want to be able to act on them and their being able to do so may require an exemption. Waite also claimed that women who were involved in plural marriages were victims of a self-delusion.[143] This false consciousness argument, where women who participate in such arrangements must be the victims of brainwashing, has not passed from the scene. It is premised on the pernicious assumption that if they really knew what was in their own best interest, then they would never choose to be a part of such relationships. As I tried to show earlier, even if some women do not choose such relationships, many do – and even many antipolygamists concede this point these days when the discussion is about what most polygynous relationships in this country are like. The fact that some are less than fully voluntary cannot entail that no adult woman may opt for such a marital arrangement under any circumstances. In the antebellum period, the kind of patriarchy that characterized plural marriage was considered worse than that of a typical traditional monogamous marriage.[144]

The Supreme Court has not overturned *Reynolds* and will not do so in the near future.[145] Justice Scalia even cites the decision in his majority opinion in *Smith*, the infamous peyote case, which limited the scope of free exercise

139 Ibid., 108. 140 Gordon, *The Mormon Question*, 89.
141 *Reynolds v. United States*, 98 U.S. 145, 162 (1878).
142 See Nussbaum, *Liberty of Conscience*, 101.
143 *Reynolds v. United States*, 98 U.S. 145, 167–69 (1878).
144 Nancy Rosenblum, "Democratic Sex: Reynolds v. U.S., Sexual Relations, and Community," in *Sex, Preference, and Family: Essays on Law and Nature*, ed. David M. Estlund and Martha C. Nussbaum (Oxford, UK: Oxford University Press, 1997), 77.
145 *Reynolds v. United States*, 98 U.S. 145 (1878).

exemptions.[146] Nonetheless, some scholars have criticized the reasoning in *Reynolds* and no thoughtful person today would eagerly accept its racist and irresponsible claims that plural marriage is contrary to "social duties and good order" and "odious among the northern and western nations of Europe."[147] As Sarah Song observes: "The *Reynolds* court both drew upon and reinforced . . . [a] discourse of racial and cultural superiority of whites over others, casting the American-born Mormon religion as foreign and other."[148] Whatever happened in the past, as I keep reminding readers, present-day FLDS polygyny is only one of the many forms a plural marriage could take.[149] First, only a small number of FLDS practice polygyny.[150] Second, the typical FLDS polygynous marriage does not facilitate other crimes, such as sexual assault and child abuse.[151] The vast majority of them are probably no better or no worse than the monogamous ones Americans idealize. If some polygynous marriages actually facilitate certain crimes, then the proper legislative response is regulation, not prohibition, as I argued in the third chapter. It surely makes little to sense for the state to continue its policy of permitting polygynous cohabitation while criminalizing polygynous "marriages" but rarely enforcing such laws. And if being married is conducive to human well-being, as traditionalists have told us repeatedly, then why should polygamists be denied the benefits a plural marriage could produce?

For many commentators, even today, the more general topic of plural marriage is only worthy of discussion as a limit case in the ongoing debate about same-sex marriage. In such discussions, people often assume the Constitution does not protect the right to plural marriage. The only puzzle is to distinguish same-sex marriage from plural marriage so one can defend a constitutional right to the former without proving too much and thereby unintentionally conceding a right to the latter. Today, FLDS polygynous marriages continue to serve as the archetype for plural marriage, but hopefully, that state of affairs will change sooner rather than later. To confine ourselves to that example is to impair our thinking about the forms that such marriage could take in a society that did not force such persons to conceal their unconventional intimate relationships. The personal cost of having to engage in such deception, which is a common theme in episodes of HBO's *Big Love*, must be extraordinary.

146 *Employment Division v. Smith*, 494 U.S. 872 (1990).

147 *Reynolds v. United States*, 98 U.S. 145, 164 (1878).

148 Sarah Song, *Justice, Gender, and the Politics of Multiculturalism* (New York: Cambridge University Press, 2007), 148–49.

149 In fact, FLDS polygyny itself is also diverse. Bennion, *Polygamy in Primetime*, xvii.

150 Ibid., 7.

151 Ibid., xvi.

F. The Origins of Opposition to Plural Marriage

This is neither the time nor the place to offer anything like a comprehensive explanation of the historical causes of antipolygamist sentiment, but it is evident that in the West, it has deep roots in the Christian tradition, which privileges opposite-sex monogamy. I also suspect that these causes are related to the narrative in this country about "appropriate" sexual behavior. As Martha Nussbaum notes, "appeal to disgust … has been a crucial part of the antigay strategy."[152] Those who are homophobic tend to fixate on the sexual dynamics of the same-sex relationship. In this respect, antipolygamy has something in common with opposition to homosexuality because many Americans still believe same-sex sex acts to be unnatural or deviant. As Will Kymlicka suggests, "The restriction on polygamy may instead be a case in which allegations of social instability are used to suppress an unpopular minority whose actions are seen as morally indecent or corrupt."[153] Perhaps many Americans believe the *New Testament* requires monogamous marriage. Or they continue to associate plural marriage with Mormonism and the worst features of FLDS polygyny. Or they continue to fear "the other." One scholar has coined the term *polyphobia* to describe prejudice against polygamists and their relationships.[154] The topic of sex still makes many Americans feel uncomfortable.[155] They may be even more wary of the idea of anyone's having multiple sexual partners or with alternative lifestyles more generally that involve unfamiliar sexual behaviors. For Nussbaum: "Americans characteristically exhibit a lot of anxiety about sexual variety. …"[156] Sexual nonexclusivity is one of the defining features of some polygamous unions.

Opposition to plural marriage may also be rooted in racism.[157] After the Civil War, the Freedmen's Bureau began to promote monogamous marriage among former slaves by going after those who practiced bigamy.[158] More recently, such opposition may reflect anti-Muslim sentiment. The

152 Nussbaum, *From Disgust to Humanity*, 8.

153 Will Kymlicka, "Rethinking the Family," Susan Moller Okin, *Justice, Gender, and the Family Philosophy and Public Affairs* 20 (1991), 77, 93–94.

154 Bennion, *Polygamy in Primetime*, 7.

155 See Michael Warner, *The Trouble With Normal: Sex, Politics, and the Ethics of Queer Life* (Cambridge, MA: Harvard University Press, 1999), 21.

156 Nussbaum, *From Disgust to Humanity*, 25.

157 See Patricia Hill Collins, *Black Feminist Thought: Knowledge, Consciousness, and the Politics of Empowerment* (New York: Routledge, 1991).

158 Brake, *Minimizing Marriage*.

Koran permits polygyny (up to four wives) but does not require it.[159] Some advocates of plural marriage point out the apparent hypocrisy that underlies the belief that such marriage does not really differ from serial monogamy or chronic infidelity. As one scholar notes: "Muslims argue that for all practical purposes a man with a mistress is engaged in polygyny and neither the law nor social opinion in the West is much exercised about it."[160] That is probably an overstatement. Although very few people in this country still believe adultery or divorce should be illegal, most of them are quick to condemn cheating on one's partner and mere allegations of such behavior create salacious scandals that many Americans never seem to tire of. This moral reaction is understandable due to the deception that infidelity usually involves and the pain it causes, but this reaction has a hidden cost: It precludes public discussion about whether the couple has an open marriage or whether having more than one long-term intimate partner might turn out to be a superior arrangement for some persons in light of their specific circumstances.

Decades ago, when *Bowers* was still good law, it would have been much more challenging to formulate a plausible constitutional argument on behalf of same-sex marriage on either privacy or equal protection grounds. *A fortiori*, it would have been even harder to argue that the Constitution requires plural marriage as an additional option. As Koppelman writes: "Together, *Lawrence* and *Romer* establish a fairly clear rule: If the law singles out gays for unprecedentedly harsh treatment, the Court will presume that what is going on is a bare desire to harm, rather than mere moral disapproval."[161] It then would follow that at minimum, the state must cease making polygamy a crime unless one does not care about other sexual minorities who are discrete and insular. Like many members of the LGBT community, those who partake in polygamous relationships live double lives; they often do not feel welcome to come out of the closet. They could lose their families, friends, jobs, and even their children in a custody dispute.[162] In some places, they could face criminal charges.[163]

Keep in mind that even today, polygamists can be prosecuted for in essence doing what married and unmarried people – straight or gay – can do without fear of incurring criminal liability. *Bowers v. Hardwick* was only decided by a

[159] Bhikhu Parekh, *Rethinking Multiculturalism: Cultural Diversity and Political Theory* (2nd ed.) (New York: Palgrave Macmillan, 2006), 282–85.

[160] Ibid., 283. [161] Koppelman, *Same Sex, Different States*, 78.

[162] On the risks of this sort of coming out, see Tristan Taormino, *Opening Up: A Guide to Creating and Sustaining Open Relationships* (San Francisco: Cleis Press, 2008), 229–31.

[163] Most states treat polygamy as a felony, but some of them treat it as a misdemeanor. Samantha Slark, "Are Anti-Polygamy Laws an Unconstitutional Infringement on the Liberty Interests of Consenting Adults?" *Journal of Law and Family Studies*, 6 (2004), 453.

single vote and today is regarded by most legal academics as an embarrassment.[164] Before this decision was overruled in 2003, it was not clear whether the failure of a state to recognize same-sex marriage would be subject to the analysis found in *Bowers* or that of *Romer*, where the Supreme Court had concluded that animus against gays and lesbians was not a legitimate state interest. Read more broadly, *Romer* stands for the proposition that the judges will be more skeptical of the rationale offered on behalf of the statute in question when a suspect group is being legally disadvantaged. One concern is that it may be hard to know when the intent that underlies the law in question is invidious. The disagreement between Kennedy and Scalia over how to properly characterize why the voters of Colorado had approved Amendment 2 in *Romer* resurfaces in *Windsor*. In his dissent, Justice Scalia complains about the implication of the majority opinion that he and others like him who continue to oppose same-sex marriage are bigots.[165]

Many of them genuinely care about preserving the symbolic meaning of traditional marriage and may believe that redefining marriage will have bad consequences. If that is the case, then not everyone who opposes same-sex marriage could be automatically labeled a homophobe. Perhaps not every voter in California who voted for Proposition 8 in 2008 had morally unacceptable reasons for doing so, even though many of them most likely did have such reasons. During the trial in *Perry*, Judge Vaughn Walker doubted that the actual individual reasons for opposition to same-sex marriage were constitutionally legitimate. What is obscured by this shallow way of looking at the issue of redefining marriage to include same-sex couples is the significant cost gays and lesbians are being asked to bear. In effect, a straight person who seeks to preserve the symbolic meaning of two-person opposite-sex marriage by excluding gays and lesbians from the institution is asking many of them to make a considerable sacrifice he or she probably would not be willing to make him or herself. No one is asking straight people who have been or are likely to be poor marital partners, not to marry to preserve the integrity of the institution. It may be true that a fair number of straight people who oppose same-sex marriage – to a greater or lesser extent – dislike gays and lesbians or are intolerant of same-sex relations more generally. It is almost impossible to ignore the fact that when they cite religious sources to support their position, they are relying on texts that hardly present a positive view of same-sex sexual relations. But like Scalia did in his dissent in *Romer*, one could argue that those who voted for Amendment 2 were not homophobic but were expressing their genuine moral

[164] *Bowers v. Hardwick*, 478 U.S. 186 (1986).
[165] *United States v. Windsor*, 570 U.S. __ (2013) (Scalia, J., dissenting).

disapproval of gays and lesbians and same-sex relationships. As Koppelman comments: "The constitutional status of laws that discriminate against gays . . . is uncertain after *Romer*."[166] That situation results from the lack of clarity with respect to the kinds of reasons the state may offer in defense of its decisions to designate sexual orientation as a relevant difference.

However, *Windsor* shows that the state cannot treat gays and lesbians differently with respect to federal marital benefits when such differential treatment is rooted in a bare desire to harm a politically unpopular group.[167] What for Scalia is genuine moral disapproval is for Kennedy animus against a sexual minority. How one describes the state's interest will determine its legitimacy and whether the law in question passes rational basis. A ban on interracial marriages, for example, can only be rationalized by a morally false belief of white supremacy – notwithstanding the sincerity and firmness with which the belief is held. The correctness of *Loving* is self-evident.[168] Although it may be offensive to some people to compare bans on interracial and same-sex marriage, discrimination against gays and lesbians mirrors racial discrimination in terms of its adverse impact on their self-worth. People who have been denied the right to marry on the basis of their sexual orientation are denied that right on the basis of a morally or legally irrelevant characteristic. It must be very painful to be told in a state that still does not permit same-sex couples to marry that no matter the quality of their relationship, as far as the state is concerned, it does not measure up to the worst opposite-sex one.

Constitutionally, lawmakers and voters may not act on the basis of animus against a discrete and insular minority. Animus is an interpretive concept. It requires the judge to not only make a factual determination with respect to the circumstances under which the law in question was enacted but to also make a moral judgment, as in what it ought to mean. While the exact meaning of "animus" (and what would count as sufficient proof of its existence) is disputed, at its core lies the belief that a legislative majority may not act on the basis of certain reasons – namely, those rooted in malice.[169] As Dale Carpenter puts it: "Animus doctrine constitutionalizes the basic concept that one should not hate any human being or class of human beings."[170] To act with malice is to not only act with the wrong intention in terms of one's subjective motivations but to also fail to treat a particular minority group fairly. Even Chief Justice John Roberts, in his dissent in *Windsor*, conceded that is

[166] Koppelman, *The Gay Rights Question in Contemporary American Law*, 7.
[167] *United States v. Windsor*, 570 U.S. __ (2013).
[168] Eskridge, *The Case for Same-Sex Marriage*, 109.
[169] Dale Carpenter, "'*Windsor* Products': Equal Protection From Animus," http://ssrn.com/abstract=2424743 (p. 184).
[170] Ibid., 185.

was constitutionally impermissible to "codify" malice.[171] In my view, it makes sense to see animus as an unarguably nonpublic reason – that is, a reason that reasonable persons would not and could not share as justification for unequal treatment. Coupled with *Lawrence*, which disqualifies mere moral disapproval as a public reason, the state has to offer a better rationale for the law to pass constitutional muster.

A law should surely not be based on hatred of anyone or any single group. Its justification would have to come from elsewhere. These days, anyone who claimed to have sincere religious or moral convictions for opposing interracial marriage (or a legal right to it) would be labeled a racist and understandably so when that sort of relationship should not precipitate a reaction of moral disapproval. There is nothing wrong with an interracial intimate relationship between consenting adults, and even if many people had sincere religious reasons to morally disapprove of it, we would still conclude that animus underlies the opposition, which is a way of saying that the moral disapproval expressed is inappropriate. By contrast, if I morally disapproved of how my imaginary neighbor abuses his intimate partner, my moral disapproval would be justified in a way that opposition to an interracial couple never could be. In that case, the behavior in question is no longer self-regarding; there is a victim.

Is opposition to same-sex marriage, then, more like opposition to interracial couples or more like opposition to my imaginary neighbor's intolerable treatment of his intimate partner? If Kennedy is right and Scalia is wrong, then the state's interest is not legitimate and a law that treats gays and lesbians unequally fails the first part of rational basis standard of review. Like it or not, *Romer*, *Lawrence*, and *Windsor* lay the foundation for a constitutional right to same-sex marriage not only because Scalia says so in his dissent in *Windsor* but also because the Supreme Court seems to believe that none of the reasons lawmakers or voters could use to support their opposition to same-sex marriage make the grade. This is the connection that Judge Robert J. Shelby recently made in striking down a Utah law that failed to give same-sex couples the same marital rights as opposite-sex couples.[172] Likewise, one might be equally skeptical of the kinds of reasons that allow states to make bigamy a crime. As Jonathan Turley writes, "the criminalization of polygamy should fail under an equal protection challenge even if it is found not to involve a suspect class or fundamental right. There is no rational basis for criminalizing the private relations of consenting adults absent proof of harm to children or others."[173]

While Turley only concerns himself with decriminalization, the reasons the state offers on behalf of keeping polygamy a crime have at least some

[171] *United States v. Windsor*, 570 U.S. __ (2013) (Roberts, J. dissenting).
[172] *Kitchen v. Herbert* (2013) (Case No. 2:13-cv-217) [173] Turley Report, p. 21.

applicability to states' not also giving competent adults the option of plural marriage. One way to argue that the state must let people marry more than one person at the same time is to make an explicit equal protection argument to support the constitutional conclusion that the state may not treat polygamists differently when it comes to marriage. According to Bedi, "the Equal Protection Clause is best understood . . . as a limit on the kinds of reasons government may invoke."[174] As such, the clause functions as a restriction on state power where the state cannot treat individuals differently unless it has adequate reasons for such treatment. The problem with what Bedi calls the "tiers-of-scrutiny" approach is that what counts as a constitutionally inadmissible rationale for a legislative classification is debatable.[175] One is free to express what he or she believes marriage should be – only between a man and a woman or not subject to dissolution under any circumstances – but is not equally free to impose that definition on the rest of us unless he or she has sufficiently public reasons. That is one way to understand the limits the Equal Protection Clause in particular and the Constitution more generally imposes on the legislative power of the state.[176] Here, the ongoing constitutional discourse over same-sex marriage is illuminating: in the *Perry v. Hollingsworth* and *Windsor* litigation, it is hard not to notice how the different judges tended not to take the state's asserted interest at face value. Instead, they questioned the sincerity of the reasons offered on behalf of laws that discriminated against same-sex couples because they appeared to provide such weak support. For Carpenter, "the flimsiness of these justifications reinforces the conclusion that the law was infected by animus."[177]

IV. THE SYMBOLIC IMPORTANCE OF MARRIAGE

In this last section, I want to underscore the extent to which the Equal Protection Clause stands for the principle that the state may not use the law to make value judgments about particular identities or ways of life. In other areas, a constitutional law, such as the Establishment Clause, a commitment to neutrality is well established.[178] According to one interpretation, the state is not supposed to take sides in religious disputes or tell members of religious minorities that their deepest religious convictions and the behaviors that

[174] Bedi, *Beyond Race, Sex, and Sexual Orientation*, 20. [175] Ibid., 72.

[176] Elsewhere, I described same-sex marriage as an easy case because those who oppose it have been unable to put forth such reasons. See Den Otter, *Judicial Review in an Age of Moral Pluralism*, especially 245–61.

[177] Carpenter, "'*Windsor* Products': Equal Protection From Animus," 192.

[178] See Andrew Koppelman, *Defending American Religious Neutrality* (Cambridge, MA: Harvard University Press, 2013).

follow from them are misguided. The focal point of many Free Exercise Clause and Establishment Clause cases is the message that the state conveys when it puts its imprimatur on certain religious symbols or practices.[179] That is no doubt a normative position, and no doubt one that is not beyond dispute, but I also believe it captures the spirit of some of the most important Equal Protection Clause decisions in American constitutional history. Critical race theorist Charles Lawrence has gone so far to argue that *Brown* is as much a free speech case as it is an equal protection case and its holding – properly understood – is premised on the constitutionally objectionable message of racial superiority that racially segregated schools convey.[180]

In this nation, marriage is not just another social institution. In Nancy Polikoff's words: " 'Marriage' has a long history of exclusion: slaves, interracial couples, and same-sex couples have been denied it."[181] Historically, the denial of the right to marry stands for the acceptability of some people's being treated as inferiors.[182] For most of our history, under the common law, marriage was predicated on coverture and thus subordinated women. Scholars continue to note how marriage "functions as a special symbolic resource."[183] Two of them write: "When people marry, they receive not only material benefits, but also a kind of official legitimacy from the state."[184] As Elizabeth Brake adds, "[marriage] also carries a rich symbolism of adulthood, full citizenship, and moral respectability."[185] This use of the "m" word would not be so worrying if marriage did not retain such a special social meaning in our society. One could imagine a different human society in which marriage did not have the same resonance and most people were indifferent as to whether a couple was married in the eyes of the law, had wed in a church, or was simply cohabitating. To let others know you are married – at the very least – is to inform them of how you see your commitment to your partner. From this perspective, the fundamental problem with the state's recognizing some marital relationships but not others is that the state should not be able to tell anyone it is better to be married than unmarried or single out some kinds of marriage for legal recognition because they are

179 *Lynch v. Donnelly*, 465 U.S. 668 (1984).

180 Charles R. Lawrence III, "If He Hollers Let Him Go: Regulating Racist Speech on Campus," in *Words That Wound: Critical Race Theory, Assaultive Speech, and the First Amendment* (Boulder, CO: Westview Press, 1993), 59–62.

181 Nancy D. Polikoff, *Beyond (Straight and Gay) Marriage: Valuing All Families Under the Law* (Boston, MA: Beacon Press, 2008), 132.

182 George Chauncey, "The Long Road to Marriage Equality," *New York Times*, June 27, 2013, A29.

183 Metz, *Untying the Knot*, 89.

184 Cass R. Sunstein and Richard H. Thaler, "Privatizing Marriage," *Monist*, 91 (2008), 382.

185 Brake, *Minimizing Marriage*, 5.

supposed to be superior. The message associated with the state's recognizing some marriages at the expense of others is that the lives of those whose intimate relationship is not accorded legal status are less worthwhile.

The growing concern over the unfairness of how same-sex couples are treated legally, then, is not just about the material benefits that accompany marriage.[186] These benefits are not trivial, but a well-written comprehensive civil union or domestic partnership law could address this worry.[187] Other democracies have already detached many of the entitlements that still do – but do not have to – come with marriage.[188] Contracts, wills, powers of attorney, and other legal instruments could also create something like a marriage-like legal relationship. In Nussbaum's words: "Marriage has ... an expressive aspect. When people get married, they typically make a statement of love and commitment in front of witnesses. Most people who get married view that statement as a very important part of their lives."[189] Instead, not treating same-sex couples as legal equals lets people know the state views being straight as more admirable.[190] In *Windsor*, in his majority opinion, Justice Kennedy reiterates this point several times.[191] Marriage law conveys multiple messages about which sexual behaviors, which identities, and which kinds of families are appropriate.[192] For an increasing number of Americans, even though gays and lesbians are not a racial minority, the unequal treatment of same-sex couples is the moral and legal equivalent of racism. The idea of "separate but equal" that civil unions for same-sex couples is premised on seems indefensible when one's sexual orientation ought to be as legally irrelevant as one's hair color.[193]

186 Such benefits include immigration, taxes, inheritance, social security and disability benefits, visitation at hospitals, and end-of-life issues. See Eskridge, *The Case for Same-Sex Marriage*, 66–67.

187 At least with respect to state law. However, prior to *Windsor*, the Defense of Marriage Act (DOMA) authorized the federal government to discriminate against same-sex couples. Under Section 4 of DOMA, a same-sex couple who married in a state that performs or permits such marriages did not count as a married couple for purposes of federal law. For example, if one of them was a citizen and one of them was not, the citizen could not sponsor his or her marital partner for citizenship. Even after *Windsor*, a same-sex couple who is not legally married in the state in which they reside may still be denied the federal benefits a married opposite-sex couple would be entitled to. In addition, many state domestic partnerships laws do not create the legal equivalent of marriage. See Mary Ann Case, "Marriage Licenses," *Minnesota Law Review*, 89 (2005), 1773–75.

188 Polikoff, *Beyond (Straight and Gay) Marriage*, especially 110–22.

189 Martha C. Nussbaum, "The Right to Marry?" *California Law Review*, 98 (2010), 669.

190 See Andrew F. March, "Is There a Right to Polygamy? Marriage, Equality and Subsidizing Families in Liberal Public Justification," *Journal of Moral Philosophy*, 8 (2011), 244–70.

191 *United States v. Windsor*, 570 U.S. __ (2013).

192 Cott, *Public Vows*, 4.

193 Bedi, *Beyond Race, Sex, and Sexual Orientation*, 2.

In 2015, few people would conclude that civil unions for interracial couples would satisfy the requirements of the Equal Protection Clause, even if all the tangible benefits paralleled those of marriage. Any judge who reviews the constitutionality of a legislative classification that treats gays and lesbians differently than straight persons must consider the symbolic effect of such unequal treatment and why it might be constitutionally objectionable. In 2008, the California Supreme Court decided that the state's failure to "designate the official relationship of same-sex couples as marriage," even with the option of domestic partnerships for same-sex couples, violates the California Constitution.[194] This concern about symbolism also underlies Judge Stephen Reinhart's belief, expressed in *Perry v. Brown*, that the state's taking away a right to marriage differs from not granting such a right in the first place.[195]

More generally, law has a well-documented symbolic or expressive function.[196] In *Windsor*, Justice Kennedy underscores the extent to which Section 3 of DOMA stigmatized same-sex marriages and denied gays and lesbians their dignity.[197] Before that decision, a number of legal scholars had made more or less the same point about the symbolism of such laws. In David Cruz's view, marriage is a unique symbolic or expressive resource.[198] Marriage can be symbolic in multiple ways. The institution could stand for love and the value of a long-term commitment in general or it could stand for the normality (and normativity) of straight relationships. How people interpret its meaning to some extent is influenced by their social context because people who grow up in the same culture internalize shared meanings. For example, normally, to refer to one's significant other as a husband, wife, or spouse differs from referring to him or her as a boyfriend or girlfriend in terms of the kind (and intensity) of the commitment. "Partner" is deliberately vague by not divulging marital status or gender.

The issue with keeping the word *marriage* in the legal code – as opposed to, say, universal civil unions or domestic partnerships – is that a break with the past may be more appropriate, given the injustices associated with the institution.[199] Rather than retaining the term and trying to rehabilitate it, it may be

194 *In re Marriage Cases*, 43 Cal. 4d 757, 780 (2008) (George, J., majority)

195 *Perry v. Brown*, 671 F. 3d 1052 (2012).

196 See, for example, Cass R. Sunstein, "On the Expressive Function of Law," *University of Pennsylvania Law Review*, 144 (1996), 2012–53.

197 *United States v. Windsor*, 570 U.S. __ (2013), pp. 20–25.

198 David Cruz, "'Just Don't Call It Marriage': The First Amendment and Marriage as an Expressive Resource," *Southern California Law Review*, 74 (2001), 925–1026. Although Cruz makes the case that marriage is an essential expressive resource on free speech grounds, I do not believe the First Amendment is the only constitutional source for such a conclusion.

199 See Polikoff, *Beyond (Straight and Gay) Marriage*, 132.

more fruitful for the state to cease to use it and in its place use a morally neutral label for all marriage-like relationships. Private religious organizations could continue to use the term *marriage* and assign it their own religious meaning and then fewer people would fail to differentiate religious marriage with the legal status the state accords to two or more persons who meet the eligibility requirements. As unromantic as what I am about to write may sound, the more people begin to see "marriage" as a more or less contractual arrangement, the less they will be inclined to confuse religious marriage with its legal counterpart. Public opinion polls show that Americans who still oppose same-sex marriage are more receptive to such nomenclature as *civil unions* and *domestic partnerships*. That reaction may be due to the "separate but equal" regime that reserving "marriage" for opposite-sex couples reinforces. With civil union status for everyone, there would be no message of inferiority being sent to gays and lesbians. That new state of affairs might engender opposition from traditionalists who are wedded to a narrower understanding of marriage (and want to keep the special legal status for themselves). But it has the virtue of allowing them to call their intimate relationship a "marriage" if they so desire without implying that the state believes it to be more worthwhile than the alternative forms.

As aforementioned, today, a ban on interracial marriages could not get off the ground even if the state provided domestic partnerships for interracial couples and such partnerships contained all the tangible benefits of marriage. This much is for certain: The belief they are being treated as less than equals is not just in their own heads.[200] The heart of Chief Justice Warren's opinion in *Brown* is that all "separate but equal" laws cannot survive a challenge to their constitutionality because the very act of segregating creates a stigma of racial inferiority.[201] In the setting of gender discrimination, one can view Justice Ginsburg's majority opinion in *United States v. Virginia* as her seeing VMI's single-gender admissions policy as a means of telling women they are not deserving of the same educational and professional opportunities.[202] By contrast, few people think that high school sports teams segregated by gender convey the same pernicious message. There was a time when some gay and lesbian rights activists did not want same-sex couples to marry because they viewed the institution of marriage as heterosexist.[203] To not marry was a way of

200 In his notorious majority opinion in *Plessy*, Justice Henry Brown blamed the victims – African-Americans – for assuming that Jim Crow laws "stamped them with a badge of racial inferiority." *Plessy v. Ferguson*, 163 U.S. 537 (1896).

201 *Brown v. Board of Education*, 347 U.S. 483 (1954).

202 *United States v. Virginia*, 518 U.S. 515 (1996).

203 On anti-assimilation, see Eskridge, *The Case for Same-Sex Marriage*, 75–80.

rejecting not only the social and legal institution itself but also the wrongs it stood for in their eyes. This point is not lost on either side of the same-sex marriage debate. Roughly, those who oppose letting same-sex couples wed maintain that the extension of the right of marriage to such couples would reflect the belief that there is nothing wrong or sinful about homosexuality. Those who favor same-sex marriage perceive the extension of this right as being predicated on – after so much discrimination – acceptance or tolerance of gays and lesbians and their constitutional right to be treated equally.

At times, it is fair to say messages associated with most laws are not always as self-evident as those, say, linked to Jim Crow laws or all-male admissions policies. In equal protection cases, the Supreme Court has not been indifferent to symbolism. According to Bedi: "The label 'marriage' is important because it adds something to the relevant union, something that goes above and beyond the tangible benefits and burdens that accompany civil unions."[204] Also, we should not dismiss the possibility of extending the term *marriage* to unconventional relationships at this moment in American history as a kind of compensation for past amatonormative discrimination.[205] Part of the appeal of having an equal right is that it reflects the belief that you are no better or no worse in the eyes of the law than anyone else. In present-day America, as Judge Walker remarks, there is nothing like marriage except marriage.[206] People who have been unfairly denied the marital partner of their choice are entitled to that legal status under the nonideal conditions that exist and will continue to exist in the near future. The most promising route to public acceptance of unconventional marital relationships is for the state – for the time being – to legally recognize them as marriage-like relationships, including plural marriages, to treat all persons with the equal concern and respect they deserve before serious consideration of abolishing the institution takes place. The arguments found in the discursive context of the ongoing debate over same-sex marriage explain why those who would marry more than one person if they had the legal right to do so are entitled to having the state treat their intimate relationships as marriages or their equivalent. To not do so is to reinforce the unfortunate but widely held belief that their deepest beliefs and the practices that follow from them are illegitimate.

Whatever else not recognizing same-sex marriage as a legal status may do, this failure preserves a status quo where legally, opposite-sex marriages are superior to all the alternatives. As Ralph Wedgwood writes: "It is widely believed that the state's purpose in honouring in this way must be to express

[204] Bedi, *Beyond Race, Sex, and Sexual Orientation*, 225.
[205] See Brake, *Minimizing Marriage*. [206] *Perry v. Schwarzenegger*, 704 F. Supp. 2d 921 (2010).

the view that married life is an especially virtuous or valuable way of life."[207] At present, in most states, same-sex intimate relationships are presumed to be less worthwhile. A woman who marries an older man just because of his wealth and an older man who marries her so she can be his trophy wife have a more socially (and legally) acceptable relationship than two women or two men who are in a long-term, committed relationship. This implication is hard to accept. Not too many of us would believe that Anna Nicole Smith's last marriage was superior to a committed same-sex relationship unless we are in the thrall of the ridiculous view that all opposite-sex romantic relationships are *prima facie* better than all same-sex romantic relationships. This view only makes sense if one cares more about the sex of the participants than the quality of their relationship or their personal reasons for marrying in the first place. If their sex is irrelevant, then unequal treatment of their relationship would not be justified under any standard of review, including the most deferential, namely rational basis. This point is also made in the *In re Marriage Cases* when Chief Justice Ronald George elaborated on why civil unions could not take the place of marriage.[208] As Wedgwood writes: "To defend same-sex marriage, then, . . . we must argue that there is a basic inequality in the fact that same-sex couples, unlike opposite sex couples, are denied the *marital status itself* [his emphasis]."[209]

That status is equally important when the state expands the range of intimate relationships it confers legal recognition on. In the context of the contemporary debate over same-sex marriage, that status is important not only due to its tangible benefits, as noted, but also because of its symbolic importance. To legally recognize same-sex marriages is not necessarily to approve of them.[210] Just because I believe that Britney Spears has a legal right to marry Kevin Federline (and more than once if she wanted) hardly implies I approve of their marriage or their reasons for marrying. Rather, it is to be committed to the view that the state must reserve judgment about its merits by leaving its determination to the individuals involved. Being married is an important part of many people's identities – that is, how they conceive of themselves; marriage may even be the paramount goal for some of them. It is evident from public debate over DOMA that those who oppose same-sex

[207] Ralph Wedgwood, "The Fundamental Argument for Same-Sex Marriage," *Journal of Political Philosophy*, 7 (1999), 227.

[208] *In re Marriage Cases*, 43 Cal. 4th 757 (2008).

[209] Wedgwood, "The Fundamental Argument for Same-Sex Marriage," 227.

[210] This is called the stamp-of-approval argument in the literature.

marriage are fully aware of what is symbolically at stake if same-sex marriages were to receive legal recognition.[211]

CONCLUSION

One way of reading out our constitutional tradition is to underscore its equal protection aspects and in doing so recognizing the equal right of all persons to live the kinds of lives they want to live without unjustified legal discrimination. In the end, assuming the state will remain in the marriage business, there are only two ways to create equal access to marriage: Let everyone in or keep everyone out.[212] As long as states continue to accord the legal status of marriage to some intimate relationships but not to others, they cannot draw arbitrary lines where one kind of marriage is privileged over all the other marriage-like possibilities. Until the state can come up with a rationale that adequately supports a numerical limitation – and in the second and third chapters, I explained why it had not done so to date – not permitting the option of a plural marriage violates the Equal Protection Clause. Recent judicial decisions indicate that substitutes for same-sex marriages, such as civil unions and domestic partnerships, are not only inadequate but also inherently demeaning due to the message of inferiority that accompanies them. The existence of such substitutes could be construed to communicate that same-sex couples are not entitled to the same kind of legal recognition that traditional opposite-sex couples already receive.

Unquestionably, a statutory substitute for marriage for interracial couples would not save a ban on interracial marriage. Historically, bans on polygamy and interracial marriage have much in common.[213] A civil union alternative for polygamists sounds too much like "separate but equal" and too little like "there is no caste system here," but it is reasonable to inquire as to why such a legal distinction should be made and someone who responds with "We have to protect the traditional definition of marriage" would still have to explain why doing so would justify unequal treatment, even though it is simple to imagine discriminatory treatment that is even worse. A sincere response would have to include an explanation of why the state has the authority to put its imprimatur on two-person but not on multiperson marriages in a country that

211 See David Cruz, "'Just Don't Call It Marriage'," 946–52.
212 Patricia A. Cain, "Imagine There's No Marriage," *Quinnipiac Law Review*, 16 (1996), 28.
213 Martha M. Ertman, "Race Treason: The Untold Story of America's Ban on Polygamy," *Columbia Journal of Gender and Law*, 19 (2010), 287–366.

is supposed to be committed to the principle that the life of one person is as important as that of anyone else.

Most plural marriage enthusiasts are not as different as they appear to be to those who have been socialized into monogamy and are unwilling to consider the possibility that the legal definition of marriage could be much more inclusive. A crucial part of the strategy of advocates of gay rights involves showing that gay and lesbian individuals are not so different despite pervasive negative stereotypes, especially about gay men. Increasingly, Americans are indifferent to sexual orientation, which supports the conclusion that it never should serve as the basis of unequal treatment. Likewise, polygamists should not be discriminated against. They have friends, families, jobs, and lives to lead. The decriminalization of polygamy and the eventual legal recognition of plural marriages will require a dramatic change in popular attitudes toward polygamists and polyamorists and tolerance of their decision to live differently. That day may not come in the near future, but it may not be as far off as most of us believe.

6

The Disestablishment of Marriage

In this final chapter, I shall explain why civil marriage should be disestablished and what form such disestablishment should take when the state legally recognizes various kinds of plural marriage. In the scholarly literature, "disestablish" usually does not mean the elimination of the status of a marriage-like relationship but the creation of a new, more inclusive legal status.[1] For liberals committed to some version of neutrality, the state is not supposed to privilege traditional opposite-sex intimate relationships without adequate justification.[2] The issue of same-sex marriage is only one problem created by the establishment of marriage.[3] Several other kinds of intimate relationships are also disadvantaged, including nonmarital caretaking relationships between or among adults, polyamorous networks, and close but platonic friendships.[4] As a number of academics note, it is not evident why the state should be able to

[1] By contrast, abolitionists advocate the complete removal of the state from the institution. See, for example, Edward A. Zelinsky, "Deregulating Marriage: The Pro-Marriage Case for Abolishing Civil Marriage," *Cardozo Law Review*, 27 (2006), 1161–220. One scholar refers to "disestablishment" as "non-marriage." Amy L. Wax, "Traditionalism, Pluralism, and Same-Sex Marriage," *Rutgers Law Review*, 59 (2007), 377–412.

[2] Adrian Alex Wellington, "Why Should Liberals Support Same Sex Marriage?" *Journal of Social Philosophy* 26 (1995), 5–32; Ralph Wedgwood, "The Fundamental Argument for Same-Sex Marriage," *Journal of Political Philosophy* 7 (1999), 225–242; Stephen Macedo, "Homosexuality and the Conservative Mind," *Georgetown Law Review*, 84 (1995), 261; Gordon Babst, *Liberal Constitutionalism, Marriage, and Sexual Orientation: A Contemporary Case for Dis-Establishment* (New York: Peter Lang, 2002).

[3] Elizabeth Brake, "Rawls and Feminism: What Should Feminists Make of Liberal Neutrality?" in *The Legacy of John Rawls*, ed. Thom Brooks and Fabian Frevenhagen (New York: Continuum, 2005), 78.

[4] In Elizabeth Brake's words: "The privileging of marriage marginalizes the unpartnered and those in non-traditional relationships – quirkyalones, urban tribes, care networks, polyamorists – and same-sex partners, where they are prohibited from marriage." Elizabeth Brake, *Minimizing Marriage: Marriage, Morality, and the Law* (New York: Oxford University Press, 2012), x.

privilege marriage or any intimate relationship if doing so advances a particular conception of the good.[5] Their concern is that the state may not act on the basis of a perfectionist rationale for preferring one kind of marriage over other kinds. As Sonu Bedi remarks, "the actual reason for a categorical ban on *all* [his emphasis] types of plural marriage, even those involving members of the same-sex, must be about the intrinsic moral superiority of two-person couplings over couplings of three or more."[6]

In *Untying the Knot*, to avoid this neutrality problem, Tamara Metz advances a powerful case for the disestablishment of marriage.[7] Although what she intends to put in its place – intimate caregiving unions (ICGUs) – is a vast improvement over the status quo, as I shall show, such a status still violates liberal neutrality, may do much less to foster gender equality than she envisions, and unnecessarily restricts personal choice. I then offer a contractual alternative, which I refer to as a "semiprivate intimate contract" (SPIC). Such a proposal would not lead to the complete privatization of marriage, as many Libertarians have long advocated.[8] Instead, it would create a marital regime that is partially contractual and partially a status, enabling people to devise most of the terms of their marriages.[9] Such a regime would not only be more consistent with liberal neutrality, but it would also better serve other liberal values, such as freedom and, perhaps counterintuitively, equality.

Metz's idea of ICGUs is not the only status-based proposal in circulation, but it represents some of the most recent sophisticated thinking with respect to what lies beyond dyadic marriage. My proposal differs from hers inasmuch as the intimate relationships recognized by the state do not have to be predicated

[5] On the former, see Steve Vanderheiden, "Why the State Should Stay Out of the Wedding Chapel," *Public Affairs Quarterly*, 13 (1999), 175–190. On the latter, see Elizabeth Brake, Review, *Untying the Knot: Marriage, the State, and the Case for Their Divorce, Philosophy in Review* 30 (2010), 418–20. Brake refers to the state's illegitimately favoring two-person amorous intimate relationships as "amatonormativity." See Brake, *Minimizing Marriage*.

[6] Sonu Bedi, *Beyond Race, Sex, and Sexual Orientation* (New York: Cambridge University Press, 2013), 224.

[7] Tamara Metz, *Untying the Knot: Marriage, the State, and the Case for Their Divorce* (Princeton, NJ: Princeton University Press, 2010).

[8] See, for example, David Boaz, *Libertarianism: A Primer* (New York: Simon and Schuster, 1997), 241–42.

[9] I borrow the term "intimate contract" from Lenore J. Weitzman, *The Marriage Contract: A Guide to Living With Lovers and Spouses* (New York: The Free Press, 1981), 227. By "semiprivate," I mean that third parties would be compelled to treat the legal relationship as if it were a marriage. Jeremy Garrett refers to this more general approach as "marital contractualism" (MC) and holds a full contractualist view, meaning civil marriage will cease to exist and those who want to "marry" can create a legal relationship via private contract. Jeremy R. Garrett, "A Prima Facie Case Against Civil Marriage," *Southwest Philosophy Review*, 25 (2009), 41.

on any sort of caregiving. It also differs from complete privatization because it would require the state to compel third parties to recognize them. Thus, even though a SPIC is largely contractual, it remains a status and makes possible trial marriages that can end when the renewable contract expires.[10] My aim is not to offer a detailed contractual alternative but to present an account of why a commitment to liberal neutrality leads to something like contractualization.[11]

This chapter will be divided into the following sections. First, I explain why having a legal status such as marriage is morally and constitutionally problematic and then elaborate on why a commitment to liberal neutrality leads to disestablishment. Second, I critically examine one of the leading alternatives – Metz's idea of ICGUs – to illustrate how replacing one substantive – albeit better – definition with another does not solve the neutrality problem. Third, I discuss SPICs, includes some thoughts on why contractualization has such a bad reputation, and bring out some of the advantages of having a menu of options to choose from. My overarching aim is to show how a society like our own could (and should) maximize marital choice by either requiring SPICs or incentivizing their use.

I. THE DEBATE OVER DISESTABLISHMENT

A. *The Legal Status of Marriage*

The recent campaign by the marriage movement in this country to promote marriage is driven by a desire to foster a parochial conception of marriage, which so-called traditionalists believe to be the best conception of marriage.[12] Married couples are already legally entitled to material and expressive benefits that unmarried couples and single persons do not receive. Typical material benefits include those related to taxes, social security, inheritance, surrogate decision making, immigration, insurance, bereavement, adoption, custody, end-of-life decisions, health care, and evidentiary privileges.

In terms of expressive benefits, family law continues to normalize some intimate relationships while it marginalizes others. As Ralph Wedgwood

[10] For an interesting discussion of temporary or trial marriages, which contractual approaches make possible, see Laurie Shrage, "Reforming Marriage: A Comparative Approach," *Journal of Applied Philosophy*, 30 (2013), especially 108–12.

[11] In Islam, marriage is contractual. Malise Ruthven, *Islam: A Very Short Introduction* (New York: Oxford University Press, 2012), 107–08.

[12] Melanie Heath, *One Marriage Under God: The Campaign to Promote Marriage in America* (New York: New York University Press, 2012), especially 1–22.

notes, the status of marriage "signals to the community that the couple wish their relationship to be viewed in light of these generally shared assumptions [sexual intimacy, domestic and economic cooperation, and mutual long-term commitment] about what married life is like."[13] In all states, the law denies single people numerous benefits that are available to married couples and adds insult to injury by informing them it is better to be married than unmarried.[14] It should not escape our attention that as long as the state gives even minimal legal recognition to any sort of intimate relationship, it will be sending a loud and clear message that it is better to be in such a relationship than to remain single. These days, liberals are not terribly concerned with single persons being legally discriminated against but understandably worry about the treatment of same-sex couples. Laws that do not treat gays and lesbians equally seem to imply their inferiority.[15] To avoid such discrimination, most liberals favor the extension of the right of marriage to same-sex couples, which would be a leap toward marital equality. One way to understand this increasingly common normative position is to see the legal recognition of same-sex marriage as a public statement that condemning same-sex couples is morally antiquated.[16]

At the same time, few liberals have recognized how their position may lead to something much more radical, namely abolition – where states no longer accord legal status to any marriage-like relationship in the name of non-discrimination.[17] The states could probably leave the marriage business without any constitutional repercussions.[18] Their endorsing only certain kinds of marriages, though, engenders two neutrality problems. First, in a minority of states, current marriage law continues to discriminate against same-sex couples who would marry if that option were available to them. Second, in all states, polygamists are not permitted to marry more than one person at the same time. According to

[13] Ralph Wedgwood, "The Meaning of Same-Sex Marriage," *New York Times*, May 24, 2012. Available at opinionator.blogs.nytimes.com/2012/05/24/marriage-meaning-and-equality/?_php=true&_type=blog&_r=0.

[14] Garrett, "A Prima Facie Case Against Civil Marriage," 47. However, precedent indicates the state cannot discriminate against unmarried couples when it comes to birth control. See *Eisenstadt v. Baird*, 405 U.S. 438 (1972).

[15] Amy Wax, "The Two-Parent Family in the Liberal State: The Case for Selective Subsidies," *Michigan Journal of Race and Law*, 1 (1996), 513; John Corvino, "Homosexuality and the PIB Argument," *Ethics*, 115 (2005), 509; Andrew March, "Is There a Right to Polygamy? Marriage, Equality and Subsidizing Families in Liberal Public Justification," *Journal of Moral Philosophy*, 8 (2011), 244–70.

[16] Andrew Lister, *Public Reason and Community* (London: Bloomsbury Publishing, 2013), 137.

[17] Andrew Lister, Review Essay, "How to Defend Same-Sex Marriage," *Polity*, 00 (2005), 1.

[18] See Anita Bernstein, "For and Against Marriage: A Revision," *Michigan Law Review*, 102 (2003), 143–46.

one scholar, polyamory represents an ethical vision of what intimate relationships should be like.[19] The neutrality problem surfaces when the state favors one vision over others, and in doing so advances a parochial conception of the good that many reasonable people reject.

At present, marriage is a legal relationship that is a contract and a public status that confers material and expressive benefits.[20] The state not only defines marriage but also creates a standard package of rights and responsibilities for married couples and compels third parties, such as employers, hospitals, and government, to accept their legal force. In doing so, the state singles out this type of intimate relationship for more favorable treatment. Even in the wake of *Windsor*, at the time of this writing, states still do not have to permit same-sex couples to marry, even when they meet all the other legal requirements.[21] If a married couple divorces or one of them dies, they are not nearly as vulnerable as those who are cohabitating because they have the protections that come with a legal relationship.[22]

There are only three possible basic changes to the legal status of marriage that could occur: (1) The state could refuse to recognize all intimate relationships, including traditional marriages, and thus relegate them to the private sector (privatization, as in state withdrawal from the institution or its analogues – known in the literature as "abolition"). However, under such a regime, the state would still enforce certain kinds of private contracts, and as a result, it would be more accurate to say that the regulatory scheme would be altered to minimize the extent to which marriage remains a legal status.[23] (2) The state could privilege a wider range of intimate relationships to promote something substantive, like caregiving.[24] (3) The state could allow people to enter voluntarily into a more explicit contractual arrangement governing the various aspects of life that currently fall under marriage and then require the state to enforce those contracts against third parties as long as those

[19] Elizabeth F. Emens, "Monogamy's Law: Compulsory Monogamy and Polyamorous Existence," *New York University Review of Law and Social Change*, 29 (2004), 320.

[20] Cott, "The Public Stake," 33–34.

[21] *United States v. Windsor*, 570 U.S. __ (2013).

[22] Cynthia Grant Bowman, *Unmarried Couples, Law, and Public Policy* (New York: Oxford University Press, 2010).

[23] Whether the institutionalization of a regime of private marital contracts would eliminate status norms from marriage is an interesting and far from simple question. For an explanation of why marriage would always remain a semi-status, notwithstanding its privatization, see Gregg Strauss, "Why the State Cannot 'Abolish Marriage': A Partial Defense of Legal Marriage Based on the Structure of Intimate Duties," *Indiana Law Review*, 1–67 (forthcoming), http://ssrn.com/abstract=2473182.

[24] Metz, *Untying the Knot*; Elizabeth Brake, "Minimal Marriage: What Political Liberalism Implies for Marriage Law," *Ethics*, 120 (2010), 302–37.

contracts do not violate other valid laws, such as those concerning child abuse, neglect, and support.[25] That approach would require the state to retain marriage as a semi-status.

At one time, no one – other than most old-school Libertarians – was pushing (1), with a few exceptions.[26] Historically, marriage has played a role in oppressing different minority groups, such as African-Americans, women, and sexual minorities. At one time, some queer theorists rejected marriage because they feared that participation in the institution would assimilate gays and lesbians into a heteronormative lifestyle.[27] The Constitution most likely does not require states to have the institution of marriage.[28] The equal protection concern only arises when a state recognizes some intimate relationships but not others and in doing so may be unjustifiably discriminating against some minority groups. To the extent that the *Windsor* decision is premised on a federalism rationale, it would seem to follow that states can decide whether they want to provide any intimate relationships with special treatment. Also, normally, constitutional rights are negative, not positive; government must not interfere with certain personal decisions and actions, but it does not have to provide certain goods or services for everyone or subsidize the exercise of their fundamental negative constitutional rights, such as free exercise of religion, freedom of expression, or gun ownership. Once the state lets some persons marry whom they want to marry but refuses to let others do likewise, it must justify the particular vision of marriage it endorses.

(1) does not violate liberal neutrality, would address the problem of how current marriage law discriminates against singles, and might drive a wedge between civil marriage and religious marriage, which many Americans continue to conflate.[29] Nonetheless, it would be terrible policy in the real world by preventing the state from using a marriage-like status to institutionalize the rights and benefits everyone should enjoy under nonideal conditions.[30] Even

25 Martha Fineman, *The Neutered Mother: The Sexual Family and Other Twentieth Century Tragedies* (New York: Routledge, 1995); Martha Fineman, *The Autonomy Myth: A Theory of Dependency* (New York: New York Press, 2004); Linda McClain, *The Place of Families: Fostering Capacity, Equality and Responsibility* (Cambridge, MA: Harvard University Press, 2006).

26 Fineman, *The Autonomy Myth*; Claudia Card, "Against Marriage and Motherhood," *Hypatia*, 11 (1996), 1–23; Zelinsky, "Deregulating Marriage, 1161–220, 1163.

27 Cheshire Calhoun, *Feminism, the Family, and the Politics of the Closet: Lesbian and Gay Displacement* (Oxford, UK: Oxford University Press, 2000), 113.

28 *Perry v. Brown*, 681 F. 3d 1065, 1081 (2012).

29 On the third point, see Cass R. Sunstein and Richard H. Thaler, "Privatizing Marriage," *Monist*, 91 (2008), 379.

30 In addition, doing so would unsettle many people's settled expectations. Cass R. Sunstein, "The Right to Marry," *Cardozo Law Review*, 26 (2005), 2086.

such a semi-Libertarian as Eugene Volokh cautions against the state's completely removing itself from the institution.[31] If marital status were irrelevant to family law, policy, and the distribution of entitlements, then it would not be as imperative to make such a status more inclusive. In other words, abolition would be more attractive if so many benefits were not filtered through civil marriage. The state could simply abolish it, provide necessary entitlements to all adults irrespective of their marital status, and not put its imprimatur on any intimate relationships.

Those who favor the disestablishment of marriage tend not to want to embark on a journey that ends with the state's removing itself completely from the institution.[32] Despite understandable reservations, they expect the state to play at least some role – if only to adjudicate disputes and enforce contracts. At present, marriage is not only a licensing scheme but also serves as a means of redistributing basic goods and services.[33] Rather than solving the equality problem by abolishing (privatizing as much as possible) marriage and thus avoiding discrimination, the state could extend its benefits more widely – even to those involved in unconventional or nonromantic close relationships. This change would encourage Americans to be more accepting of different kinds of families, living arrangements, identities, and ways of life. Nor would there be restrictions with respect to gender, the number of spouses, consanguinity (adults), or amorous feelings.

In a more just society, such an extension – at least in terms of economic benefits – would not be so pressing because the state would not need to filter them through such a legal status as marriage; it could simply provide basic material goods and services directly to each person and disregard whether he or she has a marriage-like relationship and assist children and other dependents – notwithstanding the marital status of their parents. Just imagine that John Rawls's famous difference principle or something like it were implemented and no one could be under a social minimum. In that scenario, legal rights and duties only become necessary when more than one person is involved and, say, a hospital or prison seeks to deny the opportunity for visitation. When it comes to other sorts of noneconomic marital benefits, which arise due to the relationship itself, either contract or default rules could protect the vulnerable.

(2) is more promising because it would be more inclusive than traditional or even same-sex marriage by replacing sexual intimacy with caregiving, which is Metz's view. As I shall show, though, (2) still involves unacceptable discrimination

[31] Eugene Volokh, "Why Not Get the State Out of the Marriage Business?" http://washingtonpost.com/news/volokh-conspiracy/wp/2014/04/10why-not-get-the-state-out-of-the-marriage-business.

[32] See, for example, Steve Vanderheiden, "Why the State Should Stay Out of the Wedding Chapel," *Public Affairs Quarterly*, 13 (1999), 175–90.

[33] Davis, "Regulating Polygamy," 2041.

and consequently does not solve the neutrality problem. That leaves some version of (3), which minimizes the neutrality problem without going to the extreme of ending state involvement in the institution altogether – an alternative that would be more enticing (as noted) but for the state's ongoing use of marriage as a mechanism for allocating so many essential entitlements.

The issues, then, are which kinds of intimate relationships will be covered, what the rationale for that coverage will be, and how much discretion people will have under various schemes to customize their marriage-like relationships. Political theorists and law professors who subscribe to some sort of disestablishment disagree about what should replace marriage. In advancing (2), Metz's legitimate concern is that when the state defines marriage to include same-sex couples, it still favors some intimate relationships over others, thereby violating the principle of liberal neutrality. In the case of same-sex marriage, the conventional solution to the problem of the state's treating personal relationships unequally lies in redefining marriage to also cover same-sex couples. Metz rejects this solution, proposes the elimination of marriage as a legal category, introduces a replacement rooted in the value of caregiving, and contends that such disestablishment would better serve liberal ends.

B. Liberal Neutrality

One of those ends is neutrality.[34] Neutrality comes in many shapes and sizes, but the basic idea is that it excludes appeals to controversial moral beliefs when the state enacts public laws. The state would violate such neutrality, for example, if it promoted only one kind of sexual behavior or love on the ground that it was intrinsically superior. As long as the state stays in the marriage business, I believe a commitment to neutrality implies equal treatment – understood as individualized treatment; the state must respect the right of all competent adults to choose the marital arrangement that best suits their particular needs, which is the position I developed and defended in the last two chapters. Even if most people were made healthier, wealthier, and happier by being married to only one person, the state still may not promote a parochial conception of marriage or continue amatonormative practices. Like many other liberals, Metz maintains that the state should not have the ethical authority to dictate to adults what kind of intimate relationship they

[34] For an overview of the concept of "neutrality," see Jeremy Waldron, "Legislation and Moral Neutrality," in *Liberal Rights: Collected Papers 1981–1991* (Cambridge, UK: Cambridge University Press, 1993), 143–67.

should have.[35] The classic statement of the meaning of such neutrality is found in Ronald Dworkin's view that political decisions should not be based on claims about what gives a life intrinsic worth.[36] In political theory literature, this formulation is called "neutrality of justification," as opposed to "neutrality of effect."[37] The principle of liberal neutrality implies that the state shall not "favor or take sides" over rival conceptions of the good.[38] This principle is most flagrantly violated by the state's promotion of controversial ideals.[39] Thus, the state may not deliberately advance particular conceptions of the good without adequate justification. Neutrality limits the extent to which the state may treat people's life plans unequally when the rationale for such unequal treatment is unacceptably perfectionist.

Recently, Jonathan Quong, Steven Lecce, and Howard Schweber have defended liberal neutrality.[40] Here, my aim is not to offer another philosophical defense of such neutrality but instead to see what follows from such a commitment with respect to marriage in the context of our constitutional tradition. I proceed in this manner because I believe that such neutrality is necessary under conditions of moral pluralism. Additionally, American constitutional law incorporates something similar to a neutrality requirement in which the state may not compel or even encourage people to live certain kinds of lives because one way of living is inherently better than others.[41] As Sonu Bedi writes, "there is some synergy between liberal neutrality and the Equal Protection Clause. ..."[42] For

35 Metz, *Untying the Knot*, 106–07.

36 Ronald Dworkin, *A Matter of Principle* (Cambridge, MA: Harvard University Press, 1986), 181–204. In his last book, Dworkin refers to what he calls "ethical independence" to explain why the government should not enact laws that restrict "citizens' freedom when its justification assumes that one conceptions of how to live ... is superior to others." Dworkin, *Religion Without God* (Cambridge, MA: Harvard University Press, 2013), 141–42.

37 Will Kymlicka, "Liberal Individualism and Liberal Neutrality," *Ethics*, 99 (1989), 883–905.

38 Steven Wall and George Klosko, "Introduction," in *Perfectionism and Neutrality: Essays in Liberal Theory*, ed. Steven Wall and George Klosko (Lanham, MD: Rowman & Littlefield, 2003), 6.

39 Steven Wall, *Liberalism, Perfectionism and Restraint* (New York: Cambridge University Press, 1998), 41.

40 Steven Lecce, *Against Perfectionism: Defending Liberal Neutrality* (Toronto: University of Toronto, 2008); Jonathan Quong, *Liberalism Without Perfection* (New York: Oxford University Press, 2011); Howard Schweber, *Democracy and Authenticity: Toward a Theory of Public Justification* (New York: Cambridge University Press, 2012).

41 See Sonu Bedi, "The Constitutional Argument for the Disestablishment of Marriage," 11; Wilfrid Waluchow finds this neutrality requirement in the *Canadian Charter of Rights and Freedoms*. Waluchow, "On the Neutrality of Charter Reasoning," in *Neutrality and Theory of Law*, ed. Jordi Ferrer Beltran, Jose Juan Moreso, and Diego M. Papayannis (Dordrecht, Netherlands: Springer, 2013), 203–24.

42 Bedi, *Beyond Race, Sex, and Sexual Orientation*, 15.

Wedgwood, when the purpose of the state's recognizing civil marriage is "to express the view that married life is an especially virtuous or valuable way of life," then the state may have exceeded its authority by basing "civil marriage on a controversial conception of the good."[43]

Whether the state has violated neutrality, then, depends on the rationale for the legal definition of marriage in question, which can be understood as a public justification requirement. If the aim is to promote a particular kind of intimate relationship, such as opposite or same-sex monogamy, by offering economic incentives to enter it, then the state may be advancing one way of life at the expense of others without having sufficiently public reasons that all reasonable people could share. In another commentator's words: "In crafting legislation and other legal benefits that promote marriage, the state is implicitly wielding its regulatory power in an effort to affirm the moral superiority of particular life choices."[44] Furthermore, even if the state were to expand the legal definition of marriage to cover as many marriage-like relationships as possible, its taking this route may still violate liberal neutrality. That may not be obvious but let me explain. It may be impermissible to confer the status of marriage only on some intimate relationships but not on others in the absence of sufficiently compelling reasons that would warrant differential treatment. The political liberalism or public reasons case for marriage more generally is not straightforward.[45] Traditional or same-sex marriage is just one of a number of such relationships the state could privilege as a legal status and promote accordingly. By inducing people to participate in this social institution by providing benefits that are not available to unmarried couples or to single persons, the state may be taking the position that it is better to be married than unmarried. If that position seems acceptable, then imagine if the state were to give tax credits and other benefits to members of a particular religious denomination because their religion is believed to be superior to all other belief systems.

However, under conditions of moral pluralism where people sincerely and reasonably disagree about the ends that human beings ought to pursue, marriage – as it is currently understood – may not be preferable to the alternatives.[46] As Anita Bernstein notes, the consequentialist case for marriage

[43] Wedgwood, "The Fundamental Argument for Same-Sex Marriage," 227.

[44] Steve Vanderheiden, "Why the State Should Stay Out of the Wedding Chapel," *Public Affairs Quarterly*, 13 (1999), 175, 183.

[45] Lister, *Public Reason and Political Community*, especially 135–74.

[46] Some commentators maintain that the state's endorsing marriage is necessarily is based on a nonneutral or nonpublic reason. See, for example, Lawrence G. Torcello, "Is the State Endorsement of Any Marriage Justifiable? Same-Sex Marriage, Civil Unions, and the Marriage Privatization Model," *Public Affairs Quarterly*, 22 (2008), 51.

is far from conclusive.[47] Marriage may not make people better off.[48] It is hard to take a side in this empirical debate with any confidence. Not only are the consequences hard to identify, measure, and predict, but whether they are "good" or "bad" are also not simply empirical judgments about cause and effect; they also reflect normative judgments, which are much harder to confirm – even when one believes that moral propositions are capable of being true or false. Real people may have some interest in statistical generalizations inasmuch as the data may reveal certain marital risks, based on demographics, that they were unaware of. But they will (and should) care more about their particular circumstances so the decisions they make are sufficiently personalized.

A person might not want to marry because he or she sees marriage as a patriarchical or heterosexual institution. Or he or she may want to be able to extricate him or herself from any romantic relationship as easily as possible to protect his or her financial assets or minimize emotional trauma. Different people have different personal reasons to marry or not to marry, and more often than not, they are in a better position to evaluate these reasons than anyone else is given the uniqueness of their identities, situations, and life experiences. True, the state is not requiring adults to marry, which would unambiguously violate neutrality and be unconstitutional, but by incentivizing marriage, the state is more than pointing them in a certain ethical direction. At the very least, the state's doing so should not make people feel morally uncomfortable with their life decisions. Not everyone is cut out for married life. If that were not bad enough, these incentives exist in a society where marriage "remains the most highly valued form of family life in American culture."[49]

My assumption is that many liberals adhere to some version of neutrality and that even nonliberals are conflicted over the extent to which the state may promote controversial ideals of human flourishing. Other liberals are unapologetically more perfectionist.[50] Neutrality does not mean the state cannot make legislative classifications or try to achieve certain legislative goals or that laws and policies can never have a disparate impact on certain groups. Nobody thinks neutrality means that all ways of life will prosper and then suddenly

[47] Anita Bernstein, "For and Against Marriage: A Revision," *Michigan Law Review*, 102 (2003), 129, 163.

[48] Intimate and marital stress cause depression. As such, the claim that marriage makes people happier and so on needs to be qualified.

[49] Andrew J. Cherlin, *The Marriage-Go-Round: The State of Marriage and the Family in America Today* (New York: Vintage Books, 2010), 9.

[50] Freeman refers to Rawls's view as "semi-perfectionist." Samuel Freeman, *Rawls* (New York: Routledge, 2007), 25.

dismisses the idea once he or she becomes aware that state action will impact different people differently. If that is what neutrality really means, then it would be hard to understand why anyone with any intelligence would have ever been committed to it. Whether they realize it or not, most theorists adhere to one of the many possible formulations of neutrality – unless they are perfectionists and therefore believe the state may act purposefully to further particular conceptions of the good.[51]

Those on the left who would not describe themselves as liberals do not welcome the state's advancing religion in the public sphere or excluding same-sex couples from marriage. That reaction cannot be understood apart from some concern over whether the state can promote a conception of the good at the expense of others. After all, some conservatives explicitly advocate a narrow kind of marriage – but only for some persons – as a means of fostering what they believe to be a superior way of life.[52] Everyone should worry about whether the state may favor certain ways of living and, if the state may do so, what the justification for such favorable treatment would be. Ultimately, what matters is the concept and its implications and not what name it happens to go by. My preference is to define neutrality in broadly Rawlsian, antiperfectionist terms and to understand it as a public justification requirement, which involves the kinds of reasons that would justify the state's treating some persons more favorably than others. The primary role of the judiciary, then, is to ensure that lawmakers only act on the basis of sufficiently public reasons. Elsewhere, I have given sustained treatment to this issue from a constitutional standpoint.[53]

C. *The Abolition of Marriage or Disestablishment*

Joseph Raz has the distinction of being the first political philosopher to notice that strict antiperfectionism and state recognition of monogamous marriage may not be compatible.[54] These days, there is also an ongoing debate about whether marriage itself can be justified in terms of public reason. On the one hand, there may be sufficiently public reasons for retaining marriage, such as promoting the welfare of children, ensuring social stability, and encouraging

[51] See, for example, Joseph Raz, *The Morality of Freedom* (New York: Oxford University Press, 1986).

[52] See, for example, Linda J. Waite and Maggie Gallagher, *The Case for Marriage: Why Married People Are Happier, Healthier, and Better Off Financially* (New York: Broadway Books, 2000).

[53] Ronald C. Den Otter, *Judicial Review in an Age of Moral Pluralism* (New York: Cambridge University Press, 2009).

[54] Raz, *The Morality of Freedom*, 162.

long-term commitment.[55] On the other hand, as Elizabeth Brake powerfully argues, political liberalism can only support a minimal form of marriage.[56] The even more jarring view is that the public reasons advanced to support the state's according special status to any sort of intimate relationship may be unsatisfactory. The chickens of neutrality may come home to roost in unexpected ways. Where one comes out on this issue involves how one understands what counts as a public reason in this context and the growing literature on public reason and marriage reveals that scholars are often not on the same page.

If that concern were not grave enough, constitutionally, the state may not be able to abolish marriage or marriage-like statuses so easily.[57] Carlos Ball maintains that the state may have a constitutional obligation to provide such a right.[58] He refers to *Zablocki v. Redhail* and *Turner v. Safley* as "failure to recognize" cases because they involve whether the state has to provide the right of marriage after it had tried to limit it.[59] If the state were to take away such a right by disestablishing marriage and replacing it with some sort of universal domestic partnership status or with private contracts, such a move might be unconstitutional if the state did so to discriminate invidiously against sexual minorities. Reminiscent of the closing of some public schools in the South after *Brown*, if a state were to disestablish marriage to thwart judicial decisions that same-sex marriages are constitutionally mandated, then that rationale might be constitutionally inadmissible. As I shall eventually show, with the exception of abolition, which ought to be rejected for other reasons, SPICs are more consistent with liberal neutrality than any of the other marital alternatives. As one commentator states, "the goal should be to supplement pure contractualism in a way *as least damaging as possible to the neutralist idea* [his emphasis] in order to protect the rights and interests of the vulnerable."[60] For American legal scholars, the intellectual challenge is to translate arguments of political morality, which support the disestablishment of civil marriage, into a plausible constitutional argument.[61]

[55] Lister, *Public Reason and Community*, especially 135–74. [56] Brake, *Minimizing Marriage*.

[57] See Pamela S. Karlan, "Let's Call the Whole Thing Off: Can States Abolish the Institution of Marriage?" *California Law Review*, 98 (2010), 698.

[58] Carlos A. Ball, "The Positive in the Fundamental Right to Marry: Same-Sex Marriage in the Aftermath of *Lawrence v. Texas*," *Minnesota Law Review*, 88 (2004), especially 1203–07; *Zablocki v. Redhail*, 434 U.S. 374 (1978) (involving the right to marry for those who had not paid child support); *Turner v. Safley*, 482 U.S 78 (1987) (involving the right to marry for prisoners).

[59] Ball, "The Positive in the Fundamental Right to Marry," 1197–202.

[60] Steven Lecce, *Against Perfectionism*, 267.

[61] See Bedi, *Beyond Race, Sex, and Sexual Orientation*, especially 208–51.

In all the Supreme Court's decisions involving the fundamental right to marry, the state had imposed marriage restrictions for improper purposes. If a legislature were to eliminate marriage and replace it with civil unions for everyone – without any link to religion whatsoever – in order to be neutral and expand the number of relationships that would be legally recognized, that legislation would probably not violate the Constitution. After all, this sort of change would not deny rights and benefits to those who are currently entitled to them under the institution of civil marriage but instead would expand rights and benefits to previously excluded groups.[62] From the standpoint of neutrality or public justification, what renders marriage problematic is that historically, it has discriminated against racial minorities, women, and gays and lesbians. More recently, it has been linked to the belief that it is better to be married and have a nuclear family. If it no longer had such meaning for many Americans, it is less likely there would be so much persistent opposition to same-sex marriage.

At the same time, it can be argued that promoting marriage does not have to be seen only as a means of advancing a particular conception of the good. For example, rectifying past discrimination against sexual minorities could serve as a justification for continuing to use the "m" word. Or it could lead to the use of a label for all intimate relationships that does not connote past discriminatory meanings. Legal recognition of a much wider range of such relationships can help people understand and appreciate their diversity and reject past understandings that are insufficiently inclusive. Under such circumstances, the state would not necessarily be acting to further a particular conception of the good; it would be facilitating the assimilation of sexual minorities and others into American society and finally treating them with the dignity they deserve. For many gays and lesbians, to be allowed to marry after so long means the law is no longer dictating to them that their lives are inferior to those of straight persons.

Scholars who advocate some kind of disestablishment do not see eye to eye on how the institution of marriage should be disestablished.[63] Some of them, such as Cass Sunstein, endorse more contractual approaches.[64] Additionally, disestablishment does not fit neatly into current constitutional doctrine. Disestablishment could mean the state offers a package deal to everyone who would like to form his or her own "framily," or it could mean a move toward

62 I am indebted to Carlos Ball on this point (e-mail correspondence).

63 Shrage, "Reforming Marriage," 113.

64 See, for example, Cass R. Sunstein, "The Right to Marry," *Cardozo Law Review*, 26 (2005), 2116.

a regime of SPICs, which I favor, with legal protection for minors and other dependents. In Martha Nussbaum's view, the state could continue to offer the same marital benefits or it could attach them to other legal relationships.[65] Others favor the retention of a marriage-like status but want it to be more inclusive, as in less discriminatory. Metz writes that courts have taken for granted that marriage is established and assumes that states will continue to offer at least a marriage-like status for the time being.[66] That assumption is reasonable. In a common-law system, courts frequently take small steps and disestablishment would be unprecedented. Until *Perry v. Schwarzenegger*, no federal court had ruled on the merits of whether a state's refusal to extend the right of civil marriage to same-sex couples violates any part of the U.S. Constitution.[67] That is not to say the Supreme Court has never uttered a word about same-sex marriage. In his majority opinion in *Lawrence v. Texas*, to soften the blow, Justice Kennedy explicitly differentiates laws that criminalize same-sex sex between consenting adults and those that do not extend the constitutional right of marriage to same-sex couples.[68] Nonetheless, it is hard not to see what Kennedy said as opening the door to a variety of related questions about whether states may treat same-sex couples differently than opposite-sex ones.[69] *Windsor* does not make it easier for states to continue to discriminate against gays and lesbians when it comes to marriage licenses.[70] These cases raise the question of whether a state may define marriage as narrowly as it has done in the past.

II. THE CASE AGAINST ICGUS

A. *Metz's ICGUs*

In the rest of this chapter, then, I am going to assume – without any further argumentation – that any state could disestablish marriage (making it more inclusive) if it did so for sufficiently public reasons, such as to compensate for past discrimination against sexual minorities, to promote inclusion and acceptance of difference, or to ensure equal legal treatment. I leave aside the question of whether it could abolish civil marriage or its equivalent, such as civil union status for everyone, even though my feeling is that the state could

65 Nussbaum, "Right to Marry?" 694. 66 Metz, *Untying the Knot*, 19–46.
67 *Perry v. Schwarzenegger*, 704 F. Supp. 2d 921(N.D. Cal. 2010).
68 *Lawrence v. Texas*, 539 U.S. 558 (2003).
69 See Ball, "The Positive in the Fundamental Right to Marry," 1185–86.
70 *United States v. Windsor*, 570 U.S. __ (2013).

most likely do so without too much constitutional trouble. Concerning the state's involvement with marriage-like relationships, my aim is to explain why neutrality leads to disestablishment, which Metz accepts, and, equally importantly, to defend the conclusion that such disestablishment leads to a form of contractualization, which many liberals would reject. Metz does not identify with Kant or Rawls. Instead, she relies heavily on such liberal thinkers as Locke, Mill, Okin, and Hegel (who may not be a liberal at all).[71] Nevertheless, she is committed to neutrality in the sense of opposing the state's acting as an ethical authority, which puts her squarely in the disestablishment camp.[72] She then places caregiving at the front and center of the debate about how intimate relationships ought to be defined and proposes that ICGUs should replace marriage.[73] In legally recognizing such relationships, the state would no longer require the appearance of a sexual, amorous, or romantic relationship for a couple to qualify for the legal status. Moreover, to disentangle caregiving from marriage is to "no longer unduly burden caregivers" who are ineligible for marital status and its benefits.[74] The privileges that come with ICGUs would protect more people.[75] In making this move, she shifts our attention from marriage as a proxy for caregiving to the importance of caregiving itself, a phenomenon which has been neglected by the liberal tradition.

B. *Another Neutrality Problem*

Because liberals have not had that much to say about caregiving and its place in a good human life, Metz's book fills a void. However, by arguing for the disestablishment of marriage in the name of neutrality, Metz finds herself in a precarious position. As one commentator observes: "Once state neutrality regarding comprehensive doctrines is affirmed, it becomes difficult to recognize a substantive view of any social institution."[76] A good point can stand to be overstated: There is a not-so-bright line between acting on sufficiently public reasons and acting on the basis of a perfectionist rationale. As such, a state that treats marriage as a legal status may be endorsing a particular conception of the good. That endorsement will be objectionable unless the state can justify the unequal treatment of other intimate relationships without referring to their intrinsic merits. As Metz comments, liberal neutrality means

[71] Metz, *Untying the Knot*, 47–83. [72] Ibid., 115. [73] Ibid., 14.

[74] Tamara Metz, "The Liberal Case for Disestablishing Marriage," *Contemporary Political Theory*, 6 (2007), 207; Fineman, *The Neutered Mother*, 100–42.

[75] Metz, *Untying the Knot*, 120.

[76] Jeanne Heffernan Schindler, "A New Disestablishmentarianism," *The Review of Politics*, 73 (2011), 676.

"the government will not privilege one way of life over others without good reason."[77] Unfortunately, she downplays the message associated with a marriage-like status, such as an ICGU, which is, problematically, that it is better to be in such a relationship. In the last several years, the California Supreme Court, a U.S. district court, and a U.S. Court of Appeals ruled that civil unions for same-sex couples could not substitute for marriage – not because the material benefits were not comparable but due to the meaning of having a "separate but equal" regime for same-sex and opposite-sex couples.[78] As Metz states, "marital status is conferred with the aim of altering self-understandings."[79] She does not want the state to leave the marriage business altogether and hopes the state can support even more people in caregiving relationships through ICGUs without having the state continue to play the role of an ethical authority.

Nonetheless, it might be hard to see why anyone would believe the state is sufficiently neutral when it gives people incentives to partake in a state-sponsored marriage-like institution – whatever it is called. Imagine if the state were to give them the same incentives to join religious organizations without giving the same incentives to join nonreligious ones. Marriage is already laden with social and moral meanings that are not captured by having a registered domestic partnership. Presumably, most people do not want to "civil union" their significant other when they seek to affirm their mutual commitment in the most emphatic way possible to the community. In Bedi's words, "by conferring the status of marriage, the state takes sides in a very personal decision about what constitutes a good life."[80] Continuing opposition to same-sex marriage cannot be understood without appreciating the degree to which many Americans see the extension of the right to marriage as an endorsement of behavior they believe to be sinful. The point is not that they are correct. Rather, state involvement with ICGUs or any other marriage-like status is bound to raise similar concerns about neutrality. Also, it would be natural to ask why some relationships are excluded from ICGU status. Replacing marriage with a different legal status may indicate that as far as the state is concerned, it is better to be in such a relationship than to remain a romantic free agent. Marriage by any other name is still a status unless the state withdraws itself from the institution. If the state were to treat all caregiving relationships as if they were the equivalent of

[77] Metz, *Untying the Knot*, 24.

[78] *In re Marriage Cases*, 43 Cal. 4th 757 (2008); *Perry v. Schwarzenegger*, 704 F. Supp. 2d 921 (N.D. Cal. 2010); *Perry v. Brown*, 681 F. 3d 1065, 1081 (2012).

[79] Metz, *Untying the Knot*, 115.

[80] Bedi, *Beyond Race, Sex, and Sexual Orientation*, 210.

marriages, then it also may have to treat other intimate relationships the same way or risk violating liberal neutrality.

C. *Responses*

Ultimately, I doubt anyone who predicates marriage-like relationships on something as substantive as caregiving can avoid running afoul of liberal neutrality to some degree. At the least, this objection cannot by summarily dismissed. Still, there are two tacks Metz could take to take some of the sting out of the objection that under her scheme, the state continues to act impermissibly as an ethical authority and in doing so violates liberal neutrality. First, instead of creating ICGUs, she could have the state abolish marriage by privatizing it and leaving its meaning to private organizations, such as religious ones, or to individuals. Then, the state would no longer be entangled with the institution and functioning as an ethical authority because there would be no marriage-like status available to anyone. Such a regime would more closely resemble the less-than-strict separation between church and state most Americans take for granted. At most, the state would enforce valid private contracts that would not bind third parties. The trouble with that move is it would repudiate the very point of having ICGU status – namely, to promote caregiving and to protect those who engage in it, especially women. Metz fears that a Libertarian world of private contracts is likely to exacerbate gender inequality in particular and existing (unjust) power relations more generally.[81] This understandable fear makes her less receptive to any form of contractualization than she otherwise might be.[82]

Feminists tend to have mixed feelings about marital contracts. Those who are hostile to the very idea of contracts in the context of marriage worry that the move from status to contract, which privatization would entail, would disadvantage women, who are likely to be in a worse bargaining position than their male partners. It is important to recall, though, that some kind and degree of personal choice cannot be avoided as long as "marriage" remains a status – whatever it is called. For Metz, the state cannot impose a marriage-like status on a personal relationship without the permission of those who would

[81] Metz, *Untying the Knot*, 12.

[82] Another problem with this reform would be that the state's eliminating this status for everyone may violate neutrality in a society that has engaged in so much amatonormative discrimination for so long. At one time, Elizabeth Brake believed the state's continuing to use the "m" word to cover a much wider variety of intimate relationships may be required by justice due to this sort of past legal discrimination to compensate for past marital wrongs and to level the playing field. See Brake, *Minimizing Marriage*, 186–88.

be most affected by it. Individuals who are eligible and opt for an ICGU still have to voluntarily accept this status before it will have any legal effect.[83] Alternatively, they could cohabitate and not have any relationship in the eyes of the law. Today, few states retain common-law marriage.[84] Thus, even an ICGU would function as a quasi-contract but with predetermined legal rights and responsibilities and default rules with respect to the division of the marital property upon dissolution of the relationship.[85] As far as Metz is concerned, the difference between a private contract and an ICGU is that the latter would be structured to protect the vulnerable and promote equality.[86] While a private marriage-like contract would not necessarily have an egalitarian purpose or effect, the less regulated the relationship, the less likely it would promote caregiving and gender equality in intimate relationships. People could use such an instrument for many different ends. To summarize her view of marital contracts: The rewards are not worth the risks.

Second, like Elizabeth Brake, Metz could expand on why caregiving is a primary good and therefore required by justice.[87] For Rawls, primary goods are all-purpose means to the ends that any rational person is likely to have so that he or she can flourish as much as possible.[88] Like ICGUs, Brake's minimal marriage (MM) provides a legal framework for a much wider range of caregiving relationships.[89] Within an adult care network, the participants would exchange certain rights – and such exchanges need not be reciprocal.[90] Brake roots MM in a commitment to political liberalism, so a thick, controversial conception of the good does not serve as the primary public justification for such a framework.[91] While she insists that marriage must remain a distinct legal status, only a neutral or sufficiently public reason (one independent of any conception of the good) could justify minimal state involvement with the institution.[92] According to Laurie Shrage, Brake's idea of minimal marriage "seems to collapse into a form of contractualism."[93] By contrast, Andrew Lister believes Brake's proposal retains enough status elements to render it distinct from contractualization.[94] Metz writes that Brake's MM "is about as close to [a] contract as it gets."[95]

[83] Metz, *Untying the Knot*, 138. [84] Bowman, *Unmarried Couples, Law, and Public Policy*, 5.
[85] Metz, *Untying the Knot*, 134–35. [86] Ibid., 120.
[87] Brake, "Minimal Marriage," 302–37; Brake, *Minimizing Marriage*.
[88] John Rawls, *A Theory of Justice*, revised edition (Cambridge, MA: Belknap Press of Harvard University Press, 1971), 54–55.
[89] Brake, "Minimal Marriage," 303. [90] Ibid., 307. [91] Ibid., 305. [92] Ibid., 308.
[93] Shrage, "Reforming Marriage," 114.
[94] Andrew Lister, *Public Reason and Political Community*, 153.
[95] Tamara Metz, Review, Elizabeth Brake, *Minimizing Marriage, in Social Theory and Practice*, 40 (2014), 157.

If Metz were to take what I believe to be the more promising Rawlsian route, she would have to elaborate on why caregiving, which her new marriage-like status requires, cannot be largely contractual. A contract is not necessarily at odds with the idea of care or the practice of caregiving when it could be drafted to specify the expectations of all the parties and provide remedies for breach. The formation of such a contract does not guarantee that one or both parties will live up to its terms, but that concern is equally applicable to a legal status, such as an ICGU or an MM, or any kind of legal relationship or contract for that matter. The reluctance to embrace the idea of forming legal contracts within an intimate relationship – to borrow a well-known Hegelian idea – reflects a belief about the inappropriateness of treating personal relationships as if they were arm's-length transactions. A healthy intimate relationship is not supposed to be about rights and duties but about love, affection, and selflessness. Not only is such a view sentimental, but it also misses the point, which is that a contact can never take the place of care or emotional intimacy, but it can – depending on its terms – be conducive to such intimacy.

D. *Care and Caregiving*

Initially, it may appear that we should not give the state's promoting caregiving through ICGUs a second thought if we are committed to something like liberal neutrality. At present, family law fails to value appropriately the contributions caregivers make.[96] The giving and receiving of care is necessary for human development and well-being; caregiving is often accompanied by mutual feelings that form or strengthen emotional bonds that can help people though the most difficult times of their lives. Metz and Brake deserve considerable credit for revealing the important place of caregiving to liberalism in theory and practice and emphasizing why such caregiving must be incorporated into the formulation of a well-ordered society.

However, care is a slippery concept. Real people care for one another in different ways and some of those ways of caring may be morally objectionable.[97] Furthermore, in the real world, the dynamics of a real caregiving relationship

[96] Martha M. Ertman, *Love's Promises*, chapter 6, "The Basics of Cohabitation Agreements" (April 11, 2014: draft, p. 21).

[97] Caregiving can take a wide variety of forms and presumably a liberal will hesitate to impose only one of its forms on those in a marriage-like relationship. On this point, see Peter Brian Barry, Review Elizabeth Brake, *Minimizing Marriage*, *Ethics*, 123 (2013), 352.

may leave a lot to be desired. There may be rewards, but there also may be risks and the participants may be better off on their own when the relationship is beyond repair. Appeals to care or caregiving – despite their rhetorical effects – can only perform so much labor in any normative argument without further specification. When it leads to meeting the most basic human needs, material caregiving would seem to be undeniably important, which is why it counts as a sufficiently public reason. At times, all persons depend on others and ICGUs would incentivize caregiving for those who care for dependents, such as children, the elderly, veterans, and the disabled.[98]

Even today, women who play the role of caregiver are likely to be disadvantaged because under a gendered division of labor, they bear most of the burdens of caregiving with little or no compensation.[99] In this way, Metz links the practice of caregiving to the promotion of gender equality. The legal recognition of ICGUs would clarify why the state has an important interest in influencing the dynamics of intimate relationships. She is not only concerned about child welfare but also about how to support adults – those who give and receive care – in caretaking relationships that exist outside of marriage in its present form. Different adults need different amounts and kinds of care and some of them will not be self-sufficient. They may need someone to pay their bills, buy their groceries, feed them, bath them, dress them, drive them to appointments, and make sure others do not take advantage of them.

The caregiving that is supposed to occur, though, cannot be monitored very closely, even in the best-case scenario. The law cannot afford not to be pragmatic; it has to take into account the feasibility of proposals to serve the most worthwhile of goals. The state can only enact laws that create an incentive structure for those in such relationships to facilitate the giving and receiving of care. Whether they really do it, how well they do it, and with what attitude they do it are left up to them. Presumably, the state would not take away ICGU status when someone is doing a poor job of caregiving. The dynamics of such intimate relationships will differ markedly. That in itself is not a decisive reason to reject the importance of caregiving, but it raises the question of the unintended but foreseeable consequences of the state's pushing people toward such relationships when some of them may not be prepared to fulfill their responsibilities. Just as not everyone is cut out for marriage, not everyone would be cut out for an ICGU or an MM. If the state were to provide such a status, one would have to hope that on balance, subsidizing caring relationships is socially beneficial.

98 Metz, "The Liberal Case for Disestablishing Marriage," 209. 99 Ibid.

Additionally, ICGUs would be overinclusive because they would cover unequal male–female intimate relationships. Presumably, to qualify for ICGU status, the people seeking such a status would not have to prove to the authorities that their prospective relationship would be sufficiently egalitarian. Metz acknowledges that there is no guarantee that most of these arrangements would involve equality in ongoing daily interactions. The norm would probably be some degree of inequality due to the typical structure of caretaking relationships.[100] Too much under/overinclusion casts doubt as to whether an ICGU would serve its stated aims effectively. One of the reasons why many people are uncomfortable with recent conservative pro-marriage initiatives is that it is obvious that some men will never be decent husbands or fathers and may even be abusive. To induce them to take that path may do more harm than good – at least in individual cases. One cannot simply presuppose an ideal form of marriage or intimate relationship. Too many real marriages are anything but healthy for the couple and the children – if there are any – but the state continues to privilege such relationships. Indeed, families can be very dangerous places. In high-conflict marriages, women and children would be better off in an alternative living arrangement.[101] The same concern would arise if the state were to invite people to form and maintain ICGUs that fall far short of the ideal. Many adults have dysfunctional relationships with their parents and other family members. The unmarried may be happier and healthier.[102] Thus, it may be misguided to take for granted the existence of an ideal caregiving relationship that ought to be nourished through state support when even under the best of conditions, many of these relationships will be prone to intractable problems. In promoting healthy caregiving relationships, the state will also will subsidize unhealthy ones and in doing so reduce the quality of some people's lives.

Another concern about treating caregiving as a primary good is that many noncaring intimate relationships, which have at least some subjective value and serve human happiness, will not qualify for ICGU or MM status, like a close intellectual friendship or a purely sexual relationship. For many people, sexual satisfaction and pleasure more generally is high on their list of priorities. As central as the giving and receiving of care is to human flourishing, it strikes me that noncaring personal relationships should also count as a primary good

[100] Metz, *Untying the Knot*, 122.

[101] See Judith Stacey, *In the Name of the Family: Rethinking Family Values in the Postmodern Age* (Boston: Beacon Press, 1996), 60.

[102] See Bella DePaulo, *Singled Out: How Singles Are Stereotyped, Stigmatized, and Ignored, and Still Live Happily Ever After* (New York: St. Martin's Griffin, 2006).

or at least should not be excluded without a lengthy discussion about their merits. Today, the legal status quo for two-person marriages is that the couple can have just about whatever personal reasons it wants to have for marrying. With the exception of a fraudulent marriage for immigration purposes, the state does not vet the quality of our personal reasons. Our reasons are our own and are treated as such. Oddly and perhaps counterintuitively, with respect to ICGUs and MMs, while greatly expanding the kinds of intimate relationships that would be eligible for a marriage-like status, some personal relationships that would have previously qualified for marital status – namely, those that are dyadic but noncaring – would be excluded. This situation may present a different kind of amatonormativity problem in which noncaring relationships are being unjustly discriminated against.

Along similar lines, for some persons, it may not be better for them to be in any sort of caring relationship. First, even when it is not called "marriage" but something else, a strong social message will continue to be conveyed – namely, that it is better to be in such an intimate relationship than to not be in one, although with ICGUs or MMs in place, at least people will have many more options to choose from, which is a positive development. But even ICGUs and MM would still be moralized to some degree, given conventional understandings of the role of intimate relationships in a good human life. Second, there are many subjectively important and objectively worthwhile human activities that are conducive to self-development yet do not involve other people. Why should the state not provide such potentially nonsocial "primary goods," such as leisure time, so people can be artistic, develop other skills, cope with their anxiety, read things they would like to read, meditate, be more introspective, spend more time with their pets, exercise, do yoga, or volunteer at a homeless shelter or prison? Perhaps there is much more to be said about the value or importance of solitary activities for ordinary people – and not only for hermits – to strike a better balance between the social and the nonsocial and more accurately reflect people's divergent personal preferences.

E. Internal Equality Revisited

The previous concern about under- and overinclusion implicates an even more fundamental normative problem involving how the state can use its power to influence how family members interact with one another. As I explained in the second chapter, this concern trades on an ambiguity: Promoting gender equality through antidiscrimination laws is one thing, but promoting it in personal relationships is something else. In her classic *Justice, Gender, and the Family*, Susan Okin criticizes Rawls for leaving the family out of the basic structure of a well-ordered society.[103] Rawls responds by giving ground while maintaining that the two principles do not apply directly to the inner dynamics of family life.[104] As a result, it remained obscure as to exactly how the family was supposed to fit into the basic structure.[105] The more direct the intervention by the state in how family members interact with one another, the more illiberal and controversial it would be. Such intervention might cross a boundary that should not be crossed in a liberal society. Constitutionally, even if it were well intentioned and would foster gender equality, for example, the state could not mandate a less traditional division of labor in the family.

The worry about the place of law in personal relationships is hardly unique to Okin or to someone such as Metz who advocates the abolition of marriage in its current form. Normatively, liberal feminists must recognize a distinction between the private and public spheres or else they would not be liberals. The justification for drawing the line in one place rather than in another often divides them in particular cases.[106] As such, the issue is normative and the trouble with such a distinction between what is private and what is public is that the traditional family may teach women to accept their subordination to men and socialize children inappropriately. As Mill once remarked, the family can be a school of despotism.[107]

As far as Okin is concerned, the state cannot mandate but may encourage a less gendered division of labor in the family. She offers multiple proposals – some of which are no longer as radical as they once were, such as subsidized day care and more generous parental leave.[108] Okin has a point: The state must take some interest in how couples interact with each other and how they raise their children when one cares about gender equality, future citizenship, and social justice more generally. But what the state may do about such inequality in personal relationships is complicated by the right of people to make their own choices with respect to their personal lives. On the one hand, surely, some personal choices have to be legally restricted to prevent

[103] Susan Moller Okin, *Justice, Gender, and the Family* (New York: Basic Books, 1989), 89–109.

[104] Rawls, "The Idea of Public Reason Revisited," xxxi.

[105] Cohen refers to this as the "site of justice" problem. See G. A. Cohen, "Where the Action Is: On the Site of Distributive Justice," *Philosophy and Public Affairs*, 26 (1997), 3–30.

[106] Brian Leiter, "Rethinking Legal Realism: Towards a Naturalized Jurisprudence," in *Naturalizing Jurisprudence: Essays on American Legal Realism and Naturalism in Legal Philosophy* (New York: Oxford University Press, 2007), 19.

[107] John Stuart Mill, "The Subjection of Women," in *On Liberty and Other Writings*, ed. Stephen Collini (Cambridge, UK: Cambridge University Press, 1989), 160.

[108] Okin, *Justice, Gender, and the Family*, 175–76.

undeniable harm. Arguably, if one is sympathetic to paternalistic rationales, the state may go even further in protecting people from their own shortsighted decisions. The existence of immutable or default rules with respect to the equitable division of the marital property upon dissolution of the marriage is one way of addressing gender equality concerns when the marriage is over and must be taken seriously. Everyone should be compensated for what he or she contributed to the community – whether it was paid or unpaid labor – and should not be penalized financially for leaving the relationship.

On the other hand, the rationale for restricting other personal choices, such as those that reinforce gender inequality (as an aspect of internal equality) between the couple during the relationship and how they bring up their children, is not nearly as obvious.[109] A traditional division of labor is not desirable from a feminist standpoint, but that does not mean the state may require a division of labor that is fairer to women but against their will. Above a certain moral threshold, any liberal will be reluctant to specify the kind of personal relationship that partners should have. After all, couples should be largely left alone to determine how they want to interact with each other when their relationship is inegalitarian in certain respects.

As it turns out, Metz has a similar problem. On the one hand, she is an egalitarian liberal and rejects semi-Libertarian solutions that incorporate some form of contractualization. She understandably wants the state to be able to promote gender equality through the legal recognition of ICGUs, which she sees as an indispensable means to that end. For Metz, "intimate" does not mean "sexual."[110] ICGUs would cover many types of intimate relationships, such as nonfamily households and "polygamous units," provided they function as intimate caregiving units.[111] Not only would ICGUs more accurately reflect the changes in and the challenges of the contemporary American family, but they would largely be "unmonitored by outside parties."[112] This feature provides the unit – however it may be constituted – with the freedom to "give and receive care" according to the particular needs and desires of the participants.[113] Metz adds that ICGUs are characterized not by financial transactions or compensation but by deep material, emotional, physical, and spiritual ties where the participants are motivated by love and affection.[114]

109 For an argument that public reason limits how parents may bring up their children, see Matthew Clayton, *Justice and Legitimacy in Upbringing* (Oxford, UK: Oxford University Press, 2006), especially 87–128.

110 Metz, *Untying the Knot*, 121. 111 Ibid., 121, n. 12. 112 Ibid., 121. 113 Ibid.

114 Ibid., 121–22.

F. Emotional Care

That remark indicates that Metz has a specific kind of caregiving relationship in mind, where the parties not only perform certain tasks but also have certain feelings for one another. Three related worries about this view are that reasonable people may not agree on what counts as such caregiving, why it is important, and whether the state should foster it. Metz concedes that defining caregiving "would undoubtedly provoke controversy."[115] Having to define the term more precisely leaves her with two unpalatable choices. First, she could define caregiving so expansively that it would cover all personal relationships that are characterized by a sort of intimacy and thus be nondiscriminatory. That would make it less controversial and perhaps solve the neutrality problem, but it would defeat the explicit purposes of an ICGU status, which are to foster a particular kind of caregiving, to protect the vulnerable, and to promote gender equality.

Second, she could define caregiving more narrowly to achieve these normative ends and defend the view that while ICGUs are underinclusive – that is, they do not cover other kinds of personal relationships people may want – the state may still favor them. More or less, that is how she proceeds. Like Metz, one could maintain that being in a caring relationship not only benefits people in numerous ways but such a relationship is also what most of them want. One could then conclude that personal relationships that do not involve caregiving are less valuable and therefore not worthy of ICGU status. People could still pursue them under the regime she proposes, but the state would not legally recognize them. As Metz writes, compared with friendships, ICGUs are "characterized by greater degrees of material and physical vulnerability, dependency, and risk. . . ."[116]

However, unlike Brake, Metz does not sharply distinguish between material and emotional well-being and consequently does not provide a separate defense of the latter, which is more controversial. That is not to say they are mutually exclusive. When it comes to justifying a marriage-like status, they ought to be disaggregated and analyzed separately. Comparatively, the value of material caregiving is much easier to measure and to publicly justify insofar as a typical person cannot function well without adequate material resources – whatever his or her life plan happens to be. Normally, emotional care is also essential to living well. It may not be important enough, though, to qualify as a Rawlsian primary good, beyond what children need for their psychological development, when

[115] Ibid., 136. [116] Ibid., 126.

some people do not value the particular kind of care Metz champions or they may value other goods more than such care. Others may be able to function well without it or receive the care they need from other sources. Through ICGUs, the state would be trying to nurture reciprocal emotional caring between adults in a long-term relationship and the involvement of the state would confirm that people should have such a relationship, as opposed to being alone, having relationships that lack such care, or being involved in other activities.

Just because two people in an intimate relationship do not utilize such a legal instrument as an ICGU and instead remain unregistered does not necessarily mean the state has violated neutrality. In making emotional care the normative foundation of the legal status people could choose, the state is unquestionably making a value judgment about the desirability of such care in a good life. In other words, there may not be a bright line between legitimately providing a primary good and illegitimately promoting a particular conception of the good. In terms of neutrality, Metz's proposal would still accord primacy to some intimate relationships over other intimate (without caregiving) and nonintimate (with paid caregiving) relationships with insufficient justification. Unless the fostering of emotional care between adults is a primary good, which almost all reasonable people would want, it would probably not count as a public reason.

There are many kinds of enriching life experiences human beings can have that promote their well-being but do not involve caregiving, even broadly construed. People differ in many respects and can even be quirky and that is not simply a fact about the world but a normative point about the freedom many people need to be different and flourish accordingly. Their life plans can be unconventional and they may value and desire experiments in living, à la Mill, that do not involve other persons. People who are antisocial or introverted do not necessarily need therapists; they may need less insensitivity from a society that too often tries to impose a norm of sociality on them. Most of us benefit from intellectual challenges, serious conversations, doing volunteer work, listening to music, physical fitness, leisure, travel, friendship, gardening, hobbies, interactions with our pets, and additional opportunities to develop our talents, to learn more about ourselves, and to discover what matters to us. What may be very important to one person may be trivial to another and vice versa.

Those who are sympathetic to the idea of ICGUs can still insist that their rationale relies on nothing more than a thin theory of the good, which is a fancy way of saying that any rational person who cares about how well his or her life turns out would probably want the state to support emotional care in one way or another. In this manner, they may be able to establish that an intimate relationship predicated on more than material caregiving is important enough to most people to be a primary good and independent enough of any conception of the good to count as a public reason. That is why Metz proposes that the state should provide stipends to single persons for dating (but not sexual) services.[117] That distinction also involves a value judgment and perhaps one that is more controversial than she imagines if we care about what people tell us their preferences are. For some people, sexual gratification may be at the top of their list. What makes an appeal to primary goods so attractive at the outset is that they are supposed to be as uncontroversial as possible. The moment the list is expanded to include such a social good as emotional caregiving, one has to wonder whether this expansion has come at too high a price inasmuch as the state is expressing the view that a life with such caregiving is better than the alternatives. For different reasons, many people will not have such relationships and some of them will not want them – if only to avoid causing others pain. They may value ongoing noncaring interactions. They may have made a deliberate, informed choice to live a more solitary life and not risk the possible emotional trauma that may result from being intimate with someone and then being betrayed. For some individuals, it may be better to have not loved and not lost than to have never loved at all. It is their decision – and their decision alone – and the state should not influence them one way or the other.

My view, then, is that the list of Rawlsian primary goods should be kept to a minimum so they are as uncontroversial as possible in the sense of not stemming from a thick, potentially divisive conception of the good. Also, in providing them, the state's aim would be to give everyone the resources they need to flourish or at least to have decent lives and let them make personal decisions about what kind of intimate relationship(s) – if any – that life will incorporate. After all, caring does not have to take place in an intimate relationship. The state does not have to promote care indirectly through subsidizing only caring relationships, even broadly defined. It is not evident to me that other less controversial primary goods could not put people into a situation where they could choose to form different kinds of caring relationships if they so desire or seek such emotional support or its equivalent elsewhere. What the state can (and should) do is – as long as certain material and expressive benefits remain linked to any legally recognized relationship between two or more adults – is to treat each intimate relationship equally – irrespective of whether it involves caregiving – and provide as wide a range of marital choices as possible. That is

117 Metz, *Untying the Knot*, 149.

not to say that caring relationships are not valuable; they are for the most part. Metz and other scholars are surely more right than they are wrong about the importance of such care in most people's lives.

But they are not uniquely valuable to everyone. If the personal relationship an individual has with another or others does not meet Metz's criteria, then he or she will also be denied the economic benefits and legal privileges that are automatically given to those who meet the criteria, are eligible, and choose to form an ICGU, even when his or her relationship turns out to be inegalitarian with little or no caregiving taking place. Ultimately, one problem with ICGUs involves moving too quickly from material to emotional caregiving. Almost all adults would need the former to live decently. The latter is not as obviously a primary good. The other problem lies in the weakness of the explanation for why any sort of emotional caregiving is required for such status when it would be safer to err on the side of permitting any adult to form an intimate relationship with other adults for whatever personal reasons they happen to have. Upon closer inspection, Metz's position appears to be problematically perfectionist. It may seem obvious that all she has to do with respect to the worry about neutrality is to separate material from emotional caregiving, articulate why the former is a public reason, and treat the latter as a bonus. This move is not available to her, though, not only because she believes emotional caregiving to be central to well-being but because she also has to hold this belief to advocate any legal status for two or more persons in the first place. If material caregiving were the only justification, then the state could (a) provide such support more directly through entitlement programs independent of any marriage-like status (which is more common in developed countries outside of our borders), (b) dispense with anything like a marriage-like status (c), and include single persons. By contrast, the giving and receiving of emotional care requires at least two persons.

III. THE CASE FOR CONTRACTUALIZATION

A. *SPICs*

As I have tried to show, an ideal of emotional intimacy and the caregiving that is supposed to flow from it is central to the justification of ICGUs. To acknowledge that more often than not a person's life would go better if he or she experienced love or emotional intimacy is one thing; to believe the state should foster it through a legal status is another, especially when noncaring relationships may also deserve legal recognition and caring does not have to come from an intimate relationship. With respect to marriage, if the neutrality problem boils down to the state's acting as an ethical authority by privileging a particular kind of intimate relationship with insufficient justification, then one should be equally skeptical about what the state is doing when it makes an ICGU (or any other) status available to some persons but not to others on the ground that their noncaring relationship is not as worthwhile. From the standpoint of neutrality, the fewer intimate relationships any legal status excludes, the better because the state is less likely to be singling out some of them and not others for more favorable treatment with insufficient justification. Marriage or whatever it may be called in the future should be even more contractual than it is now and that change would conform to the trend of utilizing contracts in family law more generally.[118]

As Brake writes: "The contractual view of marriage implies spouses can choose marital obligations to suit their interests."[119] According to this view, the parties to the marital contract negotiate or deliberate to come up with mutually agreeable terms they will be subject to during the duration of their legal relationship. The quasi-contractual approach I shall put forth and defend in the remainder of this chapter already seems to be under way inasmuch as contemporary marriage is far from a permanent status.[120] As Lenore Weitzman pointed out long ago, all married couples are already subject to an unwritten marital contract.[121] Not only for the most part are people unaware of its terms, but default rules are also designed for typical situations and thus may not fit individual circumstances. According to Mary Anne Case, two-person marriage "serves ... as a series of reciprocal default designations" in the event of, say, the incapacity or death of one of the individuals, thereby increasing efficiency.[122] The norm is still that almost all married couples are subject to more or less the same unwritten marriage contract they probably do not understand very well. That contract is state dictated, codified in family law, and legally enforceable.[123] Marriage is already a "status contract."[124] Unfortunately, many scholars draw too sharp a contrast between status and contract, as if Americans had to choose between two extremes; the real issue is how much we want to allow competent adults to customize their marriage-like relationships. In other contexts, their doing so is not particularly controversial. Normally, the

[118] Lenore J. Weitzman, *The Marriage Contract: A Guide to Living With Lovers and Spouses* (New York: The Free Press, 1981); Martha M. Ertman, *Love's Promises: How Formal and Informal Contracts Shape All Kinds of Families* (Boston: Beacon Press, 2015) (forthcoming).
[119] Elizabeth Brake, "Marriage," http://plato.stanford.edu/entries/marriage (2012).
[120] See Sunstein and Thaler, "Privatizing Marriage," 383.
[121] Weitzman, *The Marriage Contract*, xvi.
[122] Mary Anne Case, "Marriage Licenses," *Minnesota Law Review*, 89 (2005), 1783.
[123] Weitzman, *The Marriage Contract*, xvii–xviii. [124] Ibid., xix.

contents of a will or a trust do not concern the state and the person who devises it will be able to effectuate his or her intent.

Status is not necessarily morally praiseworthy, even though it seems to continue to be a stand-in in the literature for an egalitarian intimate relationship. In the past, the status of marriage reinforced patriarchy. If the status can be reformed along gender egalitarian lines, then it stands to reason that contractual approaches are not just about enhancing freedom of marital choice but can also be about fostering internal equality by putting mutual expectations in writing and encouraging compliance. Today, opposite and same-sex couples can already form different kinds of cohabitation agreements that – if valid – move them closer to the legal status of marriage without actually marrying. I say "quasi" because the state would have to pass legislation to compel third parties to acknowledge the marital unit the individuals choose to form. As Case writes, the main purpose of licensing by the state has been to "structure their relations with third parties."[125] In other situations, third parties may have to recognize other kinds of legal instruments, such as wills and powers of attorney. My proposal also has the advantage of covering an even wider range of intimate relationships, including polygamous or polyamorous ones, because they do not have to be premised on caregiving or any other substantive value. In that way, as much as possible, marriage-like relationships can be consistent with neutrality on the part of the state. The meaning of marriage can then be left to the couple, thruple, or moresome.[126]

That is not to say there are not critics. Among canonical political thinkers, Hegel characterizes marriage as "a contract to transcend the standpoint of contract."[127] In different forms, that basic view survives. As Weitzman writes, "marriage is typically thought of as the most intimate and private social relationship, while a contract is typically regarded as the prototype of rational business transactions."[128] One of my aims in this book is to encourage readers to be less sentimental about amorous marriage and more open to the idea that close friendship(s) could and should lie at the core of their lives. As I see it, the more people who see marriage as a legal relationship with indeterminate

[125] Case, "Marriage Licenses," 1781.

[126] Marriage can be about many things – and not just about sex. And even if it were about sex, sexual happiness is not trivial for many people. Martha C. Nussbaum, *From Disgust to Humanity: Sexual Orientation and Constitutional Law* (New York: Oxford University Press, 2010), 39.

[127] G. W. F. Hegel, *Elements of the Philosophy of Right*, ed. Allen W. Wood, trans. H. B. Nisbet (New York: Cambridge University Press, 1995), 165.

[128] Weitzman, *The Marriage Contract*, xv.

content, the better. But let me be crystal clear. First, in the marital regime I favor, people are perfectly free to opt for a traditional marriage if that is what they want. Second, although some economists utilize the concept of marriage markets in their research and ordinary people casually refer to the dating market, I am not encouraging anyone to see his or her intimate relationship exclusively through a financial or legal lens. Indeed, that perspective may miss what is most important to most people about such relationships at their best. Instead, by making marriage less sacred and focusing on the state's involvement with the institution, my hope is that more and more people will begin to appreciate why it should be as inclusive and as flexible as possible. Disestablishment is the route to the former destination. A semicontractual approach serves the latter.

At the end of the day, how receptive one is to SPICs will depend on how paternalistic one believes the state should be when it comes to allowing people to devise almost all the terms of their state-recognized intimate relationship. As I have emphasized, this concern with protecting people from their "unwise" marital choices is intelligible but misguided. And even if it were not misguided, the concern would be equally applicable to all such choices and not only those involving multiperson unions. It may seem as if SPICs depart so dramatically from the marital status quo that for that reason alone do not deserve to be part of the conversation. Some scholars allege that the privatization of marriage, which is usually understood as the transition to a more contractual marriage-like status, would produce bad consequences for women.[129]

However, there are different kinds and degrees of contractualization – some of which are not ridiculously Libertarian. Safeguards can be put in place to perhaps increase the odds that the marital decision is as voluntary as any human choice can be under imperfect conditions. Judges can invalidate SPICs that are too one sided. There is no reason why the state could not require anyone who wants to marry to have legal advice provided by the state so his or her consent is more likely to be genuine. This safeguard would probably be adequate without denying a competent adult marital choice, which would be an extreme solution, especially in such a liberal society as ours that usually favors a range of options. People often do not make wise personal decisions when they are "in love" and thus their judgment may be impaired. The tendency on the part of critics of contractual alternatives to the legal status of marriage not to address more nuanced forms of

[129] Shrage, "Reforming Marriage," 107–21.

contractualization weakens their position.[130] To deliver a knockout blow, they would have to show that some marital contracts in some situations disadvantage women or are unfair more generally.

They would also have to establish that a semicontractual approach, such as my own – which is deliberately designed to maximize marital choice while taking into account unequal bargaining positions and power differences – deserves more than a glance. After all, marriage is already partially contractual, and through prenuptial agreements, people can modify most of its terms. In most states, the parties may utilize such an agreement to predetermine support rights and property distribution upon divorce.[131] Even if one rejects my semicontractual proposal and a single legal status remained the only marital option, couples and groups would still have to decide whether to adopt the status, which raises similar worries. Those who dismiss all contractual models – even more nuanced ones – must believe that the default rules that an ideal status would impose on the participants if they marry would always minimize the problems that arise from unequal bargaining positions. If anything, the issue of how to enforce the terms of the contract during the marriage would prove to be tricky.[132] At most, perhaps the state could provide mediation services and not have one member of the marriage sue the other(s) to enforce one or more of the contractual duties. In that sense, any marital contract would be unlike, say, a typical lease or employment contract. With more and more couples cohabitating for a variety of reasons, I wonder whether even fewer of them would marry if they could not contract around at least some – but not necessarily all – of the default rules. Their being able to do so would be less problematic if all parties were required to have legal representation. If keeping a status had the perverse effect of deterring at least some people from marrying, then more individuals would be even more vulnerable when their intimate relationships end.

Not all feminists are hostile to the contractualization of marriage.[133] Robin West maintains that privatizing marriage would make the institution even less unjust.[134] Brook J. Sadler remarks: "Civil marriage ought to be replaced with

[130] See, for example, Martha Minow and Mary Lyndon Shanley, "Relational Rights and Responsibilities: Revisioning the Family in Liberal Political Theory and Law," *Hypatia*, 11 (1996), especially 9–13.

[131] Burnham, *Introduction to Law and the Legal System of the United States*, 521.

[132] See Strauss, "Why the State Cannot 'Abolish Marriage': A Partial Defense of Legal Marriage Based on the Structure of Intimate Duties," especially 33–38.

[133] See, for example, Marjorie Schultz, "Contractual Ordering of Marriage: A New Model for State Policy," *California Law Review*, 70 (1982), 207–334.

[134] Robin West, *Marriage, Sexuality, and Gender* (Boulder, CO: Paradigm Publishers, 2007), 203–04.

civil unions, which can be entered into as individualized contracts by consenting adults who choose from among a variety of legal rights and responsibilities those that they wish to exercise."[135] Metz does not go into much detail about various contractualization schemes but rejects Martha Fineman's "contract-plus" option and concedes that liberty – if it were the only relevant value – would lead to intimate contracts.[136] Her position, then, turns on a factual claim that only a legal status like an ICGU – and not a private contract – can better serve gender equality and subsidize caregiving. It remains to be seen, though, whether any status is the most effective means of achieving these normative objectives, given its past poor performance. Like some other feminists, Fineman proposes abolishing marriage and replacing it with something more contractual and does not think that such a change would disadvantage women.[137] Metz alleges that in doing so, Fineman has left "intimate caregiving relationships dangerously unprotected and unsupported."[138] But that would only be true if Metz were right about the instrumental value of ICGUs, which is an empirical matter. There are many types of intimate contracts – some of which would not undermine gender equality and caregiving and might do an even better job of fostering them if mutual expectations were as explicit as they possibly could be and the responsibilities of each party were spelled out in advance in excruciating detail. Women who opt for monogamous, opposite-sex marriages could (and should) also be informed of their comparative vulnerability.

Metz could try to impose a more egalitarian intimate relationship on the couple or group by denying them the right to create the equivalent of a prenuptial agreement, but that would seriously infringe on their personal freedom.[139] For her, ICGUs would protect caretakers, who are usually women, and the vulnerable by providing them with material and emotional benefits. Those objectives might be realized but only if most people select them and do not modify them too much contractually. Thus, when it comes to gender equality and caregiving, ICGUs may not be as effective as she believes them to be. Neither of our proposals can guarantee more egalitarian dynamics between men and women in their interactions nor preclude exploitation. At the end of the day, so much hinges on their respective strengths and weaknesses as human beings and how they behave in their personal relationships,

[135] Brook J. Sadler, "Rethinking Civil Unions and Same-Sex Marriage," *Monist*, 91 (2008), 592–93.

[136] Metz, *Untying the Knot*, 140.

[137] Fineman, *The Autonomy Myth*, 134–35.

[138] Metz, *Untying the Knot*, 140.

[139] For a nice discussion of how premarital agreements work, see Fineman, *The Autonomy Myth*, 125–28, 133–34.

particularly when they experience stress, frustration, and disappointment. There are only legal ways of trying to minimize the consequences of an unequal relationship if it ends through immutable or default rules or contracts. Metz refuses to let go of status because she expects it to do considerable equality work during the relationship, yet it is not evident that that status would make as much of a difference as she believes it would when the state would not police it closely.

The main rationale for ICGUs involves the importance of fostering the emotional well-being and building or maintaining of self-esteem of the participants. Caregiving serves as a means to that end and has to be provided by a family member, close friend, or partner who does it with the right attitude. Otherwise, the state could simply pay someone to do it, such as when it subsidizes child care for some families. However, the value of such emotional care and why the state should support it calls for a separate defense.[140] Despite how radical her proposal initially appears to be, what underlies it is a traditional ideal of love and care that some people may reasonably reject.[141] Many worthwhile relationships and activities do not directly involve such emotional states or attitudes. In not separating material from emotional caregiving and adequately defending the latter as indispensable to a decent life, Metz excludes other personal reasons people may have for not choosing caring relationships and instead engaging in other activities.

That is not to say that emotional caregiving is not valuable to many people; it is to say that others could have other serious personal reasons for being in a noncaregiving relationship, such as a close friendship (without care, even broadly defined) or a purely sexual relationship, which would not qualify for ICGU status. Or they simply may prefer to be alone and pursue nonsocial ends. Even if the state were to make some sort of caregiving a requirement of a state-recognized intimate relationship, I do not see how the state could verify that the persons who are applying for an ICGU license already have or plan to have a caregiving relationship. Basically, the state would have to take them at their word.

B. *Pateman, Shanley, and Contractualism*

I now want to share a few preliminary thoughts on contractualism, attempt to rehabilitate its reputation in the context of the debate over the disestablishment of marriage, and show why such an approach is more consistent with

[140] Brake, review of Tamara Metz, *Untying the Knot*, 420.

[141] See, for example, Michael Warner, *The Trouble With Normal: Sex, Politics, and the Ethics of Queer Life* (Cambridge, MA: Harvard University Press, 1999).

neutrality than any of the alternatives other than abolition or complete privatization. For starters, contract has a bad name in some circles due to its historical association with the domination of women and racial minorities.[142] Here, though, we are talking about SPICs, where the individuals involved are assumed to be well informed enough to bind themselves to a legal agreement and may (and probably should) receive legal advice. Mary Shanley refers to this view as "contractualism."[143] In its most extreme form, if there were no children, the parties would decide all their legal rights and responsibilities – limited only by other valid laws. For the most part, marriage law is already laissez-faire; it regulates entrance and exit and barely restricts how couples may interact with each other – except behaviors related to the welfare of the children, torts, crimes, and the economic vulnerability of the spouses upon dissolution of the marriage.

A legal contract is "[a]n agreement between two or more persons which creates an obligation to do or not to do a particular thing. Its essentials are competent parties, subject matter, legal consideration, mutuality of agreement, and mutuality of obligation."[144] Normally, in contract law, the contracting parties are empowered to create their own terms, where the contract is a promise between two or more parties that the law recognizes as binding by providing a remedy in the event of breach.[145] Most contract theories presuppose the importance of autonomy or efficiency.[146] As Case observes, the presence of more than two persons almost necessitates a more contractual approach in the absence of any default designations.[147] The option of a SPIC would probably compel people to think more deeply about what they want their intimate relationship to be like and what they expect from each other. Moreover, if current marriage law were repealed and replaced by a regime of such contracts, then the liberal neutrality problem would be mitigated. The personal choice of the participants from a long menu of different options implies the state is not endorsing a single idea of intimacy.[148] They can form a

[142] Charles Mills, *The Racial Contract* (Ithaca, NY: Cornell University Press, 1999).

[143] Shanley, "Just Marriage," 5.

[144] *Black's Law Dictionary* (5th ed.) (St. Paul, MN: West Publishing, 1979), 291–92.

[145] William Burnham, *Introduction to the Law and Legal System of the United States* (5th ed.) (St. Paul, MN: Thomson West, 2011), 398–414.

[146] Jody S. Kraus, "Philosophy of Contract Law," in *The Oxford Handbook of Jurisprudence and Philosophy of Law*, ed. Jules Coleman and Scott Shapiro (New York: Oxford University Press, 2002), 687–88.

[147] Mary Anne Case, "Marriage Licenses," *Minnesota Law Review*, 89 (2005), 1783.

[148] An analogy would be that the state does not violate neutrality in the context of religious freedom when it lets everyone choose his or her religious beliefs and practices – with the caveat that such practices cannot harm others or put them unreasonably at risk.

legal marriage-like relationship for whatever personal reasons they happen to have. That does not mean that every single possible way of life would be feasible, but they cannot complain they have been discriminated against when they can contractually create the equivalent of a marriage-like status and devise almost all its terms if they want to enter into such an arrangement with at least one other person. The drawback of permitting people such choice in these circumstances is that they may end up forming legal relationships that do not serve their own good or the freedom and equality of all persons. For women, even today, too many choices may still be a product of their false beliefs about appropriate gender roles and unequal bargaining power.[149]

That is a possibility that continues to haunt contractual models more generally. Hegel is known for attacking Kant's view of marriage as being inappropriately contractual.[150] In her famous work *The Sexual Contract*, Carole Pateman concerns herself with property in the person.[151] Because a woman's body is the subject of prostitution and surrogate motherhood contracts, for example, they are morally problematic and that same worry also applies to marriage under the common law.[152] Although Pateman's scholarship made it seem as if a contract could only conceal subordination and thus not serve feminist or egalitarian ends, SPICs do not necessarily raise the same concerns that motivated Pateman's influential critique of the social contract tradition.[153] As Okin writes: "Pateman gives up too easily on the potential uses of contract for feminism."[154] After all, no logical connection between private contracts and domination exists. Consequently, any objection to such an approach must be historical or empirical and be predicated on the prediction

[149] Catharine MacKinnon, *Feminism Unmodified: Discourses on Life and Law* (Cambridge, MA: Harvard University Press, 1987).

[150] Hegel, *Elements of the Philosophy of Right*, 71, 105, 202.

[151] Carole Pateman, *The Sexual Contract* (Stanford, CA: Stanford University Press, 1988); Carole Pateman and Charles Mills, *Contract and Domination* (Cambridge, UK: Polity Press, 2007); Daniel O'Neill et al., *Illusion of Consent: Engaging With Carole Pateman* (University Park, PA: Penn State University Press, 2008).

[152] This is a kind of Kantian argument because it relies on the normative claim that people should be treated as ends and not as means. The underlying rationale is that our autonomy gives us our dignity or value and to treat someone merely as a thing or an object is to not respect that value.

[153] Pateman's main concern is to show how the original contract, which created and justified the modern state and its power structures, is a political fiction that appears to reflect freedom but in fact conceals subordination. See Steve On, "Interview With Carole Pateman by Steve On," *Contemporary Political Theory*, 9 (2010), 247.

[154] Susan Moller Okin, Review of Carole Pateman, *The Sexual Contract*, "Feminism, the Individual, and Contract Theory," *Ethics*, 100 (1990), 658, 666.

that such contracts would be worse than whatever marriage-like status they are being compared with.

Shanley takes this route by raising two related concerns: (1) Contractualism does not take mutual aid and dependence in intimate relationships seriously enough and (2) it underplays the role of positive state action in fostering equality.[155] A marriage contract is a special contract because the state ensures that third parties have to also accept its legal effects.[156] Thus, some degree of state involvement is inevitable. Following Brake, I believe the state must enact legislation that would require third parties to recognize the legal status the adults in question have created. For Shanley, the difficulty with the privatization of marriage through a regime of contract is that marriage is "a relationship that transcends the individual lives of the partners."[157] This phrasing is a way of articulating the place of mutual trust in any healthy human relationship and the inappropriateness of conceptualizing marriage as an ongoing business partnership.

The flaw in Shanley's view lies in the false choice between contract and status it relies on. People who marry are already subject to a state-imposed unwritten contact that is codified in family law, even without their knowledge.[158] People who trust each other may still want to indemnify themselves against future loss if the relationships sours and one of the most foolish things anyone can do is to think that love at one moment in time will last forever and render any sort of insurance policy superfluous. At least part of the opposition to the contractualization of marriage is rooted in the romantic notion of what an intimate relationship at its best can be. The irony is that historically, women had many reasons to want to use a contract to alter the patriarchal institution the state had thrust on them through the common law to subordinate them. In the past, what was often referred to as the marriage contract is more aptly described as a state-imposed status whose rules severely disadvantaged women.[159] This fact should not be forgotten. Ideals of love, trust, and cooperation have hardly secured their equality and well-being. As Martha Ertman points out, the introduction of (contractual) business models into family law could promote equality.[160]

155 Shanley, "Just Marriage," 5–6.

156 David Cruz, "Mystification, Neutrality, and Same-Sex Couples in Marriage," in *Just Marriage*, ed. Mary Lyndon Shanley (Oxford, UK: Oxford University Press, 2000), 53.

157 Shanley, "Just Marriage," 6.

158 Weitzman, *The Marriage Contract*, xv–xvi.

159 See Mary Anne Case, "Marriage Licenses," *Minnesota Law Review*, 89 (2005), 1765.

160 Martha M. Ertman, "The Business of Intimacy," in *Feminism Confronts Homo Economicus: Gender, Law, and Society*, ed. Martha Fineman and Terrance Dougherty (Ithaca, NY: Cornell University Press, 2005), 493.

Contracts seem to call attention to what can go wrong in a relationship, but they can also clarify mutual expectations, facilitate communication, and make both parties aware of the possibility that things may not work out as planned.[161]

For Shanley, the state has a strong interest in enhancing equality in each marriage.[162] Her concern is that a regime of private marital contracts would let people enter into unequal marital arrangements, thereby increasing the opportunity for exploitation by the party in the better bargaining position – usually the male. That also could be said, though, about many couples who do not marry but instead cohabitate, which is increasingly common these days; their personal relationship could already be unequal, and in terms of its dynamics, it will probably not become more egalitarian if they marry. Having a contractual option would not necessarily exacerbate the existing inequality in individual cases or cumulatively. If one is concerned about protecting women, especially when the relationship ends, then the new marriage-like status should be as attractive as possible so more people enter into a legal relationship and receive its benefits.

It is always possible that one party can take advantage of another in any bargaining situation. Like any other unconscionable contract, an unconscionable intimate contract could be invalidated if its terms were egregiously unfair.[163] Legally, "[a]n offer is unconscionable when it is coercive and imposes harsh conditions on the coercee or confers unfair benefits on the coercer."[164] Compared with other areas of private law, family law is fact-driven. If an ICGU were the only option, the party in the superior position could simply decline to adopt the marriage-like status. In my view, the state has a much stronger interest in preventing inequality when the marriage-like relationship ends. That interest may mean the state will either impose default rules on everyone who enters into such a relationship or provide legal advice to anyone who is thinking about forming what I call a SPIC so he or she understands the consequences of opting out of the egalitarian default rules, such as an equitable division of the marital property.

Shanley's view, taken to its logical extreme, is illiberal.[165] Subsequently, she concedes that the choice between contract and public status left something to be desired and later endorses civil unions for same-sex and opposite-sex couples.[166]

161 Weitzman, *The Marriage Contract*, 241.

162 Shanley, "Just Marriage," 6.

163 See Weitzman, *The Marriage Contract*, 248.

164 Nicholas Dixon, "Boxing, Paternalism, and Legal Moralism," *Social Theory and Practice*, 27 (2001), 330.

165 Zelinsky, "Deregulating Marriage," 1216.

166 Shanley, "Just Marriage," 111–12.

This response does not entirely account for the more radical critiques of marriage that Metz, Brake, Bedi, and others have introduced over the past few years. Shanley goes halfway in recognizing that a single legal structure for all marriages or intimate relationships no longer works. But why not proceed even farther down that road and permit people to structure their relationship – at least as long as it lasts – in a manner that best suits their particularities? If it were more than mere conjecture that ICGUs would reduce inequality in intimate relationships and SPICs would have the opposite effect, then there would be more to be said on behalf of the former. Indeed, a much wider range of marital options for women may enhance gender equality.[167] Under my marital scheme, women would not have to choose a more traditional opposite-sex marriage but could form whatever intimate relationships they happen to prefer.

Even if ICGUs were to do better than SPICs in terms of equality, the lives of people who are not and never will be in caregiving relationships also count and their exclusion from a marriage-like status should not be overlooked. As a substitute for marriage, a SPIC is quasi-libertarian in that people would be able to act of all sort of personal reasons to marry. Additionally, unlike a private marital contract, a SPIC would force the state to treat their relationship as a status and make its benefits and burdens a matter of law. They could put emotional caregiving or just about any other purpose at its core. The specifics of the SPIC that people form are much less important than their having a menu of contractual options that would make their legal relationship as individualized as possible, thereby minimizing the liberal neutrality problem. Although the state would be providing a legal instrument for people who want to assume a status and that might qualify as state endorsement of personal relationships, their deciding on their own what the purpose(s) of their intimate relationship would be is about as much as the state can do to foster such relationships without succumbing to complete privatization.

A liberal state is also supposed to be neutral in its justification for laws and policies that impact reasonable conceptions of the good.[168] It may be illegitimate, then, for the state to advance marriage or something like it on the ground that it is better to be married than unmarried when plenty of reasonable people reject this idea. Not all liberals take this position. For example, Stephen Macedo insists that the "argument for marriage claims that more

[167] See Brake, *Minimizing Marriage*, 205.

[168] The concept of "neutrality" is anything but uncomplicated. For an excellent overview, see Jeremy Waldron, "Legislation and Moral Neutrality," in *Liberal Rights: Collected Papers 1981–1991* (Cambridge, UK: Cambridge University Press, 1993), 143–67.

stable commitments promote public as well as private welfare."[169] It follows that the state may favor marriage over nonmarriage by offering "public inducements," provided that marriage is available to all.[170] Here, Macedo has in mind same-sex couples. On its face, this proposal seems to be mild. From the standpoint of liberal neutrality, the problem is that in offering legal benefits and burdens, the state makes a judgment that being married is better than the alternatives and in doing so puts its imprimatur on a conception of the good. It may be true that statistically, marriage promotes more stable relationships and that more stable relationships are better for the development of children and "encourage responsible conduct, planning for the future, and concern for others."[171]

On the other hand, that claim might be factually false, unproven, or overstated, and even if it is more or less accurate, there are probably some people who are not prepared for the responsibilities of marriage. In such situations, the promotion of marriage by the state may end up luring people into situations that do not benefit anyone and may produce worse outcomes. Conservative pro-marriage arguments, which have not yet exited the stage, usually presuppose that the people in the marriage are psychologically untroubled, emotionally stable, and financially responsible. The truth is that some people are not marriageable; they will never be good or even decent partners and the state's creating incentives for couples to marry may have the unintended consequence of making their lives (or those of their partners) worse than they otherwise would have been. Anyone who has been in a bad marriage knows it can be a grave mistake to marry. It is not obvious to me that the state's interest in promoting marriage on empirical grounds is nearly as strong as Macedo or anyone else makes it out to be, especially when the state's purported interest in marriage involves its alleged secondary effects.

C. *SPICs*

On the one hand, privatizing marriage in the sense of removing the state completely may give private organizations too much influence over the institution.[172] Historically, status did not protect women or come close to ensuring their equality in marriages. Supporters of polygamy before and after the Civil

[169] Stephen Macedo, "Sexuality and Liberty: Making Room for Nature and Tradition?" in *Sex, Preference, and Family; Essays on Law and Nature*, ed. David M. Estlund and Martha C. Nussbaum (New York: Oxford University Press, 1997), 94.

[170] Ibid., 99. [171] Ibid., 94. [172] Shrage, "Reforming Marriage," 115.

War made contractual freedom arguments.[173] This possibility of privatization is not so disconcerting when it comes to religion because the state does not use religious affiliations as a means of filtering entitlements to those who need them. Additionally, there are thousands of religious denominations and no official or established religion but not many types of socially approved intimate relationships and even fewer kinds of marriage. Even when the state retains the legal status of marriage or its equivalent, the state can probably extricate itself from the institution without acting unconstitutionally. The right to marriage does not mean states must "offer any particular package of civil benefits to people who marry."[174]

On the other hand, it is about time we take a second look at contractual models and resist caricatures of them. As Ertman writes, "love and contracts often complement instead of oppose each other."[175] Contracts are a legal instrument and morally neutral; like any tool, they can serve the interests of one party or all parties to the marital contract. Regulating the environment in which the formation of the SPIC takes place – with legal advice – more often than not would enhance informed choice and produce better consequences than relying on a legal status that is too inflexible to accommodate individual differences. SPICs may produce greater diversity and experimentation, strengthening the institution.[176] According to another scholar: "Before the marriage, few couples have any real alternative to 'one-size-fits-all' marriage."[177] The advent of the option of a contractual alternative would alter the status quo and make "marriage" as inclusive as it ever has been and ever could be. A marriage could expire after a certain specified period (and not necessarily end via divorce, annulment, or legal separation).[178] A "wedlease" marital lease is a renewable contract in which the marriage expires after a designated period.[179] Its temporary nature might encourage people to not take their marriage-like relationship for granted. Or it might make them take their

[173] Martha M. Ertman, "Race Treason: The Untold Story of America's Ban on Polygamy," *Columbia Journal of Gender and Law*, 19 (2010), 337.

[174] See Martha C. Nussbaum, "The Right to Marry?" *California Law Review*, 98 (2010), 686.

[175] Martha M. Ertman, "Love and Contracts in *Don Quixote*," in Don Quixote: *Interdisciplinary Connections*, ed. Matthew D. Warshawsky and James A. Parr (Newark, DE: Juan de la Cuesta, 2013), 251.

[176] Zelinsky, "Deregulating Marriage," 1215.

[177] Barbara Stark, "From One-Size-Fits-All to Postmodern Marriage Law," *California Law Review*, 89 (2001), 1484.

[178] For an interesting discussion of temporary or trial marriages in an Islamic context, see Shrage, "Reforming Marriage," especially 108–13.

[179] www.npr.org/blogs/thetwo-way/2013/08/13/211700456/would-some-marriages-be-better-if-couples-signed-wedleases

marriage less seriously. The point is to let them figure out the arrangement that best suits their shared goals. Those who do not exercise the option of writing their own SPIC for whatever reason could be subject to default rules designed to make the marriage-like relationship as egalitarian as possible and protect the vulnerable in the event of divorce. Typically, default rules govern a transaction in the absence of the parties' specifying their own rules; they can be avoided by contracting around them. At present, with respect to two-person marriage, most couples do not use prenuptial agreements.[180]

It is worth pondering why they do not do so, though, given the high rate of divorce in this country and the increasing availability of inexpensive sources of legal self-help. Most people may be sentimental or, less charitably, naïve about marriage. Or they lack information or the cost of acquiring it and having to seek professional legal advice may make the option less attractive than it otherwise might be. Or they may not want to "jinx" the relationship in the sense of planning for failure. As Okin concedes, contracts can be legitimate under certain conditions.[181] Under less than ideal conditions of the real world, the other virtues of SPICs would include even greater flexibility than that of ICGUs, more respect for personal choice, more transparency, and more opportunities for informed consent.[182] First, a contractual model would maximize the opportunity of the parties themselves to shape their intimate relationship in accordance with their particular needs, desires, goals, and values. This option is important inasmuch as the success of marriages and intimate relationships more generally has a lot to do with personal compatibility, communication, honesty, compromising when necessary, letting go of control accommodating personal differences, sharing aims, making important collective decisions together, and working on personal shortcomings. SPICs can enable people to customize their marriage-like relationships – whatever name they go by – so they can achieve their individual and mutual goals.

Second, competent adults could make their own choices about the nature of their intimate relationships – no matter how idiosyncratic they might be. It may turn out to be true that maximizing individual choice in this context would lead to greater gender inequality, but for the state to restrict choice on this basis alone amounts to telling competent adults they cannot act in what they perceive to be their own best interest. To some extent, we have to take

180 Adrienne D. Davis, "Regulating Polygamy: Intimacy, Default Rules, and Bargaining for Equality," *Columbia Law Review*, 110 (2010), 2000–01.

181 Susan Moller Okin, Review of Carole Pateman, *The Sexual Contract*, "Feminism, the Individual, and Contract Theory," *Ethics*, 100 (1990), 667.

182 See Weitzman, *The Marriage Contract*, xv.

people as they are – warts and all – and not how we wish them to be. In a liberal society, there should be a strong presumption against such paternalism. That is not to say the state ought to be indifferent to the circumstances under which such contracts are formed and be unconcerned with how well informed people are about the legal relationship they are about to enter into; it is to say that the state should not be so enthusiastic about telling competent adults about how to structure their intimate lives.

Third, far too many people still do not understand that by marrying, they are establishing a legal relationship with their partner and often only learn of its consequences the hard way. The process of forming a contract – whatever other benefits it might have – should enhance informed consent.[183] As a probable result, more people would enter into a state-recognized intimate relationship with more knowledge of their rights and responsibilities and the rewards and risks, including what could happen if the relationship ends. Due to some people's well-known vulnerability in certain intimate relationships, it is particularly important for women to be well informed before they decide to take a leap of faith.[184] After being informed of certain risks, women could insert an antipolygamy clause or other safeguards into the SPIC they decide to form with their putative spouse.[185]

The future of marriage is uncertain. As one scholar writes: "Culturally, marriage no longer plays the role in our society that it once did."[186] The privatization of marriage is already under way.[187] More and more couples are cohabitating than ever before without full legal protection.[188] That does not mean even greater privatization is inevitable or desirable, but the trend indicates that this conversation about whether (and how) to disestablish marriage ought to take place in the near future. The movement toward a regime of moderate contractualism or SPICs is not as much as a departure from the status quo as it initially may seem because the state already permits prenuptial and postnuptial agreements. Also, today, same-sex couples who do not have access to marriage or civil unions in their states can form contracts concerning health care proxies, power of attorney, property, and so on.

Again, the actual content of any SPIC matters less than the more abstract point that contracts are the right approach when one is committed to some version of neutrality and personal freedom. The kinds of concerns people have

183 Garrett, "A Prima Facie Case Against Civil Marriage," 45.
184 Brake, *Minimizing Marriage*, 205.
185 On this point, see Goldfeder, *Revisiting Polygamy*, 200.
186 Zelinsky, "Deregulating Marriage," 1163.
187 Cass R. Sunstein and Richard H. Thaler, "Privatizing Marriage," *Monist*, 91 (2008), 378.
188 Bowman, *Unmarried Couples, Law, and Public Policy*, 1.

about contracts more generally – incapacity, misrepresentation, duress, undue influence, illegality, unconscionability, breach, and remedies – are not new and to advocate a more contractual approach to personal relationships is not to ignore any of them. The state simply can do what it normally does – or even go to greater lengths – to minimize unfairness in the bargaining process and to make this option as affordable as possible. State bar associations, legal publishers, and independent websites can facilitate the move from status to contract.[189] Any status – whether it is called an ICGU, MM, civil union, or marriage – is subject to similar problems when those who are eligible have to choose to adopt such a status before it will have any legal effect. Whatever else it might accomplish, a contractual approach makes more explicit what is too often hidden from view.

When it comes to marriage, one does not solve the neutrality problem by introducing new substantive values as its foundation. As I have tried to establish in this chapter, the exact nature of the state's interest in either encouraging people to marry or keeping them married – in light of the relative ease of divorce and the decriminalization of fornication and cohabitation – is far from obvious.[190] It is even less certain what the state's interest is in only providing a two-person conception of marriage, requiring the appearance of sexual intimacy, when such a conception of marriage cannot accommodate the particular needs of an increasing number of adults. My aim has not been to offer a detailed contractual alternative. Instead, it has been to explain why a commitment to liberal neutrality leads to some form of contractualization, which too many liberals summarily dismiss.

The idea that the state should support monogamous marriage by providing incentives for people to take on martial commitments so they can live better lives remains increasingly difficult to defend in the face of more inclusive, less parochial alternatives. The practice of the state's promoting a particular type of intimate association, such as an ICGU, at the expense of others of arguably equal worth violates such neutrality. The third way – SPICs – are the most promising option consistent with neutrality. They not only maximize personal choice by providing multiple contractual options to choose from, but they break the chain between the state as an ethical authority and the legal status a couple or group of persons may adopt. As such, the state would no longer be

[189] Ibid., 1183.

[190] At present, when it comes to divorce, all states have no-fault regimes. Brian Bix refers to this argument – in which the state sends mixed messages about the value of marriage – as the "coherence" argument. Brian H. Bix, "State of the Union: The States' Interest in the Marital Status of Their Citizens," *University of Miami Law Review*, 55 (2000), 26–28.

signaling that a particular kind of intimate relationship based on such a substantive value as caregiving is better than other kinds of personal relationships that people may have or may want to form. Additionally, SPICs would not be far removed from the more familiar concept of prenuptial agreements.[191]

Granted, the state's making SPICs available could be construed as the state's promoting – albeit in a rather attenuated way – such relationships. A SPIC would not enable a person to "marry" him or herself. Even under a more contractual regime like my own, the lives of those who are single and unmarried are devalued in that the state subsidizes caregiving/caretaking relationships on the assumption they are worthwhile and better than nonrelationships. Thus, single persons do not qualify for any sort of legal status. True, there are some rights they would not need, such as hospital or prison visitation rights, if they do not have at least one partner. Nonetheless, this state of affairs is troubling insofar as the state may still be advancing a particular vision of the good – namely, that it is better to be in a relationship with at least one other person. That may be unavoidable as long as the state continues to accord legal status to any intimate relationships.

Whatever else may be said against SPICs, the contractual approach I advocate minimizes the extent to which the state violates neutrality without adopting the undesirable Libertarian alternative of complete privatization and leaving vulnerable people at the mercy of market forces. In a liberal society, the problem of how to respect people's personal choices and simultaneously protect the vulnerable or promote equality will never yield a simple solution. Metz deserves considerable credit for identifying it in the context of the debate over the meaning of marriage and developing a thoughtful solution that is a vast improvement over the status quo. As I have tried to show, though, we cannot honor liberal neutrality and have a status that is supposed to foster emotional care and equality in intimate relationships without thinking seriously about noncaring relationships and solitary activities. That is not to say that SPICs can do any better when it comes to such care and equality. My point is that they may not do much worse and their inherent flexibility enables the state to respect the wide range of personal reasons people may have for wanting the state to recognize their intimate relationship. That proposal is not privatization, but it is close and should compel egalitarian liberals to see that any status – short of contractualization – comes at a very high cost – namely, personal choice.

191 For an excellent discussion of their use with respect to multiperson unions, see Mark Goldfeder, *Legalizing Plural Marriage*, especially 158–68.

CONCLUSION

In this final chapter, I explained why scholars who are committed to some version of liberal neutrality are troubled by the state's involvement with marriage. They cannot live with such involvement, but they cannot live without it. The promotion of traditional two-person opposite-sex marriage violates just about any formulation of liberal neutrality. Not as obviously, the promotion of two-person opposite or same-sex marriage also violates such neutrality by favoring a certain kind of marriage over many other alternatives that may be equally or even more worthwhile. Brake's calling for "minimal marriage" and an end to amatonormative discrimination is welcome in a society that too often fails to value marital diversity. The traditional purpose of the promotion of marriage in the United States has been to advance the view that it is better to be married.[192] In political theory terms, the state is advancing a particular way of life and justifying it with reference to a particular conception of the good.

However, under conditions of moral pluralism, the state's doing so violates a stronger – but maybe not a weaker – version of liberal neutrality. Today, in the context of the debate over same-sex marriage, almost all liberals find the status quo to be morally and constitutionally objectionable and many states have expanded their respective legal definitions of marriage to make them more inclusive. Even if the Supreme Court were to address this neutrality problem by recognizing a constitutional right to same-sex marriage and compelling every state to grant marriage licenses to same-sex couples, the state would still be favoring one form of marriage – the two-person or dyadic kind – over other possible forms.

One solution – introduced by Metz, Brake, and Bedi – is to have marital status cover a much wider range of intimate relationships, including those that do not necessarily incorporate a romantic relationship or only two persons. This reform is a considerable improvement over our current marital state of affairs because the state would be putting its imprimatur on a greater variety of intimate relationships and not singling out only a few of them for special treatment. Still, this seemingly plausible solution does not permit the participants to have the freedom to tailor its terms to their particular needs and other potentially valuable relationships are excluded from the status. Even if Americans were to reject the semicontractual approach I put forth, Metz's idea of ICGUs or Brake's idea of an MM would include various kinds of plural marriages.

[192] See Melanie Heath, *One Marriage Under God: The Campaign to Promote Marriage in America* (New York: New York University Press, 2012).

In my view, the state should not condition a marriage license on the purported or actual existence of one kind of intimacy to the detriment of others, even if most people value such intimacy and want to experience it. Because marriage is no longer linked legally to procreation, a marriage does not have to be sexually consummated. At present, in no state do couples have to love or even like each other or promise to treat each other equally or even decently in order to marry. For the most part, the state's interest in encouraging its residents to marry and keeping them married is instrumental; that is, their being married serves other public policy objectives.[193] As long as the institution exists, the state must provide equal access to it, which means it should be as inclusive as possible.

[193] Bix, "State of the Union: The States' Interest in the Marital Status of Their Citizens," 3.

Conclusion

Ultimately, this book embraces marital diversity and unapologetically argues that the law must adapt to the familial changes that are already taking place by according legal recognition to any intimate relationship that competent, consenting adults want to form. It is never too late for us to reexamine our beliefs and change them accordingly, especially when they are rooted in prejudice more than in anything else. Historically, marital norms have changed and will continue to change over time. As such, "traditional" and "nontraditional" families are more fluid than they may seem.[1] All states should make marriage as inclusive as possible because what matters above all is their respecting the importance of marital choice, given that the state's interests in disallowing such choice are so weak. As Judge Walker wrote in *Perry v. Schwarzenegger*: "Whether the belief is based on moral disapproval of homosexuality, animus towards gays and lesbians or simply a belief that a relationship between a man and a woman is inherently better than a relationship between two men or two women, this belief is not the proper basis on which to legislate."[2] The same point can be made about plural marriage enthusiasts and numerical restrictions that prevent them from having the kind of life they believe to be most fulfilling. To some supporters of same-sex marriage, discrimination against such enthusiasts may seem comparatively trivial, but that does not change the fact they are victims when the state does not have to treat them unequally. A monogamous marriage is not necessarily better than its multiperson counterpart. More may not always be merrier, but that is beside the point. The real issue is about who should decide and not about whether the decision is wise or appropriate for everyone. Although our

[1] Stephanie Coontz, *The Way We Really Are: Coming to Terms with America's Changing Families* (New York: Basic Books, 1997), 3.

[2] Perry v. Schwarzenegger, 704 F. Supp. 2d 921, 1002 (2010).

debate over same-sex marriage is usually cast in equal protection terms, one should not forget that any state that does not permit such marriage is also denying plural marriage enthusiasts a deeply personal choice on the basis of reasons that fail to be publicly justified.

By now, it should be evident that this ongoing debate is about a lot more than whether a man can marry another man or a woman can marry another woman. As Mark Goldfeder writes, "the debate over plural marriage can be properly thought of as the next frontier in the evolution of twenty-first century family law."[3] The conservative marriage movement no longer controls the narrative about marriage in this country and that is wonderful news not only for proponents of same-sex marriage but also for any American who cares about treating everyone equally. As I have explained, the understandable preoccupation with such marriage due to the existence of discriminatory policies against gays and lesbians in many states even today should not come at the expense of excluding a wide variety of multiperson intimate relationships – opposite or same sex. It should not matter that polygamists and polyamorists do not yet have the numbers and resources to advance their agenda or that their being nonmonogamous is not as central for many of them to their self-understanding as sexual orientation is for most gays and lesbians. The numbers at this moment in time are neither here nor there. The fate of legal recognition of plural marriage should not turn on whether it is more imperative than same-sex marriage. The cause of marriage equality, then, could be less sectarian and more about ending all forms of marital discrimination – irrespective of the identity of the victims.

The truth is that we already live in a country in which polygamous relationships exist and that state of affairs is not going to change. America is no more a monogamous country than it is a Christian country – just because the majority of its inhabitants are Christians. In this book, my attempt to examine marriage more closely and discern whether the current legal definition in all states is underinclusive and therefore morally unenlightened and constitutionally objectionable reflects my desire to begin a conversation that is long overdue. After all, everyone deserves to be treated fairly by the law, even when they have unconventional or unpopular ideas about how to live and what kind of intimacy is most important to them. The lives of polygamists and polyamorists also count. As Thoreau might have put it, they are a majority of one.[4] Legislative majorities should not be able to force their views on

[3] Mark Goldfeder, *Revisiting Polygamy*, 13.

[4] The famous term "majority of one" comes from Henry David Thoreau, "Civil Disobedience," in *Thoreau: Walden and Other Writings* (New York: Bantam Books, 1962), 93.

minorities in the absence of the kinds of reasons that reasonable persons could share. At the time of this writing, adult polygamists in every state still fear prosecution for their way of life. *Reynolds* would probably have to be overturned before a serious legal discussion about the legalization – understood as the legal recognition of plural marriage – could begin.

Someday, there may be a U.S. Supreme Court decision for plural marriage enthusiasts that would do for them what *Romer*, *Lawrence*, and *Windsor* have done to improve the lives of gays and lesbians in this country. In the near future, some lawmakers and judges may become more skeptical of the rationale for continuing to criminalize the mere act of being married to more than one adult at the same time and more receptive to the view that regulation is not only fair but also more humane and more effective at addressing crimes associated with certain polygynous arrangements. As it stands, women in illegal polygynous relationships are vulnerable in multiple ways. That change in thinking may pave the way for evaluating the strengths and weaknesses of the case against the constitutional right to plural marriage more objectively.

My solution to the marriage equality problem that persists in America is to "equalize" up by making the legal status as inclusive as possible and relying on a semicontractual marital model to give adults the flexibility they need to form the marital relationship they desire. In such a regime, the state would avoid vetting their personal reasons for marrying. That reform would foster legal equality among various kinds of marriages by no longer singling out monogamous, companionate marriage for preferential treatment. Constitutionally, if the reasons the state offers in support of limiting marriage to couples turn out to be inadequate, then the state must extend the right of marriage to groups of three or more persons. Internal equality is trickier because the authority of any liberal state is limited in its capacity to influence the inner dynamics of any intimate relationship in the absence of demonstrable harm.

Equally important, practically, it would be hard to imagine how the state could enforce equality within any sort of marriage once it had begun without intolerably interfering in people's personal affairs. What the state can do is make entrance as informed as possible, which SPICs can accomplish, and exit as easy as possible, which would necessitate either universal immutable or default rules, which would permit the participants to choose from among a number of divorce options to ensure fair treatment, including taking into account the value of uncompensated domestic labor, like caregiving. In many cases, the most serious concern is the economic vulnerability of one (or more) of the spouses upon dissolution of the marriage and how such vulnerability might adversely affect a person's decision not to leave the relationship, thereby undermining consent and exacerbating personal unhappiness. The use of Immutable rules, which would be a departure from the marital status quo, would reduce such vulnerability. Default rules would enhance personal choice but at the possible cost of inequality after the marriage-like relationship has ended. Like most other scholars, I believe the state has an even stronger interest in regulating exit than in regulating entrance. When we learn that a marriage has ended and try to console the person who has shared the news with us, we tell him or her we are sorry. Usually, that response reflects our desire to show empathy and acknowledge the emotional pain he or she is probably going through. We may not be sorry about the outcome; it may be best for both parties so they can move onto greener pastures. As I suggested, the state could provide something such as divorce insurance to minimize the likelihood that a person in any sort of marriage would not file for divorce due to financial hardship or would not be compensated for the unpaid labor he or she had performed while the marriage lasted. To advocate for the expansion of the legal definition of marriage is not to be indifferent to the surrounding circumstances in which such relationships either come into being or expire.

That is not the only way to address the concern that too many people would not willingly stay in plural marriages, but it is worth exploring because if equality and related concerns about consent can be minimized, then my defense of the option of plural marriage ought to be more compelling. Too often, arguments against plural marriage are really arguments against the worst sorts of unregulated polygynous marriages. Critics of plural marriage seem reluctant to engage more qualified defenses that would have safeguards in place to minimize exploitation. Such safeguards would not end all problems, but they could minimize them. These concerns about equality and financial hardship are not unique to multiperson relationships. In my view, the state must respect each adult's most important personal choices, including whom to marry, and that imperative implies he or she may marry more than one person simultaneously for whatever personal reasons he or she happens to have, which is already the case for couples. To be in favor of the right to plural marriage is not necessarily to endorse such marriage on its merits, as I have underscored, or to believe it to be superior to its monogamous counterpart. Instead, it is to believe that the decision is best left to competent adults who know themselves and what they want better than others do. Intimacy can come in many shapes and sizes. By comparison, one can be pro-choice with respect to abortion and still believe such a procedure to be wrong. The nonrecognition of plural marriage amounts to an unconstitutional denial of marital choice. Thus, the numerical restriction should be dispended with and the legal definition of marriage must cover different kinds of plural marriage. The result would be what Diane Klein envisions as "true marriage freedom."[5]

Most Americans continue to oppose plural marriage.[6] As a consequence, those who want states to be more pluralistic about marriage face a daunting task: to induce ordinary people to see plural marriage as morally acceptable – at least in most circumstances – and to begin by persuading legislators and judges to reform laws that criminalize multipartner intimate relationships or treat polygamists unequally. In the foreseeable future, it is unlikely that those who advocate same-sex marriage will make common cause with those who endorse plural marriage. Nor are the latter likely to become influential in a country that is supposed to be individualistic but often does not practice what it preaches. Nevertheless, that state of affairs could change over time, particularly when a greater number of persons become more informed about plural marriage and its variations, cease reducing it to the worst kinds of polygyny, and actually meet and interact with polygamists and polyamorists who are out of the closet. The media, which deserve partial credit for humanizing them, still have a central role to play in this drama by making the unusual less unusual. Even if the current situation remains the same, just because the public feels strongly that something is wrong does not necessarily make it so. That is a lesson Americans ought to have already learned from their past.

Some questions of political morality, such as affirmative action, capital punishment, and abortion, do not yield simple answers or lend themselves to moral compromise. Because society cannot split the difference, the default cannot be personal choice. Either the Constitution permits universities to take race into account in their admissions processes or it does not. Either the Constitution allows the state to execute people or it does not. Either the Constitution permits women to terminate their pregnancies prior to viability or it does not. By contrast, as I have argued in this book, when it comes to marriage, the state does not have to define marriage in a needlessly narrow way based on the dubious claim that some kinds of marriages are intrinsically superior or produce better overall consequences. The decision not to marry or to marry only one person or multiple partners simultaneously can be left to individuals who may have very different views of the meaning of marriage, its configuration, its dynamics, and its place in their lives. Whatever its flaws may

[5] Diane J. Klein, "Plural Marriage and Community Property Law," *Golden Gate University Law Review*, 41 (2010), 37.

[6] According to a Gallup poll from several years ago, 90 percent of them believe the practice of polygamy is immoral. Gallup poll, May 8–11, 2008, N = 1,017 adults nationwide, margin of error: +/– 3 percent. www.gallup.com/poll/108115/americans-evenly-divided-morality-homosexuality.aspx.

be, the pro-choice position I develop and defend in this book avoids the perennial problem of public justification: The state ought not to base its most important political decisions on controversial reasons that people can and do sincerely and reasonably reject. That requirement of political morality and constitutional doctrine is rooted in the belief that all of us implicitly agree to treat one another fairly when it comes to the exercise of political power.[7]

Too often, polygamy is portrayed as either good or evil.[8] However, ultimately, the quality of any personal relationship, including marriage, is a product of its particulars. One of the recurring themes of this book is that opponents of plural marriage need to stop comparing the worst kinds of polygyny with the ideal kinds of monogamy. That is not to minimize how miserable some – and perhaps many – people in polygynous marriages may be, particularly when the relationship comes about in an insular setting with no oversight. Even if, say, five in ten polygynous marriages are dysfunctional, that fact would not support denying the constitutional right to marrying more than one person simultaneously to everyone. Another common difficulty is that opponents of plural marriage generalize from populations to individuals and condemn polygamy rashly without appreciating how it can take different forms at different times and in different places depending on the participants and the background conditions under which they act. While some of the well-known objections must be taken seriously, those same objections can also be raised with respect to monogamy, resulting in an indefensible double standard. Sadly, many two-person intimate relationships leave a lot to be desired, and traditional marriage continues to be an institution that should not be revered given its well-known past and present pathologies. Americans do not have to internalize this double standard, family law does not have to incorporate it, lawmakers do not have to put up with it, and judges do not have to constitutionalize it. As I have emphasized, one cannot take the worst kind of polygynous marriages and conclude that all or most plural marriages would be characterized by the same sorts of problems. Doing so is what I call "The Argument from Warren Jeffs." The uncritical acceptance of the double standard – where critics of polygamy conveniently overlook the flaws of monogamy and put those of polygynous marriage under a microscope – is an embarrassment.

Tolstoy once observed that each family is unhappy in its own way.[9] I believe "families" can be happy in their own ways or at least happier than they would

[7] For a "communitarian" conception of public reason, see Andrew Lister, *Public Reason and Political Community* (London: Bloomsbury Publishing, 2013).

[8] Bennion, *Polygamy in Primetime*, 242.

[9] Leo Tolstoy, *Anna Karenina*, trans. David Magarshack (New York: Signet Classic, 1961), 5.

be if they had the freedom to experiment with different structures that may better suit their particular circumstances. It appears that a majority of contemporary polyamorists would marry if that option were available to them.[10] In the preceding pages, I have tried to spell out in sufficient detail why the Constitution mandates a much wider range of marital options. A regime of SPICs would make such a state of affairs possible. The Constitution lets people worship god(s) differently (or not at all), lets them raise and educate their children differently, lets them express all sorts of bizarre beliefs, and lets them have sex differently, but it does not let them marry differently. The status quo must change sooner rather than later so people can customize their respective marriage-like relationships to have the lives they want; those lives may turn out to be better lives. I do not know which way the arc of history will bend, but my belief is that the Constitution requires states, which give marriage licenses to couples, to issue marriage licenses to all kinds of polygamists to form multi-person marriages if they so desire. The meaning of marriage, then, can be in the eye of the beholder.

A liberal society is committed to leaving the most personal of personal choices to competent adults in the absence of demonstrable harm to others or unreasonable risk of such harm. At bottom, none of the arguments that opponents of plural marriage put forth are compelling. Usually, they are underdeveloped, and even when they are more fully developed, they tend to provide some support for the view that polygyny under certain conditions is morally disturbing and thus ought to be monitored more carefully. The failure on the part of antipolygamists to argue more convincingly so far does not prove they are wrong, but it casts some doubt on the correctness of their view. I suspect that as time goes by, the antiplural marriage position will lose traction because the state's discriminating against plural marriage enthusiasts – just like discriminating against gays, lesbians, and other sexual minorities – will become less socially acceptable as more and more Americans learn that some of their friends, acquaintances, colleagues, and neighbors are polygamists. Some of them are already outing themselves despite the legal risks of doing so. It is time for our society to stop treating such persons as pariahs and accord them the dignity they are entitled to as human beings even if most of us would make different marital choices. As Martha Nussbaum writes: "The object of

[10] At one time, polyamorists were not very interested in marrying. Hadar Aviram, "Make Lover, Not Law: Perceptions of the Marriage Equality Struggle Among Polyamorist Activists," *Journal of Bisexuality*, 7 (2008), 261, 264. However, that state of affairs seems to be changing. New survey data reveals that a majority of Loving More's national respondents (65.9%) would marry more than one person simultaneously if it were a legal possibility. See www.lovemore.com.

respect is the person, not the person's actions."[11] Above all, this injunction means Americans must reserve judgments about how others decide to arrange their personal lives in the absence of demonstrable harm. In reality, that is easier said than done. At times, all of us have found ourselves in the uncomfortable position of legally permitting behavior we believe to be unequivocally mistaken. But that difficulty does not excuse us for being intolerant by not respecting that individual's capacity to choose how he or she wants to live. Either on due process or equal protection grounds, the American constitutional tradition does not permit legislative majorities to subordinate unpopular minorities and invade their spheres of freedom without adequate justification.

In this book, I elaborated on why a sufficient justification for confining marriage to couples does not exist. As a result, there should be virtually no limits on the gender and the number of individuals involved in a state-recognized marriage as long as they are consenting adults and the multiperson relationships they form are administratively manageable. Not seeing the world from the perspective of plural marriage enthusiasts is a failure not only of moral imagination but also of honoring the constitutional principle that no marriage should be better or worse than any other marriage as far as the state is concerned. The institution of marriage has changed in the past and will continue to change in the future. Those who do not like those changes can be expected to sound alarm bells. There was a time when almost all Americans would have endorsed a conception of marriage that by contemporary standards would be misogynistic. Most of them probably would not have been open to the idea of interracial marriage and would have seen a much lower age of consent as acceptable. They probably could not have fathomed that someday, a man could marry another man and a woman could marry another woman in a majority of states.

In the end, the constitutional issue is inescapably normative and forces us to address how marriage should be understood (and what would be fair) under conditions of moral pluralism. As I have argued, marriage ought to be an institution that welcomes all kinds of intimate relationships. According to Adrienne Davis : "The question is not whether any of us would enter a plural marriage, but whether we should prohibit others from doing so."[12] That statement captures the most appropriate way, I believe, to conceptualize how we should approach the issue. My aim is not to destroy marriage, as I will be accused of, but to make it as inclusive as possible so even unconventional

[11] Martha C. Nussbaum, *From Disgust to Humanity: Sexual Orientation and Constitutional Law* (New York: Oxford University Press, 2010), xv.

[12] Davis, "Regulating Polygamy," 2046.

intimate relationships may receive the equal legal treatment they are entitled to constitutionally. As long as the state remains in the marriage business, then, the only way of avoiding unjustified discrimination is to have everyone use SPICs. Although I may not have convinced anyone that the Constitution requires plural marriage, which probably strikes many readers as a strange conclusion, I hope I have at least begun a more sophisticated conversation about the topic and made the pro-plural marriage position more intellectually respectable than it used to be.

References

Abbey, Ruth and Douglas J. Den Uyl. 2001. "The Chief Inducement? The Idea of Marriage as Friendship." *Journal of Applied Philosophy*, 18(1):37–52.

Ackerman, Bruce A. 1985. "Beyond Carolene Products," *Harvard Law Review*, 98 (4):713–46.

2014. *We the People: The Civil Rights Revolution*. Cambridge, MA: Belknap Press of Harvard University Press.

2014. "Dignity Is a Constitutional Principle," *New York Times*, www.nytimes.com/2014/03/30/opinion/sunday/dignity-is-a-constitutional-principle.html?_r=1.

Alexandre, Michele. 2007. "Big Love: Is Feminist Polygamy an Oxymoron or a True Possibility?" *Hastings Women's Law Journal*, 18:3–30.

Altman, Irwin. 1996. "Polygamous Family Life: The Case of Contemporary Mormon Fundamentalists." *Utah Law Review*, 367–91.

Altman, Irwin and Joseph Ginat. 1996. *Polygamous Families in Contemporary Society*. New York: Cambridge University Press.

Amato, Paul R., Alan Booth, David R. Johnson, and Stacy J. Rodgers. 2007. *Alone Together: How Marriage in America Is Changing*. Cambridge, MA: Harvard University Press.

Anapol, Deborah. 2010. *Polyamory in the Twenty-First Century: Love and Intimacy With Multiple Partners*. Lanham, MD: Rowman & Littlefield.

Anderson, Elizabeth S. 1991. "John Stuart Mill and Experiments in Living." *Ethics*, 102:4–26.

Aristotle, 1996. *The Politics*. Stephen Everson trans. Cambridge, UK: Cambridge University Press.

Arkes, Hadley. 1997. "The Role of Nature." In *Same-Sex Marriage: Pro and Con*, ed. Andrew Sullivan (New York: Vintage Books). 276–77.

Arneson, Richard J. 1980. "Mill versus Paternalism." *Ethics*, 90(4):470–89.

Arthur v. Utah, 2004 UT 76, 99 P. 3d 820 (2004).

Aviram, Hadar. 2008. "Make Love, Not Law: Perceptions of the Marriage Equality Struggle Among Polyamorist Activists." *Journal of Bisexuality*, 7:261–86.

Babst, Gordon. 2002. *Liberal Constitutionalism, Marriage, and Sexual Orientation: A Contemporary Case for Dis-Establishment*. New York: Peter Lang.

Baehr v. Lewin, 852 P. 2d 44 (Haw. 1993).

Bailey, Martha, Beverley Baines, Bita Amani, and Amy Kaufman. 2006. "Expanding Recognition of Foreign Polygamous Marriages: Policy Implications for Canada." In *Queens University Legal Studies Research Paper No. 7–12*. Prepared for Status of Women Canada. Available at http://papers.ssrn.com/sol3/papers.cfm?abstract_id=1023896.

Baker v. Vermont, 744 A. 2d 864 (Vt. 1999).

Baker v. Nelson, 409 U.S. 810 (1972).

Bala, Nicholas. 2005. "An International Review of Polygamy: Legal and Policy Implications for Canada." In *Polygamy in Canada: Legal and Social Implications for Women and Children – A Collection of Policy Research Reports* (Ottawa: Research Directorate, Status of Women Canada).

Balkin, Jack. 2007. *What Roe v. Wade Should Have Said: The Nation's Top Legal Experts Rewrite America's Most Controversial Legal Decision*. Jack M. Balkin ed. New York: New York University Press.

2011. *Living Originalism*. Cambridge, MA: Belknap Press of Harvard University Press.

2011. *Constitutional Redemption: Political Faith in an Unjust World*. Cambridge, MA: Harvard University Press.

2013. "The New Originalism and the Uses of History." Available at http://ir.lawnet.fordham.edu/cgi/viewcontent.cgi?article=4936&context=flr.

Ball, Carlos A. 2003. *The Morality of Gay Rights: An Exploration in Political Philosophy*. New York: Routledge.

2004. "The Positive in the Fundamental Right to Marry: Same-Sex Marriage in the Aftermath of *Lawrence v. Texas*." *Minnesota Law Review*, 88:1184–232.

2014. *Same-Sex Marriage and Children: A Tale of History, Social Science, and Law*. New York: Oxford University Press.

Banks, Ralph Richard. 2011. *Is Marriage for White People? How the African-American Marriage Decline Affects Everyone*. New York: Dutton.

Barash, David P. and Judith Eve Lipton. 2001. *The Myth of Monogamy: Fidelity and Infidelity in Animals and People*. New York: Henry Holt.

Barker, Meg and Darren Langdridge. 2010. "Introduction." In *Understanding Non-Monogamies*, ed. Meg Barker and Darren Langdridge. New York: Routledge. 3–20.

Barnett, Randy E. 1998. "Curing the Drug-Law Addiction: The Harmful Side Effects of Legal Prohibition." In *Drugs: Should We Legalize, Decriminalize or Deregulate?* ed. Jeffrey A. Schaler. Amherst, NY: Prometheus Books: 155–80.

2004. *Restoring the Lost Constitution: The Presumption of Liberty*. Princeton, NJ: Princeton University Press.

2006. "Scalia's Infidelity: A Critique of 'Faint-Hearted' Originalism." *University of Cincinnati Law Review*, 75:17–24.

2011. "Interpretation and Construction." *Harvard Journal of Law and Public Policy*, 34:65–72.

Barry, Brian. 2001. *Culture and Equality: An Egalitarian Critique of Multiculturalism*. Cambridge, MA: Harvard University Press.

Baum, Bruce. 1997. "Feminism, Liberalism and Cultural Pluralism." *Journal of Political Philosophy*, 5(3):230–53.

Becker, Gary S. 1993. *A Treatise on the Family*. Cambridge, MA: Harvard University Press.

Becker, Jo. 2014. *Forcing the Spring: Inside the Fight for Marriage Equality*. New York: Penguin Press.
Belle Terre v. Boraas, 416 U.S. 1 (1974).
Bedi, Sonu. 2009. *Rejecting Rights*. New York: Cambridge University Press.
2013. *Beyond Race, Sex, and Sexual Orientation: Legal Equality Without Identity*. New York: Cambridge University Press.
Bennett, Jessica. 2009. "Polyamory: The Next Sexual Revolution?" *Newsweek*, July 29, 2009: www.newsweek.com/polyamory-next-sexual-revolution-82053.
Bennion, Janet. 2012. *Polygamy in Primetime: Media, Gender, and Politics in Mormon Fundamentalism*. Waltham, MA: Brandeis University Press.
Berger, Peter. 1976. "Ideologies, Myths and Moralities." In *The Americans: 1976 (Critical Choices for Americans)*, ed. Irving Kristol and Paul Weaver. Lexington, KY: Lexington Books.
Berkowitz, Peter. 2013. *Constitutional Conservatism: Liberty, Self-Government, and Political Moderation*. Stanford, CA: Hoover Institution Press.
Bernstein, Anita. 2003. "For and Against Marriage: A Revision," *Michigan Law Review*, 102:129–212.
Bix, Brian H. 2000. "State of the Union: The States' Interest in the Marital Status of Their Citizens." *University of Miami Law Review*, 55:1–30.
Black, D. Marisa. 2006. "Beyond Child Brides: Polygamy, Polyamory, Unique Familial Constructions, and the Law." *Journal of Law and Family Studies*, 8:497–508.
Black's Law Dictionary, 1979. 5th edn. St. Paul, MN: West Publishing.
Blankenhorn, David. 2007. *The Future of Marriage*. New York: Encounter Books.
Block, Jenny. 2008. *Open: Love, Sex, and Life in an Open Marriage*. Berkeley, CA: Seal Press.
Bloom, Allan. 1987. *The Closing of the American Mind*. New York: Simon and Schuster.
Boaz, David. 1997. *Libertarianism: A Primer*. New York: Simon and Schuster.
Boddie v. Connecticut, 401 U.S. 371 (1971).
Bork, Robert H. 1990. *The Tempting of America: The Political Seduction of the Law*. New York: Simon and Schuster.
2003. *Slouching Towards Gomorrah: Modern Liberalism and American Decline*. New York: Regan Books.
Bowers v. Hardwick, 478 U.S. 186 (1986).
Bowman, Cynthia Grant. 2010. *Unmarried Couples, Law, and Public Policy*. New York: Oxford University Press.
Bozzuti, Joseph. 2004. "The Constitutionality of Polygamy Prohibitions After *Lawrence v. Texas*: Is Scalia a Punchline or a Prophet?" *Catholic Lawyer*, 43:409–42.
Bradley, Martha Sonntag. 2011. "A Repeat of History: A Comparison of the Short Creek and Eldorado Raids on FLDS." In *Modern Polygamy in the United States: Historical, Cultural, and Legal Issues*, ed. Cardell K. Jacobson and Lara Burton. New York: Oxford University Press: 3–39.
Brake, Elizabeth. 2005. "Rawls and Feminism: What Should Feminists Make of Liberal Neutrality?" In *The Legacy of John Rawls, ed.* Thom Brooks and Fabian Frevenhagen. New York: Continuum. 67–84.

2010. Review: Tamara Metz, *Untying the Knot: Marriage, the State, and the Case for Their Divorce, Philosophy in Review*, 30(6):418–21.
2010. "Minimal Marriage: What Political Liberalism Implies for Marriage Law," *Ethics*, 120(2):302–37.
2012. "Marriage." http://plato.stanford.edu/entries/marriage.
2012. *Minimizing Marriage: Marriage, Morality, and the Law*. New York: Oxford University Press.
2014. "Recognizing Care: The Case for Friendship and Polyamory." In *Syracuse Law and Civic Engagement Forum*: 1–36.
Brooks, Thom. 2009. "The Problem With Polygamy." *Philosophical Topics*, 37 (2):109–22.
Brown, Wendy. 2008. "Tolerance as/in Civilization Discourse." In *Toleration and Its Limits*, ed. Melissa S. Williams and Jeremy Waldron. New York: New York University Press. 406–41.
Brown v. Board of Education, 347 U.S. 483 (1954).
Brunson, Samuel D. 2013. "Taxing Polygamy." *Washington University Law Review*, 91:113–68.
Buck v. Bell, 274 U.S. 200 (1927).
Brown v. Buhman (2013) (Case No. 2:11-cv-0652).
Burke, Edmund. 1973. *Reflections on the Revolution in France*. Garden City, NY: Anchor Books.
Burnham, William. 2011. *Introduction to the Law and Legal System of the United States*, 5th edn. St. Paul, MN: Thomson West.
Bushman, Richard Lyman. 2008. *Mormonism: A Very Short Introduction*. New York: Oxford University Press.
Butler, Judith. 2000. "Competing Universalities." In *Contingency, Hegemony, and Universality: Contemporary Dialogues on the Left*. New York: Verso. 136–81.
Cain, Patricia A. 1996. "Imagine There's No Marriage." *Quinnipiac Law Review*, 16:27–60.
Cairncross, John. 1974. *After Polygamy Was Made a Sin: The Social History of Christian Polygamy*. London: Routledge and Kegan Paul.
Calhoun, Cheshire. 2000. *Feminism, the Family, and the Politics of the Closet: Lesbian and Gay Displacement*. Oxford, UK: Oxford University Press.
Calhoun, Calhoun. 2005. "Who's Afraid of Polygamy? Lessons for Same-Sex Marriage From the History of Polygamy." *San Diego Law Review*, 42:1023–42.
Card, Claudia. 1996. "Against Marriage and Motherhood." *Hypatia*, 11(3):1–23.
Carpenter, Dale. 2012. *Flagrant Conduct: The Story of Lawrence v. Texas*. New York: Norton.
"'*Windsor* Products': Equal Protection From Animus," pp. 183–285. Available at http://ssrn.com/abstract=2424743.
Case, Mary Anne. 2005. "Marriage Licenses." *Minnesota Law Review*, 89:1758–97.
Cave, Eric M. 2003. "Marital Pluralism: Making Marriage Safer for Love." *Journal of Social Philosophy*, 34(3):331–47.
Chamberlin, Julia and Amos N. Guiora, "Polygamy: Not 'Big Love' but Significant Harm." Available at http://ssrn.com/abstract=2395370.
Chambers, David L. 1997. "Polygamy and Same-Sex Marriage." *Hofstra Law Review*, 26:53–83.
Chapman, Steve. 2001. "Two's Company; Three's a Marriage." *Slate*, June 4.

Chatlani, Hema. 2006. "In Defense of Marriage: Why Same-Sex Marriage Will Not Lead Us Down a Slippery Slope Toward the Legalization of Polygamy." *Appalachian Law Journal*, 6:367–91.

Chauncey, George. 2013. "The Long Road to Marriage Equality." *New York Times*, June 27, A29.

Chemerinsky, Erwin. 2011. *Constitutional Law: Principles and Policies*. 4th edn. New York: Wolters Kluwer.

Cherlin, Andrew J. 2009. *The Marriage-Go-Around: The State of Marriage and the Family in America Today*: New York: Vintage Books.

2010. "One Thousand and Forty-Nine Reasons Why It's Hard to Know When a Fact Is a Fact." In *Families as They Really Are*, ed. Barbara J. Risman. New York: W.W. Norton. 10–14.

Chua, Amy. 2011. *Battle Hymn of the Tiger Mother*. New York: Penguin Group.

Church of the Lukumi Babalu Aye v. City of Hialeah, 508 U.S. 520 (1993).

Clayton, Matthew, 2006. *Justice and Legitimacy in Upbringing*. Oxford, UK: Oxford University Press.

Cleburne v. Cleburne Living Center, 473 U.S. 472 (1985).

Cleveland Board of Education v. LaFleur, 414 U.S. 632 (1974).

Cleveland v. United States, 329 U.S. 14 (1946).

Cohen, G. A. 1997. "Where the Action Is: On the Site of Distributive Justice." *Philosophy and Public Affairs*, 26:3–30.

Collins, Patricia Hill. 1991. *Black Feminist Thought: Knowledge, Consciousness, and the Politics of Empowerment*. New York: Routledge.

Compassion in Dying v. Washington, 79 F. 3d 790 (9th Circuit 1996) (en banc).

Conly, Sarah. 2013. *Against Autonomy: Justifying Coercive Paternalism*. New York: Cambridge University Press.

Coontz, Stephanie. 1992. *The Way We Never Were: America's Families and the Nostalgia Trap*. New York: Basic Books.

1997. *The Way We Really Are: Coming to Terms With America's Changing Families*. New York: Basic Books.

2005. *Marriage, A History: How Love Conquered Marriage*. New York: Penguin Books.

Copi, Irving M. and Carl Cohen. 1998. *Introduction to Logic*. 10th edn. Upper Saddle River, NJ: Prentice Hall.

Corvino, John. 2005. "Homosexuality and the PIB Argument." *Ethics*, 115 (2005):501–34.

2012. "The Case for Same-Sex Marriage." In *Debating Same-Sex Marriage*, ed. John Corvino and Maggie Gallagher. New York: Oxford University Press. 4–90.

2013. *What's Wrong With Homosexuality?* New York: Oxford University Press.

Cott, Nancy F. 2000. *Public Vows: A History of Marriage and the Nation*. Cambridge, MA: Harvard University Press.

Craig v. Boren, 429 U.S. 190 (1976).

Cruz, David. 2000. "Mystification, Neutrality, and Same-Sex Couples in Marriage." In *Just Marriage, ed.* Mary Shanley. Oxford, UK: Oxford University Press. 52–57.

2001. "'Just Don't Call It Marriage': The First Amendment and Marriage as an Expressive Resource." *Southern California Law Review*, 74:925–1026.

Cruzan v. Director, Missouri Department of Health, 497 U.S. 261 (1990).

Davis, Adrienne D. 2010. "Regulating Polygamy: Intimacy, Default Rules, and Bargaining for Equality." *Columbia Law Review*, 110:1955–2046.

Davis v. Beason, 133 U.S. 333 (1890).

De Marneffe, Peter. 2010. *Liberalism and Prostitution*. New York: Oxford University Press.

Denbow, Jennifer M. 2015. *Governed Through Choice: Autonomy, Technology, and the Politics of Reproduction*. New York: New York University Press.

Den Otter, Ronald C. 2009. *Judicial Review in an Age of Moral Pluralism*. New York: Cambridge University Press.

DePaulo, Bella. 2006. *Singled Out: How Singles Are Stereotyped, Stigmatized, and Ignored, and Still Live Happily Ever After*. New York: St. Martin's Griffin.

Dixon, Nicholas. 2001. "Boxing, Paternalism, and Legal Moralism." *Social Theory and Practice*, 27(2):323–44.

Dixon-Spear, Patricia. 2009. *We Want for Our Sisters What We Want for Ourselves: African American Women Who Practice Polygyny by Consent*. Baltimore, MD: Inprint Editions.

Dorf, Michael C. 1998. "God and Man in the Yale Dormitories." *Virginia Law Review*, 84:843–69.

Drury, Shadia B. 2005. *The Political Ideas of Leo Strauss*. Updated edition. New York: Palgrave Macmillan.

Du Bois, W. E. B. 2010. *The Souls of Black Folk*. ReadaClassic.com.

Duncan, Emily J. 2008. "The Positive Effects of Legalizing Polygamy: 'Love Is a Many Splendored Thing.'" *Duke Journal of Gender Law and Policy*, 15:315–37.

Dworkin, Gerald. "Paternalism," *Stanford Encyclopedia of Philosophy*. Available at http://plato.stanford.edu/entries/paternalism.

Dworkin, Ronald. 1977. *Taking Rights Seriously*. Cambridge, MA: Harvard University Press.

1986. *A Matter of Principle*. Cambridge, MA: Harvard University Press.

1996. *Freedom's Law: The Moral Reading of the American Constitution*. Cambridge, MA: Harvard University Press.

2013. *Religion Without God*. Cambridge, MA: Harvard University Press.

Easton, Dossie and Janet W. Hardy. 2009. *The Ethical Slut: A Practical Guide to Polyamory and Open Relationships and Other Adventures*. 2nd edn. New York: Celestial Arts.

Embry, Jessie L. 1984. "Effects of Polygamy on Mormon Women." *Frontiers: A Journal of Women's Studies*, 7(3):56–61.

Emens, Elizabeth F. 2004. "Monogamy's Law: Compulsory Monogamy and Polyamorous Existence." *New York University Review of Law and Social Change*, 29:277–376.

Employment Division v. Smith, 494 U.S. 872 (1990).

Ertman, Martha M. 2001. "Marriage as Trade: Bridging the Private/Private Distinction." *Harvard Civil Rights – Civil Liberties Law Review*, 36:123–31.

2005. "The Business of Intimacy." In *Feminism Confronts Homo Economicus: Gender, Law, and Society*, ed. Martha Fineman and Terrance Dougherty. Ithaca, NY: Cornell University Press. 467–500.

"Race Treason: The Untold Story of America's Ban on Polygamy." *Columbia Journal of Gender and Law*, 19:287–366.

2013. "Love and Contracts in *Don Quixote*." In *Don Quixote: Interdisciplinary Connections*, ed. Matthew D. Warshawsky and James A. Parr. Newark, NJ: Juan de la Cuesta. 251–70.

2015. *Love's Promises: How Formal and Informal Contracts Shape All Kinds of Families*. Boston: Beacon Press (forthcoming).

Eskridge Jr., William N. 1996. *The Case for Same-Sex Marriage: From Sexual Liberty to Civilized Commitment*. New York: The Free Press.

1999. *Gaylaw: Challenging the Apartheid of the Closet*. Cambridge, MA: Harvard University Press.

2008. *Dishonorable Passions: Sodomy Laws in America, 1861–2003*. New York: Viking Books.

2009. "A Liberal Vision of U.S. Family Law in 2020." In *The Constitution in 2020*, ed. Jack M. Balkin and Reva B. Siegel. New York: Oxford University Press.

Eskridge Jr., William N. and Darren R. Spedale. 2006. *Gay Marriage: For Better or for Worse? What We've Learned From the Evidence*. New York: Oxford University Press.

Ettlebrick, Paula. 2004. "Since When Is Marriage a Path to Liberation?" in *Same-Sex Marriage: The Moral and Legal Debate* (2nd edn.), ed. Robert M. Baird and Stuart E. Rosenbaum. Amherst, NY: Prometheus Books: 257–61.

Fainaru-Wada, Mark and Steve Fainaru. 2013. *League of Denial: The NFL, Concussions, and the Battle for Truth*. New York: Crown Archetype.

Feinberg, Joel. 1986. *Harm to Self: The Moral Limits of the Criminal Law*. New York: Oxford University Press.

Fineman, Martha Albertson. 1995. *The Neutered Mother: The Sexual Family and Other Twentieth Century Tragedies*. New York: Routledge.

2004. *The Autonomy Myth: A Theory of Dependency*. New York: The New Press.

2004. "Why Marriage?" In *Just Marriage*, ed. Mary Lyndon Shanley. New York: Oxford University Press. 46–51.

Finnis, John. 1996. "Is Natural Law Theory Compatible With Limited Government?" In *Natural Law, Liberalism, and Morality: Contemporary Essays*, ed. Robert P. George. Oxford, UK: Clarendon Press. 1–26.

2002. "Natural Law: The Classical Tradition." In *The Oxford Handbook of Jurisprudence and Philosophy of Law*. Oxford, UK: Oxford University Press.

Fleming, James E. 2013. Review: "The New Originalist Manifesto: Constitutional Originalism: A Debate." *Constitutional Commentary* 28:539–60.

Freeman, Samuel. 2007. *Rawls*. New York: Routledge.

Galston, William A. 1991. *Liberal Purposes: Goods, Virtues, and Diversity in the Liberal State*. Cambridge, UK: Cambridge University Press.

Garrett, Jeremy R. 2009. "A Prima Facie Case Against Civil Marriage." *Southwest Philosophy Review*, 25(1):41–53.

Garrow, David J. 1998. *Liberty and Sexuality: The Right to Privacy and the Making of Roe v. Wade*. Berkeley: University of California Press.

Gerhardt, Michael J., Stephen M. Griffin, Thomas D. Rowe Jr., and Lawrence B. Solum. 2013. *Constitutional Theory: Arguments and Perspectives*. 4th edn. Albany, NY: Matthew Bender.

Gerstmann, Evan. 2004. *Same-Sex Marriage and the Constitution*. New York: Cambridge University Press.

Gher, Jaime M. 2008. "Polygamy and Same-Sex Marriage – Allies or Adversaries Within the Same-Sex Marriage Movement?" *William and Mary Journal of Women and the Law*, 14:559–603.

Ginsburg, Ruth Bader. 1985. "Some Thoughts on Autonomy and Equality in Relation to *Roe v. Wade*." *North Carolina Law Review*, 63:375–86.

Gill et al. v. Office of Personnel Management, 682 F. 3d 1 (1st Cir.) (2012).

Girgis, Sherif, Robert P. George, and Ryan T. Anderson. 2010. "What Is Marriage?" *Harvard Journal of Law and Public Policy*, 34:246–87.

2012. *What Is Marriage? Man and Woman: A Defense*. New York: Encounter Books.

Goldfeder, Mark and Elisabeth Sheff. 2011. "Children of Polyamorous Families: A First Empirical Look." *Journal of Law and Social Deviance*, 150–243.

2013. "It's Time to Reconsider Polygamy." Available at www.cnn.com/2013/12/16/opinion/goldfeder-polygamy-laws/index.html?htp=op_+1.

2015. *Legalizing Plural Marriage: The Next Frontier in Family Law*. Lebanon, NH: University of New England Press (forthcoming).

Goldwater, Barry. 1960. *Conscience of a Conservative*. Shepherdsville, KY: Victor Publishing.

Golinsky v. Office of Personnel Management, 824 F. Supp. 2d 968 (N.D. Cal.) (2012).

Gonzales v. Carhart, 550 U.S. 124 (2007).

Goodridge v. Department of Health, 798 N.E. 2d 941 (Mass. 2003).

Gordon, Sarah Barringer. 2002. *The Mormon Question: Polygamy and Constitutional Conflict in Nineteenth-Century America*. Chapel Hill: University of North Carolina Press.

Gray, John. 1996. *Mill on Liberty: A Defence*. 2nd edn. London: Routledge.

2012. "Most of Our Beliefs Are Unwarranted, Even Absurd." Review: Brian Leiter, *Why Tolerate Religion?* Available at www.newstatesman.com/print/culture/culture/2012/11/giant-leaps-mankind.

Greenawalt, Kent. 2006. *Religion and the Constitution: Fairness and Free Exercise*. Princeton, NJ: Princeton University Press.

Greenberg, Mark D. and Harry Litman. 1998. "The Meaning of Original Meaning." *Georgetown Law Journal*, 86:569–619.

Greenfield, Kent. 2013. "The Slippery Slope to Polygamy and Incest." *The American Prospect*, July 15. Available at http://prospect.org/article/slippery-slope-polygamy-and-incest.

Greenwood, Arin. 2014. "Who Are 'The Polyamorists Next Door'? Q&A With Author Elisabeth Sheff." *Huffington Post*, March 5.

Grutter v. Bollinger, 539 U.S. 306 (2003).

Gunther, Klaus. 1993. *The Sense of Appropriateness: Application Discourses in Morality and Law*. John Farrell trans. Albany: State University of New York.

Gunther, Gerald. 1972. "Foreword: In Search of Evolving Doctrine on a Changing Court: A Model for a Newer Equal Protection." *Harvard Law Review*, 86:1–48.

Gutmann, Amy. 1980. "Children, Paternalism, and Education: A Liberal Argument." *Philosophy and Public Affairs*, 9:338–58.

Haag, Pamela. 2011. *Marriage Confidential: The Post-Romantic Age of Workhorse Wives, Royal Children, Undersexed Spouses and Rebel Couples Who Are Rewriting the Rules*. New York: HarperCollins.

Hagerty, Barbara Bradley. 2008. "Some Muslims in U.S. Quietly Engage in Polygamy." May 27. Available at www.npr.org/templates/story/story.php?stpryId=90857818.

Halperin, Mark and John Heilemann. 2013. *Double Down: Game Change 2012*. New York: Penguin Press.

Hamilton, Marci A. 2005. *God vs. the Gavel: Religion and the Rule of Law*. New York: Cambridge University Press.

Hart, H. L. A. 1963. *Law, Liberty, and Morality*. Stanford, CA: Stanford University Press.

Hartog, Hendrick. 2000. *Man and Wife in America: A History*. Cambridge, MA: Harvard University Press.

Hayes, Jeffrey Michael. 2007. "Polygamy Comes Out of the Closet: The New Strategy of Polygamy Activists." *Stanford Journal of Civil Rights and Civil Liberties*, 3:100–29.

Heath, Melanie. 2012. *One Marriage Under God: The Campaign to Promote Marriage in America*. New York: New York University Press.

Hegel, G. W. F. 1995. *Elements of the Philosophy of Right*. Allen W. Wood ed. H. B. Nisbet trans. New York: Cambridge University Press.

Heyd, David. "Introduction." In *Toleration: An Elusive Virtue*, ed. David Heyd. Princeton, NJ: Princeton University Press. 3–17.

Hill Jr., Thomas E. 1991. *Autonomy and Self-Respect*. New York: Cambridge University Press.

Hollingsworth v. Perry, 570 U.S. __ (2013).

Holm v. Utah, 127 S. Ct. 1371 (2007).

Honig, Bonnie. 1999. "'My Culture Made Me Do It'." In Susan Moller Okin, *Is Multiculturalism Bad for Women?* ed. Joshua Cohen, Matthew Howard, and Martha C. Nussbaum. Princeton, NJ: Princeton University Press. 35–40.

Hume, David. 1995. "Of Polygamy and Divorces." In *David Hume Essays: Moral, Political, and Literary*, ed. Eugene F. Miller. Indianapolis: Liberty Fund: 181–87.

Husak, Douglas. 2008. *Overcriminalization: The Limits of the Criminal Law*. New York: Oxford University Press.

In re Marriage Cases, 43 Cal. 4d 757, 183 P. 3d 384, 76 Cal. Rptr. 3d 683 (2008).

Jordan, Jeff. 2004. "Contra Same-Sex Marriage." In *Same-Sex Marriage: The Moral and Legal Debate* (2nd edn.), ed. Robert M. Baird and Stuart E. Rosenbaum. Amherst, NY: Prometheus Books. 163–80.

Joslin, Courtney G. 2011. "Searching for Harm: Same-Sex Marriage and the Well-Being of Children." *Harvard Civil Rights – Civil Liberties Law Review*, 46:81–101.

Kant, Immanuel. 1963. "Duties Towards the Body in Respect of Sexual Impulse." In *Lectures on Ethics*. Louis Infield trans. Indianapolis: Hackett Publishing: 162–68.

Karlan, Pamela S. 2010. "Let's Call the Whole Thing Off: Can States Abolish the Institution of Marriage?" *California Law Review*, 98(3):697–707.

Kelly, Erin and Lionel McPherson. 2001. "On Tolerating the Unreasonable." *Journal of Political Philosophy*, 9:38–55.

Kerrigan v. Commissioner of Public Health, 289 Cnn. 135, 957 A. 2d 407 (2008).

Kilbride, Philip L. 1994. *Plural Marriage for Our Times: A Reinvented Option?* Westport, CT: Bergin & Garvey.

King, Dennis. 1989. *Lyndon LaRouche and the New American Fascism*. New York: Doubleday.

Kirk, Russell. 2001. *The Conservative Mind: From Burke to Eliot* (7th revised edn.). Washington, DC: Regnery Publishing.

Kitchen v. Herbert (2013) (case no. 2:13-cv-217)

Klarman, Michael J. 2007. Brown v. Board of Education *and the Civil Rights Movement*. Abridged edition. New York: Oxford University Press.

2013. *From the Closet to the Altar: Courts, Backlash, and the Struggle for Same-Sex Marriage*. New York: Oxford University Press.

Klein, Diane J. 2010. "Plural Marriage and Community Property Law." *Golden Gate Law Review*, 41:33–89.

Knowles, Helen J. 2009. *The Tie Goes to Freedom: Justice Anthony M. Kennedy on Liberty*. Lanham, MD: Rowman & Littlefield.

Koppelman, Andrew. 2002. *The Gay Rights Question in Contemporary American Law*. Chicago: University of Chicago Press.

2006. *Same Sex, Different States: When Same-Sex Marriages Cross State Lines*. New Haven, CT: Yale University Press.

2014. "Judging the Case Against Same-Sex Marriage." *University of Illinois Law Review*, 432–65. Available at http://ssrn.com/abstract=2257557.

2010. "How Shall I Praise Thee? Brian Leiter on Respect for Religion." *San Diego Law Review*, 47:961–85.

2013. "More Intuition Than Argument." Review: Robert George, *What Is Marriage? Commonweal*, March 2013.

2013. *Defending American Religious Neutrality*. Cambridge, MA: Harvard University Press.

Krakauer, Jon. 2004. *Under the Banner of Heaven: A Story of Violent Faith*. New York: Anchor Books.

Kraus, Jody S. 2002. "Philosophy of Contract Law." In *The Oxford Handbook of Jurisprudence and Philosophy of Law*, ed. Jules Coleman and Scott Shapiro. New York: Oxford University Press. 687–751.

Kurtz, Stanley. 2004. "The Libertarian Question: Incest, Homosexuality, and Adultery." In *Same-Sex Marriage: The Moral and Legal Debate* (2nd edn.), ed. Robert M. Baird and Stuart E. Rosenbaum. Amherst, NY: Prometheus Books. 263–68.

2005. "Here Come the Brides." *The Weekly Standard*, vol. 11, issue 15, p. 3. Available at www.weeklystandard.com/Content/Public/Articles/000/000/006/494pqobc.asp.

Kymlicka, Will. 1989. "Liberal Individualism and Liberal Neutrality." *Ethics*, 99:883–905.

1991. "Rethinking the Family." Review: Susan Moller Okin, *Justice, Gender, and the Family. Philosophy and Public Affairs*, 20(1):77–97.

1995. *Multicultural Citizenship: A Liberal Theory of Minority Rights*. Oxford, UK: Clarendon Press.

Lafollette, Hugh. 1980. "Licensing Parents." *Philosophy and Public Affairs*, 9:182–97.

Lawrence III, Charles. 1993. "If He Hollers Let Him Go: Regulating Racist Speech on Campus." In *Words That Wound: Critical Race Theory, Assaultive Speech, and the First Amendment* . Boulder, CO: Westview Press. 53–88.

Lawrence v. Texas, 539 U.S. 558 (2003).

Leiter, Brian. 2007. "Rethinking Legal Realism: Towards a Naturalized Jurisprudence." In *Naturalizing Jurisprudence: Essays on American Legal Realism and Naturalism in Legal Philosophy*. New York: Oxford University Press. 15–58.

2013. *Why Tolerate Religion?* Princeton, NJ: Princeton University Press.

Lecce, Steven. 2008. *Against Perfectionism: Defending Liberal Neutrality*. Toronto: University of Toronto Press.

Levi, Edward H. 1949. *An Introduction to Legal Reasoning*. Chicago: University of Chicago Press.

Levinson, Sanford. 2005. "The Meaning of Marriage: Thinking About Polygamy." *San Diego Law Review*, 42:1049–58.

2006. *Our Undemocratic Constitution: Where the Constitution Goes Wrong (And How We the People Can Correct It)*. New York: Oxford University Press.

Levitt, Steven D. and Stephen J. Dubner. 2005. *Freakonomics: A Rogue Economist Explores the Hidden Side of Everything*. New York: HarperCollins.

Levy, David. 2007. *Love + Sex With Robots: The Evolution of Human-Robot Relationships*. New York: HarperCollins.

Lister, Andrew. 2005. Review Essay: "How to Defend Same-Sex Marriage." *Polity*, 37(3):116.

2013. *Public Reason and Political Community*. London: Bloomsbury Publishing.

Locke, John. 1993. *The Second Treatise of Government*. Peter Laslett ed. Cambridge, MA: Cambridge University Press.

Loving v. Virginia, 388 U.S. 1 (1967).

Lynch v. Donnelly, 465 U.S. 668 (1984).

Macedo, Stephen. 1995. "Homosexuality and the Conservative Mind." *Georgetown Law Review*, 84:261–300.

1997. "Sexuality and Liberty: Making Room for Nature and Tradition?" In *Sex, Preference, and Family: Essays on Law and Nature*, ed. David M. Estlund and Martha C. Nussbaum. New York: Oxford University Press. 86–101.

2002. "Against the Old Sexual Morality of the New Natural Law." In *Natural Law, Liberalism, and Morality: Contemporary Essays*, ed. Robert George. New York: Oxford University Press. 36–43.

2003. *Diversity and Distrust: Civic Education in Multicultural Democracy*. Cambridge, MA: Harvard University Press.

MacKinnon, Catharine A. 1987. *Feminism Unmodified: Discourses on Life and Law*. Cambridge, MA: Harvard University Press.

Mahoney, Jon. 2008. "Liberalism and the Polygamy Question." *Social Philosophy Today*, 23:161–74.

Maine, Henry Sumner. 1888. *Ancient Law* (3rd American edn.). Sioux Falls, SD: NuVision Publications (2009).

Mansbridge, Jane J. 1986. *Why We Lost the ERA*. Chicago: University of Chicago Press.

Mansfield, Harvey C. 2007. *Manliness*. New Haven, CT: Yale University Press.

March, Andrew F. 2010. "What Lies Beyond Same-Sex Marriage: Marriage, Reproductive Freedom and Future Persons in Liberal Public Justification." *Journal of Applied Philosophy*, 27(1):39–58.

2011. "Is There a Right to Polygamy? Marriage, Equality and Subsidizing Families in Liberal Public Justification." *Journal of Moral Philosophy*, 8:244–70.

Marx, Karl and Friedrich Engels. 1967. *The Communist Manifesto*. New York: Penguin Books.

May, Simon Cabulea. 2014. "Liberal Feminism and the Ethics of Polygamy." In *Families: Beyond the Nuclear Ideal*, ed. Daniela Cutas and Sarah Chan. London: Bloomsbury.

Maynard v. Hill, 125 U.S. 190, 205 (1888).

McClain, Linda C. 2006. *The Place of Families: Fostering Capacity, Equality, and Responsibility*. Cambridge, MA: Harvard University Press.

McGinnis, John O. and Michael B. Rappaport. 2009. "A New Theory of Interpretation and the Case Against Construction." *Northwestern University Law Review*, 103:751–801.

2013. *Originalism and the Good Constitution*. Cambridge, MA: Harvard University Press.

Metz, Tamara. 2004. "Why We Should Disestablish Marriage." In *Just Marriage*, ed. Mary Shanley. New York: Oxford University Press. 99–105.

2007. "The Liberal Case for Disestablishing Marriage." *Contemporary Political Theory*, 6:196–217.

2010. *Untying the Knot: Marriage, the State, and the Case for their Divorce*. Princeton, NJ: Princeton University Press.

2014. Review: Elizabeth Brake, *Minimizing Marriage. Social Theory and Practice*, 40:153–59.

Meyer v. Nebraska, 262 U.S. 390 (1923).

Michael H. v. Gerald D., 491 U.S. 110 (1989).

Mill, John Stuart. 1989. "The Subjection of Women." In *On Liberty and Other Writings*, ed. Stefan Collini. Cambridge, MA: Cambridge University Press.

1989. "On Liberty." In *On Liberty and Other Writings*, ed. Stefan Collini. Cambridge, MA: Cambridge University Press.

Mills, Charles. 1999. *The Racial Contract*. Ithaca, NY: Cornell University Press.

Minow, Martha and Mary Lyndon Shanley. 1996. "Relational Rights and Responsibilities: Revisioning the Family in Liberal Political Theory and Law." *Hypatia*, 11 (1):4–29.

Montesquieu. 1973. *Persian Letters*. C. J. Betts trans. London: Penguin Books.

Moore v. City of East Cleveland, 431 U.S. 494 (1977).

Moore, Mignon R. 2010. "Independent Women: Equality in African-American Lesbian Relationships." In *Families As They Really Are*, ed. Barbara J. Risman. New York: W. W. Norton. 214–27.

Murphy, Jeffrie G. and Jules Coleman. 1990. *Philosophy of Law: An Introduction to Jurisprudence*. Revised edition. New York: Westview Press.

Myers, Michael G. 2006. "Polygamist Eye for the Monogamist Guy: Homosexual Sodomy … Gay Marriage … Is Polygamy Next?" *Houston Law Review*, 42:1451–86.

Nanda, Serena and Jill Norgen. 1996. *American Cultural Pluralism and Law* (2nd edn.). Westport, CT: Praeger.

Nearing, Ryam. 1992. *Loving More: The Polyfidelity Primer*. Captain Cook, HI: PEP Publishing.

Norton, Ann. 2004. *Leo Strauss and the Politics of American Empire*. New Haven, CT: Yale University Press.

Nussbaum, Martha C. 1999. *Sex and Social Justice*. New York: Oxford University Press.

2000. *Women and Human Development: The Capabilities Approach*. New York: Cambridge University Press.

2008. *Liberty of Conscience: In Defense of America's Tradition of Religious Equality*. New York: Basic Books.

2010. "A Right to Marry?" *California Law Review*, 98(3):667–96.

2010. *From Disgust to Humanity: Sexual Orientation and Constitutional Law*. New York: Oxford University Press.

Okin, Susan Moller. 1979. *Women in Western Political Thought*. Princeton, NJ: Princeton University Press.

1989. *Justice, Gender, and the Family*. New York: Basic Books.

1990. Review, Carole Pateman, *The Sexual Contract*, "Feminism, the Individual, and Contract Theory." *Ethics*, 100(3):658–69.

1999. "Is Multiculturalism Bad for Women?" In *Is Multiculturalism Bad for Women?* ed. Joshua Cohen, Matthew Howard, and Martha C. Nussbaum. Princeton, NJ: Princeton University Press. 9–24, 587–97.

Olmstead v. United States, 277 U.S. 438 (1928).

O'Neill, Daniel I., Mary Lyndon Shanley, and Iris Young. 2008. *Illusion of Consent: Engaging With Carole Pateman*. University Park, PA: Penn State University Press.

O'Neill, Onora. 1989. "Between Consenting Adults." In *Constructions of Reason: Explorations of Kant's Practical Philosophy*. Cambridge, UK: Cambridge University Press. 105–25.

On, Steve. 2010. "Interview With Carole Pateman by Steve On." *Contemporary Political Theory*, 9:239–50.

Parekh, Bhikhu. 2006. *Rethinking Multiculturalism: Cultural Diversity and Political Theory* (2nd edn.). New York: Palgrave Macmillan.

Pateman, Carole. 1988. *The Sexual Contract*. Stanford, CA: Stanford University Press.

Pateman, Carole and Charles Mills. 2007. *Contract and Domination*. Cambridge, UK: Polity Press.

Perry v. Schwarzenegger, 704 F. Supp. 2d. 921 (N.D. Cal. 2010).

Perry v. Brown, 671 F. 3d 1052 (2012).

Pinello, Daniel R. 2006. *America's Struggle for Same-Sex Marriage*. New York: Cambridge University Press.

Planned Parenthood of Southeastern Pennsylvania v. Casey, 505 U.S. 833 (1992).

Plato, 1945. *The Republic of Plato*. Francis MacDonald Cornford trans. New York: Oxford University Press.

Plessy v. Ferguson, 163 U.S. 537 (1896).

Plyer v. Doe, 457 U.S. 202 (1982).

Poe v. Ullman, 367 U.S. 497 (1961).

Polikoff, Nancy D. 2008. *Beyond (Straight and Gay) Marriage: Valuing All Families Under the Law*. Boston: Beacon Press.

Posner, Richard A. 1992. *Sex and Reason*. Cambridge, MA: Harvard University Press.

2013. *Reflections on Judging*. Cambridge, MA: Harvard University Press.

Putnam, Hilary. 1987. *The Many Faces of Realism*. LaSalle, IL: Open Court Publishing.

Quill v. Vacco, 80 F. 3d 716 (2d Cir. 1996).

Quinton, Anthony. 1995. "Conservatism." In *A Companion to Contemporary Political Philosophy*, ed. Robert E. Goodin and Philip Pettit. Cambridge, UK: Blackwell. 244–68.

Quong, Jonathan. 2011. *Liberalism Without Perfection*. New York: Oxford University Press.

Rauch, Jonathan. 1997. "Marrying Somebody." In *Same-Sex Marriage: Pro and Con*, ed. Andrew Sullivan. New York: Vintage Books. 285–88.

2004. *Gay Marriage: Why It Is Good for Gays, Good for Straights, and Good for America*. New York: Henry Holt.

Ravenscroft, Anthony D. 2004. *Polyamory: Roadmaps for the Clueless and Hopeful*. Santa Fe, NM: Fenris Brothers.

Rawls, John. 1971. *A Theory of Justice*. Revised edition. Cambridge, MA: Belknap Press of Harvard University Press.

1996. *Political Liberalism*. New York: Columbia University Press.

1999. "The Idea of Public Reason Revisited." In *The Law of Peoples*. Cambridge, MA: Harvard University Press. 129–80.

Raz, Joseph. 1986. *The Morality of Freedom*. New York: Oxford University Press.

Regan, Milton C. 1999. *Alone Together: Law and the Meanings of Marriage*. New York: Oxford University Press.

Regnerus, Mark. 2012. "How Different Are the Adult Children of Parents Who Have Same-Sex Relationships? Findings from the New Family Structures Study." *Social Science Research*, 41:752–70.

Reynolds v. United States, 98 U.S. 145 (1878).

Richards, David A. J. 1999. *Identity and the Case for Gay Rights: Race, Gender, Religion as Analogies*. Chicago: University of Chicago Press.

2005. *The Case for Gay Rights: From Bowers to Lawrence and Beyond*. Lawrence: University of Kansas Press.

Rickless, Samuel C. 2005. "Polygamy and Same-Sex Marriage: A Response to Calhoun." *San Diego Law Review*, 42:1043–47.

Risman, Barbara J. 2010. "Families: A Great American Institution." In *Families As They Really Are*, ed. Barbara J. Risman. New York: W. W. Norton. 452–58.

Ristroph, Alice and Melissa Murray. 2010. "Disestablishing the Family." *Yale Law Journal*, 119:1236–79.

Roe v. Wade, 410 U.S. 113 (1973).

Romer v. Evans, 517 U.S. 620 (1996).

Rosenberg, Alexander. 1995. *Philosophy of Social Science* (2nd edn.). Boulder, CO: Westview Press.

Rosenblum, Nancy. 1997. "Democratic Sex: Reynolds v. U.S., Sexual Relations, and Community." In *Sex, Preference, and Family: Essays on Law and Nature*, ed. David M. Estlund and Martha C. Nussbaum. Oxford, UK: Oxford University Press. 63–85.

Rossum, Ralph A. 2006. *Antonin Scalia's Jurisprudence: Text and Tradition*. Lawrence: University Press of Kansas.

Russell, Bertrand. 1957. "Our Sexual Ethics." In *Why I Am Not a Christian*. New York: Simon and Schuster. 168–78.

1970. *Marriage and Morals*. New York: Liveright.

Ruthven, Malise. 2012. *Islam: A Very Short Introduction*. New York: Oxford University Press.

Ryan, Alan. 1974. *J.S. Mill*. London: Routledge and Kegan Paul.

1998. "Mill in a Liberal Landscape." In *The Cambridge Companion to Mill*, ed. John Skorupski. Cambridge, UK: Cambridge University Press. 497–540.

Sadler, Brook J. 2008. "Re-Thinking Civil Unions and Same-Sex Marriage." *Monist*, 91:578–605.

Sandel, Michael. 1989. "Moral Argument and Liberal Toleration: Abortion and Homosexuality." *California Law Review*, 77:521–38.

Schauer, Frederick. 2009. *Thinking Like a Lawyer: A New Introduction to Legal Reasoning*. Cambridge, Ma: Harvard University Press.

Schindler, Jeanne Heffernan. 2011. Review: "A New Disestablishmentarianism." *The Review of Politics*, 73:675–77.

Schultz, Marjorie. 1982. "Contractual Ordering of Marriage: A New Model for State Policy." *California Law Review*, 70:207–334.

Schwartz, Bernard. 1993. *A History of the Supreme Court*. New York: Oxford University Press.

Schweber, Howard. 2012. *Democracy and Authenticity: Toward a Theory of Public Justification*. New York: Cambridge University Press.

Shanley, Mary Lyndon. 2004. "Just Marriage: On the Public Importance of Private Unions." In *Just Marriage*, ed. Mary Lyndon Shanley. New York: Oxford University Press. 3–30.

Shapiro, Scott J. 2007. "The Hart-Dworkin Debate: A Short Guide for the Perplexed." In *Ronald Dworkin*, ed. Arthur Ripstein. New York: Cambridge University Press. 22–55.

Sheff, Elisabeth. 2014. *The Polyamorists Next Door: Inside Multi-Partner Relationships and Families*. Lanham, MD: Rowman & Littlefield.

Sigman, Shayna M. 2006. "Everything Lawyers Know About Polygamy Is Wrong." *Cornell Journal of Law and Public Policy*, 16:101–85.

Shilts, Randy. 1982. *The Mayor of Castro Street*. New York: St. Martin's Press.

Shrage, Laurie. 2013. "Reforming Marriage: A Comparative Approach." *Journal of Applied Philosophy*, 30(2):107–21.

Simon, Stephen A. 2014. *Universal Rights and the Constitution*. Albany, NY: State University of New York Press.

Singular, Stephen. 2009. *When Men Become Gods: Mormon Polygamist Warren Jeffs, His Cult of Fear, and the Women Who Fought Back*. New York: St. Martin's Press.

Skorupski, John. 2007. *Why Read Mill Today?* New York: Routledge.

Slark, Samantha. 2004. "Are Anti-Polygamy Laws an Unconstitutional Infringement on the Liberty Interests of Consenting Adults?" *Journal of Law and Family Studies*, 6:451–60.

Smith, Patricia. 2005. "Four Themes in Feminist Legal Theory: Difference, Dominance, Domesticity, and Denial." In *The Blackwell Guide to the Philosophy of Law and Legal Theory*, ed. Martin P. Golding and William A, Edmundson. Malden, MA: Blackwell Publishing. 90–104.

Solomon, Norman. 1996. *Judaism: A Very Short Introduction*. New York: Oxford University Press.

Solum, Lawrence B. Legal Theory Blog: "Legal Theory Lexicon 071: The New Originalism." Available at http://lsolum.typepad.com/legal_theory_lexicon/2013/02/legal-theory-lexicon-071-the-new-originalism.html.

2006. "Pluralism and Public Legal Reason." *William and Mary Bill of Rights Journal*, 15:7–23.

2010. "The Interpretation-Construction Distinction." *Constitutional Commentary*, 27(2010):95–118.

"Originalism and the Natural Born Citizen Clause." p. 3 (Draft, April 18, 2010). Available at http://ssrn.com/abstract=1263885.

2011. "We Are All Originalists Now." In *Constitutional Originalism: A Debate*. Ithaca, NY: Cornell University Press. 1–77.

Song, Sarah. 2007. *Justice, Gender, and the Politics of Multiculturalism*. New York: Cambridge University Press.

Stacey, Judith. 1990. *Brave New Families: Stories of Domestic Upheaval in Late Twentieth-Century America*. Berkeley: University of California Press.

1996. *In the Name of the Family: Rethinking Family Values in the Postmodern Age*. Boston: Beacon Press.

2011. *Unhitched: Love, Marriage, and Family Values from West Hollywood to Western China*. New York: New York University Press.

Stacey, Judith and Tey Meadow. 2009. "New Slants on the Slippery Slope: The Politics of Polygamy and Gay Family Rights in South Africa and the United States." *Politics and Society*, 37:167–202.

Stark, Barbara. 2001. "From One-Size-Fits-All to Postmodern Marriage Law." *California Law Review*, 89:1479–1548.

Stein, Edward. 2002. "Law, Sexual Orientation, and Gender." In *The Oxford Handbook of Jurisprudence and Philosophy of Law*, ed. Jules Coleman and Scott Shapiro. Oxford, UK: Oxford University Press. 990–1039.

Strassberg, Maura I. 1997. "Distinctions of Form or Substance? Monogamy, Polygamy, and Same-Sex Marriage." *North Carolina Law Review*, 75:1501–65.

2003. "The Challenge of Postmodern Polygamy: Considering Polyamory." *Capital University Law Review*, 31:439–563.

2014. "Distinguishing Polygamy and Polyamory Under the Criminal Law." In *Families: Beyond the Nuclear Ideal*, ed. Daniela Cutas and Sarah Chan. London: Bloomsbury. 160–72.

Strauss, David A. 2010. *The Living Constitution*. New York: Oxford University Press.

Strauss, Gregg. 2012. "Is Polygamy Inherently Unequal?" *Ethics*, 122(3):516–44.

2015. "Why the State Cannot 'Abolish Marriage': A Partial Defense of Legal Marriage Based on the Structure of Intimate Duties." *Indiana Law Review*, 1–67 (forthcoming) Available at http://ssrn.com/abstract=2473182.

Sullivan, Andrew. 1997. "Three's a Crowd." In *Same-Sex Marriage: Pro and Con*, ed. Andrew Sullivan. New York: Vintage Books. 278–82.

Sunstein, Cass R. 1988. "Sexual Orientation and the Constitution: A Note on the Relationship Between Due Process and Equal Protection." *University of Chicago Law Review*, 55:1161–79.

1996. "On the Expressive Function of Law." *University of Pennsylvania Law Review*, 144:2012–53.

1999. *One Case at a Time: Judicial Minimalism on the Supreme Court*. Cambridge, MA: Harvard University Press.

2004. "Of Federalism and Caste." In *Just Marriage*, ed. Mary Lyndon Shanley. New York: Oxford University Press. 41–45.

2005. "The Right to Marry." *Cardozo Law Review*, 26:1081–2120.

2009. *A Constitution of Many Minds: Why the Founding Document Doesn't Mean What It Meant Before*. Princeton, NJ: Princeton University Press.

Sunstein, Cass R. and Richard H. Thaler. 2008. "Privatizing Marriage." *Monist*, 91 (3&4):377–87.

Tamanaha, Brian. 2012. *Failing Law Schools*. Chicago: University of Chicago Press.

Taormino, Tristan. 2008. *Opening Up: A Guide to Creating and Sustaining Open Relationships*. San Francisco: Cleis Press.

Taylor, Charles. 1994. "The Politics of Recognition." In *Multiculturalism: Examining the Politics of Recognition*, ed. Amy Gutmann. Princeton, NJ: Princeton University Press. 25–73.

Thomson, Judith Jarvis. 1975. "The Right to Privacy." *Philosophy and Public Affairs*, 4:295–314.

1962. "Civil Disobedience." In *Thoreau: Walden and Other Writings*. New York: Bantam Books.

Thoreau, Henry David 1962. "Walden." In *Thoreau: Walden and Other Writings*. New York: Bantam Books.

Tolstoy, Leo. 1961. *Anna Karenina*. David Magarshack trans. New York: Signet Classic.

Torcello, Lawrence G. 2008. "Is the State Endorsement of Any Marriage Justifiable? Same-Sex Marriage, Civil Unions, and the Marriage Privatization Model." *Public Affairs Quarterly*, 22(1):43–61.

April 1: (Current Policy) http://www.acluutah.org/pluralmarriage.htm.

Tribe, Laurence H. 1988. *American Constitutional Law* (2nd edn.). New York: Foundation Press.

2004. "*Lawrence v. Texas*: The 'Fundamental Right' That Dare Not Speak Its Name." *Harvard Law Review*, 117:1893–955.

and Joshua Matz, 2014. *Uncertain Justice: The Roberts Court and the Constitution*. New York: Henry Holt.

Turley, Jonathan. 2010. Expert Report Prepared for the *Amicus Curiae*. October 20, p. 5.

Turner v. Safley, 428 U.S. 78 (1987).

Tweedy, Ann. 2011. "Polyamory as a Sexual Orientation." *University of Cincinnati Law Review*, 79:1461–515

Urist, Jacoba. 2012. "Postnups Becoming More Popular, but They're Not for Everyone." Available at www.thedailybeast.com/articles/2012/05/20/postnups-becoming-more-popular-but-they-re-not-for-everyone.html.

United States v. Virginia, 518 U.S 515 (1996).

United States v. Carolene Products, 304 U.S. 144 (1938).

U.S. Department of Agriculture v. Moreno, 413 U.S. 528 (1973).

United States v. Windsor, 570 U.S. __ (2013).

Utah v. Arthur, 2004 UT 76; 99 P. 3d 820 (2004).

Utah v. Green, 76 Utah (2004).

Utah v. Holm, 2006 UT 31; 137 P.3d 726 (2006).

Vallier, Kevin and Fred D'Agostino, 2013. "Public Justification." Available at http://plato.stanford.edu/entries/justification-public.

Vanderheiden, Steve. 1999. "Why the State Should Stay Out of the Wedding Chapel." *Public Affairs Quarterly*, 13(2):175–90.

Vasquez, Richard A. 2001/2002. "The Practice of Polygamy: Legitimate Free Exercise or Religion or Legitimate Public Menace? Revisiting *Reynolds* in Light of Modern Constitution Jurisprudence." *New York University Journal of Legislation and Public Policy*, 5:225–53.

Volokh, Eugene. 2005. "Same-Sex Marriage and Slippery Slopes." *Hofstra Law Review*, 33:1155–201.

2014. "Why Not Get the State Out of the Marriage Business?" Available at http://washingtonpost.com/news/volokh-conspiracy/wp/2014/04/10why-not-get-the-state-out-of-the-marriage-business.

Waite, Linda J. and Maggie Gallagher, 2000. *The Case for Marriage: Why Married People Are Happier, Healthier, and Better Off Financially*. New York: Broadway Books.

Waldron, Jeremy. 1993. "Legislation and Moral Neutrality." In *Liberal Rights: Collected Papers 1981–1991*. Cambridge, UK: Cambridge University Press. 143–67.

1993. "Mill and the Value of Moral Distress." In *Liberal Rights: Collected Papers 1981–1991*. Cambridge, UK: Cambridge University Press. 115–33.

2002. "One Law for All? The Logic of Cultural Accommodation." *Washington and Lee Law Review*, 59:3–34.

Wall, Steven. 1998. *Liberalism, Perfectionism and Restraint*. New York: Cambridge University Press.

and George Klosko. 2003. "Introduction." *Perfectionism and Neutrality: Essays in Liberal Theory*, ed. Steven Wall and George Klosko. Lanham, MD: Rowman & Littlefield. 1–27.

Waluchow, Wilfrid. 2013. "On the Neutrality of Charter Reasoning." In *Neutrality and Theory of Law*, ed. Jordi Ferrer Beltran, Jose Juan Moreso, and Diego M. Papayannis. Dordrecht, Netherlands: Springer. 203–24.

Ward, Cassiah M. 2004. "I Now Pronounce You Husband and Wives: *Lawrence v. Texas* and the Practice of Polygamy in Modern America." *William and Mary Journal of Women and the Law*, 11:131–51.

Warner, Michael. 1999. *The Trouble With Normal: Sex, Politics, and the Ethics of Queer Life*. Cambridge, MA: Harvard University Press.

Washington v. Glucksberg, 521 U.S. 702 (1997).

Warren, Elizabeth and Amelia Warren Tyagi. 2003. *The Two-Income Trap: Why Middle-Class Parents are Going Broke*. New York: Basic Books.

Wax, Amy. 1996. "The Two-Parent Family in the Liberal State: The Case for Selective Subsidies." *Michigan Journal of Race and Law*, 1:491–550.

2007. "Traditionalism, Pluralism, and Same-Sex Marriage." *Rutgers Law Review*, 59:377–412.

Wedgwood, Ralph. 1999. "The Fundamental Argument for Same-Sex Marriage." *Journal of Political Philosophy*, 7(3):225–42.

2012. "The Meaning of Same-Sex Marriage." *New York Times*, May 24. Available at opinionator.blogs.nytimes.com/2012/05/24/marriage-meaning-and-equality/?_php=true&_type=blog&_r=0.

Weisberg, D. Kelly and Susan Frelich Appleton, 2006. *Modern Family Law: Cases and Materials* (3rd edn.). New York: Aspen Publishers. 234–44.

Weitzman, Lenore J. 1981. *The Marriage Contract: A Guide to Living With Lovers and Spouses*. New York: The Free Press.

Wellington, Adrian Alex. 1995. "Why Should Liberals Support Same Sex Marriage?" *Journal of Social Philosophy*, 26(3):5–32.

West, Robin. 2007. *Marriage, Sexuality, and Gender*. Boulder, CO: Paradigm Publishers.

2014. "From Choice to Reproductive Justice: De-Constitutionalizing Abortion Rights." In *Philosophy of Law* (9th edn.), ed. Joel Feinberg, Jules Coleman, and Christopher Kutz. Boston: Wadsworth. 210–29.

2014. *Teaching Law: Justice, Politics, and the Demands of Professionalism*. New York: Cambridge University Press.

Whittington, Keith E. 1991. *Constitutional Interpretation: Textual Meaning, Original Intent, and Judicial Review*. Lawrence: University of Kansas Press.
1999. *Constitution Construction: Divided Powers and Constitutional Meaning*. Cambridge, MA: Harvard University Press.
2004. "The New Originalism." *Georgetown Journal of Law and Public Policy*, 2:599–613.
2013. "Originalism: A Critical Introduction." *Fordham Law Review*, 82:375–409.
Williams, Bernard. 1996. "Toleration: Impossible Virtue?" In *Toleration: An Elusive Virtue*, ed. David Heyd. Princeton, NJ: Princeton University Press. 18–27.
Wilson, Donald. 2004. "Kant and the Marriage Right." *Pacific Philosophical Quarterly*, 85:103–23.
Windsor v. United States, 570 U.S. __ (2013).
Wing, Adrien Katherine. 2003. "Polygamy in Black America." In *Critical Race Feminism: A Reader* (2nd edn.), ed. Adrien Katherine Wing. New York: New York University Press. 186–94.
Winkler, Adam. 2006. "Fatal in Theory and Strict in Fact: An Empirical Analysis of Strict Scrutiny in Federal Courts." *Vanderbilt Law Review*, 59:790–871.
2013. "Are Polygamy Bans Unconstitutional?" *Huffington Post*, December 16. Available at www.huffingtonpost.com/adam-winkler/are-polygamy-bans-unconst_b_4454076.html.
Wisconsin v. Yoder, 406 U.S. 205 (1972).
Witte Jr., John. 2012. *From Sacrament to Contract: Marriage, Religion, and the Law in the Western Tradition* (2nd edn.). Louisville, KY: Westminster John Knox Press.
2015. *The Western Case for Monogamy Over Polygamy*. New York: Cambridge University Press (forthcoming).
Wittes, Benjamin. 2006. *Confirmation Wars: Preserving Independent Courts in Angry Times*. Lanham, MD: Rowman & Littlefield.
Wolff, Robert Paul. 1970. *In Defense of Anarchism*. Berkeley: University of California Press.
Wolfson, Evan. 2004. *Why Marriage Matters: America, Equality, and Gay People's Right to Marry*. New York: Simon and Schuster.
Wollstonecraft, Mary. 1993. "A Vindication of the Rights of Woman." In *Political Writings*, ed. Janet Todd. Toronto: University of Toronto Press. 69–296.
Zablocki v. Redhail, 434 U.S. 374 (1978).
Zakaras, Alex. 2009. *Individuality and Mass Democracy: Mill, Emerson, and the Burdens of Citizenship*. New York: Oxford University Press.
Zeitzen, Miriam Koktvedgaard. 2008. *Polygamy: A Cross-Cultural Analysis*. New York: Berg.
Zelinsky, Edward A. 2006. "Deregulating Marriage: The Pro-Marriage Case for Abolishing Civil Marriage." *Cardozo Law Review*, 27:1161–220.

Index

For EU product safety concerns, contact us at Calle de José Abascal, 56–1°, 28003 Madrid, Spain or eugpsr@cambridge.org.

www.ingramcontent.com/pod-product-compliance
Lightning Source LLC
LaVergne TN
LVHW011529200926
848484LV00001B/201

* 9 7 8 1 1 0 7 0 8 7 7 1 2 *